MECHANICAL DESKTOP 5

Parametric Modeling

John E. Wilson

CMP Books
Lawrence, Kansas 66046

CMP Books
CMP Media, Inc.
1601 W. 23rd Street, Suite 200
Lawrence, KS 66046
USA

Cover art created by Audrey Welch.

Distributed in the U.S. and Canada by:
Publishers Group West
1700 Fourth Street
Berkeley, CA 94710
1-800-788-3123

ISBN: 1-57820-065-2

TABLE OF CONTENTS

CHAPTER 1

Working with Mechanical Desktop

Read this chapter to obtain an overall picture of Mechanical Desktop's capabilities and to learn the basic information you need to get started and work in 3D space with Autodesk's Mechanical Desktop.

This chapter covers the following topics.

- *Defines parametric solid modeling.*

- *Describes the components of the Mechanical Desktop window.*

- *Describes the contents of the Desktop Browser and explains how to manage it.*

- *Explains how to issue Mechanical Desktop commands.*

- *Explains how to specify preferences for the general operating characteristics of Mechanical Desktop.*

- *Describes the 3D space in which you create 3D models, and the Mechanical Desktop tools for working in 3D space.*

Parametric Solid Modeling

You will use Mechanical Desktop for designing objects that are typically manufactured by machining, molding, casting, forging, bending, and stamping processes, and you will create these designs by constructing 3D solid models. Unlike 2D drafting, in which you draw pictures of an object as it is seen from various viewpoints, 3D models are a computer version of the object itself. They are comparable to physical models made of clay or plaster, even though they consist entirely of computer data. They have length, width, and height; you can determine their physical properties, such as weight; and you can see them in realistic shaded forms from any point in 3D space. Although you cannot touch or hold computer models and you must view them on a 2D computer screen, they are easier to modify than physical models, you can make 2D multiview dimensioned drawings of them, and you can even transfer their geometry data to numerically controlled machines for manufacturing the object.

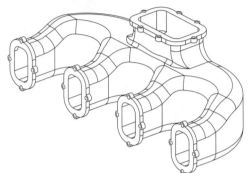

This manifold is a typical Mechanical Desktop model.

The geometry of parametric solid models is controlled by dimension and constraint parameters. Dimensions actually control sizes rather than just report sizes as they do in nonparametric modelers, while constraints maintain geometric relationships between the components of the model. You can easily change properly constructed parametric models to accommodate design changes or to create a family of parts from a basic version of a part.

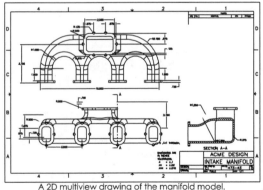

A 2D multiview drawing of the manifold model.

Mechanical Desktop's parametric solid models are based on the ACIS Geometric Modeler (sometimes referred to as the ACIS kernel). from Spatial Technology, Inc. This is a tool kit of 3D modeling routines that is licensed by Autodesk and incorporated into Mechanical Desktop. It is also used by other CAD programs, including Inventor and AutoCAD, to build solid models. AutoCAD, however, does not fully implement the kernel. Mechanical Desktop is able to create 3D solids having geometric shapes that cannot be created by AutoCAD. Also, AutoCAD's solid models are not parametric. Inventor, on the other hand, fully utilizes the kernel, and like Mechanical Desktop, is a parametric solid modeler. Its interface is altogether different from other Autodesk CAD programs, and its file format is not compatible with Mechanical Desktop.

Mechanical Desktop also has a full set of tools for creating and working with surface models. Unlike solid models, which always have thickness, surface models are created from objects that have no thickness. They have only edges and an infinitely thin surface. Shapes and forms that cannot be created as solid models can be constructed as surface models. Surface models, however, are not parametric and the steps to construct them are entirely different than those for constructing solid models. Furthermore, you will seldom need to model a part that cannot be constructed as a Mechanical Desktop parametric solid model. Therefore, this book will not describe Mechanical Desktop's surface modeling tools.

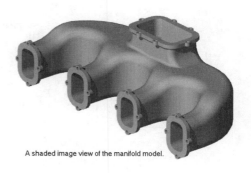

A shaded image view of the manifold model.

The Mechanical Desktop Interface

Since Mechanical Desktop is based on AutoCAD, its user interface is much like that of AutoCAD, and all AutoCAD commands can be used within Mechanical Desktop. You will use AutoCAD commands for file management, creating and editing text, drawing wireframe objects, controlling object properties, printing, and so forth. You will use Mechanical Desktop commands for creating and managing 3D models. There is not, though, a distinct boundary between AutoCAD and Mechanical Desktop.

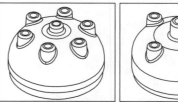

Parametrics allow you to easily change this model from the version on the left to the version on the right.

The Mechanical Desktop Window

While the overall appearance of the Mechanical Desktop window is similar to that of AutoCAD, it has some components that AutoCAD does not have, and others are modified versions of those in AutoCAD.

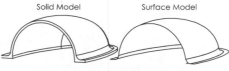

Solid Model   Surface Model

Surface model objects have no thickness.

- The graphics area, which dominates the Mechanical Desktop window, is where you create 3D models as well as 2D drawings of those models.

- Pulldown menus for initiating most AutoCAD and Mechanical Desktop commands and functions are accessed from the pulldown menu bar. Most of the Mechanical Desktop commands are in the Surface, Part, Toolbody, and Drawing menus. Also, depending on Mechanical Desktop's current operating mode, the Toolbody menu may be replaced by the Assembly menu. (Mechanical Desktop operating modes are discussed in Chapter 2.)

- The Mechanical Main toolbar is a specialized version of AutoCAD's Standard and Object Properties toolbars.

- Selecting one of the buttons in the Desktop Main toolbar displays a toolbar for either Part Modeling, Assembly Modeling, Scenes, Drawing Layout, or Toolbody Modeling.

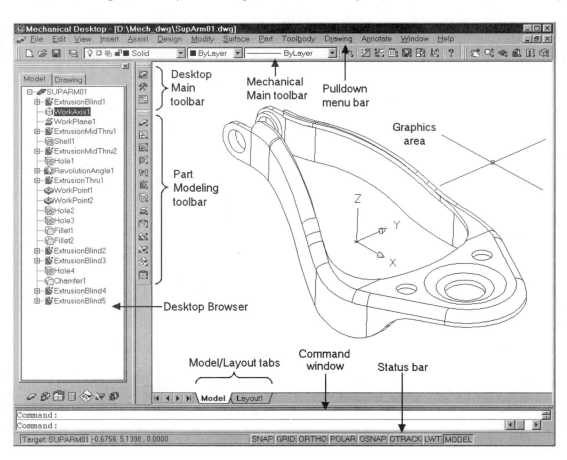

(Mechanical Desktop generally refers to the solid model of a single item as a part, and to a set of related parts as an assembly. A scene is an exploded view of an assembly.) Only one of these toolbars can be displayed at a time. When you begin a new file, the Part Modeling toolbar is displayed. By default, the docked location of the Desktop Main toolbar, as well as its subsidiary toolbar, is on the left side of the graphics area. You can, though, dock them on the right side of the graphics area by selecting Toolbars/Desktop Express (Right) from the View pulldown menu.

- The Part Modeling toolbar, which is shown in the figure, gives you quick access to commands for creating parametric solid models of individual parts. Some of the buttons launch other toolbars, with tooltip messages indicating which buttons launch toolbars. The Part Modeling toolbar can be replaced by the Assembly Modeling, Scenes, Toolbody Modeling, or Drawing Layout toolbar, as described in the previous paragraph.

- The Desktop Browser displays information about parametric models and their drawings. It does not display information for AutoCAD objects or Mechanical Desktop surface models. See "The Desktop Browser" beginning on page 5 for additional information.

- The tabs located on the bottom edge of the graphics area are for switching the graphics area between 3D modeling and 2D drawing modes.

- Mechanical Desktop prompts and messages are displayed in the Command window. The last line within this window, which is called the command line, is for user input.

- The Status line, which is always at the bottom of the Mechanical Desktop window, displays the coordinates of the screen cursor and the status of various operating modes. The button and name on the far left end of the status bar refers to subassemblies of parts, which are described in Chapter 20. If there are no subassemblies, the current drawing file name will be given as the target.

The Desktop Browser

The Desktop Browser is a multifunction component having contents that vary to match the current Mechanical Desktop operating mode, as shown in Table 1. You can switch from one mode to another by selecting a tab on the top edge of the Browser. Within Mechanical Desktop's Part environment, the tabs that are available are Model and Assembly, while the Model, Drawing, and Scene tabs are available within Mechanical Desktop's Assembly environment.

Note

See "Mechanical Desktop's Modeling Environments" on page 32 for descriptions of Mechanical Desktop's two working environments.

The Drawing mode is first discussed in Chapter 14.

The Scene mode is described in Chapter 19.

Table 1

Operating Mode	Browser Contents
Model	The names of the part's features. In Mechanical Desktop's assembly environment, the relationships between parts is also displayed.
Drawing	The names of drawing views and their relationships.
Scene	The names of the parts in the scene, and their spatial relationships.

The object names within the Browser are listed in an outline, or tree-like, format. Their names, such as ExtrusionBlind1, Hole2, and Ortho (for a drawing view), are assigned by Mechanical Desktop in the language of the Mechanical Desktop language version. You can, though, convert the names to another language with the AMBLD-FEATNM command. Suppose, for example, a model created in the German language version of Mechanical Desktop is opened in the English version. AMBLDFEATNM will convert the Browser names from German to English. The command has no options and requires no input after it has been invoked. You can also rename an object by right-clicking its name and selecting Rename from the resulting shortcut menu.

The icons on the bottom of the Browser, which vary according to the operating mode, are for initiating specific commands. Their uses are described as the command they initiate is discussed in this book.

By default, the Browser is docked on the left side of the Mechanical Desktop window. You can, though, click within its gray area and drag it to another location as you hold down the pick button of your pointing device. When the Browser is floating, you can stretch it vertically or horizontally as you can any window. When it is docked, you can stretch the Browser horizontally.

When the Browser is floating, you can click and drag in the Browser's gray area or title bar to move it. To dock the Browser, drag it to the left or right side of the Mechanical Desktop window, or double-click in the title bar of the Browser. Also, you can completely collapse the Browser by double-clicking in a gray area, and you can restore it to its full length by again double-clicking in a gray area. Clicking the ∞ in the title bar will close the Browser. You can turn it back on with the AMBROWSER command. This command acts as a toggle to turn the Browser display on or off. You can initiate this command by selecting Display\Desktop Browser from the View pulldown menu.

A shortcut menu is displayed when you right-click in the gray area of the Browser. Options within this menu allow you to turn the Browser off and to enable or disable docking. The Auto Hide option of this menu is for temporarily hiding the browser. When you select the Left or Right options, the Browser reappears when you move the screen cursor to side of your screen. When you select the Collapse option, the Browser collapses but expands when you move the screen cursor over it.

You can change the font used for the text within the Browser with the AMBROWSER-FONT command. This command displays a dialog box for you to use in selecting a font type and size.

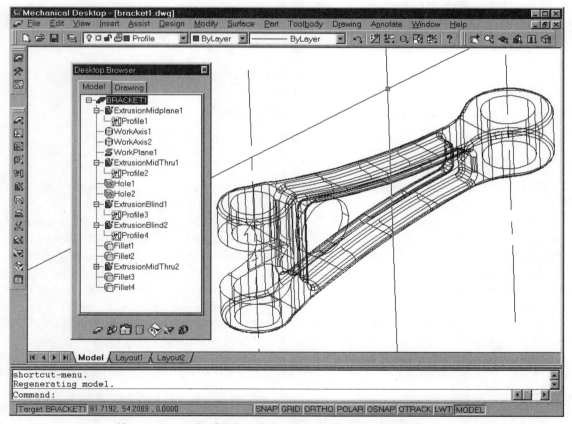

You can move the Desktop Browser from its docked location.

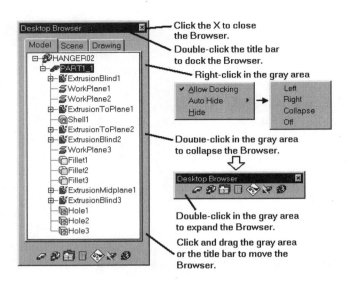

Click the X to close the Browser.

Double-click the title bar to dock the Browser.

Right-click in the gray area

Double-click in the gray area to collapse the Browser.

Double-click in the gray area to expand the Browser.

Click and drag the gray area or the title bar to move the Browser.

Issuing Commands

As with AutoCAD, virtually every Mechanical Desktop operation is initiated by a command that has a name. You can though, issue most commands in a variety of ways. Suppose, for instance, you want to modify an existing 3D solid feature. You can start the operation in any of the following six ways.

1. Select Edit Feature from the Part pulldown menu.

2. Right-click within the Graphics area to display a shortcut menu.

In this menu select Edit Features, and then Edit.

3. Right-click the feature's name in the Desktop Browser, and select Edit from the shortcut menu.

4. In the Part Modeling toolbar, select the Edit Feature button.

5. Type the letters LL on the command line and press the Enter key.

6. Type the word AMEDITFEAT on the command line and press the Enter key.

You can also use a graphics tablet, or digitizer to initiate commands. Autodesk does not, however, supply a tablet menu containing Mechanical Desktop Commands.

The method you use in starting a command will depend, for the most part, on your personal preferences. Also, since some of the menus and toolbar buttons initiate a specific option of a command, you may often use one method for some commands, and another method for others. In this book descriptions of Mechanical Desktop's operations will be based on command names, so that the focus will be on how commands work rather than on how to start them.

When you right-click in the graphics area, which is the second method in the list for starting commands, one of three context-sensitive shortcut menus will be displayed.

* When no object has been selected and no command is in progress, the menu will contain options for initiating commands.

* When an object is selected and no command is in progress, the menu will list options for editing the object.

- When a command is in progress, the menu will list options for that command.

Method 5 in the previous list uses a technique that Autodesk refers to as *accelerator keys* (and sometimes as *command aliases*). The accelerator keys for AutoCAD are stored in a file named acad.pgp, while those for Mechanical Desktop are initially stored in mcad.pgp. When Mechanical Desktop is installed, though, the contents of the mcad.pgp file are appended to those in the acad.pgp file. As a result, Mechanical Desktop letter combinations over-ride AutoCAD accelerator keys having the same letter combinations. Both files are text files, and therefore, can be modified by a text editor, such as Window's Notepad. To have any effect in Mechanical Desktop, though, you must modify the acad.pgp file that is located in the desktop support directory; not the mcad.pgp file.

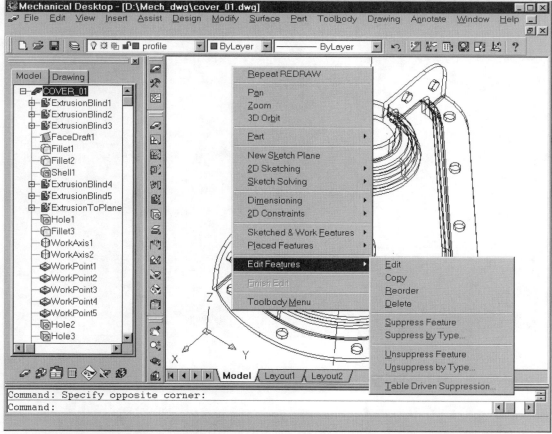

Context-sensitive shortcut menus are displayed when you right-click in the graphics area.

The Mechanical Desktop Today Window

By default Mechanical Desktop starts by displaying the `Mechanical Desktop Today` window, and this window is also displayed whenever you begin a new drawing file. This window contains three separate areas.

My Drawings   Use this area to create new drawing files and to open existing files.

Bulletin Board   You can post messages for Mechanical Desktop users in this area.

Autodesk Point A   You can connect to Autodesk sites on the Internet from this area.

If you prefer not to have this window displayed when you start Mechanical Desktop or a new drawing file, you can invoke AutoCAD's OPTIONS Command. Select the Systems tab, and then deselect Show TODAY startup dialog from the Startup list box.

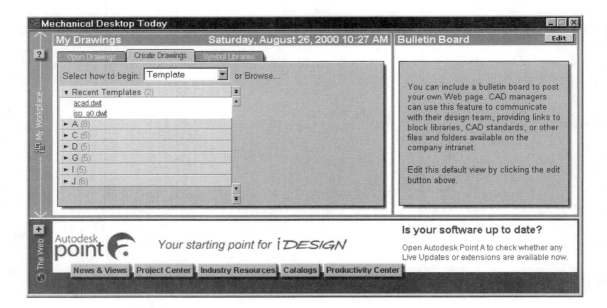

Setting Desktop Preferences

You will use AutoCAD's OPTIONS command to set the appearance of the screen and the cursor, and to set general operating preferences. Refer to the AutoCAD User's Guide supplied with Mechanical Desktop for information about the OPTIONS command.

To set your preferences for Mechanical Desktop, use the AMOPTIONS command. (A convenient way to start AMOPTIONS is to click the icon on the bottom of the Browser that looks like an index card.) This command displays a dialog box titled **Mechanical Options** that has six tabs for setting options. We will discuss the Preferences tab now. The other five tabs are for setting options in specific working areas of Mechanical Desktop, and we will discuss them as their working area is covered in this book.

Initially, the default settings in the Preferences tab will work well for you. As you become more advanced, though, and begin to customize Mechanical Desktop, you will change some of them to fit your preferences. The options within the Preferences tab are described in the following paragraphs.

Snap Settings

The Snap Defaults button displays the **Power Snap Settings** dialog box. You can also display this dialog box by invoking the AMPOWERSNAP command. The four tabs in this dialog box, which have identical contents, allow you to set up different object snap settings, and you can switch between these settings with the AMPSNAP1, AMPSNAP2,

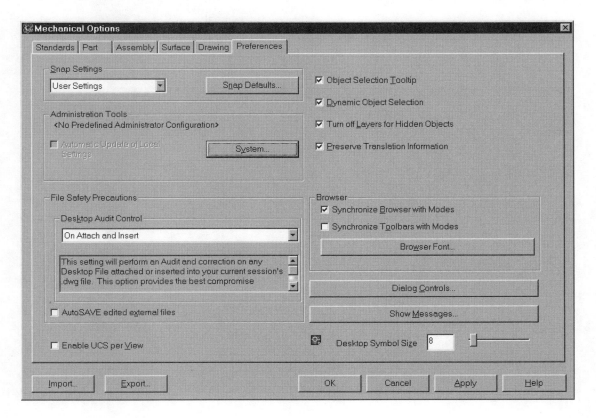

AMPSNAP3, and AMPSNAP4 commands. (When you open this dialog box through the AMPOWERSNAP command, a fifth tab showing the current snap settings is displayed.) The dropdown list box has three options.

- System Settings enables the snap settings you specified in the `Power Snap Settings` dialog box, as well as those assigned to AutoCAD commands.

- User Settings enables the snap modes you specified in the `Power Snap Settings` dialog box and disables the snap modes assigned to AutoCAD commands.

- Suppress Object Snaps disables the Power Snap settings.

Administration Tools

These options are for using Mechanical Desktop within a networked system. The button labeled System displays a dialog box containing tree-structured list setting configuration variables.

File Safety Precautions

The three options in the Desktop Audit Control list box control the extent to which Mechanical Desktop checks files for errors when they are inserted or attached to the current open file. When you select Never, inserted and attached files are not audited; when

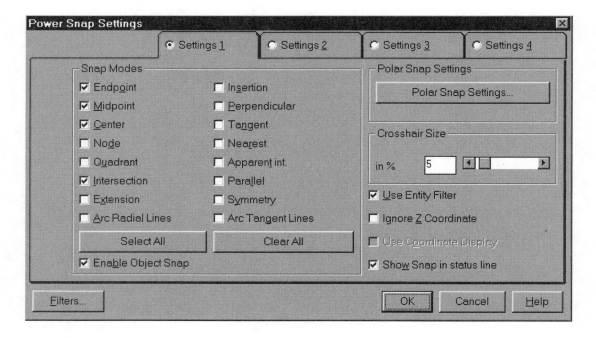

you select On Attach and Insert, files are audited only at the time they are inserted or attached; and when you select Always, Mechanical Desktop audits them when they are inserted or attached, and continues to audit them.

When you select the AutoSAVE edited external files option, external files of parts within an assembly will automatically be saved if the part is modified. See Chapter 17 for a discussion of external files.

Enable UCS per View	When this check box is selected, each viewport can have its own UCS. When this check box is cleared, the UCS is always the same in all viewports.
Object Selection Tooltip and Dynamic Object Selection	When these check boxes are selected, certain Mechanical Desktop commands will highlight potential selection objects and display the Browser's name of the object whenever the AutoCAD pickbox touches the object (you do not need to pick a point on the object). If the `Tooltip` box is cleared, however, the name of the potential selection object will not be displayed; and, if the `Dynamic` box is cleared, potential objects will not be highlighted and their object name will not be displayed.
Turn off Layers for Hidden Objects	This option turns off new created layers for hidden objects.
Preserve Translation Information	When this option is selected, system text strings are provided with internal information that allows them to be translated to another language by the AutoCAD Mechanical 2000I Language Converter. By itself, Mechanical Desktop does not contain the Language Converter.

Browser

When the Synchronize Browser with Modes check box is selected the items listed in the Browser will be coordinated with the current mode. Thus, when Model mode is active the items listed in the Browser will relate to Model mode, and when Drawing mode is active they will relate to Drawing mode.

When the Synchronize Toolbars with Modes option is selected, the vertical toolbar under the Desktop Main toolbar will match the current mode. For example, when the Scene operating mode is active the Scenes toolbar will be displayed; and in Model Mode, the Part Modeling toolbar will be displayed.

The Browser Font button Initiates the AMBROWSERFONT command for changing the font used for the Browser's text.

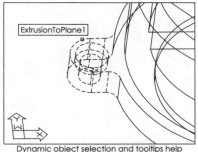

Dynamic object selection and tooltips help you identify Mechanical Desktop objects.

Dialog Controls

When you select this option, the **Dialog Controls** dialog box is displayed for you to use in controlling the displayed values offered in Mechanical Desktop dialog boxes that contain edit boxes for specifying distances and angles.

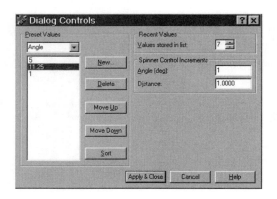

Preset Values Dialog boxes with options for specifying distance or angle often have right-click shortcut menus in which you can select a preset value. To create these preset values, select the value type—Distance, Angle, or Draft Angle—from the dropdown list box in the **Dialog Controls** dialog box, and then click the New button. A small secondary dialog box will appear for you to use in entering the preset values. Use the Delete, Move Up, Move Down, and Sort buttons in the **Dialog Controls** dialog box to arrange and manage the preset values you have created. As an example, the following figure shows the shortcut menus of the AMEXTRUDE command's dialog box.

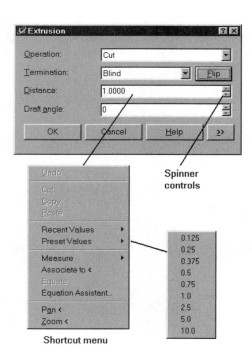

Spinner controls

Shortcut menu

Recent Values Dialog box shortcut menus for specifying distance or angle values also have an option to select a recently used value. The number of recent values offered is controlled by this edit box.

Spinner Control Increments The two edit boxes in this cluster control the display of values in dialog box edit boxes having spinners—up and down arrows—for specifying lengths or angles. (The dialog box shown in the previous figure has spinners for both the Distance and the Draft angle edit boxes.) The increment of the number displayed in such edit boxes after each click on a spinner is controlled by the **Angle** and **Distance** edit boxes. For example, if you enter 5 for **Angle**, every Mechanical Desktop dialog box with a spinner box for setting angles will offer angle values in increments of 5 degrees.

Show Messages   This option opens a **Show Messages** dialog box that gives you control over whether or not certain Mechanical Desktop messages for file updates and maintenance will automatically be displayed.

Desktop Symbol Size   In assemblies of parts, Mechanical Desktop will on demand display a symbol, which is referred to as the Degrees of Freedom (DOF) symbol, indicating the possible movement directions of an individual part. This edit box sets the relative size of the symbol. See the discussion on constraining parts in assemblies in Chapter 18 for information about degrees of freedom and the DOF symbol.

Working in 3D Space

Coordinate Systems

AutoCAD and Mechanical Desktop identify the location of every point in 3D space by its distance from three invisible, mutually perpendicular lines. These three lines, which intersect at a point called the origin, are referred to as the X, Y, and Z axes. Each of the axes extends an infinite distance in the positive and negative directions from the origin. The three distances from the axes to the point are generally written together, separated by commas, and are called the point's coordinates. This system is called the *World Coordinate System* (WCS). It is fixed in space, and the locations of points used in defining AutoCAD and Mechanical Desktop objects are stored in the drawing database as WCS coordinates. The accompanying figure show the coordinates of selected points on a 3D model. Notice that some of the coordinate values are preceded by a minus sign, indicating they are in the negative direction from the origin.

Of the infinite number of planes in the WCS, the three planes defined by (1) the X and Y axes, (2) the X and Z axes, and (3) the Y and Z axes are especially important. They are referred to as the *principal planes*, and in several Mechanical Desktop commands they are used as a reference for establishing other planes. The XY plane is the most important principle plane, because your pointing device can operate only on the XY plane.

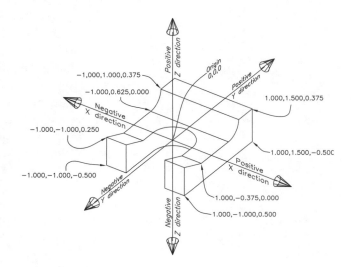

You must either enter coordinates with the keyboard or use object snaps to specify points off of the XY plane. The XY plane is often considered to represent a horizontal plane, with the terms up, down, above, and below being relative to the XY plane—up and above refer to the positive Z axis direction, while down and below refer to the negative Z axis direction.

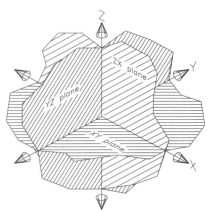

The three principal planes

To enable you to more efficiently use your pointing device, AutoCAD has a secondary coordinate system called the *User Coordinate System (UCS)*. The UCS is identical to the WCS, except that you can move it and orient it as you like. Typically in creating 3D models you will move the UCS origin to some point, orient its XY plane to some desired position, and draw objects on the UCS XY plane with your pointing device. When your work on that plane is finished, you will move the UCS XY plane to another location, draw more objects, and continue this move-and-draw process until your model is finished.

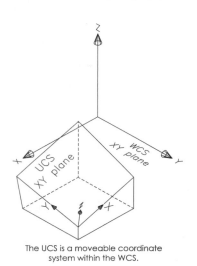

The UCS is a moveable coordinate system within the WCS.

The name of the command that manages the User Coordinate System is UCS. Since UCS is an AutoCAD command, you should refer to your AutoCAD documentation for information on using it. Unless you are building surface models, however, you will not use the USC command extensively in building parametric models, because Mechanical Desktop uses a specialized moveable plane, called the *sketch plane*, rather than the UCS in building them. Most Mechanical Desktop commands that establish planes, though, have options that permit you to locate and orient sketch planes and working planes according to WCS and UCS planes. Therefore, you should review the AutoCAD documentation about the WCS and the UCS. Chapter 3 of this book describes Mechanical Desktop sketch planes and work planes.

Both Mechanical Desktop and AutoCAD have an icon, which is called the *UCS icon*, that helps you visualize coordinate system directions in 3D space. This icon is managed by AutoCAD's UCSICON command. Through this command, you can turn the display of the icon on and off, and you can cause the icon to be positioned either on the UCS origin or in the lower left corner of the viewport. If the origin is not within the viewport, the icon automatically positions itself in the viewport's lower-left corner.

You can change the appearance of the UCS icon by selecting the Properties option of the UCSICON command. This option displays the **UCS Icon** dialog box, which allows you to choose either a flat icon or 3D icon, as well as to specify its color and its relative size.

The 2D UCS icon has two arrows that indicate the positive direction of the X and Y axes. Other features on the icon indicate whether the WCS or the UCS is in effect, whether or not the icon is on the origin, and whether or not the view is looking down on the XY plane. When the view direction is within 1 degree of the XY plane, the icon assumes the form of a broken pencil.

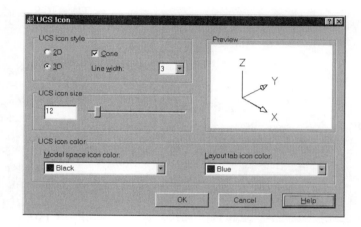

The 3D UCS icons have arrows on the X and Y axes, while the Z axis is simply a line that is perpendicular to the XY plane. When the viewing direction is down toward the XY plane, the Z axis is a solid line; when it is up toward the XY plane, the Z axis is dashed; when it is directly toward the XY plane, the Z axis is not displayed. The X axis will be clockwise from the Y axis when the viewing direction is from above the XY plane, and it will be counterclockwise from the Y axis when the viewing direction is from below the XY plane.

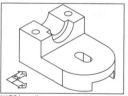

WCS is active.
UCS icon is not located at the origin.
The viewpoint is from the positive Z direction.

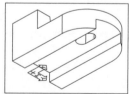

WCS is active.
UCS icon is located at the origin.
The viewpoint is from the negative Z direction.

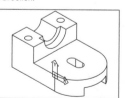

UCS is active.
UCS icon is located at the origin.
The viewpoint is from the positive Z direction.

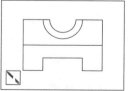

The viewpoint is within one degree of the XY plane.

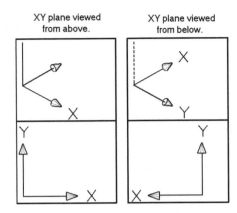

XY plane viewed from above.   XY plane viewed from below.

Controlling the Appearance of 3D Solids

Most of the time the surfaces of the 3D solid models you make will be transparent, with their geometry being indicated by lines and curves. This viewing mode is often called the *wireframe mode*, and sometimes the models themselves are referred to as *wireframes*, even though they are not true wireframe models. Although this is a good mode for selecting objects, the screen is often cluttered and it is difficult to visualize the model.

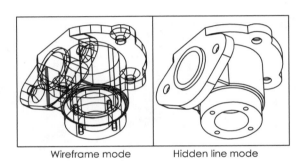

Wireframe mode   Hidden line mode

AutoCAD's HIDE command, which makes surfaces opaque, is one way to improve visualization. The resulting views are often referred to as *hidden line views*. Surfaces continue to be opaque until some operation causes a screen regeneration. A drawback to the HIDE command is that the real-time options of ZOOM and PAN are disabled when HIDE is in effect.

AutoCAD's SHADEMODE command displays 3D solids in wireframe, hidden line, and shaded modes. Unlike HIDE, the SHADEMODE viewing modes are not cancelled by a screen regeneration, and they work with real-time zooms and pans.

In shaded views, surfaces are colored-in according to their object color and the intensity, or relative brightness, of their color varies according to the orientation of the surface to the light source. Surfaces are at their brightest when they directly face incoming light beams, and the more inclined they are to incoming light, the dimmer they become. In the shaded views of SHADEMODE, AutoCAD aims a single light, by default, over the left shoulder of the viewer, toward the model.

SHADEMODE has five options, each of which establishes a specific viewing mode.

With the exception of the 2D Wireframe mode, all of these modes display the UCS icon as three mutually perpendicular cone shaped arrow heads on cylindrical shafts. Each arrow has a label and a distinctive color to help you identify the X, Y, and Z directions.

This option cancels the other SHADEMODE viewing modes and restores the normal AutoCAD viewing mode.

2D wireframe

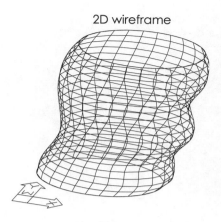

In this wireframe viewing mode, noncontinuous linetypes are displayed as continuous, and lineweights cannot be displayed.

3D wireframe

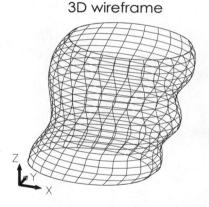

In this mode, surfaces become opaque.

Hidden

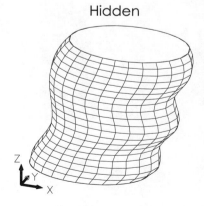

Flat shading

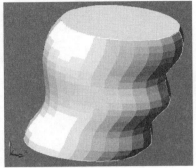

Surfaces are shaded. Rounded and curved surfaces are divided into facets, with the intensity of shading on each facet being uniform.

Gouraud shading

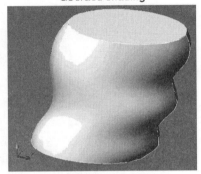

Surfaces are shaded. Rounded and curved surfaces are smoothly shaded—they are not facetted.

Flat shading plus edges

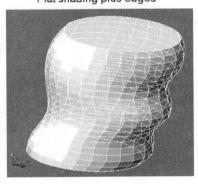

Surfaces are shaded, with rounded and curved surfaces displayed as facets. In addition, model and facet edges are displayed in the object's color.

Beginning with Mechanical Desktop 5, you have limited control of the light properties and direction in SHADE-MODE. AMLIGHT controls the light properties and AMLIGHTDIR controls the light direction. You can, though, initiate AMLIGHT-DIR from AMLIGHT. AMLIGHT displays a dialog box that has one slider bar for setting ambient light, and another for setting direction light.

By default, ambient light is low and direct light is high. As you increase ambient light, shaded objects become brighter and, if edges are displayed, more transparent looking. As you decrease direct light, shaded objects become darker and highlights decrease in intensity.

In the AMLIGHT dialog box, select the button with the light-bulb icon to initiate the AMLIGHTDIR command. You will be prompted from the command line to specify the light's direction by picking a point. The light will be aimed from the point you picked toward the center of the viewport.

Surfaces are shaded and edges are displayed in their object color. Rounded and curved surfaces are not facetted.

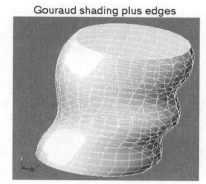

Gouraud shading plus edges

The appearance of 3D solids, whether they are AutoCAD solids or Mechanical Desktop parametric solids, is controlled by the following four AutoCAD system variables.

isolines isolines controls the relative number of lines and curves displayed on curved and rounded surfaces of 3D solids in wireframe views. They are a visualization aid. They do not affect the accuracy of the surfaces, are invisible to object picks, and do not appear on planar surfaces. You can assign any integer number from 0 to 2047 to **isolines**.

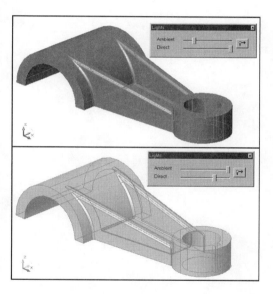

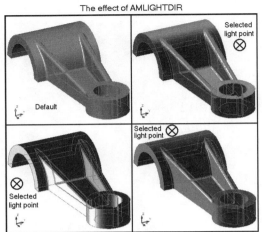

The effect of AMLIGHTDIR

dispsilh This system variable has a value of either 0 or 1. When **dispsilh** is set to 0, curved surfaces of 3D solids are delineated solely by isolines in wireframe views and they are faceted in when the HIDE command is in effect. When **dispsilh** is set to 1, profiles of curved surfaces are shown in addition to isolines in wireframe views, and the surfaces are not faceted in the hidden line views of the HIDE command.

isolines=4

isolines=8

facetres The relative size and number of the facets used for curved and rounded surfaces of 3D solids in hidden line views is controlled by this AutoCAD system variable. **Facetres** accepts any value between 0.0 and 10.0, with larger values resulting in more but smaller facets than lower values. The accuracy of surfaces is not affected by **facetres**—only their appearance in hidden line views.

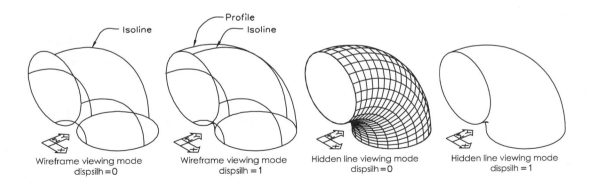

Wireframe viewing mode dispsilh=0

Wireframe viewing mode dispsilh=1

Hidden line viewing mode dispsilh=0

Hidden line viewing mode dispsilh=1

facetratio AutoCAD's **facetratio** system variable controls the relative number of lengthwise facets on cylindrical and conical surfaces of solids when **dispsilh** is set to 0. When it is set to 0, the side surfaces of cylinders and cones have facets that extend from one end to the other in hidden line views. On the other hand, when **facetratio** is set to 1, each facet will be divided lengthwise into at least two facets.

Setting Viewpoints in 3D Space

Unlike 2D drafting, in which you invariably look straight down toward the XY plane, you will frequently change viewpoints as you build 3D models and you will seldom look perpendicularly toward the XY plane. Although the word "viewpoint" is commonly used when referring to 3D views, most of the commands and techniques for establishing them set a viewing direction, or line of sight, rather

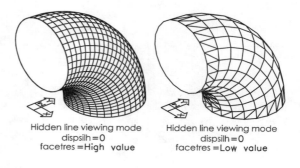

Hidden line viewing mode
dispsilh = 0
facetres = High value

Hidden line viewing mode
dispsilh = 0
facetres = Low value

than a specific observation point in 3D space. Through the years, AutoCAD and Mechanical Desktop have introduced numerous commands for establishing viewpoints. All of these commands still exist, and as described in the following paragraphs, most of them still have useful features.

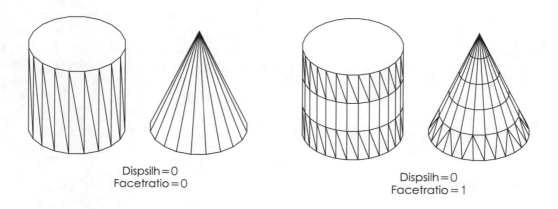

Dispsilh = 0
Facetratio = 0

Dispsilh = 0
Facetratio = 1

The VPOINT Command

AutoCAD's VPOINT command has two useful options for setting viewpoints: Vector and Rotate. (A third option—the compass and axis option—is not useful.) With the Vector option, you enter three numbers separated by commas. These numbers are the coordinates of the end of an invisible line, or vector, that begins at the WCS origin. Since the vector represents a direction, rather than a distance, the ratios between the numbers are important, while their magnitude is not. For example, there is no difference between the direction coordinates of 2.70,-1.50, 2.10 and 1.35, -0.75, 1.05. Furthermore, the resulting view always has the same zoom level regardless of the magnitude of the coordinates, and the model is always centered in the view regardless of its location relative to the WCS origin.

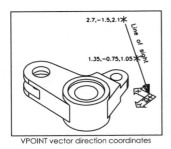

VPOINT vector direction coordinates

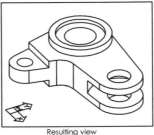

Resulting view

You specify two angles when you use VPOINT's rotate option. The first angle is the line of sight's angle *on* the XY plane, and the second angle is the line of sight's angle *from* the XY plane. We will sometimes give VPOINT vector coordinates or rotation angles in this book so that you can exactly duplicate the viewpoint used for a figure in an exercise.

The DVIEW Command

DVIEW is a multipurpose AutoCAD command for setting-up and working with views. A newer command, 3DORBIT, does almost everything that DVIEW can do, and it does it more conveniently. However, DVIEW has an option named Twist that 3DORBIT does not have. With this option, you specify an angle that represents the rotation of vertical lines (in the Z axis direction) about the view's line of sight. Thus, to straighten a view to an upright position, you would enter 0 as the twist angle.

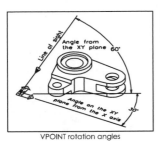

VPOINT rotation angles

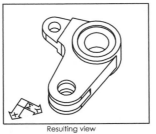

Resulting view

The PLAN Command

AutoCAD's PLAN command sets a line of sight that looks perpendicularly toward the positive side of the XY plane. This view direction is often referred to as a *plan view*. Options allow you to specify whether the plan view is for the WCS or the UCS XY plane.

The AMVIEW Command

The AMVIEW command of Mechanical Desktop has options for rotating the current view direction by a set angle in one of four specified directions—up, down, right, or left. It also has an option for setting the view rotation angle, and for setting a plan view. You will seldom use AMVIEW directly, but its rotation options can be invoked from Mechanical Desktop's acceleration keys, and its option for setting a plan view can be invoked by selecting the Sketch View button in the Mechanical View toolbar.

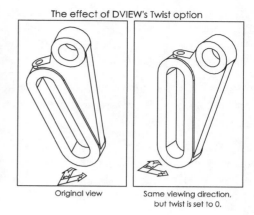

The effect of DVIEW's Twist option

Original view   Same viewing direction, but twist is set to 0.

The 3DORBIT Command

3DORBIT is the command you will most often use in setting viewpoints because it sets the line of sight in real time. When you start 3DORBIT, a large circle, which is called the *arcball,* is displayed in the center of the current viewport. As you move your pointing device while holding its pick button down, the image of the model rotates about an axis that passes through the center of the arcball, and the orientation of that axis depends on the location of the screen cursor, as described in the following paragraphs. Also, the appearance of the screen cursor changes to indicate the rotation axis orientation.

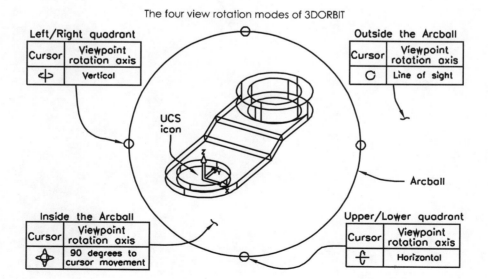

The four view rotation modes of 3DORBIT

Left/Right quadrant	
Cursor	Viewpoint rotation axis
⬍⬌	Vertical

Outside the Arcball	
Cursor	Viewpoint rotation axis
↻	Line of sight

Inside the Arcball	
Cursor	Viewpoint rotation axis
✥	90 degrees to cursor movement

Upper/Lower quadrant	
Cursor	Viewpoint rotation axis
⊢⊣	Horizontal

UCS icon

Arcball

- When the screen cursor is within the arcball, it assumes the shape of a sphere encircled by both a horizontal and a vertical arc-shaped arrow, and the viewpoint rotates about an axis that is perpendicular to the movement of the screen cursor. For example, if you move the cursor down and to the right 30 degrees from the horizontal edges of the viewport, the view rotation axis is inclined 60 degrees relative to the horizontal edges.

- When the cursor is outside the arcball, the screen cursor changes to a dot encircled by an arc-shaped arrow, and the model rotates about the viewport's line of sight as you move the cursor.

- When you move the screen cursor within either of the small circles on the top and bottom quadrants of the arcball and hold down your pointing device's pick button, the view rotation axis is horizontal. The appearance of the screen cursor will assume the form of a horizontal line within a vertical arc-shaped arrow.

- When you depress the pick button of your pointing device as the cursor is within either of the small circles on the right and left quadrants of the arcball, the screen cursor becomes a vertical line within a horizontal arc-shaped arrow, and the view rotation axis is vertical.

When you right-click during 3DORBIT, a shortcut menu offering additional options is displayed. As shown in the next figure, many options in this menu lead to options in secondary menus. Notice that a few of the options invoke other commands (which often have a name beginning with 3D) that are related to 3DORBIT.

When the current view is zoomed-in to an extremity of your model, setting a viewpoint with 3DORBIT may be confusing because the view rotation axis is centered in the current viewport, rather than in the center of the model. Therefore, Mechanical Desktop has two commands that specify the center of the rotation axis and then invoke 3DORBIT.

- AMROTCENTER calculates the geometric center of the model from the current view direction, pans to that point without changing the current zoom level, and starts 3DORBIT.

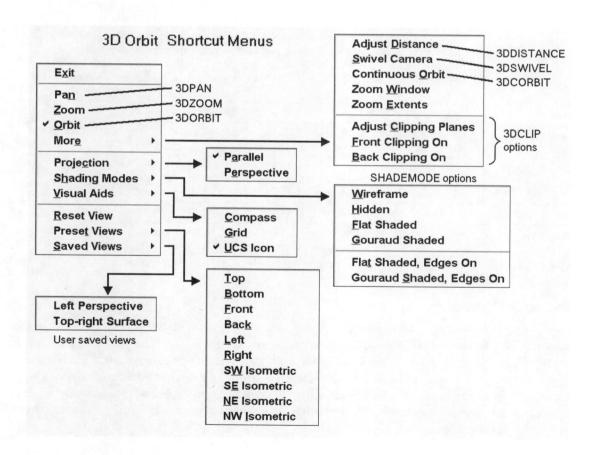

- AMSELROT prompts for a user specified center of rotation, and initiates 3DORBIT. You can specify the point by picking it with your pointing device or by entering its coordinates.

Options in the 3D Orbit Shortcut Menus	
Exit	Ends the 3DORBIT command. (You can also end 3DORBIT by pressing the Enter or Esc keys.)
Pan	Invokes the 3DPAN command for moving the image of the model in real time.
Zoom	Invokes 3DZOOM for increasing or decreasing the size of the model's image in real time.
Adjust Distance	Invokes 3DDISTANCE for adjusting perspective views.
Swivel Camera	Invokes 3DSWIVEL to set a viewpoint as if you were looking through a camera's viewfinder. Similar to swiveling (rather than moving) the camera, the image of the model will shift to the left when you move the cursor to the right, and the image will shift down when you move the cursor up.
Clipping	The three Clipping menu selections are for specific options of the 3DCLIP command, which creates and manages clipping planes. The two clipping planes are invisible planes perpendicular to the line of sight. The front clipping plane can hide everything from the plane toward the viewer. The back clipping plane can hide everything that is behind it.
Projection	Toggles between the parallel and perspective viewing modes.
Shading Modes	See the description of the SHADEMODE command earlier in this chapter for information on shading modes.
Visual Aids	The Grid and UCS Icon options turn the display of these features on and off. When the Compass option is selected, three concentric circles representing the three principal planes will be displayed inside the arcball.
Reset View	This option restores the view that existed when 3DORBIT was first invoked.
Preset Views	Sets the viewpoint to one of the six orthographic views or to one of the four isometric views that look down and at an angle toward the XY plane.
Saved Views	Restores a view that has been saved by AutoCAD's VIEW command.

Using Multiple Viewports

To help you visualize and select objects, AutoCAD enables you to divide the graphics area into multiple sections that are called viewports. Autodesk often refers to them as *tiled viewports*, because, similar to ceramic floor and wall tiles, they always abut each other. Unlike operating system windows, tiled viewports do not have title bars, cannot overlap, be dragged to other locations, or be stretched to another size or shape. In addition to fitting tightly against each other, tiled viewports are always rectangular and combined they always fill the entire graphics area.

Each viewport can have its own view direction, zoom level, snap and grid settings, and even its own UCS. (Generally, however, you will use the same UCS in all viewports when you are constructing parametric models.) You can work in just a single viewport, called the *current viewport*, in any instance in time. Additions and changes to the model made in the current viewport, though, are instantly shown in the other viewports, provided the additions or changes are in an area shown within the viewport. The current viewport is the one that contains the screen cursor crosshairs, and has a slightly thicker border than the others. In the accompanying figure, the upper left viewport is the current viewport.

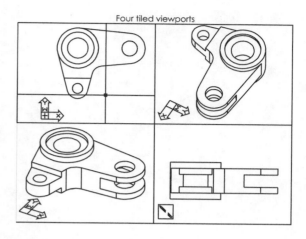

Four tiled viewports

You move from one viewport to another by moving the screen cursor crosshairs to the desired viewport and pressing the pick button of your pointing device. You can do this even in the middle of most commands. For example, you can select a base point for a move or copy operation in one viewport and select the destination point in another. You cannot, however, change viewports during commands affecting views—such as ZOOM, PAN, and 3DORBIT. AutoCAD's REDRAW and REGEN commands affect only the current viewport. To clean-up the display in all viewports, use the REDRAWALL and REGENALL commands.

Tiled viewports are created by AutoCAD's VPORTS command. You can create up to four viewports during a single use of VPORTS, but since you can create viewports within viewports, you can have a total of more than four. Seldom, though, will you need more than four viewports. VPORTS has options for setting orthographic and isometric viewpoints as the viewports are created. However, orthographic viewpoints are generally not suitable for 3D work. Isometric viewpoints are better, and viewpoints that are askew to true isometric viewpoints are often even better.

CHAPTER 2

Parametric Modeling Overview

Most of the chapters in this book concentrate on giving you detailed information for performing specific Mechanical Desktop operations. To give you some insight as to how those operations are related and where they fit within the process of constructing and using Mechanical Desktop models, this chapter gives you an overall look at parametric modeling.

This chapter covers the following topics.

- *Explains the purposes and characteristics of the two Mechanical Desktop modeling environments.*

- *Describes how parametrics, in the form of geometric and dimensional constraints, control the size, geometry, and proportions of part models.*

- *Introduces you to the feature-based technology of Mechanical Desktop.*

- *Demonstrates step-by-step how parametrics and features are used to construct a typical part model.*

- *Explains the relationship between a 3D part model and a 2D drawing of the model.*

- *Gives you a preview of Mechanical Desktop's assembly modeling module.*

A part model

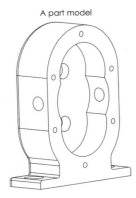

Mechanical Desktop's Modeling Environments

In manufacturing industries, a part is defined as an item that cannot be divided, while an assembly is a collection of related parts. For example, a gear pump assembly might consist of nine different parts: a body, a driving gear, a driven gear, four bushings, a gasket, a cover, a gland, a seal, and six screws. In line with these two definitions, Mechanical Desktop has two working environments. One environment is for modeling a single part, and the other is for modeling an assembly of parts.

An assembly model

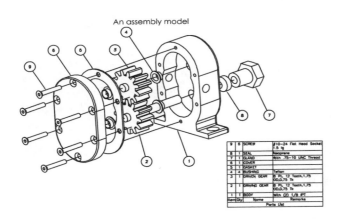

Item	Qty	Name	Remarks
9	6	SCREW	#10–24 Flat Head Socket 1.5 lg
8	1	SEAL	Neoprene
7	1	GLAND	With .75–10 UNC Thread
6	1	COVER	
5	1	GASKET	
4	4	BUSHING	Teflon
3	1	DRIVEN GEAR	B Pl, 12 Teeth,1.75 OD,0.75 Tk
2	1	DRIVING GEAR	B Pl, 12 Teeth,1.75 OD,0.75 Tk
1	1	BODY	With (2) 1/8 iPT
Item	Qty	Name	Remarks

Parts List

Which modeling environment is activated depends on how you start a new Mechanical Desktop drawing file. Selecting New from the File pulldown menu or selecting the New button from the Mechanical Main toolbar starts a new drawing in the Assembly Modeling environment. On the other hand, selecting New Part File from the File pulldown menu or selecting the New Part File button from the Mechanical Main toolbar starts a new drawing in the single Part Modeling environment.

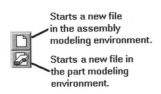

Starts a new file in the assembly modeling environment.

Starts a new file in the part modeling environment.

Assembly Modeling Environment

When you work in this environment, you have full access to all Mechanical Desktop commands and you can work in three different operating modes: Model, Scene, and Drawing. Tabs for these modes are on the top edge of the Desktop Browser, and you can switch from one mode to another by selecting a tab. Model mode is for working with parts and building assemblies, Scene mode is for exploding assemblies to obtain an unobstructed view of the assembly's individual parts, and Drawing mode is for creating 2D drawings of assemblies.

Part Modeling Environment

This environment is for working with a single part. Consequently, the Mechanical Desktop commands for creating and working with assemblies are not available. You can work in two different operating modes: Model and Drawing. Model mode, which is a fully 3D space, is for creating and working with a 3D part model. Drawing mode is for creating and working with 2D drawings of the part. You can switch from one mode to another by selecting the Model or Drawing tab at the top of the Browser. You will notice that the Assembly pulldown menu is replaced by the Toolbody menu in the part modeling environment. Toolbodies are described in the section on combining parts in Chapter 12.

Assembly modeling environment

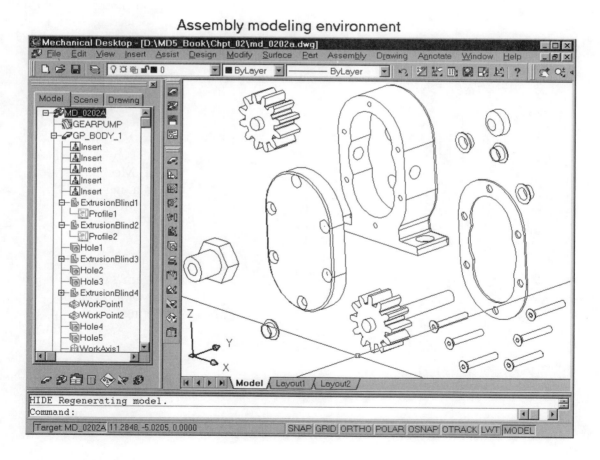

Even though the single part environment is more restrictive than the assembly environment, it is the environment you should use for creating a single part. Parts created within this environment can, as described in Chapter 17, be inserted into an assembly modeling file, but you cannot easily insert parts created within the assembly modeling environment into an assembly.

Part Models

Mechanical Desktop incorporates both parametric and feature-based technology in the construction of part models. The parametric technology enables you to construct 3D models that can easily be modified, while the feature based technology enables you to construct those models in a logical, step-by-step manner.

Part modeling environment

Parametrics

Parametrics control the size, geometry, and proportions of Mechanical Desktop part models. They come in two forms—*geometric constraints* and *dimensional constraints.* Geometric constraints (Mechanical Desktop sometimes calls them *2D constraints.*) control the geometry of a part. Through geometric constraints, for example, you can specify that two straight adjoining edges will always be perpendicular to one another, that the radius of two specified arc-shaped edges will always be equal, that a straight edge will always be tangent to an adjacent arc-shaped edge, and so forth.

Geometric constraints are invisible most of the time, but you can direct Mechanical Desktop to temporarily display them as symbols on or near the objects they control. By default, Mechanical Desktop automatically establishes some geometric constraints as objects are created, but you can both remove and add geometric constraints manually.

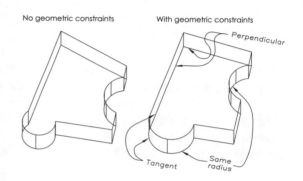

Dimensional constraints, on the other hand, control the size of objects. Although they look like ordinary AutoCAD dimensions, their relationship with objects is reversed—rather than just showing the size of objects, Mechanical Desktop's parametric dimensions actually control the size of objects. For example, the diameter of a cylinder is 23.5 mm because that is the value you assigned to its diameter dimension, not because you drew it to have a diameter of 23.5 mm.

Parametrics makes your approach to both drawing and modifying objects different in Mechanical Desktop than in AutoCAD. First of all, because of geometric constraints, you do not need to draw objects precisely or accurately. In fact, you will sometimes deliberately draw objects inaccurately and perhaps out-of-position, so that you can see them better and more readily make object selections. Moreover, almost all editing and modification operations are done by changing dimension values, rather than by stretching and moving objects as is done in conventional 2D drawings. For instance, to change the diameter of the cylinder mentioned in the previous paragraph from 23.5 mm to 18.0 mm, you would simply change the diameter dimension value to 18.0 mm. The cylinder's diameter will shrink to match the new dimension value.

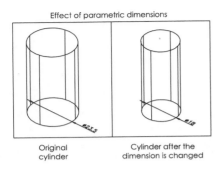

Effect of parametric dimensions

Original cylinder

Cylinder after the dimension is changed

It is possible to build a Mechanical Desktop part without using geometric and dimensional constraints, but you will seldom do that because the resulting model cannot be easily modified or edited. You can also add most geometric constraints and dimensions after a part has been partially, or even completely, constructed. As a rule, though, you should add constraints as you go, and you should advance to the next construction step only after the current feature is fully constrained.

Features

Features are the building blocks of a Mechanical Desktop part. They are used for a wide variety of purposes and they come in a wide variety of forms, ranging from a simple point to a complex 3D solid. Some features—such as work planes, round holes, and fillets—are generated directly by Mechanical Desktop (although they are based on user input), while others—such as profile and 2D path sketches—are based on user drawn objects. Some typical features are labeled on the part model shown in the following figure.

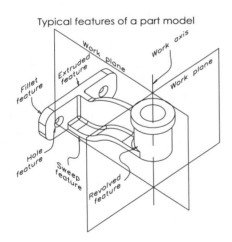

Typical features of a part model

Work plane

Work axis

Work plane

Extruded feature

Fillet feature

Hole feature

Sweep feature

Revolved feature

Every feature of a part is listed in Mechanical Desktop's Browser in an outline-type format that indicates what the feature is, the order in which the features were created, and how they are related. The following figure shows the Browser for the part in the previous figure. Notice that each feature has a name, such as Hole1 or ExtrusionBlind1, that is preceded by an icon. This icon is the same as the one on the toolbar button for creating the feature. You can change the generic names that Mechanical Desktop assigns to features to more specific names, such as No8screwHole or Manifold_flange.

Regardless of their purpose and form, all features are connected to one another through geometric or dimensional constraints. Because of these constraints you can, for example, easily change the length of the sweep feature of the part we have been discussing and the revolved feature will remain fixed at the end of the sweep feature.

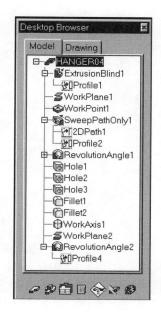

Steps in Constructing a Part Model

To give you an overall picture of the use of parametrics and features, we will step through the construction of a typical Mechanical Desktop part model. This example will serve both as an introduction to part modeling, and as a preview of some of the commands and operations used in constructing parts. While these steps will demonstrate some typical operations in constructing a part, they will not show you specifically how to perform those operations. Chapters 3–13 will explain and show you in detail everything you need to know for constructing Mechanical Desktop parts, including the operations used in this example.

The example part, which could be used as part of a hand crank assembly, is shown in Figure 1-1. This figure shows the completed part in the Gouraud Shading Plus Edges mode of AutoCAD's SHADEMODE command.

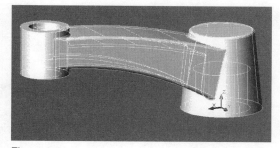

Figure 1-1

A Profile Feature

Generally, the first feature of a part will be a profile. (Mechanical Desktop sometimes refers to them as sketches.) The profile for our example part is shown in Figure 1-2. It consists of four AutoCAD wireframe objects—two arcs and two lines—that have been transformed into a profile feature by Mechanical Desktop's AMPROFILE command. The objects must be on a Mechanical Desktop sketch plane, which is comparable, but not equivalent, to AutoCAD's User Coordinate System. We have elected to draw this particular profile on the World Coordinate System's ZX plane, and therefore, the sketch plane is on the ZX plane of the WCS.

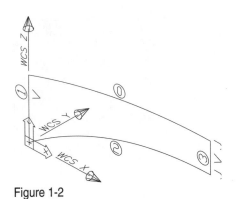

Figure 1-2

Even though the profile is made of ordinary AutoCAD objects, its components have relationships with one another that do not exist in AutoCAD. These relationships are the geometric constraints of the profile. In this profile, the two lines are constrained to always be parallel with the sketch plane's Y axis, and the centers of the two arcs are constrained to be in-line with the right-hand vertical line of the profile. (References to directions in Mechanical Desktop profiles use the word vertical to indicate the sketch plane's Y direction and horizontal to indicate the X direction.) Most of the time, geometric constraints are invisible. You can have Mechanical Desktop temporarily display symbols, as shown in Figure 1-2, that indicate the geometric constraint types and relationships.

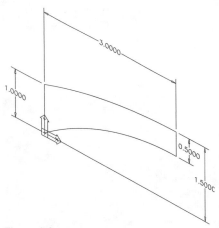

Figure 1-3

In addition to geometric constraints, most profiles need one or more dimensional constraints. This profile needs the four dimensions shown in Figure 1-3 to be fully constrained, which means that its geometry and size is fixed. You can change any or all of the four dimension values to change the size and shape of the profile. Notice that because of the geometric constraints, no radius dimensions are needed for the two arcs.

An Extruded Feature

Once the profile has been fully constrained, we use Mechanical Desktop's AMEXTRUDE command to push the profile one unit in a direction that is perpendicular to the profile to make the 3D feature shown in Figure 1-4. (This figure shows the 3D feature in the hidden line mode.)

AMEXTRUDE displays a dialog box for you to enter the parameters, such as the extrusion distance and direction, of the extruded feature. The profile and its dimensions disappear when the 3D feature is created, but you can restore them if you need to edit them. The first 3D feature that is created, such as this extruded feature, is the base feature of the part. All subsequent features directly or indirectly modify the base feature, and they are dependent to it.

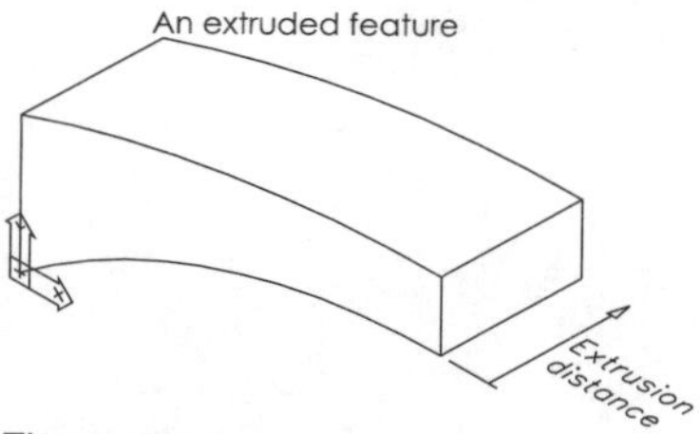

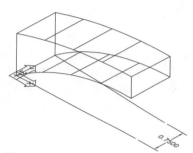

Figure 1-4

A Second Profile Feature

After moving the sketch plane to the XY plane of the WCS, we draw the two lines shown in Figure 1-5 for the profile of a 3D feature that will modify the base feature. Even though most profiles must form a closed loop, only two lines are needed for this particular profile because Mechanical Desktop allows you to close profiles with edges of existing 3D features (even if they are in different planes, as they are here).

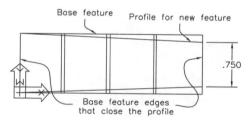

Figure 1-5

Figure 1-6 shows the plan view of the part to give you a better idea of the profile's relative position to the base feature. Constraints have been added to force the two lines of the profile to have the same length. As a result, only the one dimension shown in Figures 1-5 and 1-6 is needed to fully constrain this profile.

Figure 1-6

A Second Extruded Feature

Next, the profile is extruded up and through the base feature using a Boolean intersection operation to leave just the common, or intersecting, volume of the two features. The results are shown in a wireframe viewing mode in Figure 1-7. Extrusion is just one of the ways that a profile can be transformed into a 3D feature. Sweeping the profile along a path or revolving it about an axis are two other often used methods. You can also create a 3D feature by using two or more offset profiles to define its cross section.

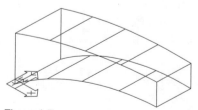

Figure 1-7

A Shell Feature

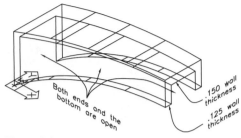

Figure 1-8

The next feature we will add to the part is a type that is often called a *placed feature*. Unlike the first two features of this part, placed features are not based on a profile. Instead, you specify the parameters of the feature (usually within a dialog box) and then you select the faces or edges that are to be modified by the placed feature. The placed feature we will add now is a *shell feature*. It hollows-out existing solid features, leaving an outer wall, or shell. In addition to specifying the overall resulting wall thickness, you can specify that some walls are a different thickness than others, and you can specify that some faces are to be open.

For our part, we specify an overall shell thickness of 0.125, but we make the upper curved face of the part 0.150 inches thick, and we specify that the bottom and both ends of the part are to be open. The results are shown in Figure 1-8.

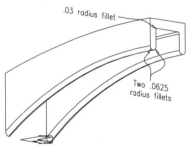

Figure 1-9

Fillet Features

We will use fillets, which are another type of placed feature, to round the bottom edge of the two vertical walls on the part. Since the walls are 0.125 thick, we specify that the radius of the fillets is to be 0.0625, and then simply pick each wall's two bottom edges. We also round the two inside corners of the part with fillets having a radius of 0.03. When you view the part from its lower side and with hidden lines removed, it looks like the one in Figure 1-9.

A Revolved Feature

The next 3D feature we make for this part will, as were the first two, be based on a profile. These are often called *sketched features*. The sketch plane is moved to the large end of the part, and a profile consisting of four lines is drawn, as shown in Figure 1-10. As is often the case, the part is becoming cluttered and it is difficult to distinguish objects. In this figure you can identify the four line of the profile by their dimensions. With the models you build, you will probably use layers with distinctive colors to help you recognize objects.

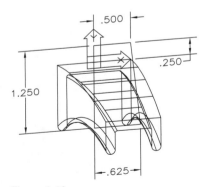

Figure 1-10

The purpose of the 0.250 dimension is to tie the profile to the existing part, rather than help define the geometry of the profile. A geometric constraint, which is not visible in Figure 1-10, also helps constrain the profile to the existing part.

This profile is rotated about the 1.250 line to make the revolved 3D feature shown, with hidden lines removed, in Figure 1-11.

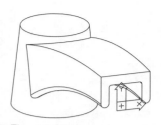

Figure 1-11

Another Revolved Feature

Next the sketch plane is moved to the vertical face on the opposite end of the part, where four lines are drawn for another profile. The profile and the three dimension that fully constrain it are shown in Figure 1-12. The right-hand vertical line of the profile is constrained to be collinear with the right-hand vertical edge of the face. Although this geometric constraint is not visible, it, along with the 0.125 dimension, ties the profile to the part.

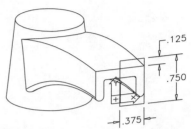

Figure 1-12

A 3D feature is created from this profile by revolving the profile about its left-hand vertical line. The part now looks like the one in Figure 1-13.

Hole Features

Since round holes are so common, Mechanical Desktop has a command that specializes in making them. While the command, AMHOLE, has provisions for making countersink and counterbore holes, we need

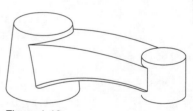

Figure 1-13

just two simple holes in this part. One is a 0.50 diameter hole completely through the center of the small revolved feature. The other is a 0.875 diameter hole 0.625 deep in the bottom surface of the large revolved feature. The parameters for each of these holes is specified in a dialog box, their locations are pointed out to Mechanical Desktop, and each hole is centered in the feature without further input. The two holes are shown in Figure 1-14 from a viewpoint that looks up toward the part from below the WCS XY plane.

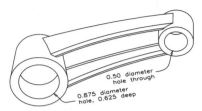

Figure 1-14

More Fillet Features

The part is finished by rounding some of its sharp edges and corners with fillet features. It looks like the one shown in Figure 1-1 at the beginning of this demonstration on page 37.

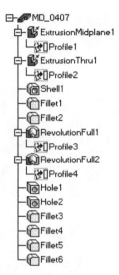

Figure 1-15

The Desktop Browser for this part is shown in Figure 1-15. Notice that every feature of the part is included and is shown in the order it was created. The model for this example is in file md02e101.dwg on the CD-ROM that comes with this book. If you retrieve and open this file, you can use Mechanical Desktop's AMREPLAY command to step through each of the construction steps we've described. This command is easy to use and requires no user input, other than to press the Enter key to advance to the next step. If you have trouble, though, you can read about AMREPLAY in Chapter 13.

Even though this part is reasonably complex, it is not difficult to construct because it is built one feature as a time. Since its features are linked together and are based on geometric and dimensional constraints, the part is readily modified when design changes are needed. Also, the part can be used in the model of an assembly in which a knob would be attached to the crank through the 0.50 diameter hole and the crank itself would be attached to the part it is to turn.

2D Drawings from Part Models

You can create 2D multiview drawings from 3D part models, such as the example one we just constructed. As you would surmise, this is done in Mechanical Desktop's Drawing mode. Virtually no drafting is required to make these drawings. You specify the views, and Mechanical Desktop draws the part as it appears in those views. You can create any of the standard six orthographic views (such as the top view, front view, right side view, and so forth), as well as auxiliary views and section views. You can also even create isometric views.

Mechanical Desktop automatically adds most of the dimensions in the drawing views. They are based on the dimensions used to constrain the profiles and on data you entered in dialog boxes, such as extrusion lengths, when you created the features. You do have to add a few dimensions, such as those for holes and fillets, manually. Even then, though, Mechanical Desktop will supply most of the dimension values for you.

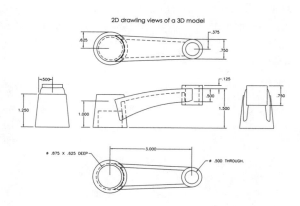

The 2D drawing are also parametric because they use the same database of geometric and dimensional constraints used by the 3D model. Therefore, when you make changes to a part in Model mode, the drawing views and their dimensions for that part are automatically updated to reflect the changes. Conversely, when you change dimension values in drawing views, the 3D model is updated. Compare the views and dimensions in the figures to the right with those in the previous figure to see the relationship between the model and its dimensions in drawing views. AutoCAD editing operations, such as moving, stretching, and trimming, are not needed, nor are they even allowed. User editing input consists simply of entering new dimension values, and telling Mechanical Desktop to update the model and its drawing.

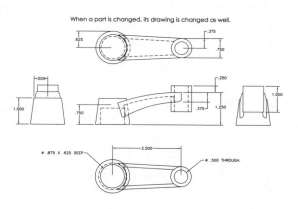

Assembly Modeling

Since a single part is usually connected in some way with other parts to form an assembly, Mechanical Desktop has an assembly modeling module for you to use in creating and working with multiple parts and with assemblies of parts. Among the features of Mechanical Desktop's assembly modeling module are the following.

Part Management Although the parts that are used in an assembly can reside in the assembly's file, they more often are in external files. To accommodate this practice, Mechanical Desktop has a full set of tools for importing parts into assembly files and for maintaining relationships between part files and assembly files.

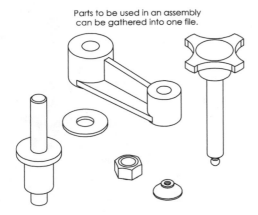

Parts to be used in an assembly can be gathered into one file.

Part Constraints Individual parts in an assembly always fit together in specific ways. For instance, a nut will fit on a similarly sized bolt, and the bolt will be within a round hole through one or more parts. Therefore, Mechanical Desktop has a set of commands for constraining one part with another part. Mechanical Desktop often calls them *3D constraints* to distinguish them from the 2D geometric constraints of feature profiles.

Exploded Views Mechanical Desktop can make assembly views in which the individual parts are spread apart (exploded) so that you can better see their form and the relationships between parts. Mechanical Desktop refers to an exploded view as a scene, and you can make more than one scene from an assembly.

Assembly Drawings Just as with individual parts, you can make 2D drawings of assemblies. The drawings can have orthographic and section views, plus views of scenes. They can also list the parts in the assembly, and the parts can be identified by part numbers and balloons.

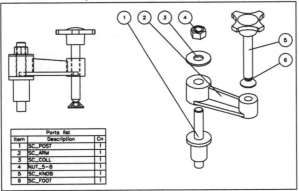

Assembly drawings can contain orthographic and exploded views, as well as a parts list.

Ports list		
Item	Description	Cn
1	SC_POST	1
2	SC_ARM	1
3	SC_COLL	1
4	NUT_5-8	1
5	SC_KNOB	1
6	SC_FOOT	1

CHAPTER 3

Profiles and Sketch Planes

Virtually all of the 3D solid features that make up a part model are based on profile features. Profiles, which are based on 2D wireframe objects, have considerable control over how easily parts are constructed and modified. The objects you select for a profile must lay on the current sketch plane. While sketch planes have some similarities with the AutoCAD User Coordinate System's XY plane, they are a unique Mechanical Desktop plane for drawing 2D objects.

This chapter covers the following topics.

- *Introduces you to the sketch feature types.*

- *Explains how to create profiles for constructing 3D features.*

- *Describes the uniqueness of the base feature of a part.*

- *Tells you how to close profiles with edges of existing 3D features.*

- *Describes how to create open profiles and shows you examples of the features you can create from them.*

- *Tells you how to transform text into a profile.*

- *Explains how sketch planes differ from the UCS, and how to position and orient sketch planes.*

- *Describes Mechanical Desktop's commands for working with the UCS.*

Sketches

Profiles belong to a class of features called sketches. Altogether, there are five different types of sketches, and five different commands for creating them, as shown in the following table.

Mechanical Desktop Sketch Types

Sketch Type	Command	Purpose
Profile	AMPROFILE	To make the profile of a 3D feature
2D Path	AM2DPATH	To make a planar path for sweeping a profile in making a 3D feature
Splitline	AMSPLITLINE	For splitting faces of 3D features, and for splitting a part into two separate parts
Cutting Line	AMCUTLINE	To make an offset section view through a model that is to be shown in a 2D drawing
Break Line	AMBREAKLINE	To make a breakout section within a model for a 2D drawing section view

While these five sketch types serve different purposes and have different shape criteria, they are all based on ordinary AutoCAD objects, such as lines and arcs, that are drawn on a plane. They are referred to as sketches because you can draw them imprecisely and then use geometric and dimensional constraints to obtain the exact sizes and shapes you want. We will focus on profile sketches in this chapter, and we will discuss the other four sketch types in subsequent chapters as we cover the operations in which they are used.

Profiles

At least three steps are needed to create most Mechanical Desktop 3D features. First, you must sketch the outline of the 3D feature using ordinary AutoCAD wireframe objects, such as lines and arcs. Next, you must turn those objects into a Mechanical Desktop profile with the AMPROFILE command, and use geometric and dimensional constraints to fully constrain it. Finally, you must use one of the five methods shown in the following table to transform the profile into a 3D feature. Mechanical Desktop often refers to these 3D feature types as *sketched features*, because they are based on profiles, which in turn, are based on sketches.

Methods for Creating a 3D Feature from a Profile

Method	Command	Operation
Extrusion	AMEXTRUDE	Pushes the profile perpendicularly from its plane

Method	Command	Operation
	Methods for Creating a 3D Feature from a Profile (Continued)	
Extrusion	AMRIB	Pushes the profile in its plane to an existing 3D feature
Rotation	AMREVOLVE	Revolves the profile about an axis
Sweep	AMSWEEP	Pushes the profile along a path
Loft	AMLOFT	Two or more profiles serve as cross sections of the 3D feature

Most sketches for profiles form a closed loop, but the sketch does not have to be made from a single object—it can consist of any number of open objects that touch (or, because of constraints, almost touch) end-to-end to form a closed loop. Valid AutoCAD objects for sketches include lines, circles, arcs, ellipses, planar splines, and any member of the 2D-polyline family. You can also use edges of existing 3D features as sketch objects. Regions, 3D-polylines, non-planar splines, and self-intersecting objects (such as four lines that form a bow-tie figure) cannot be used.

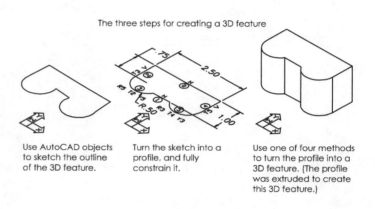

The three steps for creating a 3D feature

Use AutoCAD objects to sketch the outline of the 3D feature.

Turn the sketch into a profile, and fully constrain it.

Use one of four methods to turn the profile into a 3D feature. (The profile was extruded to create this 3D feature.)

Note: Prior to Release 4, Mechanical Desktop used the name "sketch" rather than "profile" in the Desktop Browser, and often used the words "sketch" and "profile" interchangeably in its prompts and documentation. That is also true in the current Mechanical Desktop release, although not to the extent it was in earlier releases. In this book, we will use the word "sketch" to mean the AutoCAD objects used to draw the outline of a 3D feature, and we will use the word "profile" to refer to those same objects after they have been transformed into a profile feature.

A profile can contain multiple loops. When one loop is within another (larger) loop, the volume of the inside loop is subtracted from the volume of the outside loop when the 3D feature is created. When the loops are separated, their volume is combined into one 3D feature, even though there is empty space between the components of the feature.

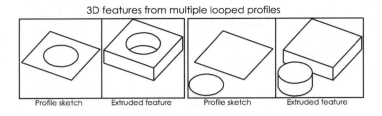

3D features from multiple looped profiles

Profile sketch   Extruded feature   Profile sketch   Extruded feature

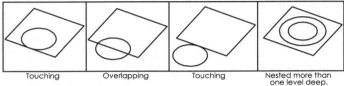

These configurations of multiple looped profiles are not allowed.

Touching   Overlapping   Touching   Nested more than one level deep.

Individual loops, however, cannot touch one another, overlap, or be nested more than one level deep. Actually, the AMPROFILE command permits you to make such profiles, but attempts to use them to create a 3D feature will fail.

Profiles with multiple loops are convenient for making 3D features that are complicated to set up, such as sweep features. Multiple looped profiles have significant limitations, though; they cannot be used to create lofted features or in making 3D features based on certain types of 3D paths. Also, the options for using planes and faces to terminate extruded and revolved features are not available with profiles having multiple loops. As we discuss those operations, we will remind you of the multiple looped profile limitations.

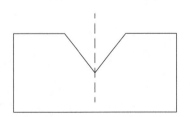

Objects with non-continuous linetypes can be included in a profile to help constrain and dimension the profile.

By default, profile objects must have a CONTINUOUS linetype. (You can change this default by changing the contents of Mechanical Desktop's **amskstyle** system variable, but you are not likely to ever do this.) You can, though, include objects that are drawn in a non-continuous linetype, such as HIDDEN, or CENTER. These objects, which are often referred to as construction geometry, become part of the profile, but they are not used to close or form the feature. Rather, they are used in constraining and dimensioning the profile. Construction geometry is used in conjunction with dimensions, as well as for controlling shapes and as rotation axes. Chapter 5 contains a detailed discussion of construction geometry.

When you invoke the AMPROFILE command, Mechanical Desktop will prompt you to select the objects for the profile. Depending upon the settings of some system variables that we will discuss in Chapter 4, the sketch objects may shift and realign themselves as gaps are closed and geometric constraints force slightly sloped lines to be horizontal, lines that are almost parallel to be parallel, and so forth.

Mechanical Desktop's Part/ Sketch Solving pulldown menu and its Profile toolbar contain an option called Single Profile that invokes an AutoLISP based menu macro for turning the most recently created AutoCAD object into a profile. For this option to successfully work, the most recently created object must be a closed object, such as a circle, an ellipse, or a closed 2D polyline.

Existing AutoCAD dimensions, provided they are associative dimensions, can be included in the selection set of objects for the profile. In most cases, these will be incorporated into the profile as Mechanical Desktop dimensional constraints.

Even though the objects comprising a profile are still individual objects, and AutoCAD's LIST command will continue to describe them as ordinary AutoCAD objects, they form a unique Mechanical Desktop feature. AutoCAD editing and modification commands that affect the sketch's constraints either do not work, or they work in a way that will not compromise the constraints. Moving a single object in a sketch, for instance, will generally cause the other objects in the sketch to move and rearrange themselves to accommodate the object's new location.

As a rule, any changes you make in the profile's geometry will be done through constraints and dimensions, rather than through AutoCAD editing operations. If, however, you need to change the number

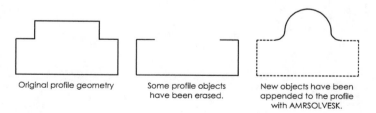

Original profile geometry

Some profile objects have been erased.

New objects have been appended to the profile with AMRSOLVESK.

or the type of the profile's objects—such as to replace an arc with a straight line—you can erase objects in the profile, draw new objects, and incorporate them in the profile with the AMRSOLVESK command. When you invoke this command, the existing profile objects will be highlighted to help you distinguish them from the new objects, and a command line prompt will ask you to select the objects that are to be added to the profile. Constraints and dimensions that already exist will be retained, and Mechanical Desktop will report the number of constraints and dimensions needed to fully constrain the re-solved profile.

The Base Feature

The very first 3D feature you create from a profile is called the base feature. It serves as a foundation to be built on and modified by subsequent features in making a finished part. Since all other features are dependent on the base feature, deleting it deletes the entire part. Also, you cannot make copies of base features, and you cannot suppress them. (Copies of features are discussed in Chapter 12, and feature suppression is discussed in Chapter 13.)

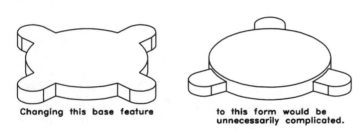

Changing this base feature   to this form would be unnecessarily complicated.

Drawing the profile sketch for the base feature is not only the first step in constructing a model, it has a great deal of control over how easily the part is made and how easily it can be modified. It should have a form that will not cause problems if the model is modified. The base feature shown on the left in this figure, for example, is not a good one because it would be difficult to change the number of lobes or to make their thickness different than the center disk. A simple round disk would be a much better base feature. You should consider the base feature as raw stock material that is to be carved, added to, and supplemented by other features.

Using Existing Feature Edges to Close Profiles

If the objects you select for the profile of a dependent feature do not form a closed loop, AMPROFILE will prompt you to select the edges of existing 3D features to close the profile. These

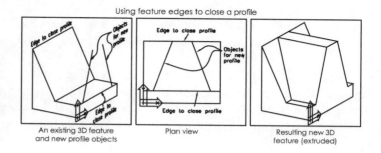

Using feature edges to close a profile

An existing 3D feature and new profile objects   Plan view   Resulting new 3D feature (extruded)

edges do not have to be on the same plane as the sketched profile objects, because Mechanical Desktop projects the selected edges perpendicularly onto the sketch plane. Therefore, as illustrated in this figure, the edges need only appear to close the profile when seen from a plan view.

The side of a rounded feature, such the side of a cylinder, can also be used to close sketches, but you must take a couple extra steps before Mechanical Desktop will recognize them. First, you must assign a value of 1 to the AutoCAD system variable **dispsilh**. This causes the profile, or silhouette, of curved and rounded surfaces of 3D features to always be displayed in wireframe views, regardless of the viewpoint. Second, you must select the silhouette edge within a plan view of the sketch plane.

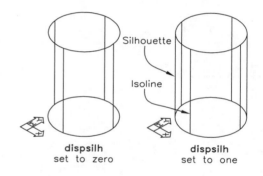

dispsilh set to zero   dispsilh set to one

As an example, the panel on the left in this figure shows a cylindrical shaped base feature, plus three lines of a profile sketch for making a groove (such as one for a retaining ring) around the cylinder. **Dispsilh** has been set to 1, and consequently the silhouette of the cylinder is shown in all views. Even though the open side of the sketch is closed by an isoline,

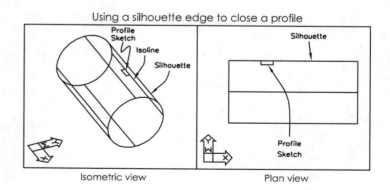

Using a silhouette edge to close a profile

Isometric view   Plan view

Mechanical Desktop will not recognize the isoline as a closing edge. Therefore, as shown on the right in this figure, you must switch to a plan view of the sketch so that the silhouette of the cylinder's side is on the sketch plane. AMPROFILE will then accept the silhouette as a closing edge.

Using existing feature edges to close a profile is a convenience, not a requirement, that reduces the number of sketch objects you must draw and reduces the number of constraints you must add to the profile. You cannot, however, copy profiles that have been closed with a feature edge, nor copy 3D features based on such profiles.

Open Profiles

Beginning with Release 5, Mechanical Desktop permits open profiles. These are created by the same command that creates closed profiles—AMPROFILE. When the objects you select for a profile do not form a closed loop, AMPROFILE will prompt for a part edge to close the profile, and when you press the Enter key in response to this prompt, AMPROFILE will create an open profile. Open profiles have Browser names such as OpenProfile1, OpenProfile2, and so forth.

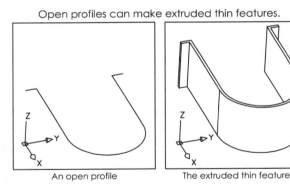

Open profiles can make extruded thin features.

An open profile   The extruded thin feature

You can only use the AMEXTRUDE and AMRIB commands in creating 3D features from open profiles. Both of these commands make planar solid features that are referred to as *thin features*, and you specify the feature's thickness as you implement the commands.

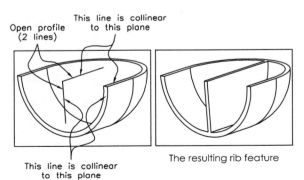

This line is collinear to this plane

Open profile (2 lines)

This line is collinear to this plane

The resulting rib feature

One of these two figures shows an example of an extruded thin feature, and the other shows an example of a rib feature. Notice that the profile for the rib feature does not need to extend to the existing 3D feature's edges. Chapter 8 explains how to use open profiles to make thin features.

Another use of open profiles is in making bend features with the AMBEND command. This command is useful in creating models of sheet metal parts. As shown in this figure, one open profile, which is always a single straight line, is used for the bend feature, and the open profile is constrained or dimensioned to an existing part edge. Bend features are discussed in Chapter 8.

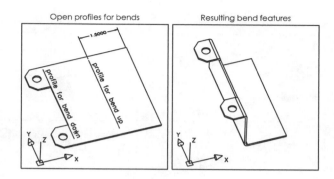

Open profiles for bends   Resulting bend features

Text Sketch Profiles

Text based profiles have been introduced with Mechanical Desktop Release 5. They are created with the AMTEXTSK command, and they can be extruded or revolved. Text sketches are especially useful for creating identification text, such as a model number or manufacturer's name, on a part. When you invoke AMTEXTSK, the `Text Sketch` dialog box is displayed for you to use in specifying the text within the sketch and its properties. Enter the text in the edit box labeled Text. You can enter only one line of text. Select a font for the

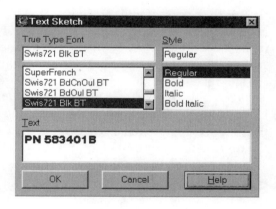

text from the dropdown list box. As you select a font the text you have entered will assume the font's form, and the font's name will be displayed in the upper-right corner of the dialog box. You can also specify a style, such as bold or italic, for the text.

When the text, font, and style are as you want them, click the OK button of the dialog box. Mechanical Desktop will issue the following command line prompts.

```
Specify first corner: (Specify a point on the current sketch plane.)
(As you move the screen cursor, a rectangle that has one corner anchored on the specified
    point will change size to indicate the boundaries of the text.)
Specify opposite corner or [Height/Rotation]: (Specify a point or enter a H or R.)
```

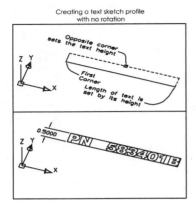

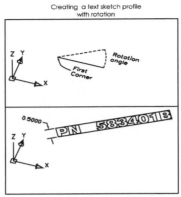

If you specify a point, it is used as the height of the sketch. You cannot specify a text length directly, (and usually the text rectangle will extend beyond the opposite corner location) because it is controlled by the text height. If you select the Height option, you will be prompted to enter the height of the text on the command line. If you select the Rotation option, the text rectangle will be replaced by a pie-shaped image that dynamically indicates the inclination of the text rectangle from the X axis. You can enter the inclination angle on the command line, or you can specify it with your pointing device. You can also switch the angle from its default counterclockwise rotation to clockwise. After you specify an angle, you will be prompted to specify the text height.

The text rectangle continues to enclose the text sketch, and you will use the sides of this rectangle to constrain and dimension the profile. Also, Mechanical Desktop automatically places a dimension on the rectangle to indicate the text height. In the Browser, text profiles use TextSketch as their name prefix. See Chapter 8 for information on transforming text sketches into 3D features.

Sketch Planes

Positioning the Sketch Plane

The sketch objects you select for a profile must be located on the current sketch plane. Mechanical Desktop's sketch plane is similar to the XY plane of AutoCAD's User Coordinate System (UCS).

- It is a flat work area on which you can use your pointing device to specify point locations.

- The plane can be located anywhere in 3D space, and it can be oriented in any position.

- The orientation of the X and Y axes, along with the location of the origin, is indicated by AutoCAD's UCS icon.

Despite these similarities, the sketch plane is not the same as the UCS XY plane, and the two planes do not necessarily have the same location and orientation. When you move or reorient the sketch plane, the UCS XY plane automatically moves and reorients itself to match the sketch plane. However, the reverse is not true—the sketch plane does not move when you move the UCS XY plane.

The initial location of the sketch plane in Mechanical Desktop's template drawings is on the World Coordinate System XY plane, so you can often create the profile for the base 3D feature without moving the sketch plane. Typically, once you have created the base 3D feature, you will move the sketch plane to a flat face somewhere on the feature, create another profile and 3D feature, move the sketch plane to a position suitable for creating a third 3D feature, and so forth until your part is completed. Mechanical Desktop stores the sketch plane location and orientation of every profile, and whenever you edit a profile, its sketch plane is automatically restored.

The Mechanical Desktop command that manages the sketch plane is AMSKPLN, which uses two steps in establishing the sketch plane. The first step sets the position of the plane, and the second step establishes the directions of its X and Y axes. AMSKPLN starts by issuing the following command line prompt.

```
Select work plane, planar face or [worldXy/worldYz/worldZx/Ucs]: (Enter an option, select a
    work plane, or select a planar face.)
```

Your response to this prompt establishes the location of the sketch plane. Notice that there are four basic options for establishing its location.

1. You can place the sketch plane on one of the three principal planes of the WCS. These planes, which AMSKPLN refers to as the worldXy, worldYz, and worldZx planes are sometimes useful for setting up the profile sketch or path sketch of a base feature.

2. Select a work plane by picking a point on one of its edges. (Work planes are described in Chapter 7.)

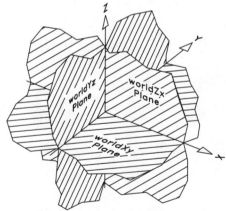

The three principal WCS planes

3. Select the planar face of an existing feature. You can select the face by either picking a point on its edge or by picking a point on its surface. Moreover, you can pick a point on the face surface even in wireframe views where you cannot see the surface. If the selection point is such that it could specify any of several different planes, Mechanical Desktop will highlight the edges of one of the faces and issue command line prompts for you to accept it, or to switch to another possible face. When the face you want is highlighted, press Enter to accept it. An animated cursor, which we will describe shortly, will also be displayed to help you specify a face.

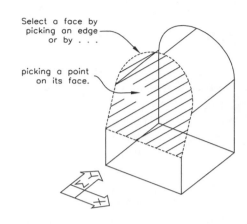

Select a face by picking an edge or by . . .

picking a point on its face.

4. Place the sketch plane in the same location as the XY plane of AutoCAD's User Coordinate System (UCS). This is the method you will use when none of the other three methods meet your needs.

Once the plane of the sketch plane has been established, AMSKPLN will issue a command line prompt for establishing the orientation of the X and Y axes.

```
Select edge to align X axis or [Flip/Rotate/Origin]<accept>: (Enter F, O, or R, select an
    edge, or press Enter.)
```

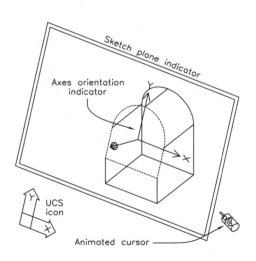

Sketch plane indicator

Axes orientation indicator

UCS icon

Animated cursor

In conjunction with this prompt Mechanical Desktop will display a double-edged rectangle on the sketch plane, and will indicate the X, Y, and Z directions by three mutually perpendicular arrows located on the rectangle. Furthermore, when you move the screen cursor away from the part, an icon containing two rotating arrows will appear. This icon, which is called the *animated cursor*, indicates that you can rotate the X and Y axis by pressing the pick button of your pointing device. Each time you press the pick button, the X and Y axes will rotate about the Z axis 90 degrees. Press Enter to signal your acceptance of the present orientation.

The animated cursor is offered as a convenience for reducing keyboard input. You can ignore it by picking a straight edge on the model to set the orientation of the X axis, or by entering the letter R to rotate the X and Y axis 90 degrees about the Z axis. Enter the letter F if you need to flip the direction of the Z axis. Most people orient the sketch plane so that the X axis points to the right, but that is not really necessary. You can even have the Z axis pointed into the screen, rather than toward you, but dimensions and text will be difficult to read because you will be seeing them from their reverse side. Usually, the location of the sketch plane origin (the point having the coordinates of 0,0) is not important. You can specify its location by selecting the Origin option, and then specifying a point.

AMSHOWSKETCH is a utility command that helps you locate objects on the current sketch plane. It will issue a command line prompt for you to select the objects that are to be considered. If you press the Enter key in response to this prompt, all objects will be considered. All wireframe objects that are on the current sketch plane will be highlighted, until you press Enter to end the command. 3D feature edges that are on the sketch plane will not be highlighted.

The UCS and the Sketch Plane

Mechanical Desktop chooses its own location for the origin of the sketch plane, and the origin might not even be on the face you selected. (It will, though, always be on the same plane as the selected face.) Usually the location of the origin is not important, but if you do want the sketch plane origin located on a specific point, use AutoCAD's UCS command to position the origin and the XY plane exactly as you want, and then use the Ucs option of AMSKPLN to match the location and orientation of the sketch plane with the UCS.

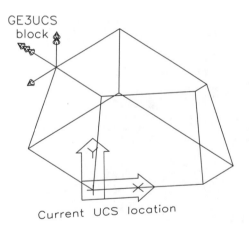

You will usually use AutoCAD's UCS and UCSMAN commands in working with the UCS. Mechanical Desktop, though, has the following four additional commands for working with the UCS.

Command	Description
AMUCSFACE	Moves the UCS to a selected planar face on a Mechanical Desktop 3D solid feature. As soon as you specify the face, the UCS will move to it. No additional prompts are issued, and you have no choice as to the location of the UCS origin or the directions of the X and Y axes.

Command	Description
AMUCSPERP	Moves the origin of the UCS to a selected line or straight edge on a 3D feature. The origin will be on the end nearest the object selection point, the Z axis will be along the selected edge, and the X axis will be parallel with the WCS XY plane. This command also has an option that moves the sketch plane to the newly established UCS.
AMCAPTUREUCS	Use this command to save the current UCS location and orientation. No prompts are issued. Mechanical Desktop creates and inserts a block named GE3UCS on the UCS origin. This block has three mutually perpendicular lines tipped with cone-shaped arrowheads. One arrowhead indicates the X axis, the second indicates the Y axis, and the third indicates the Z axis. This command, which was introduced in Mechanical Desktop Revision 4, is not supported in Revision 5.
AMRESTOREUCS	Restores a UCS saved by the AMCAPTUREUCS command. A command line prompt will ask you to select a GE3UCS block, and a second prompt will ask if you want the sketch plane moved to the restored UCS. This command, which was introduced in Mechanical Desktop Revision 4, is not supported in Revision 5.

CHAPTER 4

Geometric Constraints

Geometric constraints are a key component in creating 3D features and parts that can be readily modified. Therefore, learning the concepts that constraints are based on, what they can do, and how to work with them is vital in mastering parametric part modeling in Mechanical Desktop.

This chapter covers the following topics.

- *Introduces you to geometric constraints.*

- *Describes each of the 15 geometric constraint types.*

- *Explains how to view, add, and delete geometric constraints.*

- *Explains how to establish the rules Mechanical Desktop uses in creating sketches and constraints.*

Constraints

As you have learned, creating a profile feature that can be extruded, revolved, swept, or lofted to make a Mechanical Desktop 3D feature is quite simple. You use ordinary AutoCAD objects, such as lines and arcs, to make a 2D sketch that represents the outline of the 3D feature you intend to make, and then you turn the sketch into a profile feature with the AMPROFILE command. Such a profile, however, is not ready to be transformed into a 3D feature. Its size and shape should first be completely fixed, or constrained. Although nothing prevents you from using unconstrained profiles to make 3D features, such features are not easily modified and the advantages of parametric modeling are lost.

Usually, but not always, both geometric and dimensional constraints are needed to fully constrain a profile. *Geometric constraints* (Mechanical Desktop sometimes calls them *2D constraints*) control orientations and relationships between objects in a profile, while *dimensional constraints* control the sizes of profile objects. In its prompts and messages, Mechanical Desktop refers to a partially constrained profile as *under constrained*, and to a completely constrained profile as *fully constrained*.

We will focus on geometric constraints in this chapter, and we will focus on dimensional constraints in Chapter 5. Even though we are concentrating on constraints for profile features in these two chapters, constraints, along with the commands for creating and managing them, also apply to 2D path, splitline, cutting line, and break line sketches.

When a profile is transformed into a 3D feature, it, along with its dimensional and geometric constraints, disappears. Mechanical Desktop says that it has been *consumed*. Consumed profiles can be retrieved, though, and constraints, both geometric and dimensional, can be added and modified. (The discussion in Chapter 9 about editing sketched features explains how to do this.) Although it is generally best to fully constrain profiles before they are consumed, you may occasionally create a 3D feature from an under constrained sketch when you are uncertain as to what characteristics of the part are important, or what direction the design will take.

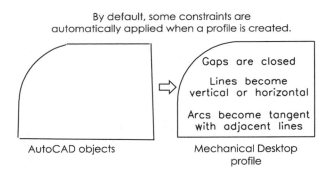

By default, some constraints are automatically applied when a profile is created.

Gaps are closed

Lines become vertical or horizontal

Arcs become tangent with adjacent lines

AutoCAD objects

Mechanical Desktop profile

An Introduction to Geometric Constraints

Altogether, Mechanical Desktop has 15 different types of geometric constraints. By default, Mechanical Desktop applies some of these constraints when AMPROFILE creates a profile. As a result, lines that are slightly askew to the X and Y axes become exactly parallel with those axes, gaps between adjacent object endpoints close, rounded corners become tangent with adjacent lines, and so forth. Mechanical Desktop has commands (which we will discuss later in this chapter) for both adding and removing constraints.

If the endpoints of two adjacent objects in a sketch fit within the AutoCAD pickbox, Mechanical Desktop, by default, joins the two objects at their endpoints when they are transformed into a sketch. The size of the pickbox is controlled by the AutoCAD system variable **pickbox**, which can be set directly or within the Selection tab of the Options dialog box that is displayed by the AutoCAD OPTIONS command.

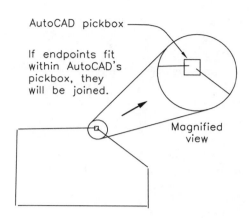

AutoCAD pickbox

If endpoints fit within AutoCAD's pickbox, they will be joined.

Magnified view

Usually constraints are not visible. You can, though, use Mechanical Desktop's AMSHOWCON command to view them. They are also visible when you use the commands that work with constraints. They appear as symbols that give the identification number of each profile object and the object's constraints. For instance, a letter H and a circled number 5 next to a line in a profile means that the line is profile object number 5 and that the line is constrained in a horizontal position (parallel with the X axis).

Symbols for constraints that control relationships between two objects have a number following the constraint symbol letter. P3 near a line that is object 0, for instance, means that the line is parallel to object number 3. The other object in this pair, object number 3, will have P0 as a constraint symbol. While constraints between pairs of objects occur most commonly between objects within the

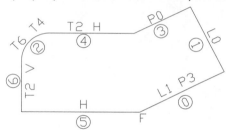

On demand, Mechanical Desktop will display a profile's constraints as symbols.

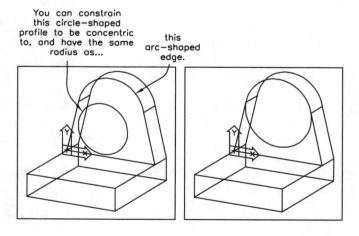

You can constrain this circle-shaped profile to be concentric to, and have the same radius as...

this arc-shaped edge.

outline of a profile, constraints can also exist between profile objects and construction geometry objects. Moreover, profiles for dependent features can have constraints between their objects and the edges of a solid feature, as shown in the accompanying figure. Constraint pairs cannot exist, however, between objects in different sketches.

AMSHOWCON uses command line prompts, that offer options for you to view all of the constraints of a profile, or to view the constraints that affect just certain objects in the profile. This can be helpful when the profile is complex, and its constraints are crowded. Constraint symbols and object numbers are displayed in AutoCAD's standard font (txt.shp) using the linetype and color of the current layer. Their size is controlled by Mechanical Desktop's **amcondspsz** system variable. (See "Setting Part Options" on page 71 for more information about constraint symbol size.) The symbols are strictly for temporary on-screen viewing. You cannot print them or select them.

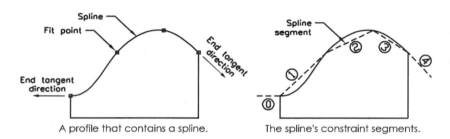

A profile that contains a spline. The spline's constraint segments.

For constraint purposes, spline curves within profiles are divided into straight-line segments connecting the points that were specified by the user in drawing the spline within AutoCAD's SPLINE command. (AutoCAD often refers to these points as the spline's *fit points*.) There will be one spline segment between each fit point, plus a segment extending from each end of the spline that indicates the directions of the end tangents. These segments are only visible when the Mechanical Desktop commands for working with geometric and dimensional constraints are in use, and they, rather than the spline curve itself, are used to constrain the spline.

Geometric Constraint Types

Constraint	Symbol	Definition	Details
Horizontal	H	A line, ellipse axis, or spline segment is parallel with the sketch plane X axis.	Horizontal Not constrained / Constrained

Geometric Constraint Types (Continued)

Constraint	Symbol	Definition	Details
Vertical	V	A line, ellipse axis, or spline segment is parallel with the sketch plane Y axis.	
Perpendicular	L	Two lines, ellipse axes, or spline segments that are askew to the sketch plane X and Y axes are 90 degrees to one another.	Usually the two objects adjoin one another, but this is not a requirement. Often one of the two objects will be the straight edge of a feature.
Parallel	P	Two lines, ellipse axes, or spline segments that are askew to the sketch plane X and Y axes have the same slope.	Usually the two objects are not adjoining, but they can be. A straight edge of an existing feature can be used as one of the two objects.

Geometric Constraint Types (Continued)

Constraint	Symbol	Definition	Details
Tangent	T	Any of the following three constraint conditions can exist. • Two adjoining arcs or partial ellipses have the same slope (tangent) at the point where they join. • An arc or partial ellipse that is joined to a line or spline segment has the same slope as the line or spline segment at the point where they join. • The side of a line or spline segment touches the perimeter of a circle, arc, or ellipse.	Tangent In constraining profiles for dependent sketched features, one of the two objects is often a curved edge on an existing feature.
Collinear	C	Two lines or spline segments share the same general line, as if the general line was divided into two pieces.	Collinear Often, one of the two objects will be the straight edge of an existing feature.
Concentric	N	Any combination of two arcs, circles, and ellipses have the same center point.	Concentric One of the two objects is often a circular edge on an existing feature. One of the two objects, as described in Chapter 7, can be a work point.

Geometric Constraint Types (Continued)

Constraint	Symbol	Definition	Details
Project	J	A point on one object is projected to another object. The point to be projected can be on a line, circle, arc, ellipse, or spline segment. It can also be the center of a circle or an arc. An endpoint or centerpoint object selection must be used to specify the point that is to be projected. The point can be projected to a line, circle, arc, ellipse, or spline segment.	**Project** Project this line's endpoint ...to this line. Not constrained Constrained The project constraint symbol, which is the letter "J", appears only on the object the point was projected to. You can also project a work point. See Chapter 7 for details.
Join	None	A point on one object is joined to a point on another object. The objects can be lines, spline segments, circles, arcs, or ellipses. An endpoint or centerpoint object selection method must be used in specifying each point.	**Join** Join this line's endpoint to ...this arc's centerpoint. Not constrained Constrained The first object selected can be a work point. See Chapter 7 for more information about constraining work points.
Radius	R	Two arcs or circles have the same radius.	**Radius** Not constrained Constrained Often, one of the base arc or circle will be an edge on an existing 3D feature.

Geometric Constraint Types (Continued)

Constraint	Symbol	Definition	Details
X Value	X	The centerpoint of two arcs or circles, or the endpoints of two lines or spline segments have the same X coordinate.	X Value for arcs Not constrained / Constrained X Value for lines Pick this line near this end / Pick this line near this end Not constrained / Constrained You do not need to use object snaps in specifying the points. When you select an arc or circle, its centerpoint is automatically selected; and when you select a line or arc segment, its endpoint nearest your pick point is selected.
Length	E	Two lines or spline segment have the same length.	Length Not constrained / Constrained

Geometric Constraint Types (Continued)

Constraint	Symbol	Definition	Details
Y Value	Y	The centerpoint of two arcs or circles, or the endpoints of two lines or spline segments have the same Y coordinate.	You do not need to use object snaps in specifying the points. When you select an arc or circle, its centerpoint is automatically selected; and when you select a line or arc segment, its endpoint nearest your pick point is selected.
Mirror	M	A selected line, spline segment, circle, ellipse, or arc becomes the mirror image of a selected object of the same type across a selected axis.	The mirror axis must be either a line that is part of the sketch—such as a construction geometry line—or a straight edge on an existing feature. You cannot use this constraint to change an object type. For instance, you cannot replace a line within a sketch by mirroring an arc.

Geometric Constraint Types (Continued)

Constraint	Symbol	Definition	Details
Fix	F	A point on a sketch object is fixed in space. All movement and stretching of objects within the sketch are from this point.	

Mechanical Desktop always places one fix constraint somewhere in the profile of a base feature. It will be at the endpoint of a line, spline segment, arc, or elliptical arc; or on the centerpoint of a circle or ellipse. In adding a fix constraint, picking a point near the end of an open object, such as a line or arc, will cause the constraint to be positioned on the object's endpoint. You can insert more than one fix constraint in a profile, but you are not likely to ever need to do that.

Working with Geometric Constraints

Adding Constraints

By default, Mechanical Desktop automatically adds radius, parallel, tangent, vertical, horizontal, concentric, perpendicular, and collinear constraints to profile objects that fit the particular constraint definition. Furthermore, Mechanical Desktop applies tolerances in determining if a constraint applies. For example, if a line is within 4 degrees of being parallel with the sketch plane X axis, the horizontal constraint is applied to the line when the profile is created. See "Setting Part Options" on page 71 for more information on automatically added constraints.

You can manually add constraints to specific profile objects with Mechanical Desktop's AMADDCON command. Often you will start AMADDCON by picking the button for a particular constraint from the **2D Constraints** toolbar. Mechanical Desktop will then display the symbols of the existing constraints on the profile and issue command line prompts for you to select the object, or objects, to be constrained.

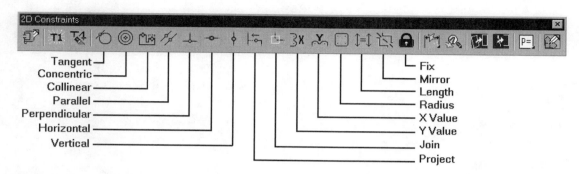

As soon as you add a constraint, Mechanical Desktop will report, on the command line, the number of constraints and dimensions still needed to fully constrain the profile, and prompt you to select another object to receive that same type of constraint. If you press the Enter key in response to this prompt, Mechanical Desktop will display the following command line menu for you to use in selecting another type of constraint or in exiting the command.

```
[Hor/Ver/PErp/PAr/Tan/CL/CN/PRoj/Join/XValue/YValue/Radius/Length/Mir/Fix]<eXit>:
```

You can right-click within the graphics area to display a shortcut menu offering these same options. When you add a type of constraint that affects two profile objects, such as the equal radius constraint, the first object you select will be the one that is moved, reoriented, or resized. Therefore, the order in which you select objects to be constrained is important. For example, if you want a line to be tangent to an arc, and the fix constraint is on one endpoint of the line, you must select the arc first.

More than one profile can exist at the same time, and you can freely switch between profiles as you add constraints. You cannot, however, constrain objects in one profile to objects in another one. For instance, you cannot constrain an arc in one profile to be concentric to an arc in another profile.

You can and often will, though, constrain objects in a profile to objects in an existing feature. Suppose, for example, you want to add a boss (a round protrusion) to the right end of the base feature shown in the following figure. After moving the sketch plane to the top surface of the base feature, you would draw a circle and turn it into a profile. Mechanical Desktop will report that 3 dimensions or constraints are needed to fully constrain the profile.

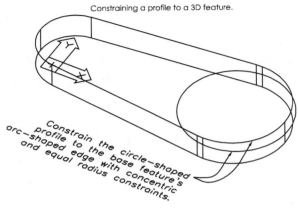

Constraining a profile to a 3D feature.

Constrain the circle-shaped profile to the base feature's arc-shaped edge with concentric and equal radius constraints.

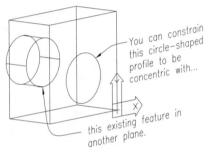

You can constrain this circle-shaped profile to be concentric with...

this existing feature in another plane.

You would then add a concentric constraint between the circle-shaped profile and the arc-shaped edge of the feature, and add an equal radius constraint between them. These two constraints will fully constrain the profile, and you can then extrude the profile to make the boss. Because its profile is constrained to the base feature, the location and the diameter of the boss will change to match any modifications made to the base feature.

A profile object can be in a different plane than that of the 3D feature object it is being constrained to. As shown in this figure for example, you can constrain a circle-shaped profile to be concentric with a circular feature even if the circular feature does not touch the plane that the profile is on.

Deleting Constraints

Sometimes you will change your mind about a constraint you have added, or Mechanical Desktop may place geometric constraints on your profile that you do not want. For instance, in the profile shown in the following figure, you may not want line 4 to be collinear with line 6, or line 0 to be parallel with line 3. Either or both of these constraints can be removed with the AMDELCON command.

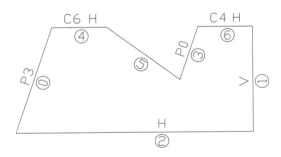

AMDELCON is a straightforward command to use; it does not involve a dialog box. If more that one sketch exists, the command will prompt you to select the one you want to edit. All of the constraints for the selected sketch will then be displayed, and a command line menu will let you to delete all of the constraints at once, or delete just selected constraints. AMDELCON also has an option for adjusting the size of the constraint symbols.

Setting Part Options

The Part tab of the **Mechanical Options** dialog box that AMOPTIONS command displays contains options for Mechanical Desktop settings related to sketches and their constraints, plus some miscellaneous settings related to parts.

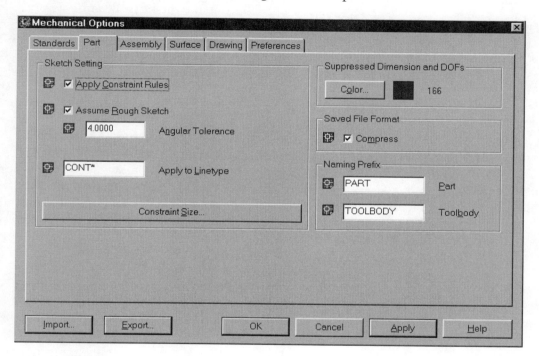

Apply Constraint Rules   If this box is checked, Mechanical Desktop automatically applies geometric constraints according to the constraint requirements and tolerances when AutoCAD objects are transformed into sketches. If this box is cleared, geometric constraints are not applied, except to join endpoints,

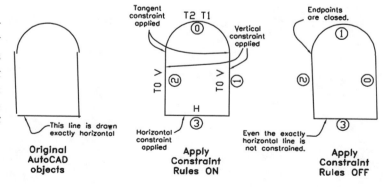

even if the AutoCAD objects fall within the tolerances. This check box turns Mechanical Desktop's **amrulemode** system variable on and off. Its default setting is on (a numerical value of 1).

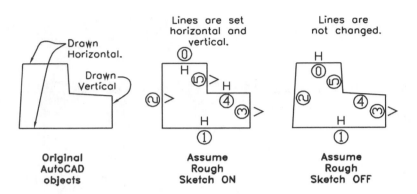

Original AutoCAD objects

Assume Rough Sketch ON

Assume Rough Sketch OFF

Assume Rough Sketch When this box is checked, objects within the sketch are forced to conform to the constraint requirements as long as they fall within the tolerances established by the **amskangtol** and **pickbox** system variables. When this box is cleared, no changes are made to the AutoCAD objects when they are transformed into a sketch. For example, a line drawn at a angle of 2.56 degrees would not become a horizontal line. Also, gaps between object endpoints are not closed. Constraints, however, are applied to objects that meet the constraint requirements. Thus, a horizontal constraint will be applied to a line that is parallel with the sketch plane X axis. Mechanical Desktop's **amskmode** system variable, which has a default setting of 1 (meaning that it is on), is set by this check box.

Angular Tolerance The edit box for angular tolerance sets the maximum angle at which lines are considered to be horizontal, vertical, parallel, and perpendicular. You may specify any angle from 0.001 to 10 degrees. The default angle is 4 degrees. This edit box sets the value of Mechanical Desktop's **amskangtol** system variable. Tangent constraints are also affected by angular tolerance, using a tolerance that is twice the value in **amskangtol**.

Apply to Linetypes By default, the boundary of all profiles must be made from objects drawn in a continuous linetype. If you would rather use some other AutoCAD linetype for boundary objects, enter the linetype's name in this edit box. You are not likely to ever have a need to use a different linetype for sketch boundaries. This edit box sets the contents of Mechanical Desktop's **amskstyle** system variable.

Constraint Display Size   For large sketches the object numbers and symbols can be too small to be easily readable, and for small sketches they can be so large that they crowd, or even overlap, one another. The Constraint Size button allows you to set the size of the numbers and symbols to one that is appropriate for your sketch. Constraint symbol display size is stored in Mechanical Desktop's **amcondspsz** system variable.

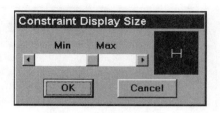

Suppressed Dimensions and DOFs   This button sets the color Mechanical Desktop uses for dimensions between suppressed and unsuppressed features and for the Degree of Freedom symbol used to indicate the possible movements of parts in assemblies. Suppressed Features are discussed in Chapter 13, and degrees of freedom are discussed in Chapter 18.

Saved File Format   When the toggle button labeled Compress is checked, Mechanical Desktop will use a compressed file format whenever the file is saved (through AutoCAD's SAVE and QSAVE commands). These files take up less disk space and load faster than non-compressed files, but the first update performed on the file will take longer. The default setting is to use compressed files. This check box controls whether the value in the Mechanical Desktop **amcompsv** system variable is 1 (compressed file format is used) or 0 (compressed file format is not used).

Naming Prefix   The edit box labeled Part holds the name that the Mechanical Desktop Browser uses in naming base features. In most cases you will accept the default name of PART, but you can choose another name if you like. It can have no more than six characters. Once a part has been created, you can still change the name that the browser has assigned to it. The edit box labeled Toolbody is for the name that is assigned to a part that is combined with another part. Toolbody names can have no more than nine characters. Combined parts and toolbodies are discussed in Chapter 12.

Tips for Constraining Profiles
1. Use the Mark option of AutoCAD's UNDO command before you begin constraining a profile and at strategic steps during the constraining process. Then, if the profile becomes wildly distorted when you add a constraint or if you don't like the direction you are going in adding constraints, you can easily restore the profile to an earlier condition.

Tips for Constraining Profiles (Continued)
2. Deliberately use sizes and proportions in sketching a profile that are different from what they will ultimately be. For instance, if two lines are to be parallel to each other, deliberately draw them so they are not parallel. Then the sketch objects will shift and relocate as you add a constraint, giving you visual evidence that the constraint produced the results you intended. Also, if the sketch is a profile for a dependent feature, draw it in a slightly different location from where it will ultimately be, so that you can more easily see and select objects in the profile.
3. Use restraint, however, when you use tip number 2. Sketch objects should be drawn in the neighborhood of their intended size and shape. Otherwise, the profile may become wildly distorted as you add geometric and dimensional constraints.
4. Each time you add a geometric constraint, Mechanical Desktop tells you the number of constraints and dimensions that are still needed to fully constrain the sketch. If that number does not decrease when you add a constraint, then the constraint you just added was not needed, and you should either remove it or remove the constraint that causes it to be redundant.
5. You do not have to add all of the necessary geometric constraints to a profile before adding its dimensions. Dimensions sometimes help preserve the proportions of the profile and prevent the profile from becoming overly distorted.
6. Usually you will enter your intended value for each dimension as you add the dimension. However, if the size or proportions of your profile objects are significantly different from your intended values, the profile may become overly distorted and out of control. In those cases, you should accept the as-drawn dimension values, and assign the correct values to them later. (Assigning and modifying dimension values is discussed in Chapter 5.)
7. Keep a notebook or file of profiles and their constraints and dimensions that you can refer to when you are creating a profile similar to one you have created in the past, or to one a co-worker has encountered. Such a record of constraint solutions is especially helpful when you are working with a profile that is difficult or tricky to constrain, when solutions are not obvious, and when you have discovered a particularly efficient and unique solution to a profile configuration.

Exercise 1

Creating and Constraining a Simple Profile

This is an introductory exercise in the process of creating a profile and then adding geometric constraints to it. You will apply one horizontal, two tangent, and two equal length constraints. You will also gain some experience in viewing and deleting constraints. Since this is the first exercise, we will describe every step in creating the profile and adding the constraints.

Start a new Mechanical Desktop part drawing file using the default English template (acad.dwt). You do not need to keep the results of the exercise, so the initial setup of the drawing file is not important. You may, though, want to turn on the AutoCAD grid and set its spacing to one unit to help you judge the sizes of the lines as you draw them.

Somewhere on the World Coordinate System XY plane, draw the three lines and one arc shown in Figure 1-1. Use any method you like in drawing the objects. It is not important that they be drawn precisely, except that their endpoints should touch or come very close to one another. The grid in Figure 1-1 is to help you judge sizes, and should not be drawn.

When you have drawn the four objects, open the Part Tab of the `Desktop Options` dialog box (which is displayed by the AMOPTIONS command), and clear the button labeled Apply Constraint Rules. Most of the time you will not do this, but for this exercise it will ensure that we all start out with approximately the same conditions. While you have the dialog box open, you may also want to increase the size of the constraint symbols. When you are finished, click the OK button to leave the dialog box.

Use the AMPROFILE command to transform the three lines and one arc into a profile. The command line sequence of prompts, input, and messages will be:

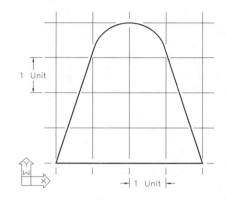

Figure 1-1

```
Command: AMPROFILE (Enter)
Select objects for sketch: (Use any method
    to select the three lines and one arc.)
Computing
Solved under constrained sketch requiring 7
    dimensions or constraints.
```

If AMPROFILE creates an open profile, use AutoCAD's UNDO command to back up, because there is too much space between at least one pair of sketch components. Then, either (1) use any of several AutoCAD methods to close or reduce the size of the gap, (2) increase the value of the **pickbox** system variable, or (3) zoom out so that the gap will fit within the present pickbox. Then invoke AMPROFILE again to create a closed profile.

Once you have created the profile, use AMSHOWCON to view its constraints.

```
Command: AMSHOWCON (Enter)
Enter an option [All/Select/Next/eXit]: A (Enter)
Enter an option [All/Select/Next/eXit]: (Refer to the following text.)
```

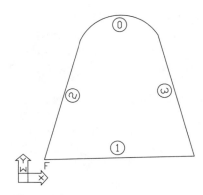

Figure 1-2

A number within a circle, similar to those shown in Figure 1-2, will appear next to each object in the profile. Your objects may be numbered in a different order than in Figure 1-2. That is not important. Since you turned off all of the constraint rules, only a fix constraint is present. When you have finished viewing the profile, press the Enter key to exit the AMSHOWCON command.

Now you will begin adding constraints to the profile. You will first constrain the bottom line of the profile to be parallel with the X axis.

```
Command: AMADDCON (Enter)
Enter an option [Hor/Ver/PErp/PAr/Tan/CL/CH/PRoj/Join/
XValue/YValue/Radius/Length/Mir/Fix/eXit]<eXit>: H
```

```
(Enter)
Valid selections: line, ellipse or spline segment
Select object to be reoriented: (Pick a point on the bottom line of the profile.)
Solved under constrained sketch requiring 6 dimensions or constraints.
```

The line will become horizontal, and a letter H will appear just below the line, as shown in Figure 1-3. Notice that each time you add a constraint, Mechanical Desktop will report the number of constraints, either dimensional or geometric, still needed to fully constrain the profile. As soon as the constraint is added, Mechanical Desktop will prompt you to select another object to be constrained horizontally.

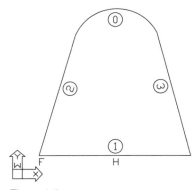

Figure 1-3

```
Valid selections: line, ellipse or spline segment
Select object to be reoriented: (Enter)
Enter an option [Hor/Ver/PErp/PAr/Tan/CL/CH/PRoj/Join/
XValue/YValue/Radius/Length/Mir/Fix/eXit]<eXit>: (Enter)
```

Pressing the Enter key when you were prompted to select an object to be reoriented brought up a menu for you to choose another constraint type. Pressing Enter again ended the command.

Next you will constrain the arc to be tangent to each of its adjacent lines. Rather than use the command line version of AMADDCON, launch the **2D Constraints** tool bar by clicking its button in the Part Modeling toolbar, and from it pick the Tangent button. Mechanical Desktop will issue a command line message as to the types of objects suitable for tangent constraints and prompt you to pick an object.

```
Valid selections: line, circle, arc, ellipse or spline segment
Select object to be reoriented: (Pick a point on the arc.)
```

```
Select object to be tangent to: (Pick a point on the right-hand line.)
Solved under constrained sketch requiring 5 dimensions or constraints.
Valid selections: line, circle, arc, ellipse or spline segment
Select object to be reoriented: (Pick a point on the arc.)
Select object to be tangent to: (Pick a point on the left-hand line.)
Solved under constrained sketch requiring 4 dimensions or constraints.
Valid selections: line, circle, arc, ellipse or spline segment
```

Your profile should now look similar to the one shown in Figure 1-4.

Now you will constrain the two lines that adjoin the arc to have the same length. Click the Equal Length button on the **2D Constraints** toolbar.

```
Valid selections: line or spline segment
Select object to be resized: (Pick a point on the right-hand line.)
Select object to base size on: (Pick a point on the left-hand line.)
Solved under constrained sketch requiring 3 dimensions or constraints.
Valid selections: line or spline segment
Select object to be resized:
```

Press the Enter key twice to exit the AMADDCON command. That is all of the constraints you will add to the profile. Three dimensions are needed to establish sizes and fully constrain the profile. When you invoke AMSHOWCON your profile should look similar to the one shown in Figure 1-5. This exercise is finished, and since we will do nothing further with this profile you do not need to save you file. On the CD-ROM that comes with this book, though, the profile at this stage is in file md04e105.dwg.

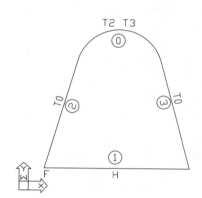

Figure 1-4

Before you abandon this profile, you should consider how you could completely constrain the profile. Based on your experience in dimensioning 2D drawings, you might suppose that the dimensions needed to fully constrain the profile would be (1) the length of the horizontal line, (2) the distance from the horizontal line to the center of the arc, and (3) the radius of the arc. You would be correct, although we will not add those dimensions since we will not discuss dimensioning until Chapter 5.

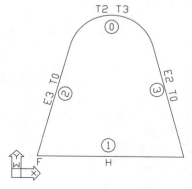

Figure 1-5

Exercise 2

Creating and Constraining a Profile

You will gain additional hands-on experience in this exercise as you create a profile and add horizontal, vertical, parallel, perpendicular, collinear, and project constraints to it. Start a new Mechanical Desktop part file, using the default English template (acad.dwt). You will not need to save this drawing file after you complete the exercise, so its initial setup is not important. You may, though, want to activate AutoCAD's grid with a spacing of 1 unit to help you judge sizes as you draw the profile's objects.

Use any method to draw the profile, consisting of seven lines and one arc, shown in Figure 2-1 somewhere on the XY plane of the WCS. Other than ensuring that adjoining object endpoints fit within the AutoCAD pickbox, it is not important that the profile be drawn precisely. The one-by-one grid in Figure 2-1 is to help you judge the size of the profile and should not be drawn.

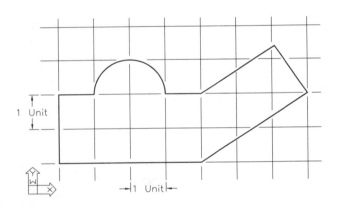

Figure 2-1

Once you have drawn the objects, clear the Apply Constrain Rules in the Parts tab of the **Mechanical Options** dialog box. Although you will not normally do this, it will ensure that your profile is in the same initial condition as the one we will describe in this exercise. Start the AMPRO-FILE command and use any method to select the seven lines and one arc as the profile's objects. Verify by the Browser's name for the profile that you have created a closed, rather than an open, profile.

Mechanical Desktop will report that 15 dimensions or constraints are needed to fully constrain the profile. Your profile should look similar to the one shown in Figure 2-2, although the object numbering sequence will most likely be different and the fix constraint may be on a different endpoint.

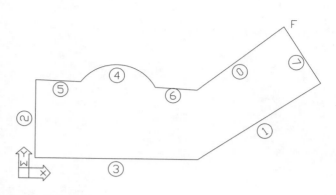

Figure 2-2

Now you will begin adding constraints to the profile. Since you have some experience in adding constraints we will not show the command line prompts and input you will use in adding them. We will just list the constraint type and the numbers of the objects that are to be constrained. First, you will constrain three of the lines to be horizontal. Select the Horizontal option of AMADDCON. When you are prompted to select an object pick object number 3 in Figure 2-2, then select object 5, and lastly select object 6. If the objects in your profile are numbered differently, use the comparable object in your profile when you add these horizontal constraints.

Your profile should look similar to the one in Figure 2-3. Next, constrain object 2 to be vertical. Then constrain objects 5 and 6 to be collinear with each other. (You may find that once you have started AMADDCON the graphic area right-click menu is an especially convenient way to initiate constraint operations.) After these constraints have been added, Mechanical Desktop will report that 10 dimensions or constraints are needed to fully constrain the profile. Your profile and its constraints should look similar to the one in Figure 2-4.

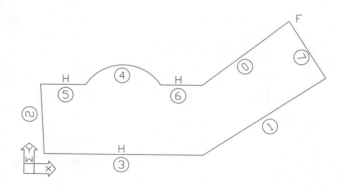

Figure 2-3

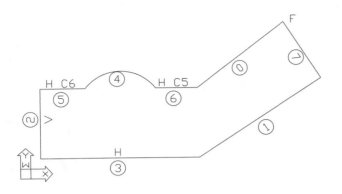

Figure 2-4

Constrain objects 1 and 0 to be parallel with one another and constrain object 7 to be perpendicular to object 0. The number of dimensions and constraints still needed to fully constrain the profile will drop to 8, and your profile should look similar to the one shown in Figure 2-5.

Lastly, you will use a project constraint to force the center of the arc to be in line with objects 5 and 6. This will make the arc become a semicircle (180 degrees) by setting the Y component of its center coordinate to equal that of its adjacent lines. When you start the Project option of AMADDCON, Mechanical Desktop will prompt for you to specify the point to be projected. Use an AutoCAD centerpoint object snap to pick the center of the arc. You will then be prompted to select an object to which that point is to be projected. Pick a point on object 5 or 6. You do not need to use an object snap to select this point.

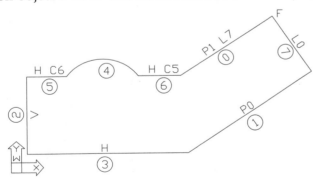

Figure 2-5

Your profile should now look similar to the one shown in Figure 2-6. Seven dimensions or constraints are still needed to fully constrain the profile. You could make objects 5 and 6 have equal lengths to keep the arc centered between them, and you could make objects 2 and 7 have equal lengths so that the thickness of the profile is the same throughout. We will not add either of those constraints though. Often, your choice of constraints to add to a profile will depend on your design intent and on the anticipated design changes. In this profile, for example, the design criteria might not call for the arc to be centered or the two ends have the same length.

You are finished with this exercise. Since you will not use this profile in any other exercises you do not need to save its file. On the CD-ROM that accompanies this book the profile is in file md04e206.dwg.

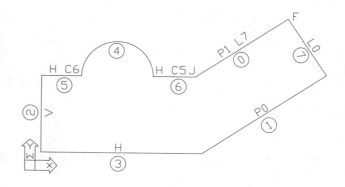

Exercise 3

Creating and Constraining a Complex Profile

Figure 2-6

In this exercise you will create a profile and add tangent, equal radius, equal length, same Y value, and concentric constraints to it. Start a new Mechanical Desktop part file using the default English template (acad.dwt). You may find it helpful to turn on the AutoCAD grid, using a spacing of one unit to help you estimate distances as you draw the profile's objects. Otherwise, the initial setup of the file is not important. On the WCS XY plane draw the four arcs and four lines shown in Figure 3-1.

Clear the Apply Constraint Rules check box in the Part tab of the **Mechanical Options** dialog box so that no constraints (other than a fix constraint) will be applied when the profile is created. Then use the AMPROFILE command to transform the four arcs and four lines into a profile feature.

We want to relocate the fix point of this profile. Therefore, you should use the AMDELCON command to delete the fix con-

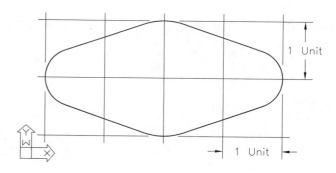

Figure 3-1

straint. Mechanical Desktop will report that 20 dimensions or constraints are now needed to fully constrain the profile. Your profile should resemble the one shown in Figure 3-2.

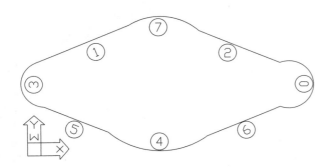

Figure 3-2

Constraint	First Object	Second Object
Tangent	1	3
Tangent	1	7
Tangent	2	7
Tangent	2	0
Tangent	6	0
Tangent	6	4
Tangent	5	4
Tangent	5	3
YValue	0	3
YValue	7	3
Radius	0	3
Radius	4	7
Concentric	4	7
Length	1	2

Use AMADDCON, through any of its interfaces, to add the constraints listed in the following table using the object numbers in Figure 3-2. If the object numbers in your profile are different, which they most likely will be, use the comparable object in your profile when you add a constraint. Since you have experience in adding constraints, we will not go through the steps required to add them.

Lastly, add a fix constraint to the profile. When you select the Fix option, AMADDCON will prompt for an endpoint to set the locked location, but you will select the centerpoint of an arc instead. At the prompt to select an endpoint, use a center object snap and select object number 4 or 7.

When you have added these constraints, your profile and its geometric constraints should be similar to the one in Figure 3-3. Mechanical Desktop will report that 3 dimensions or constraints are needed to fully constrain the profile. They will all be dimensions, and you will add those dimensions in Exercise 1 of Chapter 5. Therefore, you should save your file of this exercise, using any name you choose. On the CD-ROM that comes with this book, the completed exercise is in file md04e303.dwg.

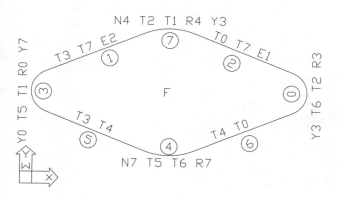

Figure 3-3

Dimensional Constraints

Every profile, except for some very simple ones for dependent features, must have dimensional as well as geometric constraints to be fully constrained. Mechanical Desktop's dimensional constraints look like ordinary AutoCAD dimensions, but they are parametric so that they actually control sizes rather than simply report them. While this chapter will focus on the techniques for adding dimensions to profile sketches, it applies equally well to 2D path, splitline, cutting line, and breakline sketches.

This chapter covers the following topics.

- *Describes the properties of Mechanical Desktop's dimensional constraints.*

- *Explains how to use the AMPARDIM and AMMODDIM commands to apply and modify linear, angular, diameter, and radius dimensional constraints.*

- *Demonstrates how the AMAUTODIM command can semi-automatically add parametric dimensions to a profile.*

- *Explains how to use construction geometry to provide additional control of a profile.*

Dimensional Constraints

Geometric constraints, as you saw in Chapter 4, control the geometric relationships of objects in profile features. Dimensional constraints, on the other hand control the size and orientation of the profile's objects—such as the length of a line, the radius of an arc, or the angle of an inclined line. Although Mechanical Desktop's dimensional constraints look like AutoCAD dimensions and even share some properties and characteristics, they are not equivalent. AutoCAD dimensions merely *show* the size and orientation of an object, while Mechanical Desktop's dimensions are parametric; they actually *control* the object's size and orientation. For instance, if you increase the value of a Mechanical

Desktop dimension of an arc radius from 1.00 inches to 1.25 inches, Mechanical Desktop will redraw the arc using the new radius value, and will stretch and move other objects in the profile to match the new radius.

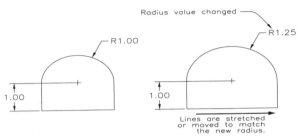

Changing a dimension value cause sizes to change.

While we will concentrate on dimensions within profile features in this chapter, parametric dimensions also apply to 2D path, split-line, cutting line, and break line sketches. Moreover, dimensions are used to control the location and orientation of dependent feature profiles to objects of existing features. You cannot, however, add dimensions between objects in one sketch and those in another.

You are likely to most often use the AMPARDIM command in adding dimensions, and that command will receive most of the space in this chapter. In using this command you manually specify each object or distance to be dimensioned. Two other Mechanical Desktop parametric dimensioning commands, AMAUTODIM and AMPOWER-DIM are able to add dimensions to a sketch semi-automatically. Although they offer some short-cuts and format options that AMPARDIM does not have,

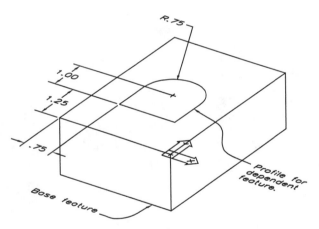

Dimensions control profile locations relative to existing 3D features as well as internally.

AMPARDIM is the more basic and flexible command. We will discuss those commands in the Automatic Dimensioning section of this chapter.

Working with Dimensions

Like AutoCAD, Mechanical Desktop has linear, angular, diameter, and radius dimensions to fit a variety of geometric shapes. Unlike AutoCAD, though, just a single command—

AMPARDIM—is used for all of these dimension types. This command is able to identify the appropriate dimension type from (1) the object, or objects, selected for a dimension, (2) the location of the selection points on the objects, and (3) the specified location of the dimension text.

When you add a dimension, AMPARDIM will display the current dimension value, and you can either accept it or enter a new value. If you enter a new value, the sketch geometry will automatically adjust to accommodate it. As each dimension is added, Mechanical Desktop will report the number of dimensions and constraints that are still needed to fully constrain the sketch. When a dimension is added that causes a sketch to become fully constrained, the message "Solved fully constrained sketch." will be displayed.

If you attempt to add a dimension that conflicts with or duplicates an existing dimension, the command line message "Adding this dimension would over constrain the sketch." will be displayed, and the redundant dimension will not be added. For example, the vertical dimension in this profile will not be allowed, because the already dimensioned arc controls the width of the profile. Conversely, if the vertical dimension had been added first, the arc could not be dimensioned.

Once dimensions have been added to a sketch, their values can be changed through the AMMODDIM command.

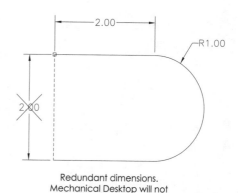

Redundant dimensions.
Mechanical Desktop will not
allow the vertical dimension.

This command will ask you to select the dimension you want changed, and to enter a new value. Mechanical Desktop will then automatically redraw the sketch to match the new dimension value. Also, you can freely use AutoCAD's ERASE command to remove dimensions—the sketch will not be invalidated.

Usually, you will enter your intended value of each dimension when you use AMPARDIM. However, if the size or proportions of the sketch objects are significantly different from your intended values, the sketch may become overly distorted and out of control. In those cases, you should accept the current, or as drawn, dimension values, and assign the correct values to them later with AMMODDIM.

Mechanical Desktop places parametric dimension in a layer named AM_5, regardless of which layer is current, and automatically creates that layer, if it does not exist, the first time a dimension is added. Most of AutoCAD's dimension variables apply to Mechanical Desktop dimensions. Consequently, you can use AutoCAD's DDIM command to set the size of arrowheads, the size and style of dimension text, and so forth.

Mechanical Desktop's parametric dimensions eventually serve as the basis for the dimensions in 2D drawings. You should, though, consider dimensions to be controls for the size and shape of a 3D model, rather than as drawing annotation. Dimensions in drawing views are discussed in Chapter 16.

Applying Linear Dimension

Like AutoCAD, Mechanical Desktop has linear dimensions that are one of the following.

Horizontal   The dimension is parallel with the sketch plane X-axis.

Vertical   The dimension is parallel with the sketch plane Y-axis.

Aligned   The dimension is parallel with the distance being dimensioned.

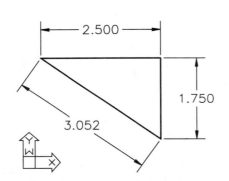

Horizontal, vertical, and aligned dimensions

All three of these linear dimension types are created with the AMPARDIM command. This command is also able to create ordinate dimensions and linear diameter dimensions (for objects that will be revolved in making a 3D feature—such as a cylinder).

AMPARDIM issues command line prompts for you to specify up to two objects for the dimension, plus a point for the dimension location.

`Select first object: (Pick a point on an object or press Enter.)`

`Select second object or place dimension: (Select a point on a second object, or pick a point for the dimension text location.)`

The first prompt is redisplayed after every dimension has been added. Pressing Enter in response to it will end the command. If a second object is selected, AMPARDIM will display the following prompt.

`Specify dimension placement: (Pick a point for the dimension line location.)`

Objects must be selected by picking a point on them. You cannot use general selection methods, such as windows or crossings. You do not, however, need to use object snap points. For example, if you wanted to dimension the distance between the ends of two lines, you would pick each line somewhere

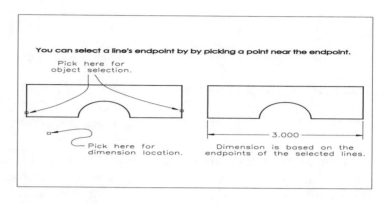

near a line endpoint. Mechanical Desktop would base the dimension on the line endpoints that are closest to the pick points.

If in response to the second prompt, you pick a point that is not on an object, AMPARDIM will use the point to establish the location of the dimension line. The point selected for the dimension line also determines

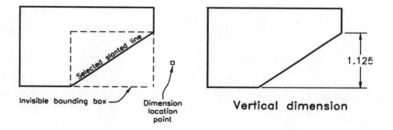

whether the dimension is to be horizontal, vertical, or aligned. This is done through an invisible box that has its opposite diagonal corners on the endpoints of the line that is to be dimensioned. If you pick a dimension location point that is to the right or left of this box, the dimension will be vertical.

When you pick a dimension line location that is below or above the invisible bounding box, Mechanical Desktop will create a horizontal dimension.

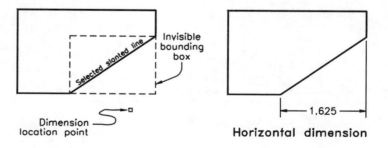

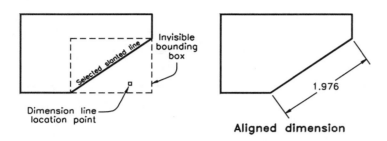

If you want the dimension to be aligned with a slanted line, pick a point inside the invisible bounding box for the dimension line location.

Mechanical Desktop also uses an invisible box to determine the linear dimension type when points near the ends of two lines have been selected. And, when a line and a circle or arc have been selected for a dimension distance, the center of the circle or arc serves as one corner of the invisible bounding box.

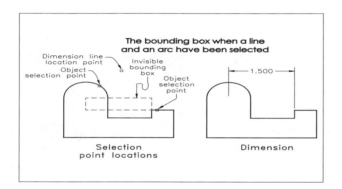

Centerpoints are also used as corners of the invisible bounding box when both selected objects are circles or arcs.

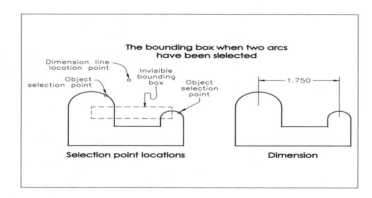

If you select a single line that is either horizontal or vertical, and pick the dimension location point to be in the direction of that line, Mechanical Desktop will draw an ordinate leader from the line and use the leader as the base for ordinate dimensions on the profile. We will discuss ordinate dimensions in detail shortly.

Whenever (1) a single line is selected, (2) two lines are selected by picking points near their endpoints, (3) one line and a circle or an arc is selected, or (4) two circles or arcs are selected, Mechanical Desktop will issue the following prompt related to linear dimensions.

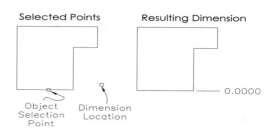

Selected Points   Resulting Dimension

Object Selection Point

Dimension Location

0.0000

```
Enter dimension value or [Undo/Hor/Ver/
   Align/Par/aNgle/Ord/Diameter/pLace]
   <current>: (Specify an option, enter a
   dimension value, or press Enter.)
```

These options are also available from the shortcut menu displayed when you right-click in the graphics area during AMPAR-DIM. If you press Enter, Mechanical Desktop will place the dimension in the specified location, using the current dimension value. If you enter a new dimension value, Mechanical Desktop will use it rather than the current one, and will redraw the sketch to match it. The user-entered dimension can be an absolute value, an equation, or the name of a design variable. (Chapter 6 discusses dimension equations and design variables.) As soon as a dimension has been added, Mechanical Desktop will report how many more constraints or dimensions are required to fully constrain the sketch, and will prompt you to select an object for another dimension.

The Undo option of the prompt cancels the currently displayed dimension, and returns to the 'Select first object' prompt. The Hor, Ver, and Align options allow you to override the current linear dimension type. For instance, if you want a dimension to be horizontal, but the displayed dimension is vertical, you can use the Hor option to force the dimension to be parallel with the X-axis.

Two objects must have been selected to use the Par (parallel) option. It reorients the displayed dimension so that it measures the perpendicular distance between two objects that are parallel to each other and askew to the sketch plane X and Y axes.

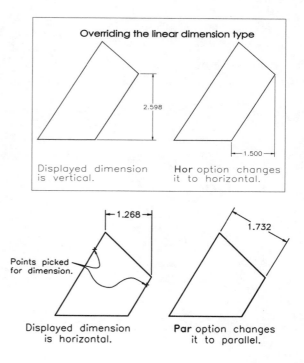

Overriding the linear dimension type

2.598

1.500

Displayed dimension is vertical.

Hor option changes it to horizontal.

1.268

Points picked for dimension.

Displayed dimension is horizontal.

1.732

Par option changes it to parallel.

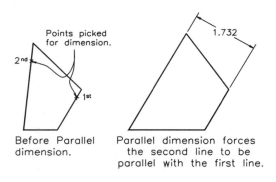

Before Parallel dimension.

Parallel dimension forces the second line to be parallel with the first line.

If the two lines are not actually parallel, this option will force the second line that was selected for the dimension to become parallel with the first line that was selected. Notice that the parallel dimension option corresponds to the parallel geometric constraint.

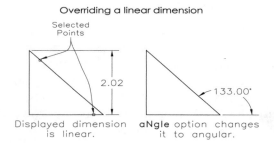

Overriding a linear dimension

Displayed dimension is linear.

aNgle option changes it to angular.

Angle is another option that can be used only when two lines have been selected. It changes the dimension type from linear to angular. We will describe another method for making angular dimensions later in this chapter.

The Ord option, which is applicable only when a single object has been selected, initiates an ordinate dimensioning mode. Mechanical Desktop will draw an ordinate leader that is parallel to the sketch plane X or Y axis from the object toward the dimension text location point. This leader serves as the base ordinate. Then, Mechanical Desktop will issue the following prompt.

```
Enter dimension value or [Undo/Placement point]: (Enter U or P, or press Enter)
```

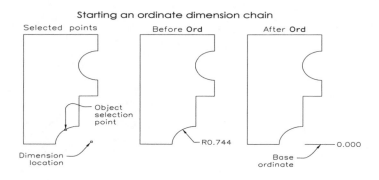

Starting an ordinate dimension chain

Selected points

Before **Ord**

After **Ord**

Pressing the Enter key places the current originate dimension value at the selected dimension location. The Undo option cancels the operation, while the Placement option allows you to pick a new point for the dimension text. If necessary, Mechanical Desktop will add a dogleg to the ordinate leader to accommodate the new text location.

After creating the ordinate dimension, Mechanical Desktop will display the following prompt.

```
Select next object for ordinate
    dimension: (Select an object, or
    press Enter.)
```

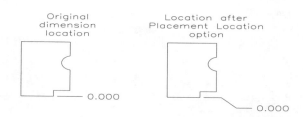

When you select an object, AMPARDIM will add a new ordinate dimension to the profile and will repeat the "Enter dimension value or [Undo/Placement point]" prompt. Pressing the Enter key will end the ordinate dimensioning mode.

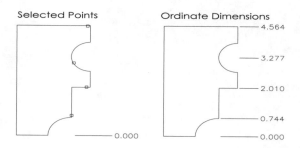

The Diameter option is for creating linear diameter dimensions on profiles that are to be revolved into a 3D feature. Two objects must have been selected, with the first object selected representing the axis of the revolved feature. The linear dimension will extend from the end of the second object selected to its symmetrical counterpart across the axis of revolution (the centerline of the revolved feature). A diameter symbol will precede the dimension text. Linear diameter dimensions will be displayed

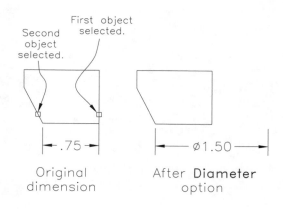

during editing operations on the revolved feature and in 2D drawing views of the model. See the discussion of the AMAUTODIM command later in this chapter for another method of adding diameter dimensions to a profile sketch. (Revolved 3D features are created with the AMREVOLVE command, which is described in Chapter 8. Editing operations on 3D features are discussed in Chapter 9, and dimensions in 2D drawings are discussed in Chapter 16.)

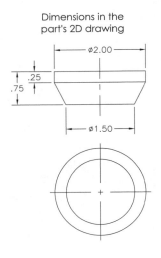

Dimensions in the part's 2D drawing

The Place option of the linear dimension prompt allows you to specify a dimension line location that is different from the originally selected location. It can be especially helpful for aligned dimensions that have their dimension text too close to the sketch object. You can also relocate a Mechanical Desktop parametric dimension through its grips, just as you can an AutoCAD associative dimension.

Applying Diameter and Radius Dimensions

When you select an arc in response to AMPARDIM's "Select first object" prompt, Mechanical Desktop will display the following command line prompt.

```
Enter dimension value or [Undo/Diameter/
Ordinate/Placement point] <current>:
(Select an option, enter a value or press
Enter.)
```

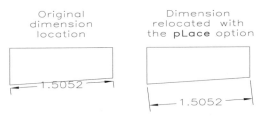

Original dimension location

Dimension relocated with the **pLace** option

These options are also displayed in the shortcut menu that appears when you right-click in the graphics area. Pressing the Enter key will place the current radius dimension value in the specified location. The Undo option cancels the current dimension. The Diameter option changes the dimension type from a radius to a diameter dimension. The dimension value will double, and it will be preceded with a diameter symbol rather than with

Changing from a radius to a diameter dimension

Dimension before **Diameter** option

Dimension after **Diameter** option

the letter "R". When a circle has been selected for a dimension, the Diameter option in the command line prompt will be replaced by a Radius option, which will transform the diameter dimension to a radius dimension.

The Ordinate option initiates the ordinate dimensioning mode, just as in linear dimensions. The Placement point option allows you to change the location of the radius or diameter leader and the dimension text. This option will continue to prompt for a new placement point until you press Enter. As with linear dimensions, entering a radius or diameter value that is different from the current value will cause the profile to be redrawn so that it matches the specified size. After any of the radius or diameter options have been completed, the "Select first object" prompt of AMPARDIM is re-displayed.

A special form of radius dimensioning is used with Ellipses. You must select two points for the dimension, with a quadrant object snap being used to select one of the points, and a third point for the dimension location. Mechanical Desktop will then display the following prompt.

```
Enter dimension value or [Undo/Ordinate/Placement point] <current>: (Select an option,
    enter a value or press Enter.)
```

These options work the same as those for radius and diameter dimensions.

Applying Angular Dimensions

Angular dimensions are created when two non-parallel lines are selected by picking points near their midpoints. AMPARDIM will display the command line prompt:

```
Enter dimension value or [Undo/Placement point] <current>: (Select an option, enter a
    value, or press Enter.)
```

The Undo option cancels the current dimension, while the Placement point option allows you to change the location of the angular dimension text. Extension lines will automatically be added to keep the angle dimension less than 180 degrees. If you enter a new dimension angle,

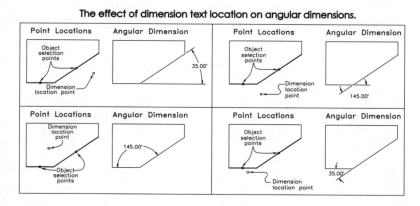

The effect of dimension text location on angular dimensions.

Mechanical Desktop will redraw the sketch in accordance with the specified angle. You can accept the present dimension angle by pressing Enter.

Selecting the Angle option from the linear dimension prompt, as we described earlier in this chapter, can also create angular dimensions.

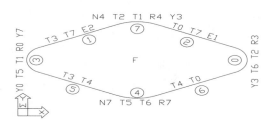

Figure 1-1

Exercise 1

Adding Dimensions to a Profile

This exercise will introduce you to Mechanical Desktop's parametric dimensions. In it we will give you the command line prompts and responses for adding the dimensions that will completely constrain the profile you created in Exercise 3 of Chapter 4. Open your file that contains that profile, or else retrieve file md04e303.dwg from the CD-ROM that accompanies this book and open it. The profile, with its geometric constraints, is shown in Figure 1-1. Three dimensions are required to fully constrain this profile.

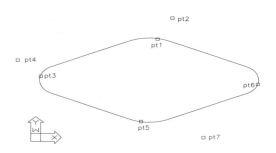

Figure 1-2

Use AutoCAD commands or system variables to set the parameters for the dimension features—such as text style and height, arrowhead size, and so forth—to suitable values. Then, start the AMPARDIM command and add dimensions to the profile in accordance with Figure 1-2 and the following command line input.

```
Command: AMPARDIM (Enter)
Select first object: (Pick pt1 in Figure 1-2.)
Select second object or place dimension: (Pick pt2 in Figure 1-2.)
Enter dimension value or [Undo/Diameter/Ordinate/Placement point] <.9909>: 1.0 (Enter)
```
Solved under constrained sketch requiring 2 dimensions or constraints.
```
Select first object: (Pick pt3 in Figure 1-2.)
Select second object or place dimension: (Pick pt4 in Figure 1-2.)
Enter dimension value or [Undo/Diameter/Ordinate/Placement point] <.3357>: .50 (Enter)
```
Solved under constrained sketch requiring 1 dimensions or constraints.
```
Select first object: (Pick pt5 in Figure 1-2.)
Select second object or place dimension: (Pick pt6 in Figure 1-2.)
Specify dimension placement: (Pick pt7 in Figure 1-2.)
Enter dimension value or [Undo/Hor/Ver/Align/Par/aNgle/Ord/Diameter/pLace] <1.6940>: 1.5 (Enter)
```

```
Solved fully constrained sketch.
Select first object: (Enter)
```

Your profile, which should look similar to the one shown in Figure 1-3, could now be extruded to make a 3D base feature. On the CD-ROM that comes with this book, the fully constrained and dimensioned profile is in file md05e103.dwg. We will do nothing more with this profile, though, so you do not need to save it.

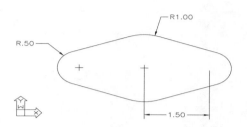

Figure 1-3

Exercise 2

Creating and Constraining a Profile

This will be a more complex exercise in which you will create a new Mechanical Desktop profile feature and add both geometric and dimensional constraints to completely constrain it. In Chapter 8, you will create a 3D feature from this profile. Begin a new Mechanical Desktop part file based on the default metric template (acad-iso.dwt). Create an AutoCAD layer having

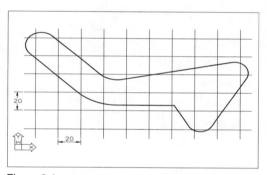

Figure 2-1

a name such as Outline or Profile, assign any color you like to it, and make it the current layer. Then, on the WCS XY plane, draw the six lines and five arcs shown in Figure 2-1. The 20 mm by 20 mm grid is to help you judge sizes, and should not be drawn.

Although it is not essential that you do so, you may want to clear the Apply Constraint Rules check box, which is in the Parts tab of the **Desktop Options** dialog box, so that you will start with a profile that is similar to the one we will describe. Use the AMPROFILE command to transform the eleven AutoCAD objects into a

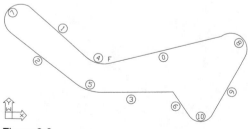

Figure 2-2

Mechanical Desktop profile. Your profile should look similar to the one shown in Figure 2-2.

Constraint	First Object	Second Object
Horizontal	3	
Tangent	7	2
Tangent	7	1
Tangent	4	1
Tangent	4	0
Tangent	8	0
Tangent	8	9
Tangent	10	9
Tangent	10	6
Tangent	5	2
Tangent	5	3
Parallel	2	1
Concentric	5	4
Equal Radius	8	10

Use AMADDCONS, in any of its various forms, with the object numbers in Figure 2-2 to add the constraints listed in this table to your profile. If your object numbers are different from those in Figure 2-2 (and they probably will be), use the comparable object in your profile when you add a constraint.

Now your profile, and its constraints, should be similar to the one shown in Figure 2-3. Mechanical Desktop will report that 10 dimensions or constraints are still needed to fully constrain the profile. They will all be dimensions.

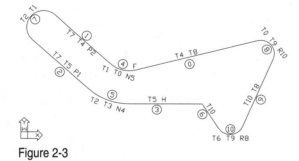

Figure 2-3

Set your dimension parameters—such as text style and height, arrowhead size, number of digits to the right of the decimal point, and so forth—to your preferences. Then use AMPARDIM to add the dimensions shown in Figure 2-4. This will give you experience in adding all three types of linear dimensions, as well as angular and radius dimensions.

When you are prompted for a dimension value, enter the value shown in Figure 2-4, or else accept the default value and use AMMODDIM after all ten dimensions have been added to enter the correct value. The following table gives the value and type of each of the ten dimensions in the order in which we added the dimension.

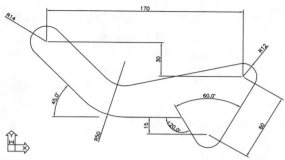

Figure 2-4

Your fully constrained profile should look similar to the one in Figure 2-4. Do not be concerned if the layout and placement of your dimensions are not as you would have them in a 2D drawing view. These are working dimensions that control the parametrics of the model that is to be created from this profile. They are not manufacturing dimensions. You are finished with this exercise, and you should save your file so that you can use this profile in Exercise 1 of Chapter 8 to create an extruded 3D feature. On the CD-ROM that comes with this book, the fully constrained profile is in file md05e204.dwg.

Dimension Value	Type
14 mm	Radius
170 mm	Horizontal
50 mm	Radius
30 mm	Vertical
60 mm	Aligned
12 mm	Radius
120 degrees	Angular
60 degrees	Angular
15 mm	Vertical
45 degrees	Angular

Automatic Dimensioning

The AMAUTODIM command will almost automatically dimension some profiles. You need only to specify the objects to be dimensioned, and the general direction of the extension lines. This command can handle horizontal and vertical linear dimensions, ordinate dimensions, and linear-diameter dimensions, it cannot however handle aligned, radius, circular-diameter, or angle dimensions. The dimensions are fully parametric. However, since they reflect the existing distances, you must eventually change the dimension values unless you have precisely drawn the profile.

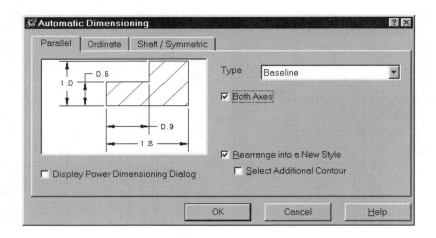

AMAUTODIM displays a dialog box with tabs for you to choose between Parallel (horizontal and vertical linear), ordinate, and Shaft/Symmetric (linear diameter) dimension types, and for setting dimensioning parameters. When you click the OK button of the dialog box, command line prompts guide you in adding dimensions to the profile.

A command related to AMAUTODIM is AMPOWERDIM. Although AMPOWERDIM is able to create parametric dimensions on sketches, it is better suited for dimensioning 2D drawing views of 3D parts. It is especially useful in adding tolerances and fit symbols to dimensions. Therefore, we will not discuss AMPOWERDIM until Chapter 14.

Exercise 3

Automatic Dimensioning

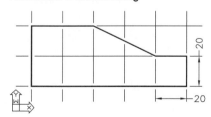

Figure 3-1

In this exercise, you will learn how AMAUTODIM works by trying it out on a simple profile sketch. Start a new part drawing file using the default metric template (acadiso.dwt). Sketch a profile similar to the one shown in Figure 3-1, using the 20 mm grid in the figure as a guide in sizing the sketch. Then turn the six lines into a profile with AMPROFILE. Mechanical Desktop will report that five constraints or dimensions are needed to fully constrain the profile.

Start the AMAUTODIM command. Select the Parallel tab. In this tab select Baseline as the dimension type, and click the Both Axes check box. This will cause both horizontal and vertical dimensions to be added to the sketch. Make certain that the other check boxes are cleared, and then click OK to dismiss the dialog box. Mechanical Desktop will issue the following command line prompts.

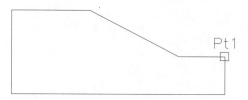

Figure 3-2

```
Select objects: (Use any method to select all six lines.)
First extension line origin: (Use an endpoint object snap to pick Pt1 in Figure 3-2.)
Second extension line origin (RETURN for previous point): (Enter)
Place dimension line [Options/Pickobj]: (Move the screen cursor up. Dimension and extension
    lines for three horizontal dimensions will appear. Drag them a suitable distance away
    from the sketch and press the pick button of your pointing device.)
Solved underconstrained sketch requiring 2 dimensions or constraints.
Starting point for next extension line (RETURN for 2nd axis): (Enter)
Place dimension line [Options/Pickobj]: (Move the screen cursor to the right to drag the
    two vertical dimensions a suitable distance from the sketch, and click your pointing
    device.)
Solved fully constrained sketch.
Starting point for next extension line: (Enter)
```

Your sketch should look similar to the one in Figure 3-3. A sketch such as this is suitable for being extruded to create a 3D feature. Next you will dimension the sketch as a shaft that would be created by using the bottom line of the sketch as an axis for revolving the profile.

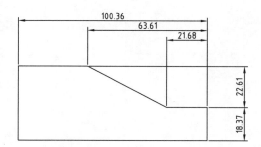

Figure 3-3

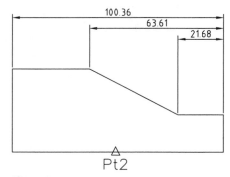

Figure 3-4

Erase the two vertical dimensions, and start AMAUTODIM again. This time, select the Shaft/Symmetric of the Automatic Dimensioning dialog box. Select Full Shaft as the dimension type, clear the tab's check boxes, and click the OK button. Mechanical Desktop will issue the following command line prompts and messages.

```
Select objects: (Use any method to select all six
    lines.)
Select revolution axis: (Use a midpoint object
    snap to select Pt2 in Figure 3-4.)
Place dimension line [Options/Pickobj]: (Move the
    screen cursor to the right. Dimension and
    extension lines for two linear diameter
    dimensions will appear. Drag them to the right
    a suitable distance and click your pointing
    device.)
Solved fully constrained sketch.
Starting point for next extension line: (Enter)
```

Your sketch should now look similar to the one in Figure 3-5. We will do nothing more with this sketch, so you do not need to save it.

Construction Geometry

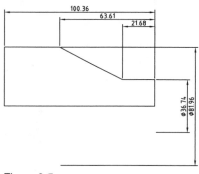

Figure 3-5

Sometimes, boundary objects alone are not able to properly constrain and dimension a profile. Consider, for example the fully constrained and dimensioned profile shown in Figure 4-1. Since Mechanical Desktop accepts only lines for angle dimensions, the angle of the curved arm in the profile must be based on lines that connect the two arc centers. These lines, which are drawn in AutoCAD's CENTER linetype, are *construction geometry* objects.

Construction geometry consists of one or more objects—such as lines, arcs, or circles—that are included in a profile for additional control or for dimensions. Even though construction geometry objects are part of a profile, they do not appear in 3D features or in drawings. A linetype that is different from that used for other sketch objects is used to identify construction geometry objects. By default, Mechanical Desktop considers objects drawn in AutoCAD's CONTINUOUS linetype to be profile boundaries, and considers objects drawn in a non-continuous line-

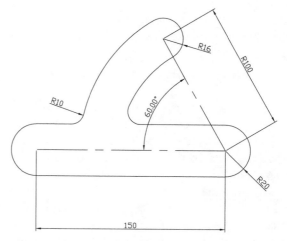

Figure 4-1

type—such as HIDDEN, CENTER, or PHANTOM—to be construction geometry objects. This interpretation is controlled by Mechanical Desktop's **amskstyle** system variable, which can be set directly or through the Part tab of the `Mechanical Options` dialog box that is displayed by the AMOPTIONS command. You are not likely, though, to ever need to change this variable. The CONTINUOUS linetype for sketch boundaries and non-continuous linetypes for construction geometry is a combination that works well.

To incorporate construction geometry into a profile, you simply include the objects in the AMPROFILE, AMPATH, AMCUTLINE, AMBREAKLINE, or AMSPLITLINE selection set, or add them through AMRSOLVESK. Since you are already familiar with the commands needed for construction geometry, we will demonstrate their use through two exercises.

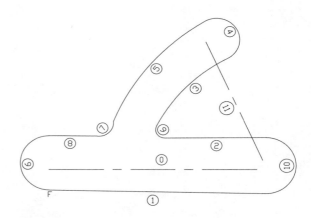

Figure 4-2

Exercise 4

Using Construction Geometry

In this exercise, you will create, constrain, and dimension the sketch shown Figure 4-1, as an example of construction geometry. Start a new Mechanical Desktop part file, using the standard metric template (acadiso.dwt), and draw the profile of the sketch using the dimensions shown in Figure 4-1 as a guide. The profile consists of three lines and seven arcs. Then use a non-continuous linetype, such as AutoCAD's CENTER linetype, to draw the two lines that are to be used for construction geometry. Be certain that these two lines, as shown in Figure 4-2, do not touch.

To ensure that we all start with a sketch that is roughly in the same condition, set the **amrulemode** system variable to 0, so that no constraints will be applied. You can do this directly, or by clearing the Apply Constraint Rules check box in the Parts tab of the **Mechanical Options** dialog box displayed by the AMOPTIONS command. Then, use AMPROFILE to turn the boundary objects and the two construction geometry lines into a sketch. Mechanical Desktop will report that 29 dimensions or constraints are needed to fully constrain the sketch.

Use AMADDCONS, in any of its various forms, to add the constraints shown in the table on page 105 to the sketch. If your object numbers are different from those in Figure 4-2 (and they probably will be), use the comparable object number in your sketch when you add a constraint. You should apply the constraints in the listed order to avoid extreme distortions in the sketch.

When you have added these constants, Mechanical Desktop will report that six dimensions or constraints are still needed to fully constrain the sketch. Use ADPARDIM to add the six dimensions, using the values shown in Figure 4-1. When you have finished dimensioning the profile, you should verify that the profile behaves as you expect it to by using AMMODDIM to change the angle dimension. When you have finished, save the profile because you will use it in Exercise 1 of Chapter 6 to demonstrate equation based dimensions. On the CD-ROM that accompanies this book, this profile is in file md05e401.dwg.

Constraint	First Object	Second Object
Horizontal	0	
Horizontal	1	
Horizontal	2	
Horizontal	8	
Collinear	2	8
Tangent	6	1
Tangent	10	1
Tangent	10	2
Tangent	2	9
Tangent	9	3
Tangent	3	4
Tangent	4	5
Tangent	5	7
Tangent	7	8
Tangent	8	6
Concentric	10	3
Concentric	10	5
Join	end 0	cen 6
Join	end 0	cen 10
Join	end 11	cen 10
Join	end 11	cen 4
Equal Radius	7	9

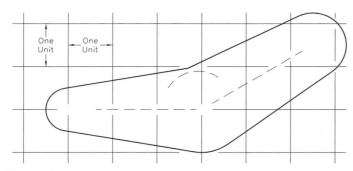

Figure 5-1

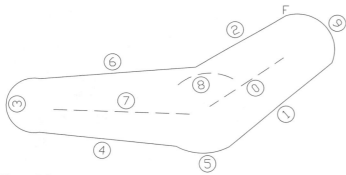

Figure 5-2

Exercise 5

Another Use for Construction Geometry

Start a new Mechanical Desktop part file using the standard English template (Acad.dwt), and draw the profile shown in Figure 5-1 using the one-by-one grid as a guide in sizing and positioning the objects. The profile consists of three arcs and four lines. Draw also the construction geometry arc and two lines, using a layer that has a HIDDEN linetype.

When you have drawn the objects, initiate the AMOPTIONS command to bring up the **Mechanical Options** dialog box; select the Part tab, and clear the Apply Constraint Rules check box. This will ensure that we all start with a profile that is in the same condition. Then invoke the AMPROFILE command to turn the objects into a profile. Be certain that you include the three construction geometry objects in the AMPROFILE selection set. Mechanical Desktop will report that 22 dimensions or constraints are needed to fully constrain the profile.

Use the AMADDCON command to add the constraints listed in this table, using the object numbers shown in Figure 5-2. If the object numbers in your sketch are different, use the comparable object in your sketch when you add a constraint. Since the sketch objects may shift dramatically as the constraints are applied, you should add them in the listed order to avoid an overly distorted sketch.

Constraint	First Object	Second Object
Horizontal	7	
Concentric	8	5
Radius	8	5
X Value	end 6	end 4
Select the left end of both lines		
Tangent	3	6
Tangent	4	5
Tangent	5	1
Tangent	1	9
Tangent	9	2
Project	cen 3	7
Project	cen 5	7
Project	cen 5	0
Project	cen 9	0
Tangent	6	8
Tangent	8	2

Now, Mechanical Desktop will report that six dimensions or constraints are needed to fully constrain the sketch. Use the AMPARDIM command to add the dimensions shown in Figure 5-3. These six dimensions will fully constrain the profile. We will not use this profile in future exercises, so you do not need to retain it. On the CD-ROM that accompanies this book, the constrained profile is in file md05e503.dwg.

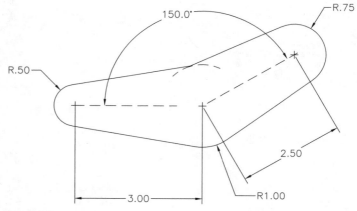

Figure 5-3

CHAPTER 6

Equations and Design Variables

In addition to the constant dimension values you used in the previous chapter, Mechanical Desktop has an assortment of tools that add flexibility to dimensions and gives you more control over them. You can even base dimensions on design variables, which enables you to create a family of parts that share the same basic geometric shape, but vary in size and, perhaps, even in proportions.

This chapter covers the following topics.

- Shows how dimensions can be based on equations that contain mathematical operators, such as addition and multiplication, and are even able to relate one dimension with another.

- Describes design variables and explains the difference between active part variables and global variables.

- Explains how to create design variables and how to incorporate them in dimensions.

- Shows you, step by step, how design variables can be linked to spreadsheet files for conveniently creating a family of parts.

Equation Based Dimensions

A powerful and very useful feature of Mechanical Desktop's parametric dimensions is that they can be based on equations. Furthermore, these equations can relate one dimension with another. The width of a rectangle, for instance, can be based upon the rectangle's length. As a result, whenever the length of the rectangle is changed, its width is changed also.

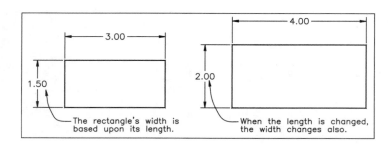

Mechanical Desktop assigns a name, which is sometimes also referred to as a *tag* or as a *parameter*, to each dimension, and this name can be used in other dimensions. The name consists of the letter 'd' (Mechanical Desktop always shows the letter in lower case.), followed by a number. For example, the name of the horizontal dimension of the profile in the following figure is d0, and the name of the vertical dimension is d1. The value of d1 has been set to equal one-half the value of d0. Thus, no matter what value is assigned to the horizontal dimension, the vertical dimension is half its length.

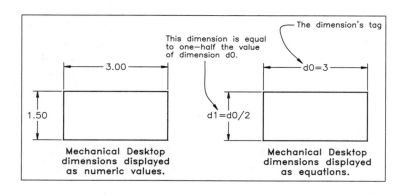

Equation based dimensions for sketches are created by the AMPARDIM and AMMODDIM commands, while equation based dimensions for 3D features, such a the height of an extrusion (which we will discuss in Chapter 8) are created when the parameters for the 3D feature are specified, or through the AMEDITFEAT command. Equations for dimensions can contain:

- Absolute values, such as 5.15625 or 3.

- Other dimension names, such as d0 or d73.

- Mathematical operators, such as * or +.

- Design variables. We will describe design variables later in this chapter.

Mechanical Desktop has 23 mathematical operators that you can use in equations. Of these, the operators that you are most likely to use are shown in the accompanying table.

Operator	Description	Example
+	Add	4.625+1.375
-	Subtract	4.625-1.375
*	Multiply	1.75*2
/	Divide	4.745/2
^	Exponent (Power)	d6^3
sqrt()	Square root	sqrt(d2)
tan()	Tangent	tan(45)
cos()	Cosine	cos(60)
sin()	Sine	sin(30)
atan()	Arctangent (Inverse Tangent)	atan(d6/d7)
acos()	Arccosine (Inverse Cosine)	acos(0.5)
asin()	Arcsine (Inverse Sine)	asin(0.5)

The arguments for the tan(), cos(), and sin() operators use angular degrees as units. The atan(), acos(), and asin() operators return numbers that represent degrees, but they do not have to be used as degrees. For instance, acos(0.5) returns 60, which can represent either an angular or linear dimension; whichever you choose. Mechanical Desktop also has an operator for the constant pi. Surprisingly, though, pi has a value of 180, rather than 3.14159....

Equations are created by entering them in response to a Mechanical Desktop prompt for a dimension value. You need to enter only the right-hand side of the equation—Mechanical Desktop will supply the equal sign as well as the dimension name on the left-hand side of the equation. Parentheses may be used in equations to group operations, and are required to enclose the arguments of operators, such as square root, that are based on functions. Spaces are permitted between components. Examples of equations are:

```
d1=2 * d0
d4=d1+d2+(d3/2)
d5=(d2^3)/d1
d7=sqrt(d5 *
d6/3)
d8=asin(d4/d5)
```

Mechanical Desktop has a dialog box titled Equation Assistant that you can use in entering a dimension equation. You can bring this dialog box up any time Mechanical Desktop is expecting you to enter a value by clicking the right button on your pointing device, and selecting Equation Assistant from the shortcut menu. The dialog box has a calculator type keypad of numbers and operators that you can use to enter an equation, and the resulting value of the equation is displayed as the equation is entered. Two additional options for assigning dimension values are available from a right-click shortcut menu within the edit box at the top of the dialog box. With one of these options you can set the dimension value by picking two points or by selecting an existing straight edge. The other option allows you to associate the dimension value to an existing dimension or to a previously dimensioned object. The Active Part and Global variables that are shown as tabs in this dialog box are described later in this chapter.

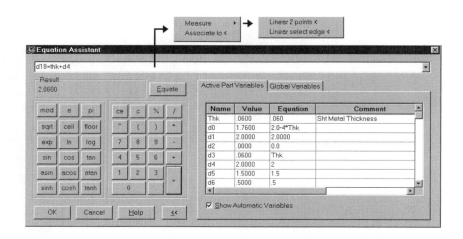

By default, dimension equations are not displayed, but you can use the AMDIMDSP command to have them displayed. From the command line, AMDIMDSP has options for displaying Mechanical Desktop parametric dimensions in any of three formats.

Numeric   Only the value of the dimension is shown. This is the default option.

Parameters   Only the dimension name, or tag, is displayed.

Equations   Dimensions are displayed in an equation format. The name of the dimension is shown on the left side of an equal sign, while its equation or constant numerical value is shown to the right.

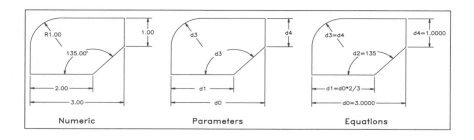

The selected dimension display mode applies to all dimensions. You cannot have some dimensions displayed in one mode, while others are in another. If you plan on using equations in dimensions, you will want to display them as equations.

Exercise 1

Using Dimension Names and Equations

This exercise will demonstrate how equations can link one dimension with another. Open the drawing file that contains the profile sketch you created in Exercise 4 of Chapter 5. On the CD-ROM that comes with this book, this profile is in file md05e401.dwg. Use the AMDIMDSP command, either directly or through one of its toolbar or menu equivalents, to display dimensions as equations. Your profile should be similar to the one shown in Figure 1-1, although the dimension names in your sketch might not refer to the same dimensions; and, if you erased and reapplied

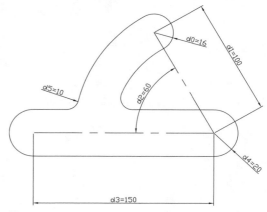

Figure 1-1

some dimensions, you may even be missing some dimension names. Dimension names are assigned by Mechanical Desktop, and cannot be changed.

When you increase the radius of the curved arm (dimension d1 in the figures) the arm moves to the left, and it is possible to give the radius a dimension value that is so large that the arm is forced off of the horizontal bar it is attached to, as shown in Figure 1-2. To prevent that from happening, we will set the bar to a length that is equal to one and one-half the radius of the arm. Then, whenever the radius changes, the length of the bar changes as well.

Use the following command line sequence of prompts and input to set the length of the bar to an equation. Use your equivalent dimension name if your names are different from those in Figure 1-1.

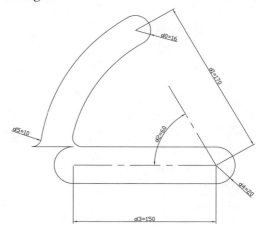

Figure 1-2

```
Command: AMMODDIM (Enter)
Select dimension to change: (Pick the d3 dimension.)
New value for dimension <100>: d1*3/2 (Enter)
```

`Select dimension to change: (Enter)`

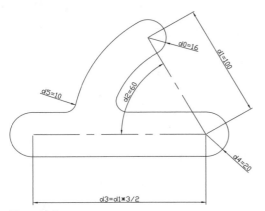

Figure 1-3

As shown in Figure 1-3, dimension d3 is now equal to one and one-half times (3/2) the length of dimension d1, which is the radius dimension. This change does not affect the shape and size of your profile sketch, but it does change the way the profile responds to changes to the radius of the curved arm. Compare Figure 1-4 with Figure 1-2. You should use AMMODDIM to change the radius of the curved arm to verify that the length of the bar does change in response to changes in the radius. You do not need to retain your drawing file for the sketch since we will not use it in any other exercises in this book. On the CD-ROM supplied this book, the profile with its equation based dimensions is in file md06e103.dwg.

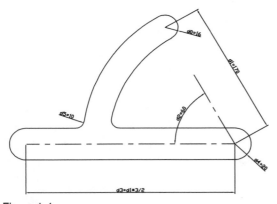

Figure 1-4

Design Variables

Sometimes you will have a family of 3D solid models, with each model in the family representing a specific style or version of a basic design. Pipe fittings, gears, fasteners, and electrical enclosures are just a few examples of objects that typically come in families. Mechanical Desktop helps manage the design and documentation of such a family of models through *design variables*. These variables control dimensions, which in turn control sizes, shapes, and proportions, as well as parameters for 3D features, such as extrusion lengths, angles of revolution, and pattern spacing. Design variables are also useful when working with parts that are to match other parts. Critical dimensions on the matching parts can be expressed as design variables that are used by both parts; thus ensuring that mating dimensions will be the same.

Individual design variables have a format similar to algebraic equations—the name of the variable is on the left side of the equal sign, while a mathematical expression representing the value of the variable is on the right side of the equal sign. Variable names may contain letters, numbers, and the underscore character. You cannot, however start a variable name with the letter d followed by a number

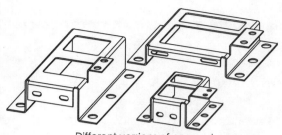

Different versions of one part.

(Mechanical Desktop uses those names for dimensions.), or with the letter c followed by a number (Mechanical Desktop uses those names for pattern parameters.) Mechanical Desktop does not distinguish between upper and lower case letters. Thus, the variable names of BASELEN, baselen, and BaseLen are the same. Although you can have very long names, you will generally want to keep them only two to six characters long to cut down on screen clutter when the names are displayed, and to reduce the possibility of input errors.

The mathematical expressions that the variables are to equal may contain the names of other design variables, any of the mathematical operators listed previously in this chapter, and constant numerical values. They cannot, however, contain the name of the variable that is to the left of the equal sign. Nor can they contain Mechanical Desktop dimension or array parameter names, such as d2 or c1. The equations can have spaces between operators and components, and they can contain parenthesis. Some examples of design variable names and their mathematical expressions are:

```
LENGTH = 3.35
dv01=.75
Height = dv01 / 2
d_01=length/sqrt(height)
v1 = (Height/3) * length
bisect=3*atan(height/length)
```

When more than one part exists in a drawing file, you can have design variables that apply to all parts and you can have design variables that apply just to a specific part. The first type are called *global variables*, while the second type are called *active part variables*. Design variables are primarily created and managed through the AMVARS command, which displays a dialog box titled Design Variables that has two tabs—one for global variables, and another for active part variables. The best way to see how the two types of variables work and interact is to actually try them out. Therefore, you should work through Exercise 2 to see how AMVARS is used to create and use both global and active part design variables.

You can create design variables from the Equation Assistant dialog box.

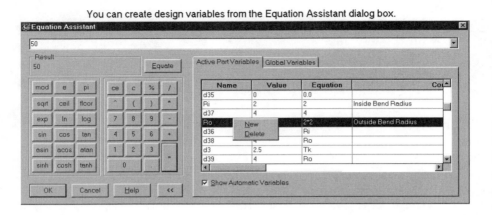

The **Equation Assistant** dialog box displays design variables, and you can use that dialog box to both create and delete design variables. To create a variable, right-click within the variables list area and select New from the shortcut menu. A blank line will appear for you to enter the parameters of the variable. To delete a variable, highlight it, right-click within the variables area, and select Delete from the shortcut menu.

Exercise 2

Becoming Acquainted with Design Variables

In this exercise, you will create three simple profile sketches for three different parts. In addition to learning how to create and use design variables, you will learn:

- How global variables can be used by all of the parts in a drawing file;
- That active part variables can be used only by a specific part;
- How active part variables can reference global variables;
- How copies of global variables can be incorporated into active part variables.

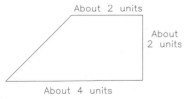

Figure 2-1

The exercise will also serve as an introduction in working with multiple parts. Begin the exercise by using the default English template (acad.dwt) to open a new Mechanical Desktop assembly file (not a part file). This is not going to be a file that you will want to save, so its name and other setup parameters are not important. Begin the exercise by drawing four lines similar to those in Figure 2-1, and then use AMPROFILE to transform them into a profile sketch.

Mechanical Desktop will report that 3 dimensions or constraints are required to fully constrain the sketch. Start the AMVARS command, and click the Global tab in the **Design Variables** dialog box. Then click the New button, which is located on the right side of the dialog box, to define a new design variable. A supplementary dialog box titled **New Part Variable,** as shown in Figure 2-2, will be displayed. In this dialog box,

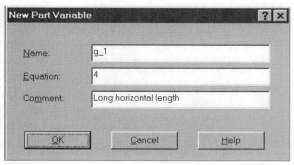

Figure 2-2

enter g_1 as the variable's name, 4 as its equation, and "Long horizontal length" as a comment. Then click the OK button to return to the main dialog box.

Follow those same steps to create two more global variables that have the following parameters:

Name	Equation	Comment
g_2	2	Width
g_3	45	Angle

All three of these variables will now be listed in the Global tab of the **Design Variables** dialog box, as shown in Figure 2-3. Click the OK button to end the AMVARS command. You can modify entries in this dialog

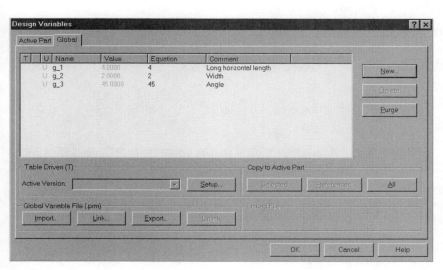

Figure 2-3

box by double-clicking within the cell you want to work in, and then editing its contents.

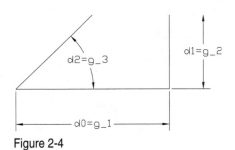

Figure 2-4

Now, use AMPARDIM to add dimensions to your profile sketch. Every time you are prompted for a dimension value, enter the name of the appropriate global variable. Your sketch, which is now fully constrained, should be similar to the one in Figure 2-4 when AMDIMDSP is set to display dimensions as equations.

This sketch will be shown in the Desktop Browser as PART1_1. Begin a new part by entering AMNEW on the command line and selecting the Create a new Part option. The command line sequence of prompts and input to do this is:

```
Command: AMNEW (Enter)
Enter an option [Instance/Part/Scene/subAssembly]<Instance>: P (Enter)
Select an object or enter a new part name <PART2>: (Enter)
```

The browser will now list PART2_1 in addition to PART1_1. The shape of the profile for this part will be similar to that of PART1_1, and you should locate it near PART1_1. Use AutoCAD's LINE command to draw the long horizontal line about 3 units long, and the vertical line about 1.5 units long. Use AMPROFILE to make a profile sketch from the four lines. Invoke AMVARS, select the Active Part tab, and define three variables having the following parameters:

Name	Equation	Comment
p2_1	3	Long horizontal length
p2_2	p2_1/2	Width
p2_3	60	Angle

Notice that we set the width of the sketch to be equal to one-half its overall length. Click the OK button in the Design Variables dialog box to exit AMVARS. Do not apply these dimensions. Instead, create a new part (PART3_1), draw a profile having the shape and size of the first one, turn it into a profile sketch with AMPROFILE. Your three sketches should be similar to those in Figure 2-5.

Start AMVARS again, and select the Active Part tab. You will notice that the variables you defined for PART2_1 are not listed. Use the following parameters to define three new variables:

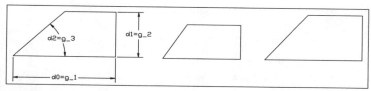

Figure 2-5

Name	Equation	Comment
p3_1	g_1*.75	Long horizontal length
p3_2	2	Width
p3_3	50	Angle

Notice that variable p3_1 uses a global variable in its equation. While you can freely reference global variables in the equations for active part variables, you cannot reference variables belonging other parts. Close the `Design Variables` dialog box by clicking its OK button. You will now dimension PART2_1, but you must first make it the active part. Click on its name in the browser to highlight it, and then press the right-hand button on your pointing device. Select Activate Part from the resulting shortcut menu. Then, invoke AMPARDIM, and dimension the sketch using the p2_1 as the dimension value for the long horizontal side, p2_2 for the vertical side, and p2_3 for the angle.

Next, activate PART3_1. Use its active part variable p3_1 for the dimension value of the long horizontal line, and use p3_2 as the dimension of the width of the profile sketch. For the angle

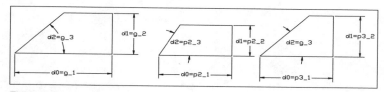

Figure 2-6

dimension, though, use the global variable g_3, rather than the part variable p3_3. This demonstrates that you can use global variables in any part. Your three dimensioned sketches should be similar to those in Figure 2-6 when AMDIMDSP is set to display equations. Notice that each part has its own d0, d1, and d2 dimension names.

You can copy global variables to an active part's list of variables. To see how this is done, make certain that PART3_1 is the active part, and start AMVARS. Click the Global tab. In the lower right-hand corner of the dialog box are three buttons labeled Selected, Referenced, and All. Click the one labeled Referenced, and then click the Active Part tab.

You will see that the variables g_1 and g_3 are now active part variables (as well as global variables). The variable g_1 was referenced in the equation for p3_1, while g_3 was referenced in the part's dimension d2. If you want to copy all of the global variables to the active part, click the button labeled All in the Global tab's dialog box, and if you want to copy just specific variables, click on their names to highlight them, and click the button labeled Selected.

You will notice that the Active Part tab has three columns that are labeled T, D, and U. The letter T in a variable's row indicates that the variable is table driven. We will discuss table driven variables shortly. The letter D signifies that the active part variable has the same name as a global variable, and the letter U indicates that the variable is not referenced—that is, it is unused. Since you defined but did not use the p3_3 variable, it will have a U.

That finishes our experiments with multiple parts, active part variables, and global variables. You do not need to save the drawing file for this exercise.

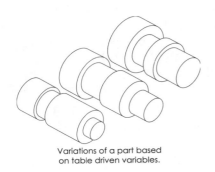

Variations of a part based
on table driven variables.

Table Driven Variables

The real power and flexibility with variables comes from being able to link them to a table that holds different values or has different equations for a variable. Suppose, for instance, you have a profile sketch for a shaft that has steps of various diameters and lengths. You could express the dimensions of the profile as variables, and have any number of different sets of variable values for making different versions of the shaft. Even after the profile has been revolved into a 3D feature, you can specify different versions of the variables, and the shaft will change shape accordingly. Also, the 2D drawing of it will be redrawn and re-dimensioned to reflect the parameters of the selected version. Moreover, you can edit the table to modify the equations of existing variables, as well as create additional versions of the part. Table driven variables can also be used to control 3D features—such as extrusion distance and taper, hole sizes, and array parameters. In this chapter, though, we will confine our discussion of table driven variables to dimensions for profiles.

Mechanical Desktop uses Microsoft Excel spreadsheets to manage table driven variables. Consequently, Microsoft Excel must be installed on your computer for you to use table driven variables. You can create the Excel file and the Mechanical Desktop file separately, and link them together; or you can create the variables in a drawing file and have Mechanical Desktop create a spreadsheet file for them. You can use active part variables and global variables as table driven variables, but you cannot include both in the same table. Relationships between a drawing and a spreadsheet are managed through the Active Part tab of AMVARS's `Design Variables` dialog box.

Version names are down

	A	B	C	D	E	F	G	H
1		Ri	Ro	Tk	BaseW	BaseL	BaseR	BaseH
2	Version01	2	2*2	2.5	50	40	(2/5)*BaseL	36
3	Version02	Tk	Tk*2	1.5	40	32	(2/5)*BaseL	24
4	Version03	3	5.5	2.5	54	40	32	32
5	Version04	2.5	5	2.5	48	44	34	34

The default format of the spreadsheet is to have each column represent a variable while each row contains data for a particular version of the variables. The first row (row 1) in the spreadsheet contains the names of the design variables, and the first column (column A) contains the names of the versions. You can,

Version names are across

	A	B	C	D	E	F	G	H
1		Version01	Version02	Version03	Version04			
2	Ri	2	Tk	3	2.5			
3	Ro	2*2	Tk*2	5.5	5			
4	Tk	2.5	1.5	2.5	2.5			
5	BaseW	50	40	54	48			
6	BaseL	40	32	40	44			
7	BaseR	(2/5)*BaseL	(2/5)*BaseL	32	34			
8	BaseH	36	24	32	34			

though, reverse this arrangement by clicking the Table Setup button in the `Design Variables` dialog box. A dialog box titled `Table Driven Setup` that has a radio button labeled Down and another labeled Across will appear. If the Down button is checked, each row represents a different version; and if Across is checked, each column represents a different version. Down is the default setting.

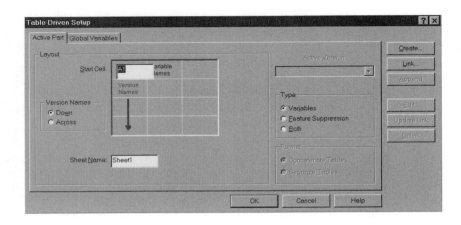

There is no limit to the number of variables and versions in a spreadsheet. However, each version must have an entry for each variable—no blank cells are allowed. In the **Design Variables** dialog box, each variable that is linked to a spreadsheet is preceded by the letter T. You can transform a table driven part to a standard parametric part by unlinking the spreadsheet. This is done by clicking the Unlink button in the **Table Driven Setup** dialog box. The resulting dimensions will be those of the last active version.

The steps to create table driven design variables from Mechanical Desktop are:

1. Initiate AMVARS.

2. Define one set of design variables. either global or active part. Unless at least one feature exists, the Active Part tab will not be available.

3. Press the Setup button in the **Design Variables** dialog box to bring up the **Table Driven Setup** dialog box.

4. Select either Down or Across for Version Names, and make certain that the radio button labeled Variables is checked. Click the create button.

5. A file-list type dialog box will appear. In this dialog box specify the spreadsheet file name and its location. Its filename extension will be XLS.

6. A Microsoft Excel spreadsheet will appear in a window over the Mechanical Desktop window. The variable names you created in Step 2 will appear across one row or down one column (whichever you specified in Step 4). The version name given to these variables will be "Generic." You can change the name to one of your choice, and you can add other sets of design variables as you wish; following the Excel methods for entering data, and the Mechanical Desktop rules for design variable equations.

7. When you are finished with the Excel file, save and close it to return to Mechanical Desktop's **Table Driven Setup** dialog box. Click the Update Link button, and click OK to return to the **Design Variables** dialog box.

8. The pull-down list box labeled Active Version will contain the names you created in the Excel spreadsheet. You can click on any of these names to have its set of design variable values become the active set. Then, click OK to exit the AMVARS command. Dimensions that have been set to the design variables will then assume the values of the active set. The version names will also appear in the Desktop Browser, and you can right-click a version name to bring up a menu that will make that version the active one.

You can also create the Excel spreadsheet first and then link it to a Mechanical Desktop drawing file. The steps to do this are:

1. Open an Excel spreadsheet. Enter the variable names along one row (usually row 1) or down one column (usually column A). Enter the version names down one column or across one row to correspond to the variable names. Enter the equations for each version and variable. Save the spreadsheet file, using a name and location of your choice.

2. Open a Mechanical Desktop drawing file. Create the profile that is to be dimensioned according to the design variables. If you do not have a profile, only global variables can exist.

3. Start AMVARS. Choose the variable type by clicking either the Active Part or Global tab. Then click the Setup button to bring up the `Table Driven Setup` dialog box. Set the layout parameters (Down or Across) to match that of the spreadsheet you created in Step 1. Then, click the Link button to bring up a dialog box for locating files that is titled `Link Table`. In this dialog box, locate the Excel file and click the Open button to link the Excel file to the Mechanical Desktop file. The `Table Driven Setup` dialog box will reappear. Click OK to return to the `Design Variables` dialog box.

4. The variable names you created in the spreadsheet will appear in the dialog box, along with the version names. The version names will also appear in the Desktop Browser.

5. Incorporate the variable names into the sketch's dimensions, through AMPARDIMS or AMMODDIM. You can change versions of the design variables through the AMVARS command or through the right-click menu of the browser.

Once a spreadsheet has been created, you can add to it or modify its contents as with any Excel spreadsheet. To update the Mechanical Desktop drawing file: be certain that the spreadsheet has been saved, start AMVARS, click Setup, and then click the button labeled Update link. If you changed the name of some variables or if you deleted some from the spreadsheet, you will need to delete them manually from the Mechanical Desktop `Design Variables` dialog box.

The type of relationship between the part and the spreadsheet is controlled by the three radio buttons labeled Variable, Feature Suppression, and Both in the cluster labeled

Type. The type of relationships that are described in this chapter are all Variable. The other two relationship types, Feature Suppression and Both, are for *version suppressed features*. Feature suppression is discussed in Chapter 13.

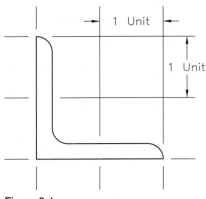

Figure 3-1

Exercise 3

Creating and Working with Table Driven Variables

In this exercise you will create a set of active part variables and then link them to a Microsoft Excel spreadsheet that stores the data to make a family of profile sketches suitable for making models of structural steel angles. Start a new Mechanical Desktop part file, using the default English template (acad.dwt). Draw the profile objects, consisting of four lines and three arcs, using Figure 3-1 as a guide.

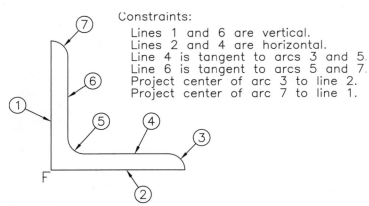

Constraints:
   Lines 1 and 6 are vertical.
   Lines 2 and 4 are horizontal.
   Line 4 is tangent to arcs 3 and 5.
   Line 6 is tangent to arcs 5 and 7.
   Project center of arc 3 to line 2.
   Project center of arc 7 to line 1.

Figure 3-2

Turn the objects into a profile sketch with AMPRO-FILE. Use AMSHOWCON to display the sketch's constraints. If they are not the same as those shown in Figure 3-2, use AMDEL-CON and AMADDCON to make them so. Mechanical Desktop will report that five dimensions or constraints are needed to fully constrain the sketch.

Start AMVARS to bring up the **Design Variables** dialog box. Click the Active Part tab, and define five variables as follows:

Name	Equation	Comment
v0	2	horizontal leg length
v1	2	vertical leg length
v2	.25	horizontal leg thickness
v3	v2	vertical leg thickness
v4	v2	arc radius

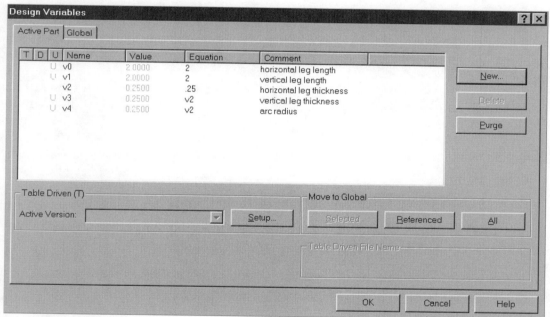

Figure 3-3

Your entries in the **Design Variables** dialog box should be similar to those shown in Figure 3-3. Press the OK button of the dialog box to end the AMVARS command. Then use AMPARDIM to dimension the profile sketch. When you are prompted for a dimension value, enter the name of the corresponding active part variable. These five dimensions will fully contain the sketch. When AMDIMDSP is set to show dimensions as equations, your sketch should look similar to the one shown in Figure 3-4.

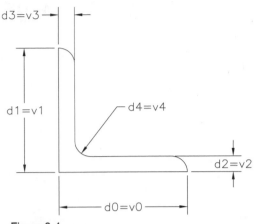

Figure 3-4

Next you will have Mechanical Desktop create a Microsoft Excel spreadsheet for the active part variables. Invoke AMVARS again, and click the Setup button in the Active Part tab to display up the `Table Driven Setup` dialog box. Accept the default layout of version names down, verify that the radio button labeled Variables is checked, and click the Create button. A dialog box will appear for you to use in specifying the name and location for the Excel file. Choose any name you like.

	A	B	C	D	E	F	G
1		v0	v1	v2	v3	v4	
2	Generic	2	2	.25	v2	v2	
3							
4							
5							
6							
7							
8							
9							

Microsoft Excel - md06e805.xls

File   Edit   View   Insert   Format   Tools   Data   Window   Help

Sheet1 Sheet2 Sheet3

Ready   NUM

Figure 3-5

As soon as the filename has been specified, the spreadsheet will open in a window over the Mechanical Desktop window. As shown in Figure 3-5, the names of the active part variables will be in the first row of the spreadsheet, while their equations will be in the second row. Also, the first cell in the second row will be labeled Generic.

In the spreadsheet, you will change the name of the first set of equations to a more meaningful name, and you will add two more sets of design variables. Move the spreadsheet cursor to the first cell in the second row, and replace 'Generic' with '2x2x0.25.' Then add the following two rows to the spreadsheet, beginning with cell A3:

```
3x3x0.375      3      3      .375    v2      v2
2x2.5x0.25     2      2.5    .25     v2      v2
```

Save the spreadsheet (Simultaneously pressing the Ctrl and S keys is one way to do this.), which should look similar to the one in Figure 3-6, and click somewhere in the Mechanical Desktop graphics area to return to the `Table Driven Setup` dialog box. Click the Update Link button to connect the data you added to the spreadsheet with the drawing file, and then click the OK button to restore the `Design Variables` dialog

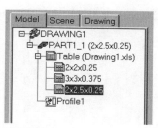

Figure 3-6

box. Each of the design variables will now have a T to signify they are table driven. The names you assigned to the additional sets of variable data (versions) will appear in the Active Version list box and also, as shown in Figure 3-7, in the Desktop Browser.

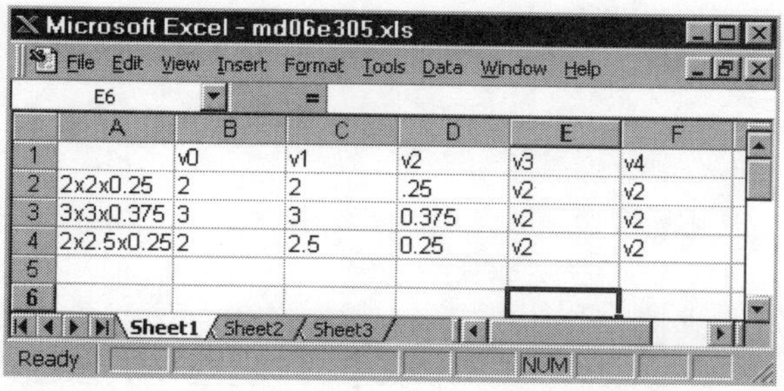

To change from one set of variables to another, click the version you want in the Active Version list box, as shown in Figure 3-8. It will be highlighted, and when you click the OK button in the `Design Variables` dialog box, the sketch will automatically update to match the selected set of variables. You can also change from one version to another by right-clicking the version's name in the browser, and selecting Activate from the shortcut menu.

Figure 3-7

When the dimension display is set to display values, your 2x2.5x0.25 version of the sketch should be similar to the one shown on the left in Figure 3-9, and the 3x3x0.375 version should be similar to the one on the right. (You, however, will not be able to display both versions at the same time, as is done in this figure.) That finishes your work with this exercise.

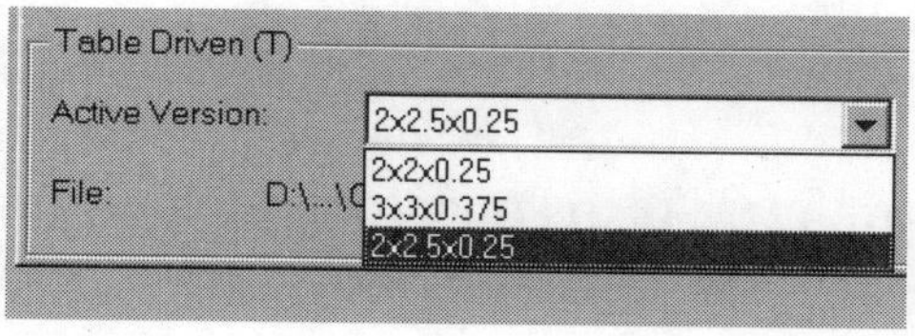

Figure 3-8

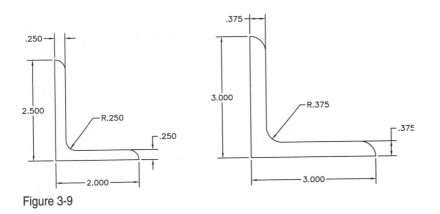

Figure 3-9

We will not use this sketch again, so you do not need to save it or its Excel file. On the CD-ROM that accompanies this book, the Mechanical Desktop profile sketch is in file md06e305.dwg and the Excel spreadsheet is in file md06e305.xls. If you use these two files, you will probably have to start AMVARS, open the Setup dialog box, and reestablish the link between the Mechanical Desktop file and the Excel file.

Global Variable Parameter Files

Before R3, Mechanical Desktop could not link global design variables to a spreadsheet file for creating multiple versions of a part's dimensions, but you could link them to files called parameter files, that contained data for a single version of the variables. Although you are not likely to need parameter files now, Mechanical Desktop is still able to use them. The files, which have a filename extension of PRM, are in ASCII format. Therefore, they can be created and read by a text editor, such as Windows' Notepad. In these files, each global variable is listed on a separate line as an equation—the name of the variable is on the left, the value the variable is to assume is on the right, and an equal sign is between them. You may include comments by enclosing them between the /* and */ characters.

The relationships between a Mechanical Desktop drawing file and a global variable parameter file is handled through the Global tab of AMVARS' `Design Variables` dialog box. This tab has buttons for selecting the following four options.

Import Use this button to import the contents of an existing parameter file into the current drawing. Mechanical Desktop will display a dialog box to help you locate the file. The variables in that file will be added to those currently in the drawing. Mechanical Desktop will not, however, maintain a relationship with the parameter file.

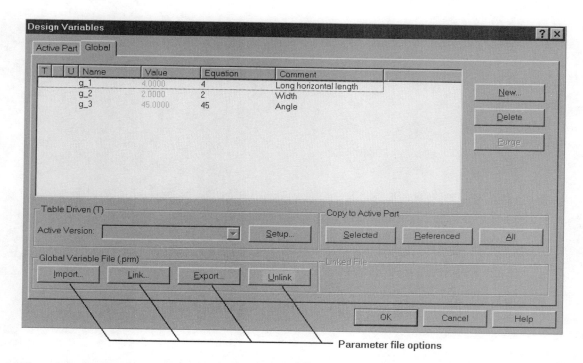

Parameter file options

Link   Use this button to relate the contents of a parameter file to the current Mechanical Desktop drawing file, rather than import the contents of the parameter file. Mechanical Desktop maintains a relationship with the parameter file, and if the parameter file is changed, the drawing's global variables are also changed. (You must invoke AMUPDATE to trigger the changes in the drawing.) The option will display a dialog box for you to use in locating the parameter file, and the variables in that file will be added to those currently in the drawing.

Export   This option exports the global variables currently in the Mechanical Desktop drawing to an external file. A dialog box will be displayed for you to use in naming and locating the file. The file will be in ASCII format.

Unlink   This button breaks the relationship between the Mechanical Desktop drawing and the parameter file. The global variables will be retained, but they will no longer be linked to a parameter file.

CHAPTER 7

Work Features

Work features are tools that help you construct and control 3D features. They are Mechanical Desktop created features that are based on your input, and you will find them to be indispensable as you construct part models and make 2D drawings of those models.

This chapter covers the following topics.

- *Shows you how to insert work points, how to constrain them, and what you can do with them.*

- *Explains the usefulness of work axes, and how to create them.*

- *Describes the many uses of work planes, their properties, and how to fix their positions.*

- *Explains the differences between parametric and non-parametric work planes.*

- *Introduces Mechanical Desktop's basic work planes to you and explains how they can be useful.*

Using Work Features

Just as construction geometry helps constrain and dimension profiles internally, work features help constrain and dimension profiles externally. As shown in Table 1, four different types of work features exist, and four different Mechanical Desktop commands are used to create them.

Table 1 Mechanical Desktop Work Features

Work Feature	Applicable Command	Typical Uses
Work Point	AMWORKPT	Parametrically locating holes and surfcut features. Adding dimensions between two profiles. Rotation axis for polar arrays.
Work Axis	AMWORKAXIS	Dimensioning and constraining profiles. Placing work planes. Axis for a revolved feature or a polar array. Center of a 3D helix path.
Work Plane	AMWORKPLN	Parametrically locating sketch planes. Termination planes for 3D features. Dimensioning and constraining profiles. Making full section views in 2D drawings. Placing other work planes. Splitting faces and parts.
Basic Planes	AMBASICPLANES	Quickly establish planes for creating the base feature of a new part.

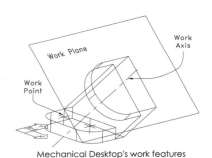

Mechanical Desktop's work features

You can control the visibility of work features through a Desktop Browser shortcut menu.

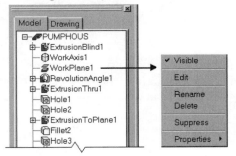

Unlike construction geometry, you do not need to draw anything in creating work features (except for sketched work axes); you simply specify their location, and (for work planes) their orientation. They are real objects, though, and they can be selected just as a line or a 3D feature edge can be selected. In most cases work features are parametric. That is, they move and reorient themselves as the features they are associated with are modified, moved, and re-oriented.

Mechanical Desktop places work features in the AM_WORK layer, which is automatically created the first time a work feature is created. They are also displayed in the Desktop Browser with names such as WorkAxis1 or WorkPlane3. If your part becomes too cluttered, you can either globally or selectively turn the display of work features on and off through the AMVISIBLE command, as well as through a Desktop Browser right-click shortcut menu. This menu also allows you to rename work features, as well as to delete them. Work features can also be deleted through the AMDELFEAT command.

Work Points

Work points are displayed as three mutually perpendicular lines that intersect at the work point. They are created by the AMWORKPT command, which issues a command line prompt for you to specify the point's location on the current sketch plane. Typically, once the point is created, you will dimension or constrain it to existing features, such as path or profile sketch objects, existing 3D feature edges, and so forth. However, if you intend to dimension a work point dimensioned to a sketch feature, such as a profile, it must be created before the sketch.

The effect of constraints between work points and arcs and circles depends on whether the arc or circle is part of a 3D feature or part of a sketch. With arc and circular shaped edges of a 3D feature, you can fix a work point to the center with a concentric constraint, and you can fix it on the edge with a project constraint. With circular and arc shaped objects in a sketch, however, the concentric constraint does not accept work points. You can, though, use the project constraint to fix a work point to the circumference of a circle or arc in a sketch. When selecting a work point for a project constraint, you do not need to use an object snap.

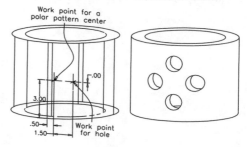

Work points are useful as hole and polar pattern centers on non-planar surfaces.

One common use of work points is in positioning round holes on non-planar surfaces, and another is to serve as an axis of revolution for a polar pattern on a non-planar surface. See Chapter 11 for more information about hole features, and Chapter 12 for a discussion on pattern features. Work points can also be used

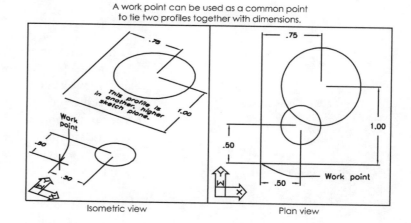

A work point can be used as a common point to tie two profiles together with dimensions.

Isometric view   Plan view

to tie two sketches together by dimensioning objects in both sketches to a single work point. This is sometimes helpful for tying profile sketches to path sketches, and for tying profile sketches that are to be used for lofted 3D features together. When work points are used to specify hole locations and array axes, and are used with sketches to make sweep and lofted 3D features, they will be consumed when the 3D feature is created. Additional uses of work points will be pointed out as we discuss other Mechanical Desktop features.

Work Axes

Work axes are centerline type objects extending along the axis of any 3D feature that is geometrically capable of having an axis, such as a round hole or a cylinder. You can also draw your own work axes. Once a work axis has been created, it remains with the feature, regardless of how the feature is located or oriented. They are created by the AMWORKAXIS command, which will issue the following command line prompt.

```
Select cylinder, cone, torus or [Sketch]: (Select a circular edge or enter an S.)
```

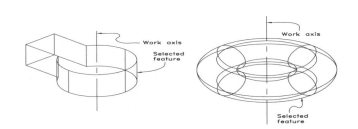

The default option is to select the edge or curved face of a cylindrical, cone, or torus shaped 3D feature. The work axis will be created along the axis of the 3D feature. You can select just one feature with each call to AMWORKAXIS.

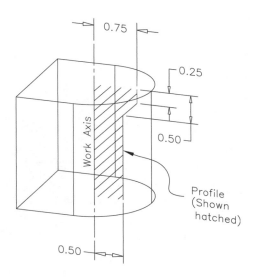

Often, you will use these work axes for constraining and dimensioning profile sketches, as shown in the accompanying figure. Although you cannot use a work axis to close a sketch, you can tie the sketch to the axis with a collinear constraint. Incidentally, notice in this figure that the arc-shaped edges of the base feature have been used to close the top and bottom sides of the profile.

A work axis can also serve as an axis of revolution when making a revolved feature, and it can serve as the center of a polar pattern. See Chapter 8 for information on revolved features and Chapter 12 for information on pattern features. Moreover, work axes can serve as edges in positioning work planes.

When you select the Sketch option of AMWORKAXIS, you can draw your own work axis anywhere on the current sketch plane, just as if you were drawing a line. Typically, though, you will use object snaps to tie the work axis to existing geometry. Sketched work axes can be used for the same purposes as those in the center of cylindrical, cone, or torus shaped 3D features. They can also be used as the center of a helix path sketch, as we will describe in Chapter 9.

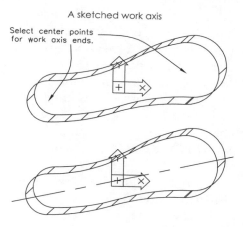

Work Planes

Using Work Planes

You may find it helpful to visualize a work plane as a rigid flat surface, such as a sheet of plywood. When you set a plywood sheet on certain objects, such as four posts or table legs, it will be stable and it will also move when the supporting objects are moved. The plywood sheet, however, will be unstable if it is placed on some objects. You would not, for example, expect it to be stable if it were placed on a horizontal cylinder or on just two posts; and you would certainly not try to rest it on the point of a cone. Once the sheet of plywood has been placed in a stable position, though, it can be used for a variety of purposes, such holding books and papers, or even a computer.

Similar to a sheet of plywood, you can place a work plane on objects, and when those objects are moved, the work plane will move accordingly. Also like a sheet of plywood, a work plane will not be stable when it is placed on certain objects, such as the side of a cylinder, or on the sharp end of a cone. In fact, Mechanical Desktop will not allow you to place a work plane in an unstable position, or in a position that would warp or bend the work plane. Unlike a sheet of plywood, though, work planes are infinite in size and are not affected by gravity. You can lay it "on" objects even if the objects are "above" the work plane.

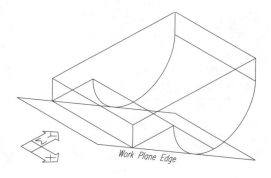

Often you will use work planes as the foundation of a sketch, especially a profile sketch. This is because you generally construct Mechanical Desktop parts on a plane-by-plane basis. You create a 3D feature from a 2D profile, and then you move to another plane to draw another 2D profile for another 3D feature. When you are analyzing your model to see how you can set up the next plane, you will first look for planar faces that can be used to establish a sketch plane. If there is nothing suitable, you will then look for ways to establish a work plane.

Although work planes are flat and unbounded, they are not a coordinate system plane. If you want to draw objects on a work plane, you must first place the sketch plane on it. The dialog box you use in establishing a work plane's parameters (which is displayed by the AMWORKPLN command) has an option for placing the sketch plane on the work plane as soon as it is created.

Another popular use of work planes is as a termination for 3D features. For instance, rather that extrude a profile a specified distance, you can extrude it until it meets a work plane. If you later move the work plane, the end of the extruded feature will move with it. Chapter 8 completely describes the role of work planes in creating 3D features. Work planes are also used as slicing planes in making section views in 2D drawings of parts. See Chapter 15 for details on section views. A work plane can be used also as a slicing place to split a face on a 3D feature into two faces, or to even splice a part into two parts. Chapter 11 explains how faces and parts can be split.

Work planes are displayed as rectangles that are automatically sized to fit the 3D model, and you can pick the edges of the rectangle for placing dimensions and constraints. However, since the displayed edge is not actually the edge of the work plane (and in fact, work planes have no edges), dimensions and constraints only work when they are perpendicular to the work plane.

Most work planes are parametric. That is, they are attached to one or more objects or features, and they move in accordance with the movement or modifications of those objects. You can, however, place a work plane on one of the three World Coordinate System (WCS) principle planes, or on the XY plane of the User Coordinate system (UCS). Since those work planes are related to space, rather than to a feature, they are referred to as non-parametric work planes.

Work Plane Modifiers

Work planes are created by the AMWORKPLN command. This command uses a dialog box for you to select the parameters for locating the work plane, and it uses command line prompts for you to select the objects that are to position it. The dialog box has two main clusters of radio buttons. One is labeled *1st Modifier*, and the other is labeled *2nd Modifier*. The effect of modifiers in fixing the position of the work plane is similar to constraints. By themselves, none of the 1st and 2nd modifiers can define a work plane's position. A single axis or edge, for instance, only partially fixes the position of a work plane because the plane is free to rotate; therefore, a second modifier is needed to stabilize it.

Generally, you will initially select a 1st modifier. Then the 2nd modifiers that are not appropriate for use with the 1st modifier will be grayed-out. When the Normal to Start, On UCS, World XY, World YZ, and World XZ modifiers are selected, all of the 2nd modifier buttons will be grayed-out. Descriptions of the 1st and 2nd modifiers are given in Table 2, and the allowable combinations of modifiers are shown in Table 3.

Table 2 Work Plane 1st and 2nd Modifiers

On Edge/Axis	This modifier forces the work plane to lie on the straight edge of a feature, on a work axis, or on one of the three WCS principle axes. A command line prompt will ask you to specify an edge or axis.
On Vertex	The work plane will be attached to the point of a 3D feature at which three or more edges meet. The point of a cone is not accepted. A command line prompt will be issued for you to select a vertex.
Tangent	The work plane will be tangent to a cylindrical or conical surface. Spherical surfaces are not allowed. AMWORKPLN will ask from the command line for you to select a rounded surface. If there are two choices available for the location of the work plane (such as on a cylinder), the possible locations of the work plane will be displayed for you to specify the location you want.

Table 2 Work Plane 1st and 2nd Modifiers (Continued)

Planar Parallel	The work plane will be parallel to a specified plane. A command line prompt will ask you to specify the plane as one of the WCS principle planes, as the XY plane of the UCS, or to select a planar surface or another work plane.
Planar Normal	The work plane will be perpendicular to a specified plane. From the command line, you will be asked to specify the plane as one of the principal WCS planes, the XY plane of the UCS, or to select a planar surface or another work plane.
Planar Angle	This modifier is only available as a 2nd modifier when On Edge/Axis has been selected as a 1st modifier. The Angle edit box will be activated for you to enter the number of degrees that the work plane is to be inclined from a specified plane. The On Edge/Axis selection will serve as the rotation axis. A command line prompt will ask you to select the plane. Your choices will be one of the WCS principal planes, the XY plane of the UCS, a planar surface, or another work plane. Then, a rotation angle direction will be displayed as a arrow on the part model, and you can accept it or switch to the reverse angle.
On 3 Vertices	This is a 2nd modifier that is only available when On Vertex has been selected as a 1st modifier. The work plane will lie on the four vertices. From the command line, Mechanical Desktop will prompt for three different vertices. You can make your selections by picking an edge near the corner of three or more edges or by picking work points. When selecting a vertex from an edge, you do not need to use object endpoint snaps.
Offset	The work plane will be constrained to be parallel to and offset from a planar face. Offset is available only as a 2nd modifier and only when Planar Parallel has been selected as a 1st modifier. The Offset edit box will be activated for you to enter the offset distance. When the dialog box has been dismissed, one of the two possible directions from the base plane will be shown, and you can accept it or switch to the other direction.
Normal to Start	This modifier creates a work plane that is located on the start point of a 2D or 3D path sketch and is oriented so that it is perpendicular (normal) to the plane of the path sketch and to its starting direction. A work point will also be placed at the start point of the path sketch. See Chapter 9 for a discussion of path sketches. The Normal to Start modifier also works with sketched work axes. No other modifiers are used, and no command line prompts are issued when just one path sketch exists. If more than one path exists, you will be prompted to select one of them; and if a sketched work axis exists you will be prompted to select one end of it.

Table 3 Allowable Combinations of Work Plane Modifiers

1st Modifier Selection	Allowable 2nd Modifiers
On Edge/Axis	On Edge/Axis
	On Vertex
	Tangent
	Planar Parallel
	Planar Normal
	Planar Angle
On Vertex	On Edge/Axis
	Planar Parallel
	On 3 Vertices
Tangent	On Edge/Axis
	Tangent
	Planar Parallel
	Planar Normal
Planar Parallel	On Edge/Axis
	On Vertex
	Tangent
	Offset
Planar Normal	On Edge/Axis
	Tangent

The following figures show the resulting work plane location and orientation from various combinations of 1st and 2nd modifiers.

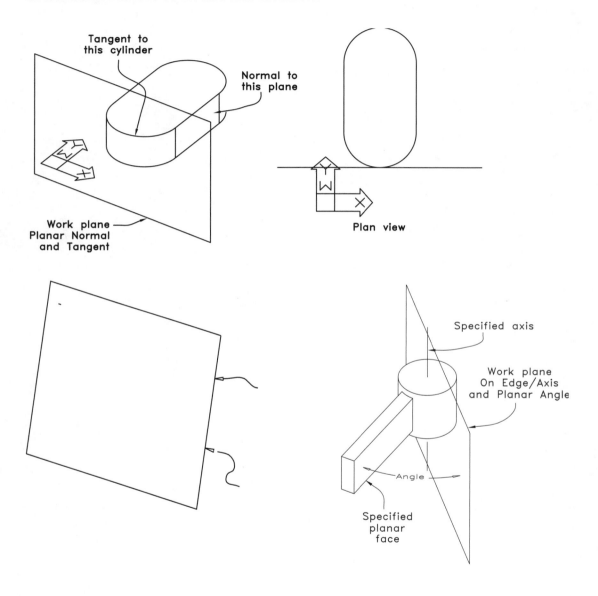

Tangent to this cylinder

Normal to this plane

Work plane Planar Normal and Tangent

Plan view

Specified axis

Work plane On Edge/Axis and Planar Angle

Angle

Specified planar face

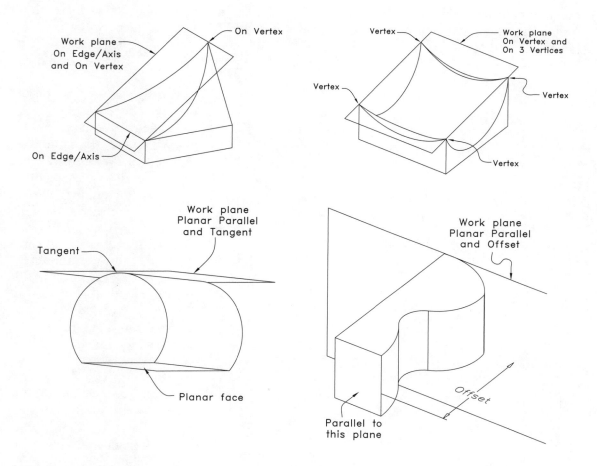

Non-Parametric Work Planes

The On UCS modifier places the work plane on the XY plane of the current UCS, while the World XY, World YZ, and World ZX modifiers place it on the stated principal plane of the WCS. These are referred to as non-parametric work planes, and no other modifiers are used with

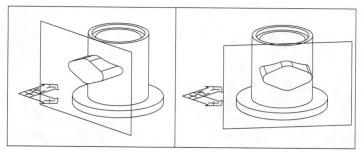

A worldZX work plane will move off of the WCS ZX plane when the part it is associated with is moved or rotated.

them. When the work plane is created, it is placed on the stated plane, but once it has been created, its relative position and orientation with the 3D part is fixed, rather than its position and orientation with the WCS. For instance, a work plane installed on the World ZX plane will move off of the World ZX plane if the part is moved or rotated, as shown in the accompanying figure.

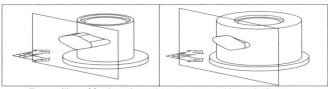

The position of features based on nonparametric work planes does not change as the more basic features are changed.

In this figure, the flat end of the dependent feature that is based on the work plane will always remain the same distance from the center of the base feature. Consequently, as the diameter of the base feature is increased, the flat face on the dependent feature will become closer to the base feature, as shown in the next figure, and it could even be engulfed by it.

There is nothing wrong with that behavior if the distance between the center of the cylinder and the dependent feature's face is an important characteristic of the design. If, on the other hand, the distance from the surface of the cylinder to the face is important, you would first place a work plane on the surface of the cylinder using the Planar Parallel (based on the WCS ZX plane) and

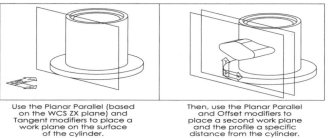

Use the Planar Parallel (based on the WCS ZX plane) and Tangent modifiers to place a work plane on the surface of the cylinder.

Then, use the Planar Parallel and Offset modifiers to place a second work plane and the profile a specific distance from the cylinder.

Tangent modifiers, and then use the Planar Parallel and Offset modifiers to position a second work plane a specific distance from the first work plane (and the surface of the cylinder). The profile for the dependent feature is positioned on this work plane, and the end of the feature will move as the diameter of the cylinder increases or decreases.

Basic Work Planes

Mechanical Desktop's AMBASIC-
PLANES command creates three
work planes, one work point, and
the definition of a new part in one
step. The work planes, which are
non-parametric, will be parallel
with the WCS principal planes, and
the work point will be located at the
intersection of the work planes. As
soon as you invoke the command,
Mechanical Desktop will switch to
the WCS if a UCS or sketch plane is
being used, display the three work
planes and the work point, and
issue a command line prompt for
you to select the point at which the
planes will intersect. While
AMBASICPLANES is not a com-

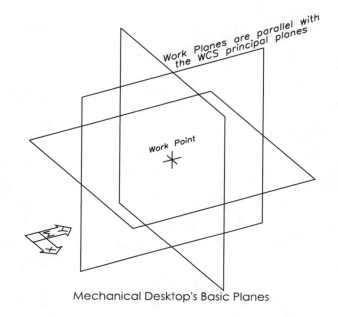

Mechanical Desktop's Basic Planes

mand you will often use, it can be useful when you want to start a new part that will have
a base feature that is not on the WCS XY plane. After you create the basic planes, you
must use the AMSKPLN command to position the sketch plane on one of them.

CHAPTER 8

Sketched Features

You will enter the 3D world of Mechanical Desktop in this chapter as you learn how to transform 2D profiles into 3D features. The 3D features are referred to as sketched features because the profiles they are based on have been drawn, or sketched, by the user. Your steps in constructing a part model will be to first create a base 3D feature and then to add-to or cut-from that base feature until you achieve the geometry you want.

This chapter covers the following topics.

- Explains the join, cut, intersect, and split operations and shows you how to use them to shape the geometry of your 3D part models.

- Describes the options Mechanical Desktop provides for ending, or terminating, the movement of profiles through space as they create 3D features.

- Explains how to create a 3D feature by moving, or extruding, a profile linearly through space.

- Explains how to create a 3D feature by revolving a profile about an axis.

- Explains how a set of profiles can serve as cross sections to define and create a 3D feature by a process referred to as lofting.

- Shows you how to use single line profiles to bend existing 3D features.

- Describes how to use single line profiles to easily make thin walled ribs on existing 3D features.

A Mechanical Desktop part is constructed in a series of steps.

| A part starts with a base 3D feature | which is modified and supplemented | with sketched and placed features | to make the finished part. |

Constructing a Mechanical Desktop part is done in a series of steps in which you use certain operations to create 3D features and you use other operations to supplement and modify those features. Mechanical Desktop places these operations into two broad categories—*sketched features* and *placed features*. The operations for sketched features are more fundamental than those placed features, because they create 3D solid features. Mechanical Desktop refers to them as sketched features because they are based on user drawn profile sketches, and sometimes on path sketches as well. Placed features, on the other hand, need at least one existing sketched feature in order to work. For the most part, placed features are created by entering data in a dialog box, and then specifying objects or locations on a 3D feature. For example; when you use the fillet placed feature, which rounds sharp edges on a 3D feature, you specify the fillet's parameters in a dialog box, and then pick the edges that are to be rounded. Placed features are discussed in Chapter 11.

Unlike some 3D solid modeling programs, Mechanical Desktop has no ready-made primitive (fundamental) geometric shapes of spheres, cylinders, and so forth, that can be combined to create a 3D solid model. Every 3D feature is created by either extruding, revolving, sweeping, or lofting a profile. Which of the four methods you use depends upon the shape you want the feature to have. Table 1 briefly describes the methods for making sketched features and lists the Mechanical Desktop commands that make them. The rib and bend methods in this table, which are new with Mechanical Desktop 5, are based on open profiles and require an existing sketched feature. Because swept features are more complex than the other sketched features—requiring a path feature as well as a profile feature—we will devote an entire chapter, Chapter 10, to them.

Table 1 Methods for Creating Sketched Features

Method	Mechanical Desktop Command	Description
Extrusion	AMEXTRUDE	A 3D solid feature is made by pushing a profile in a perpendicular direction from the sketch plane.
Revolving	AMREVOLVE	A 3D solid feature is made by revolving a profile about an axis.

Table 1 Methods for Creating Sketched Features (Continued)

Method	Mechanical Desktop Command	Description
Sweeping	AMSWEEP	A 3D solid feature is made by pushing a profile along a path. The path must have been created by the AM2DPATH or AM3DPATH command.
Lofting	AMLOFT	The cross section of a 3D solid feature is defined by two or more profiles.
Lateral extrusion	AMRIB	An open profile is assigned a width and pushed on the sketch plane to an existing face.
Bend	AMBEND	An open profile is used as a folding line to bend and existing sketched feature.

Interaction between 3D Features

The commands for creating extruded, revolved, swept, and lofted sketched features use a dialog box for you to enter the options and parameters of the feature, and each of the four dialog boxes has a list box, titled Operation. This list box has five types of operations for controlling how the feature that is to be created will interact with existing features. The five operation types are summarized in Table 2.

Table 2 Operation Types

Operation Type	Result
Base	Creates the first 3D feature of a part.
Join	The volume of the new feature is combined with the volume of the existing 3D features. Volume shared by the new feature and the existing features is absorbed by the existing features.
Cut	The volume that the new feature shares with existing 3D features is removed from the existing 3D features.
Intersect	The volume shared by existing 3D features and the new feature is retained, while volume that is not shared is deleted from both the new feature and the existing features.
Split	The volume shared between existing 3D features and the new feature is removed from the existing features and a new part (not just a new feature) is created from the shared volume.

If no 3D feature exists, base is the only operation type available—the others will be grayed out in the dialog box. Conversely, when a 3D feature does exist, the base operation type will be grayed out. Every Mechanical Desktop part model can have only one base 3D feature. In the Desktop Browser, the base feature is always at the top of the feature tree, and it cannot be moved. Often the subsequent sketched features are referred to as *dependent features*, and as you would expect, several levels, or generations, of dependent features can exist. Sometimes the words *parent* and *child* are used to indicate the relationship between two features.

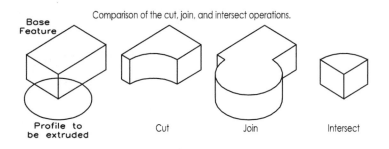

Comparison of the cut, join, and intersect operations.

The differences between the cut, join, and intersect operations are illustrated in the next figure. These interactions are sometimes referred to as Boolean operations. The name is in honor of George Boole, a mathematician who developed theories on logic and sets that are widely used in computer operations. You will see Boolean operations again in Chapter 12 when we discuss the AMCOMBINE command.

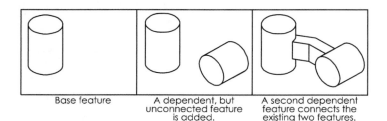

Join Operations

You will use join operations whenever you want to add to existing geometry. The joined feature can be noncontiguous with the existing 3D features, as shown in the center panel of the accompanying figure. The two objects in this figure are one feature, even though there is a space between them. In most cases, you will eventually add a feature that will connect the parts, as shown in the right panel. As you build the part, though, it is sometimes convenient to have noncontiguous features.

Cut Operations

During cut operations, on the other hand, if the dependent feature does not share any volume with existing features, the profile sketch for the dependent feature will be consumed, yet no new 3D feature will appear. Nevertheless, the dependent feature does exist. Its name will appear in the browser, and if you were to move its profile so that the dependent feature shares some volume with the other features, that volume will be removed. There is no reason for you to ever perform a cut operation in which none of the dependent feature's volume intersects the volume of existing features. Furthermore, if the volume of the dependent feature completely engulfs the existing features, an error will occur, and the cut operation will fail.

Intersect Operations

Although intersect will most likely be the operation type that you use the least, it enables you to efficiently make in one step some 3D shapes that would take several steps when only join and cut operations are used. Consider, for example, the part shown without dimensions in the figure to the right as a 2D, two view drawing.

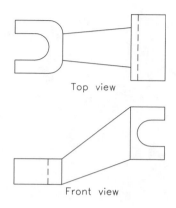

Top view

Front view

You can use the outline of the part in the top view as the profile for the base feature, and its outline in the front view as the profile for the dependent feature. On the left side of the figure below, the base feature has been created as an extrusion, and the profile for the dependent feature has been drawn on a sketch plane that is located in the center of the base feature and is parallel with the WCS ZX plane. These are shown in wireframe mode. The result of
an extruded intersect operation with the dependent
feature profile is shown on
the right in hidden line
mode. If the dependent
feature does not share any
volume with the existing
features, an error will
occur and the intersect
operation will fail.

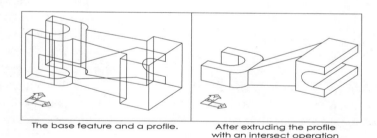

The base feature and a profile.   After extruding the profile
                                        with an intersect operation

Split Operations

Split operations are a combination of cut and intersect operations. The shared (or inter-secting) volume between existing 3D features and the dependent feature is removed from the existing geometry, while a new part is created from the intersecting volume. A command line prompt will ask you to specify a name for the new part. (If you are working in Mechanical Desktop's single part environment, the new part will be called a toolbody.)

The figure below shows a before-and-after example of a split extrusion with a wedge shaped base feature and a triangle shaped profile.

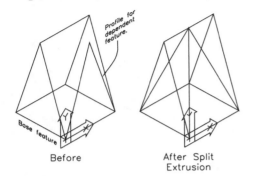

Before | After Split Extrusion

The newly created part will be inside the original part, so the split operation results will not be obvious. In the following figure, the new part has been moved away from the original part. Notice that the operation on the original part was equivalent to cut, while on the new part the operation was equivalent to intersect.

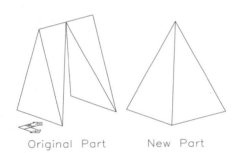

Original Part | New Part

Feature Terminations

Extruded, revolved, and swept sketched features are created by moving a profile through space to define the 3D feature's shape—an extruded feature is made by moving the profile in a direction that is perpendicular to the plane of the profile; a revolved feature is made by revolving the profile about an axis; and a swept feature is made by pushing the profile along a path. To give you additional control over the 3D feature's geometry, the AMEXTRUDE, AMREVOLVE, and AMSWEEP commands have options for establishing the end, or termination, of the feature. In making an extruded feature, for instance, you can specify that the profile is to be moved a specific distance in one direction (a blind termination), and an alternative is that you can specify that the profile is to be moved a specific distance in both directions (a midplane termination).

The command for making lofted features, AMLOFT, also offers termination options, even though lofted features are created by filling the space between profiles, rather than by moving profiles. You can, for example, have the lofted feature end when it intersects the face of an existing 3D feature, even though one or more of the profiles is beyond the face.

Mechanical Desktop has a total of thirteen different options for establishing feature terminations. However, any one 3D feature type does not offer all thirteen options. Swept features, for example, have only three termination options. Table 3 shows you which termination options are available for each of the four 3D feature types. Also, the Face,

Plane, Extended Face, and From-To terminations are not available with profiles that have multiple loops.

Some of these options use existing geometry to terminate a dependent feature. This is usually preferable to ending it on a set point (based on a distance or angle) because the feature will change as the more basic (or parent) features change. For instance, if an extruded dependent feature terminates on a specified face, it will become longer or shorter whenever the face is moved. On the other hand, when the dependent feature's profile is extruded for a certain distance (blind termination), a gap may appear when the base feature is lengthened.

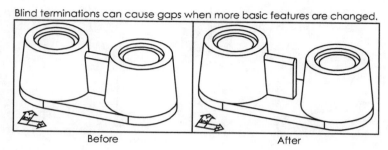

Blind terminations can cause gaps when more basic features are changed.

Before   After

In this table, a checkmark (✓) in a termination option's row indicates the option is available for the column's feature type.

Table 3 Available Termination Options by 3D Feature Type

Termination	3D Feature Type			
Option	Extruded	Revolved	Swept	Lofted
Blind	✓			
Through	✓			
Mid-Through	✓			
By Angle		✓		
MidPlane	✓	✓		
Path Only			✓	
Plane	✓	✓	✓	
Face	✓	✓	✓	
Next	✓	✓	✓	
Extended Face	✓	✓	✓	
From-To	✓	✓	✓	✓
Sections				✓
To Face/Plane				✓

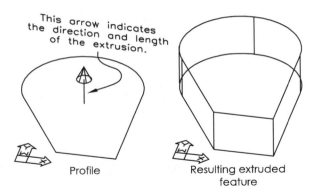

Profile

Resulting extruded feature

Termination Option Descriptions

Blind terminations are only available for extruded features. The profile is extruded in one direction for the length specified in the Distance edit box of the **Extrusion** dialog box. An arrow, extending from the geometric center of the profile, points in the extrusion direction, and its length indicates the extrusion length. You can reverse the extrusion direction with the Flip button of the **Extrusion** dialog box, and you specify the extrusion length in the dialog box's edit box that is labeled Distance.

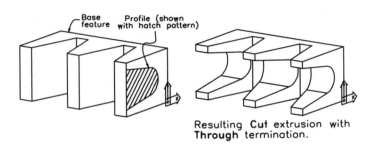

Resulting **Cut** extrusion with **Through** termination.

The *Through termination* option is available only for cut, intersect, and split operations on extrusions. It causes the extruded profile to pass through all existing features in the extrusion direction. Mechanical Desktop indicates the extrusion direction with an arrow on the profile. Select the Flip button of the Extrusion dialog box to reverse the direction.

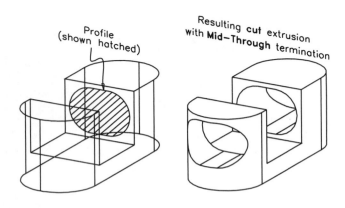

The *Mid-Through termination* can be used only with cut, intersect, and split operations of extruded dependent features. The profile is extruded in both directions through all existing features.

By Angle terminations are available only for revolved features. The profile is revolved in one direction by the angle entered in the Angle edit box of the **Revolution** dialog box.

The revolution direction is indicated by an arrow on the profile. Click the Flip button in the **Revolution** dialog box to reverse its direction.

MidPlane terminations can be used with both extruded and revolved features. In making a revolved feature the profile is revolved in both directions from the profile for a total angle equal to the value entered in the **Revolution** dialog box's Angle edit box. In making an extruded feature, the profile is extruded in both directions from the profile for a total distance equal to the value in the Distance edit box of the **Extrusion** dialog box.

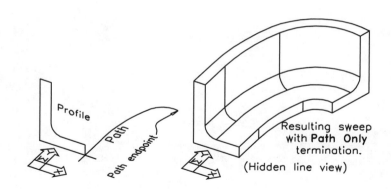

Path Only terminations, which are available only for sweep features, push the profile from the start of the path to the end of the path.

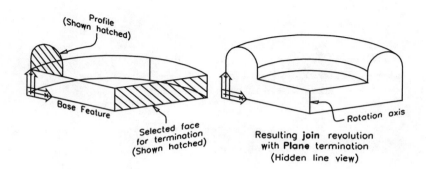

Plane terminations are based a plane that extends in an infinite distance in all directions. You will be prompted from the command line to select a face or a work plane. If you select a face, it must be planar (flat). However, the profile that is to be extruded, revolved, or swept does not have to actually intersect the face selected as a termination plane.

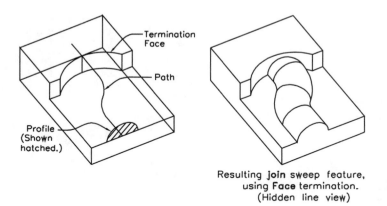

Resulting **join** sweep feature, using **Face** termination. (Hidden line view)

Face terminations end extruded, revolved, and sweep features on a selected face. A face is a continuous surface on a 3D feature that has either sharp edges or tangent edges with its adjoining faces. Unlike Plane terminations, the profile must completely intersect the face as it travels in its specified direction through space. If any part of the profile extends beyond the face, due to size or location, the operation will fail.

If the face you select is curved to the extent that more than one termination is possible, Mechanical Desktop will display the possible terminations and issue command line prompts for you to select the one you want.

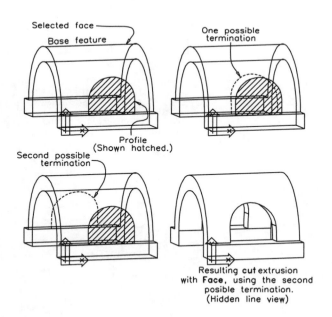

Resulting **cut** extrusion with **Face**, using the second posible termination. (Hidden line view)

The *Next termination* is similar to the face termination in that it ends the extruded, revolved, or sweep feature on an existing feature's face. You do not, however, select a face. Mechanical Desktop indicates the direction of the operation (for extruded and revolved features), and terminates the feature on the first face it encounters in that direction. As an option, you can reverse the indicated direction. This termination type is new with Mechanical Desktop Release 5.

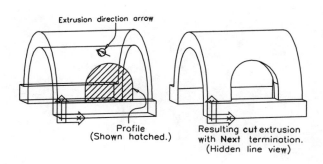

Profile
(Shown hatched.)

Resulting **cut** extrusion
with **Next** termination.
(Hidden line view)

Extended Face terminations also end extruded, revolved, and sweep features on a selected face. If the selected face is smaller than the profile, though, Mechanical Desktop extends the curvature of the face to accommodate the profile. You will be prompted from the command line to select the termination face to be extended. Extended face terminations were introduced in Mechanical Desktop Release 5.

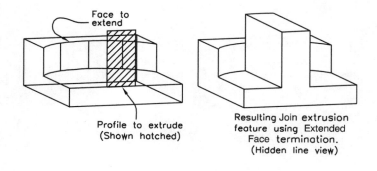

Face to
extend

Profile to extrude
(Shown hatched)

Resulting Join extrusion
feature using Extended
Face termination.
(Hidden line view)

The *From-To termination* option establishes both ends of a feature. The 3D feature will begin at the surface of one face or plane and end at a second face or plane. The From and To list boxes in the dialog box that creates the 3D feature will be activated, and in each list box you can choose between Plane, Face, and Extended Face as a termination. The profile can be located between the two faces or planes, or it can be behind one of them.

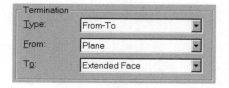

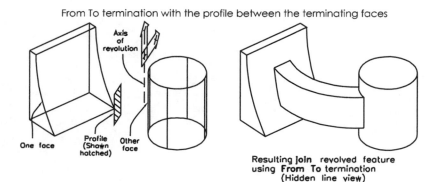

From To termination with the profile between the terminating faces

Axis
of
revolution

One face

Profile
(Shown
hatched)

Other
face

Resulting **Join** revolved feature
using **From To** termination
(Hidden line view)

The *Sections termination* option is specific to lofted features. The 3D feature will begin on the first specified profile and end on the last specified profile.

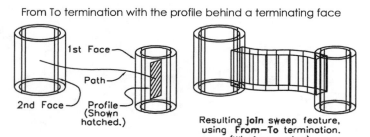

From To termination with the profile behind a terminating face

1st Face

Path

2nd Face

Profile
(Shown
hatched.)

Resulting **Join** sweep feature,
using **From—To** termination.
(Wireframe view)

The *To-Face termination* option is unique to lofted features. It causes a lofted feature to end on the selected face of a 3D feature. The face does not have to be planar, but it does have to be within the sections that are to be lofted; that is, it cannot be in back of the first or beyond the last section. You can also select a work plane as the termination face.

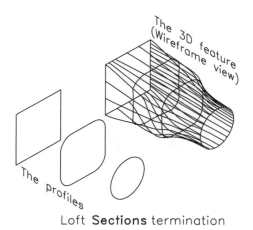

The 3D feature
(Wireframe view)

The profiles

Loft **Sections** termination

Creating Extruded Features

Extrusion will probably be your most often used method in making 3D features. It is also the most straightforward method, because no objects other that a single profile feature are involved. The 3D feature is created within the volume defined by pushing the profile through space in a direction that is perpendicular to the plane of the profile. An option allows you to have the cross section area of the profile become larger or smaller as it is extruded, which results in a solid having tapered sides. Mechanical

Desktop refers to the angle of the tapered sides as *draft angle*; a term that comes from the molding and casting industries.

Extruded features are made with Mechanical Desktop's AMEXTRUDE command, which uses a dialog box for you to enter the extrusion parameters. The options in this dialog box are described in the following text.

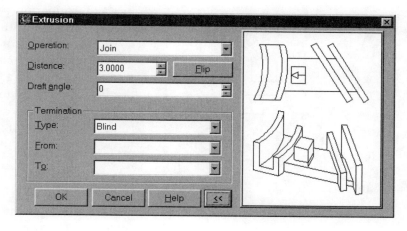

Operation This option will be disabled when you are creating a base 3D feature, because only the Base operation type is applicable. When you are creating a dependent 3D feature; the Cut, Join, Intersect, and Split operation types are offered.

Termination The available termination types are: Blind, Through, MidPlane, Mid-Through, Face, Extended Face, Plane, Next, and From-To. For profiles having multiple loops, only Blind, Through, MidPlane, and Mid-Through termination are offered. If you select a termination type

Blind extrusion direction

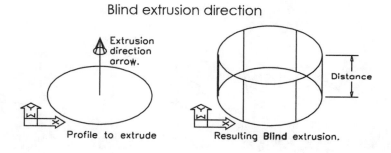

that uses a face (other than Next) or plane, Mechanical Desktop will ask you to specify the terminating object, or objects, after you exit the **Extrusion** dialog box. If you select a termination type that is direction specific, such as Blind, Mechanical Desktop will display an arrow on the profile that points toward the extrusion direction. Click the Flip button in the dialog box to reverse the direction.

The Distance edit box shortcut menus.

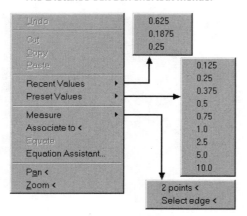

Distance   This edit box is enabled when Blind and MidPlane have been selected as the Termination type, so that you can enter the extrusion distance, or length. The length of the extrusion direction arrow that extends from the profile automatically adjusts according the value entered to visually indicate the extrusion distance. To better discern the direction and length of the arrow, you should work in an isometric-type viewpoint as you create an extrusion.

When you right-click within the Distance edit box, a menu for accessing recent and preset distance values appears. If you select the Associate to option, you will be prompted to select an existing edge or dimension, and that dimension or the dimension of the edge is used as the extrusion distance. Thus, if you selected a dimension having the name d47, the value entered in the Distance edit box will be d47, and the value of d47 will be used as the extrusion distance.

The effects of Draft angle

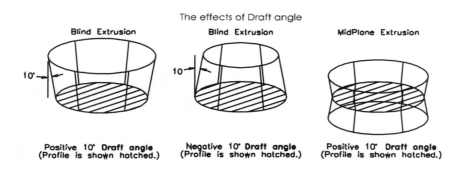

Draft Angle
The sides of the extrusion will taper according to the angle within the Draft Angle edit box. When a positive draft angle is specified, the cross-section area of the profile increases as it is extruded, and when a negative draft angle is specified, the extrusion's cross-section become smaller as it is extruded. The taper begins at the profile, even when the MidPlane termination is in effect. If the specified draft angle is so large that the sides of the 3D solid will intersect, Mechanical Desktop will issue an error message stating that the draft angle would result in a self intersecting body, and no feature will be created.

Thin Features When the profile is open, a cluster of buttons and edit boxes is added to **Extrusion** dialog box for setting the parameters of an extruded thin feature. Specify the thickness of the extrusion by entering a value in the Thickness edit box. This thickness can represent a equal distance on each side of the profile, or it can all be on one side of the profile; and you can flip the thickness from one side to the other. You can also enter two distances; one for one

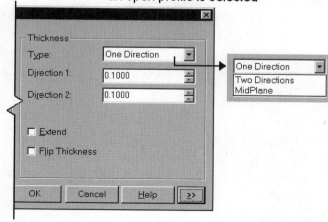

side of the profile, and one for the other. As you select these options and enter a thickness value, Mechanical Desktop displays the results on the profile.

The open profile automatically lengthens on each end to meet existing faces when you select the Extend option in

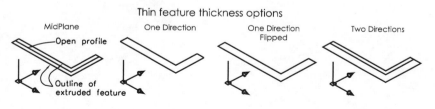

this dialog box. Therefore, for some open profiles for dependent features you do not need to draw them to their full length or constrain their endpoints.

The extrusion distance, draft angle, and thickness values are dimensions, the same as those created by AMPARDIM. Therefore, they have names, or tags, and you can use other dimensions, as well as equations and design variables

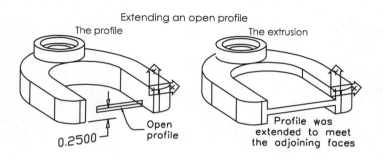

when setting their values. An example of the selected extrusion parameters is displayed in the dialog box's image tile. When you are satisfied with the parameters, click the OK button of the dialog box . Mechanical Desktop will prompt from the command line for termination planes or faces if necessary, and create the extruded feature.

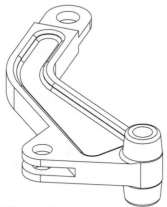

Figure 1-1

Exercise 1

Creating Extruded 3D Features

In this exercise, you will create the sketched features, which will all be extrusions, of the part shown in Figure 1-1. You created and fully constrained the profile for the base feature of this part in Exercise 2 of Chapter 5. Since this part is symmetrical across a plane, you will construct just the sketched features on one side of the part in this exercise. You will finish the part in Exercise 3 of Chapter 12 by making a mirror image copy of the part and combining the copy with the original.

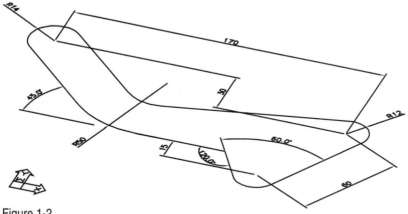

Figure 1-2

Open your file that contains the profile you created and fully constrained in Exercise 2 of Chapter 5, or else retrieve file md05e204.dwg from the CD-ROM that is supplied with this book, and open it. Use any method to set a viewpoint of the profile similar to the one in Figure 1-2. (This figure uses the VPOINT command's rotation coordinates of 290 degrees from the X axis and 35 degrees from the XY plane.)

Create a layer for the solid object you are about to make, and make it the current layer. Then start the AMEXTRUDE command. In the **Extrusion** dialog box, set Termination to Blind, enter 8 as the extrusion Distance, and enter 0 as the Draft angle. (Operation will be grayed out because no other 3D

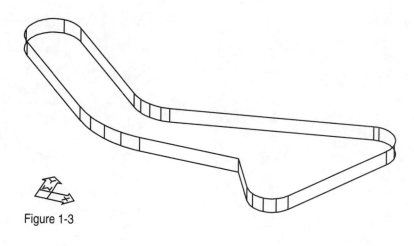

Figure 1-3

features exist.) Verify that the extrusion direction arrow points in the positive Z direction, and click the OK button of the dialog box. The profile and its dimensions will disappear and Mechanical Desktop will create the extrusion feature, as shown in Figure 1-3.

Switch to a plan view of the part. Then draw the single horizontal line shown in Figure 1-4, and turn it into a profile feature with AMPROFILE. Use the edges of the base feature to close the profile. Add a horizontal constraint if Mechanical Desktop hasn't already added it, and use AMPARDIM to set the distance of the line from the center of the arc-shaped feature edge to be 12 mm. This dimension and the horizontal constraint on the line will fully constrain the profile.

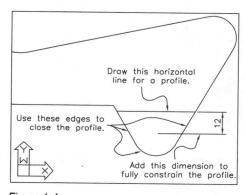

Figure 1-4

Change the viewpoint to that of an isometric-type view, and invoke AMEXTRUDE. Set Operation to Cut and Termination to Blind, enter 3 as the extrusion Distance, and enter 0 as the Draft angle. Make certain that the extrusion direction arrow points in the positive Z direction, and click the OK button of the Extrusion dialog box to create the extruded feature. Your part should look similar to the one shown in Figure 1-5.

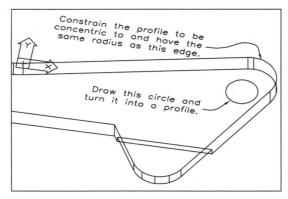

Figure 1-5

Move the sketch plane to the upper surface of the part. Then draw a circle somewhere on the new sketch plane. The circle's location and size is not critical. Turn the circle into a profile and constrain it to be concentric to, and have the same radius as, the right-hand arc-shaped edge on the part, as shown in Figure 1-5.

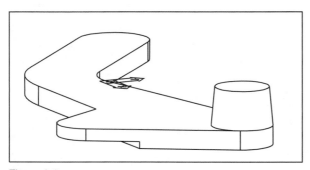

Figure 1-6

Start AMEXTRUDE to bring up the **Extrusion** dialog box. and select the circular profile. Set Operation to Join and termination to Blind. Make certain that the extrusion direction arrow points away from the part; enter 16 as the extrusion Distance, enter −5 as the draft angle, and click the OK button of the dialog box to create the extrusion. In a hidden line view, your part should now be similar to the one shown in Figure 1-6.

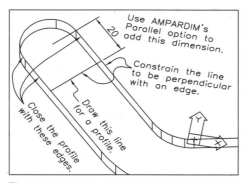

Figure 1-7

Leaving the sketch plane where it is, pan to the other end of the part and draw a line across it as shown in Figure 1-7. Turn the line into a profile; using the edges of the part to close the profile. Constrain the line to be perpendicular to either of the straight edges that are adjacent to it, and then add the 20 mm dimension to fully constrain the profile. Use the parallel option of AMPARDIM when you add the dimension. (Otherwise you will end up with an aligned dimension from the center of the arc to one end of the line.)

Invoke AMEXTRUDE. In the `Extrusion` dialog box, set Operation to Cut, Termination to Blind, Distance to 5, and Draft angle to 0. Make certain that the extrusion direction arrow points into the part, and click the dialog box's OK button. This extrusion will create a step in the left end of the part, as shown in Figure 1-8.

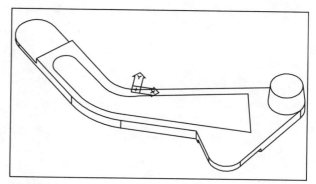

Figure 1-8

Figure 1-8 also shows the profile for the next, and last, extruded feature you will add to this part. Without moving the sketch plane, draw these five lines and three arcs, and turn them into a profile. Fully constrain the profile as shown in Figure 1-9. The top panel of Figure 1-9 identifies the geometric constraints of the profile, while the bottom panel shows the dimensional constraints. Use AMPARDIM's Parallel option in making all of the dimensions.

Initiate the AMEXTRUDE command. In the `Extrusion` dialog box set Operation to Cut, Termination to Blind, Distance to 4, and Draft angle to −5. Verify that the extrusion direction arrow points into the part, and click the OK button of the dialog box to create the pocket in the part that is shown in Figure 1-10.

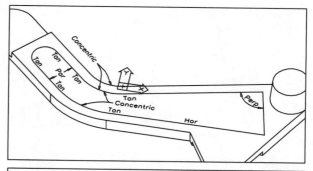

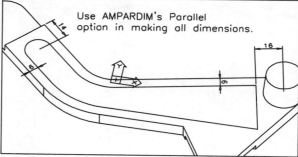

Figure 1-9

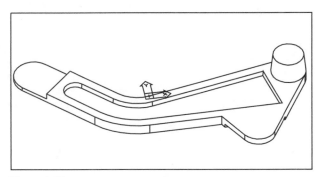

Figure 1-10

That finishes this exercise. You should save the file that contains your part model so that you can complete the part in an exercise in Chapter 12. On the CD-ROM that accompanies this book, the model at this stage is in file md08e110.dwg.

Creating Revolved Features

Revolved features are made by rotating a profile (created with the AMPROFILE command) about an axis. They are slightly more complicated to make than extruded features, since an axis must be specified in addition to the profile.

AMREVOLVE creates a solid feature by rotating a profile about an axis.

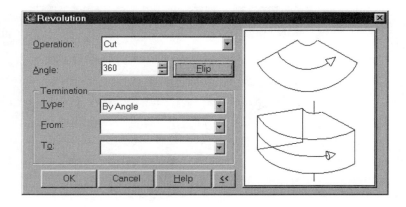

Revolved features are made through the AMREVOLVE command. This command first prompts you to select an axis of revolution, and then displays the **Revolution** dialog box for you to use in setting the revolution parameters. An image tile, which changes according to the parameters selected, shows you a preview of the operation. The options of the **Revolution** dialog box are as follows.

Operation   When making a base feature this list box is disabled, because only a Base operation is allowed. When you are creating a dependent feature, this option will offer Cut, Join, Intersect, and Split operation types.

Termination   By Angle, MidPlane, Next, Plane, Face, Extended face and From-To termination types are offered. The From and To list boxes are activated when you select From-To as the termination type. For profiles having multiple loops, only By Angle and Midplane terminations are available. If you select the By Angle or To Face/Plane types, Mechanical Desktop will display a direction arrow on the profile that points in the rotation direction. You can reverse this direction by clicking the Flip button of the dialog box.

Angle   Enter the angle through which the profile is to be revolved in this edit box. It will be grayed out for terminations using faces and planes. An angle up to 360 degrees may be entered for By Angle terminations, but the angle for MidPlane terminations must be less than 360 degrees. Since the angle of rotation is a dimension, you can use the names of other dimensions, design variables, and equations in assigning it a value. Shortcut menus for establishing angle values appear when you right-click within the Angle edit box.

Dependent revolved features can use a straight edge on an existing 3D feature, a work axis, a construction geometry line, or a straight segment on the profile boundary for an axis of revolution. When making a base feature, your only choice for an axis is either a straight segment of the profile boundary or a construction geometry object. The axis must be situated so that the revolved profile will not intersect itself.

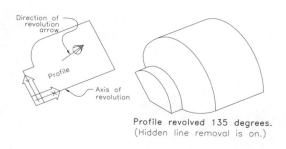

Profile revolved 135 degrees.
(Hidden line removal is on.)

The following figure shows which objects are acceptable for an axis in a profile that has construction geometry, and which objects are not acceptable.

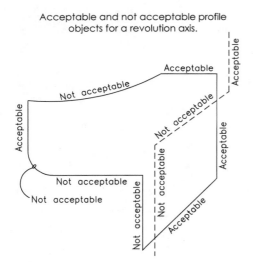

Acceptable and not acceptable profile objects for a revolution axis.

Click the OK button in the Revolution dialog box after you have set the revolution parameters. Mechanical Desktop will issue command line prompts for termination planes if necessary, and create the revolved feature.

Exercise 2

Creating a Revolved 3D Feature

You will construct the model of a pulley in this exercise by revolving a profile. Start a new Mechanical Desktop part file using the default English template (acad.dwt). On the WCS XY plane draw a cross section of the pulley, using the dimensions in Figure 2-1.

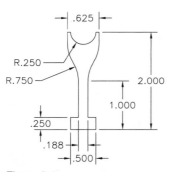

Figure 2-1

This cross section consists of eleven lines and five arcs. Turn it into a profile feature, and fully constrain the profile by adding the dimensions shown in Figure 2-1 and the geometric constraints given in Figure 2-2. If the object numbers in your profile are different than those in Figure 2-2, substitute your object numbers for those in Figure 2-2 when you add the geometric constraints. Constraining this profile may be a challenge, and if you have problems you can use the fully constrained profile in file md08e201.dwg from the CD-ROM that accompanies this book.

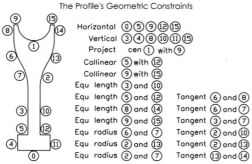

Figure 2-2

Switch to an isometric-type view, and invoke the AMREVOLVE command. When you are prompted for a revolution axis, select the 0.500 long line of the profile. In the Revolution dialog box, Operation type will be grayed out, because no other 3D features exist. Select By Angle as the Termination type, enter 360 as the Angle, and click the OK button. Mechanical Desktop will create the revolved feature without issuing any command line prompts or messages. Your pulley model should look similar to the one in Figure 2-3, when you view it in the Gouraud Shading, Edges On, shading mode.

That completes your work in this exercise. Save you file, because you will add a rib to the pulley in Exercise 5 of this chapter. On the CD-ROM that accompanies this book, the model is in file md08e203.dwg.

Creating Lofted Features

Lofted features have their cross section shape defined by two or more profile sketches. This, as show in the below figure, gives you close control over the shape of the 3D feature—not only does the cross section of the solid in this figure change from rectangular to elliptical to circular, the solid also has a dogleg bend. The four profiles this feature is based on are shown to the left in the figure.

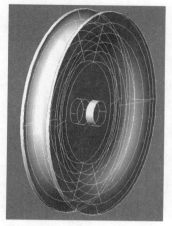

Figure 2-3

Solid lofted 3D features are created with the AMLOFT command. Usually, their cross sections consist of closed profile features made by the AMPROFILE command. Profiles that have multiple loops, however, cannot be used to create lofted features. The first and

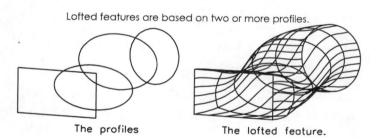

Lofted features are based on two or more profiles.

The profiles   The lofted feature.

the last sections of the lofted feature can be planar 3D feature faces, rather than profile sketches. You can also use a work point as a cross section, as long as it is the first or the last section. Every lofted feature must have at least two cross sections. While there is no maximum number of cross sections, you will want to keep their quantity as low as you can, since numerous sections make complicated features that are hard to manage, require extensive computer computations, and result in large file sizes.

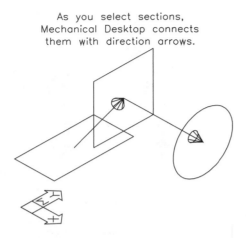

As you select sections, Mechanical Desktop connects them with direction arrows.

When you initiate AMLOFT, command line prompts will direct you to select the cross sections of the lofted feature. Mechanical Desktop will draw a direction arrow from one cross section to another as you select them. You must select the cross sections in order.

When you have selected the last cross section, press the Enter key. AMLOFT will display a dialog box for you to use in setting the parameters for the lofted feature. An image tile in the dialog box gives you a lengthwise cross section example of the loft's parameters. The options in the dialog box are:

Operation   When you are creating a base 3D feature, this option will be disabled. When you are creating a dependent 3D feature, the Cut, Join, Intersect, and Split operation types are available.

Termination   The Sections, To Face/Plane, and From-To termination options are offered in this list box.

Type   The three options in this list box control how the surface of the lofted feature blends between the sections. See the figures that follow for examples.

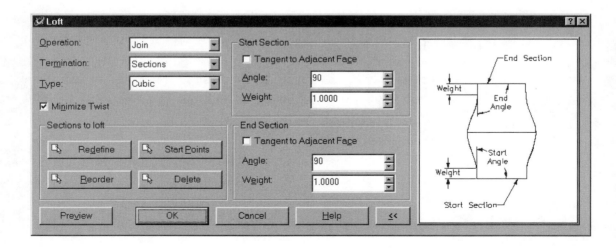

Linear Creates lofted features that have a lengthwise profile between the cross sections that, in most cases, consist of straight lines. Only two cross sections are allowed for linear lofts.

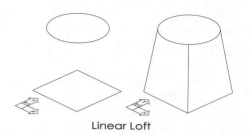

Linear Loft

Cubic Gradually blend the feature's surface between the cross sections. You can have as many cross sections as you like.

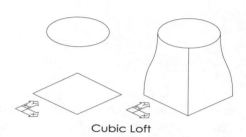

Cubic Loft

Closed Cubic Closes the lofted feature by having the starting cross section serve also as the last cross section. The minimum number of cross sections needed for a closed loft is three.

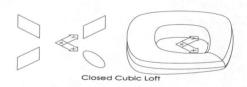

Closed Cubic Loft

Minimize Twist The surface of a lofted feature sometimes tends to twist as it is formed between the cross sections. When this check box is active, Mechanical Desktop uses techniques in creating the lofted feature that minimize twist.

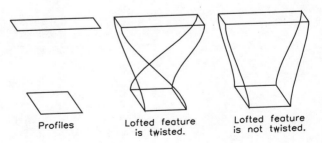

Profiles   Lofted feature is twisted.   Lofted feature is not twisted.

Redefine   When you select this option Mechanical Desktop will temporarily dismiss the dialog box and issue command line prompts for you to reselect the sections of the lofted feature. You must reselect all sections that are profile features. You can, though, omit sections that are work points or 3D feature faces.

Start Points   If you are having problems with twist, you can use this option to help reduce or eliminate it. Mechanical Desktop will temporarily dismiss the dialog box, and will display the current start point of each profile. When you move the screen cursor over a section, other possible start point locations will be displayed and you can select one by picking a point near it. Twist in the lofted feature will be minimized when the start points on the profiles are aligned as closely as possible.

Reorder   This option, which is available only when you are editing an existing lofted feature, switches the order of two cross sections. The lofted feature must have at least three sections. You will be prompted from the command line to select a section, and then to select the section that is come after it.

Delete   You can remove cross sections with this option. It is only available when you are editing an existing lofted feature that has three or more sections. A command line prompt will ask you to select the sections that are to be deleted.

Start/End Section   One of these sets of options is for the first, or start, cross section, and the other is for the last, or end, section. They are available only for Cubic and Closed Cubic lofts.

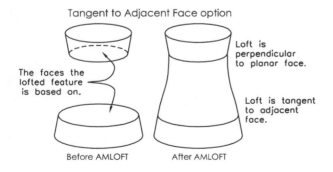

Tangent to Adjacent Face   This check box is activated when the start or the end section is a planar face. When it is selected, the surface of the loft will be tangent to the faces adjacent to the section face.

Angle   This option controls the angle between the surface of the lofted feature and the first and end sections. The default angle is 90 degrees, which is perpendicular to the cross section. You can specify any angle between 0 and 180 degrees, but you should keep it between 45 and 135 degrees.

Weight   This option controls the relative length that the start and end angles are held before the loft's surface begins to blend with the next cross section. Allowable weights range from 1 to 10.

Preview   Select this option to see a preview of the lofted 3D feature.

When you have established the parameters for the lofted feature, click the OK button of the Loft dialog box. If you chose the To-Face or From-To terminations, Mechanical Desktop will prompt you to specify a plane or face after you exit the Loft dialog box.

Exercise 3

Creating a Lofted 3D Feature

You will construct the model of a steel 3 inch by 2 inch eccentric pipe reducer for welded, schedule 40 steel pipe in this exercise. (An eccentric pipe reducer has one flat side—the centerlines of the two ends do not match. Concentric reducers, on the other hand, have ends with matching centerlines.)

Begin a new Mechanical Desktop part file, using the default English template (acad.dwt). Before you draw anything, invoke the AMWORKPNT command. When you are prompted for the work point's location, pick any point on the WCS XY plane. This work point will serve as a connection between the two profiles you will make for the lofted feature.

Draw a circle on the WCS XY plane that is 3.50 inches in diameter and centered near the work point. Turn the circle into a profile with AMPROFILE. Delete the fix constraint of the profile. Mechanical Desktop will report that 3 dimensions and constraints are needed to fully constrain the sketch.

Start the AMPARDIM command, pick the circle as the object to dimension, and assign it a diameter of 3.50 inches. Add a horizontal and a vertical dimension between the circle and the work point; assigning both a dimension value of zero to center the circle on the work point. Notice that you can pick any of the work point's axes as dimension objects. Switch to a right-front isometric viewpoint. The work point, your circle, and the circle's dimensions should look similar to those in Figure 3-1.

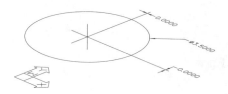

Figure 3-1

Invoke the AMWORKPLN command. A dialog box titled Work Plane Feature will appear. In the cluster of radio buttons labeled 1st Modifier, click the Planar Parallel button; and, in the cluster labeled 2nd Modifier, click the Offset button. Enter a value of 3.00

in the edit box labeled Offset. This offset, which acts like a dimension, will control the distance between the two profiles, and therefore, the length of the eccentric reducer. Be certain that the Create Sketch Plane toggle is active, and then click the dialog box's OK button.

The dialog box will close, and Mechanical Desktop will issue the following command line prompts for placing the work plane and the sketch plane:

```
worldXy/worldYz/worldZx/Ucs/<Select work plane or planar face>: X (Enter)
(A rectangle, which has arrows pointing in the Z direction at each corner, will appear on
    the screen to indicate the offset direction from the WCS XY plane.)
Enter an option [Flip/Accept]<Accept>: (Enter)
(Another rectangle will appear; this one will have arrows pointing in the X, Y, and Z
    directions.)
Select edge to align X axis or [Z-flip /Rotate/Origin] <Accept>: (Enter)
```

The first prompt was for the plane that the work plane was to be parallel to—you chose the WCS XY plane. The second prompt was for the offset direction from the reference plane—you chose the positive Z direction. Then a prompt was issued to establish the orientation of the sketch plane. You accepted the default.

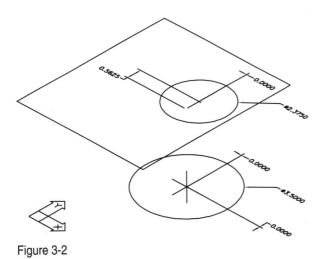

Figure 3-2

Draw a circle (It does not have to be within the rectangle representing the work plane.), turn it into a profile sketch, remove its fit constraint, and give it a diameter dimension of 2.375. Tie the circle to the work point with a horizontal dimension of zero, and vertical dimension of 0.5625. (This value represents the radius of the large circle minus the radius of the small circle.) The fact that the profile and the work point are in different planes does not affect these dimensions. One quadrant of the small circle will now be tangent (but in a different plane) to one quadrant of the large circle. Your two fully constrained profiles should look similar to those in Figure 3-2.

Initiate the AMLOFT command. Mechanical Desktop will issue command line prompts for the loft feature's profiles:

```
Select profiles or planar faces to loft: (Pick the edge of either profile.)
Select profiles or planar faces to loft: (Pick the edge of the other profile.)
(An arrow will extend from the center of the first profile to the center of the second
    profile.)
Select profiles or planar faces to loft or [Redefine sections]: (Enter)
```

The **Loft** dialog box will appear. Set its parameters as follows.

Termination	Sections
Type	Cubic
Minimize Twist	On
Start Section	
Angle	90
Weight	2
End Section	
Angle	90
Weight	2

Select the OK button to create the 3D feature and end the AMLOFT command.

Wireframe views will not adequately show the side surface of the 3D solid with the default settings. For more definitive wire frame views, increase the value of AutoCAD's **isolines** system variable to eight or more. A screen regeneration is needed for the new settings to have an effect. In wireframe form, your base feature should then look similar to the one in Figure 3-3 when seen from the view direction coordinates of 1,0,1.

You now need to hollow-out the pipe fitting model. Although you could use AMSHELL, which we will discuss in Chapter 11, to hollow-out the base feature, we want the wall

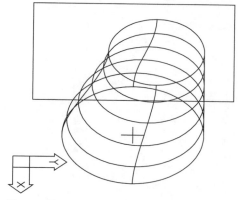

Figure 3-3

thickness of the fitting to vary so that it is the correct thickness for 3 inch pipe at the large end and for 2 inch pipe at the small end. Therefore, you will create a circular profile sketch at each end, make them concentric with the base part ends, and use AMLOFT as a cut operation to hollow-out the part.

Place the sketch plane on the large circular end of the feature. The orientation of its X axis is not important. Then, draw a circle, turn it into a profile, constrain it to be concentric with the large circular end of the base feature, and dimension its diameter to be 3.068. (This is the standard inside diameter of 3 inch steel pipe.) Move the sketch plane to the small circular end of the base feature, draw a circle, turn it into a profile, constrain it to be concentric with the small circular end of the base feature, and give it a diameter dimension of 2.067. (Which is the inside diameter of standard 2 inch steel pipe) Your two profile sketches should look similar to those in Figure 3-4.

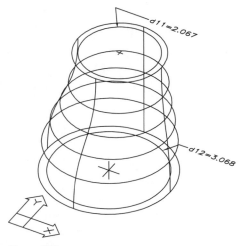

Figure 3-4

Start AMLOFT, and select the two circular profiles as objects to loft. It makes no difference which circle you select first, since their angle and weight settings will the same. Set the following parameters in the **Loft** dialog box:

Operation:	Cut
Termination:	Sections
Type:	Cubic
Minimize Twist:	On
Start Section Angle:	90
Start Section Weight:	2.0
End Section Angle:	90
End Section Weight:	2.0

Click the OK button of the dialog box to end the command and create the loft feature. Your model should now look similar to the one in the Figure 3-5. On the accompanying CD-ROM, the model at this stage is in file md08e305.dwg. That finishes this exercise. In Chapter 11, you will chamfer the ends of the fittings, as is typically done with pipe fittings that are to be welded to pipe or to other fittings.

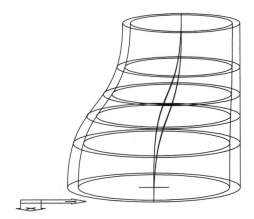

Figure 3-5

Creating Bend Features

Bend features were introduced in Mechanical Desktop Release 5. Unlike the other sketched features, they modify, rather than create, 3D features. They are, nevertheless, classified as a sketched feature, because each bend requires a profile that has been created by AMPROFILE. This profile must be open, and it must consist of a single straight line. The profile does not have to extend completely across the feature it is to bend, because Mechanical Desktop extends the bend line in both directions to the nearest edge. If there is a break in the feature to be bent, you can create two profiles and make two bends that have different bend parameters.

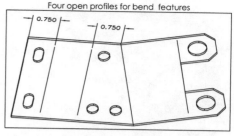

Four open profiles for bend features

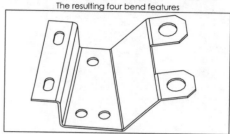

The resulting four bend features

Bend features are created by the AMBEND command. This command first asks you to select one open profile to serve as the bend line, and then displays the **Bend** dialog box. In this dialog box you select one of three combinations for specifying the bend's size parameters: (1) angle and radius; (2) radius and arc length; or (3) arc length and angle. In most cases you will choose the angle and radius combination. Edit boxes appropriate for your selected combinations will be activated for you to enter their values.

Two open profiles for bend features

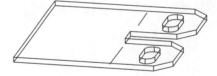

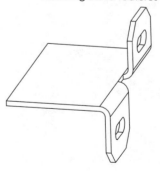

Resulting bend features

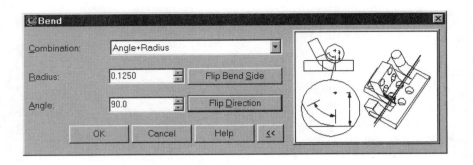

As you select and enter parameters in the **Bend** dialog box, Mechanical Desktop displays the results on the part. The section of the part that will be bent is highlighted with a blue outline. This bend side is further identified by a straight arrow anchored on the open profile and pointing toward the bend side. The direction of the bend is indicated by a curved arrow. You can independently flip these directions from the dialog box.

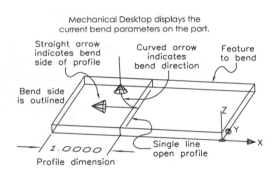

The plane of the bend profile can be on the top surface of the part to be bent, on the bottom surface, or within the part. You will need to set the bend radius to match the part's thickness and the plane of the profile relative to the part. The inside bend radius for 90 degree bends must be equal or larger than the maximum thickness of the part's cross section.

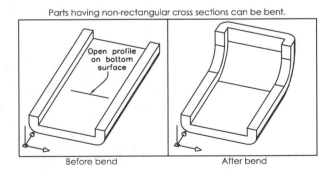

For example, if you intend to bend a part with a rectangular cross section that is 6 mm thick and the profile is on the bottom surface of the part, you must specify a bend radius of at least 6 mm for 90 degree bends down, and at least 12 mm for 90 degree bends up. Bends always start at the open profile—the profile becomes one of the bend's two tangent lines. The parts you bend can have any cross section shape, provided the bend radius accommodates the cross section thickness.

To precisely position flanges and holes on bend features, you must adjust the location of the profile to account for the curved length through the bend. You can make this adjustment by adding a factor to the dimension of the profile on the bend side of the parent feature. For 90 degree bends this factor, which is derived from the arc length of the bend, is 0.5707963 multiplied by the bend radius.

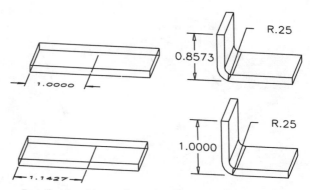

To adjust for distance through the bend arc add a factor to the dimension that positions the profile. For 90 degree bends this factor is 0.5707963 times the bend radius.

Exercise 4

Creating a Sheet Metal Part

Retrieve file md08e401.dwg from the CD-ROM that accompanies this book and open it. This file, which is based on Mechanical Desktop's acad.dwt template file for English sizes, contains the part model shown in Figure 4-1. You will make three bends in this part—the two rounded tabs will be bent down and the area of the part that has slanted edges will be bent up.

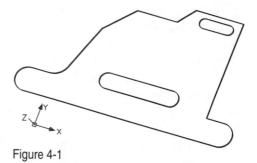

Figure 4-1

Before you make those bends, though, invoke the AMVARS command to display the **Design Variables** dialog box. You will notice in this dialog box that four active part design variables have been defined: Thk, Ri, Ro, and Delta. Thk, which represents the material thickness of the part, was used as the height of the base extrusion and as the basis for the bend radii. You will use Ri as the radius for bends down and Ro for bends up. Delta is a length adjustment factor that was added to certain dimensions of the base feature's profile to compensate for the curved length through the bends. (Note: You may want to read the Editing Sketched Features section in Chapter 9 now to find out how you can view the profiles, along with their constraints and dimensions, of the existing features of this part.) When you have looked over the design variables, press the Cancel button to leave the **Design Variables** dialog box without making any changes.

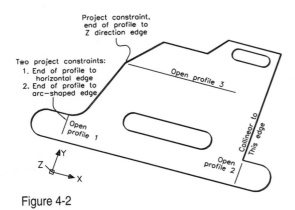

Figure 4-2

Verify that the sketch plane is on the bottom surface of the base feature. Then, draw three lines as shown in Figure 4-2 and transform each one of them into an open profile with AMPROFILE. The length of these profiles is not important, other than that they should fit within the part's edges. Constrain each of the open profiles as described in Figure 4-2.

Your first bend will use profile labeled open profile 1 in Figure 4-2 as the bend line. You should zoom in close to this area of the model so that you will be able to see the bend direction arrows Mechanical Desktop will display as you establish the bend parameters. Initiate the AMBEND command and select open profile 1 as the bend axis. In the **Bend** dialog box, select Angle+Radius from the Combination list box, enter Ri as the radius, and enter 90 as the angle. Use the Flip Bend Side button if necessary to highlight the rounded tab on the part, and the Flip Direction button to bend the tab down (in the minus Z axis direction). Then click the OK button of the dialog box to create the bend feature.

Follow these same steps using open profile 2 to bend the right-hand tab down.

Your third, and final, bend will use open profile 3. Zoom in close to that area of the model, invoke AMBEND, and select open profile 3 as the bend axis. In the Bend dialog box, set Combination to Angle+Radius, Radius to Ro (not Ri), and Angle to 90. If necessary click the Flip Bend Side button to highlight the area of the base feature containing the small slot and the slanted edges, and click the Flip Direction button until the curved bend direction arrow points in the Z axis direction. Click the OK button to dismiss the dialog box and create the bend feature.

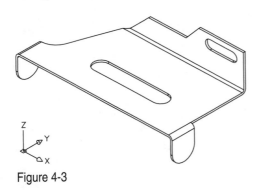

Figure 4-3

That completes this exercise. Your model should now look similar to the one shown in Figure 4-3. We will not do any subsequent work on this part, so you do not need to retain it. On the CD-ROM included with this book, the model is in file md08e403.dwg.

Creating Rib Features

Rib features are new in Mechanical Desktop Release 5. The characteristics of rib features are as follows.

- Rib features can only be used as dependent features.

- They only work with open profiles, and the length of the profile automatically extends in both directions to an adjacent face. The profile can contain multiple open objects— lines, arcs, and so forth.

- You specify the thickness of the rib in a dialog box.

- The rib is formed by pushing the profile along the plane of the sketch plane, rather than perpendicular to the sketch plane.

- The rib feature terminates when it meets a face or faces of an existing 3D feature.

- Rib features are created with the AMRIB command.

Although you can use AMEXTRUDE to create the geometry of a rib feature, AMRIB is much easier to use. Often you will make polar or rectangular patterns of a rib feature. (Pattern features are described in Chapter 12.) A limitation of rib features is that you cannot give them a draft angle.

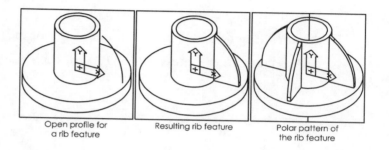

Open profile for   Resulting rib feature   Polar pattern of
a rib feature   the rib feature

Your first step in creating a rib feature will be to draw its profile. The profile must be open, but it can contain multiple objects. You do not have to draw the entire length of profile, because Mechanical Desktop will extend it to meet adjacent faces when it creates the rib. Also, you will add just enough constraints and dimensions to fix its position on an existing feature and to fix important points within the profile.

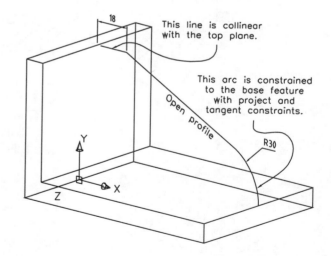

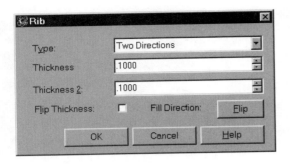

Once you have created a profile for your rib feature, invoke the AMRIB command. The **Rib** dialog box will appear for you to use in specifying the thickness of the rib's profile and the direction it is to be extruded. There are three options for specifying the thickness type.

1. The thickness can be entirely on one side of the of the profile. Use the dialog box's Flip Thickness button to choose the offset side.

2. The thickness can be offset evenly on both sides of the profile.

3. You can specify two thickness values; one for each side of the profile.

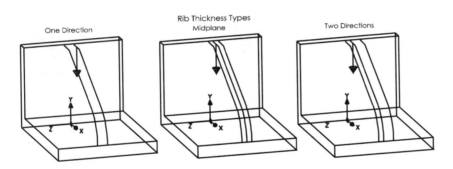

Mechanical Desktop displays the profile using the specified thickness type and values, and points an arrow in the direction of the extrusion.

Click the Fill Direction button to point the arrow in the direction. Click the OK button when you have established the rib parameters for Mechanical Desktop to create the rib feature.

Exercise 5

Creating a Rib Feature

You will add a rib to each side of the pulley you created in Exercise 2 of this chapter. Open your file of this model, or else retrieve and open file md08e203.dwg from the CD-ROM that is supplied with this book. Verify that the sketch plane passes through the center-line of the pulley.

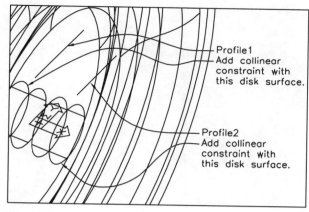

Figure 5-1

Draw two short lines as shown in Figure 5-1. These lines are on opposite sides of the pulley. Use AMPROFILE twice to turn each one of them into an open profile. Then, one at a time, add a collinear constraint between the profile and the disk-like surface of the pulley's hub. A collinear constraint works even though the edge of the surface is not linear. This and a vertical constraint are the only constraints necessary for these profiles, and you will not add any dimensions to them.

Invoke the AMRIB command and select either of the open profiles. In the **Rib** dialog box, choose Midplane as the Thickness type and enter 0.10 as the Thickness value. As shown in Figure 5-2, Mechanical Desktop will draw a rectangle around the profile to indicate the thickness of the rib and point an arrow in the direction the rib will extend. If this arrow points away from the pulley, click the Flip Direction button in the dialog box. Then select the OK button to dismiss the dialog box and create the rib feature.

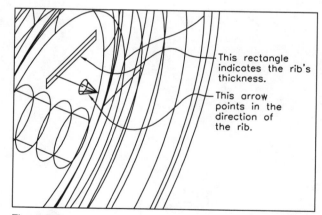

Figure 5-2

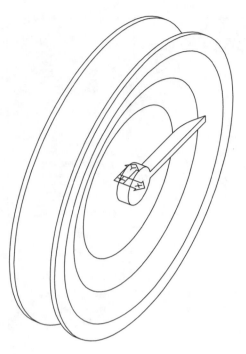

Figure 5-3

Repeat the procedure listed in the previous paragraph to create a rib feature on the other side of the pulley. Your model should now look similar to the one shown in Figure 5-3 when hidden line removal is activated. You should save your file of this part. because you will add some features to it during an exercise in Chapter 12. On the CD-ROM that accompanies this book the model at this stage is in file md08503.dwg.

CHAPTER 9

Working with Sketched Features

You will acquire some tools for working with sketched 3D features in this chapter. These tools will not only help you modify existing 3D sketched features, they will help you create new ones.

This chapter covers the following topics.

- *Describes the commands and procedures for modifying 3D features.*

- *Explains how you can turn the edges of 3D features into planar wireframe objects that can be used for creating sketches.*

- *Shows you how to make a copy of a sketch, even if it is a profile sketch that has been transformed into a 3D feature.*

Editing Sketched Features

Change and parametrics go hand in hand. Change allows you to perfect the design of a part, as well as to adapt the design to meet other conditions and serve other purposes; while parametrics—that interrelationship between dimensions and geometry—allows you to easily make changes. You do not edit 3D features by directly modifying geometry, as you do with objects in 2D drawings. Instead of making changes by stretching or trimming objects, you edit the geometry of 3D features by changing their dimensions. You do this through the AMEDITFEAT command, which displays the following command line prompt.

```
Enter an option [Sketch/surfCut/Toolbody/select Feature] <select Feature>: (Pick a point on
    a feature or enter an option.)
```

We will describe the option for surfcut features in Chapter 11, and the option for tool-bodies in Chapter 12. For editing 3D features, you will either select a 3D feature or choose the Sketch option. This chapter will focus on the use of AMEDITFEAT to modify sketched features, but the command also works on the features that are discussed in Chapters 11 and 12. Editing operations for those features are explained as the feature is discussed.

Editing Operations for a 3D Feature

Selecting a 3D feature for editing by AMEDITFEAT is done by picking a point on one of its edges or on one of its surface faces. All dimensions related to the feature will be displayed; those for the profile and those for the 3D parameters of the feature—such as extrusion distance and draft angle—along with the dialog box that was used in creating the feature. Through the dialog box, you can change such parameters as Termination, Angle of revolution, and the end section Type and Weight values (for lofted features). You can, for example, change the termination of an extruded feature from Blind to MidPlane. After you change any dialog box parameters you want, dismiss the dialog by selecting its OK button. Mechanical Desktop will then prompt you to change any of the dimensions that are displayed on the 3D feature itself. Press Enter to end the editing operation.

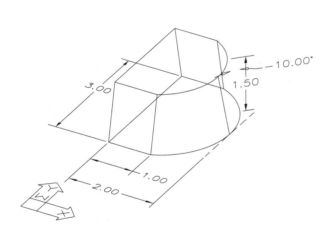

The following figure shows the dimensions that would be displayed on a typical extruded 3D feature. The 1.50 dimension is for the extrusion distance, and the –10 degree dimension is for the extrusion draft angle. Both of these dimensions were added to the feature by Mechanical Desktop from the data entered in the **Extrusion** dialog box. The other dimensions were supplied by the user in constraining the profile. For sweep features, the path sketch and its dimensions will also be displayed.

As the dimensions are displayed, AMEDITFEAT issues a command line prompt for you to select an object. This prompt intends that you select a displayed dimension of the feature, by picking a point anywhere on it. When you select a dimension, Mechanical Desktop will display the dimension's current value on the command line, and prompt for a new value. Note that you do not use the AMMODDIM command to change the dimension values.

Editing Operations on a Profile

When you choose the Sketch option of the AMEDITFEAT command, you will be asked to select a 3D feature. The 3D feature you select will disappear, and just its underlying profile sketch, or profiles for lofted features, will be displayed. Any construction geometry the profile has will also be displayed, and if the 3D feature is a sweep feature, its path sketch will be shown in addition to its profile sketch. 3D features, sketched or placed, created after

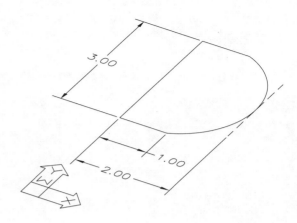

the selected feature will also temporarily disappear. When the Sketch option is used with the 3D feature shown in the previous figure, you would see only the objects and dimensions shown in the accompanying figure.

In effect, the 3D feature is rolled-back to its pre-3D state. You can add to and edit the dimensions and geometric constraints of the roll-back profile just as you would with any profile. AMEDITFEAT's Sketch option is especially useful for adding dimensions and constraints to a sketch that was not fully constrained when the 3D feature was created. In this state, you will use AMPARDIM to add dimensions, and AMMODDIM to modify dimension. You can even delete sketch objects, and replace them with new ones through the Append option of the AMRSOLVESK command.

Updating Edited Features

When you have completed your editing operations on a 3D feature, regardless of which AMEDITFEAT option you used, you must update the feature before the changes take effect. This is done with the AMUPDATE command, which has options that vary according to the current Mechanical Desktop operating mode. You will accept the default Active Part option to initiate feature changes in model mode. Generally, you will invoke AMUPDATE through one of the several buttons that have an icon of a lighting bolt, rather than from the command line. You are not allowed to perform any operations on an edited feature that has not been updated.

Using the Desktop Browser

Every time you create a feature, a corresponding entry is added to the Mechanical Desktop Browser. 3D features show up with names related to the technique used in creating the feature, while the feature's underlying profile, or profiles, is shown as a component of the feature. Typically, 3D features have names such as Sweep1, RevolutionAngle1, or ExtrusionBlind1, while Profiles have names such as Path1, OpenProfile1 or Profile3.

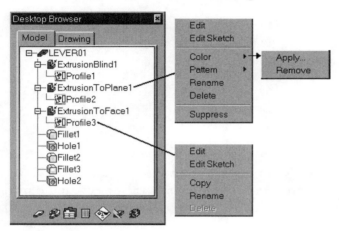

Browser shortcut menus for editing features

When you right-click one of these names in the browser, a menu appropriate for the feature will be displayed. For sketched features and their profiles, the menu includes items for changing the Browser's name of the feature, for deleting the feature, and for editing it. Selecting the Edit option in these menus is a shortcut for implementing the select Feature option of AMEDITFEAT, and selecting the Edit Sketch option is a shortcut for implementing the command's Sketch option. An even more direct shortcut is to double-click the name of a feature in the Browser. This initiates the select Feature option of the AMEDITFEAT command, and when you dismiss the dialog box and press Enter in response to the command's prompt to select an object, the feature will automatically be updated.

The feature shortcut menu's Color option enables you to assign a unique color to the feature. The operation initiated by the menu's Pattern option is discussed in Chapter 12, and that of the Suppress option is discussed in Chapter 13.

The browser menu for lofted features contains an extra option named Edit All Sketches. If you select that option, the lofted solid will disappear, leaving just the profiles, which can be edited individually. Moreover, the browser menu for each profile in a lofted feature also has an Edit Sketch option, and when it is selected, the lofted 3D solid feature disappears along with the other profile sketches. You can then edit just the displayed profile. The Edit option in this menu invokes the AMEDITFEAT command, and you will be prompted to select an object.

In the Browser, the name of a feature that has been edited but not yet updated will have a yellow background. If you made any changes to a feature that would not have been allowed when the feature was being constructed, such as an extrusion draft angle that creates a self intersecting body, the background of the feature's name in the Browser will turn red when the part is updated, and a command line message will instruct you to use AutoCAD's UNDO command until you return to a stable model.

Browser shortcut menus for editing lofted features

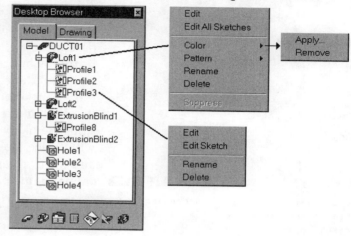

Exercise 1

Editing an Extruded Feature

This exercise will give you hands-on experience in editing operations on a 3D feature. Start a new Mechanical Desktop part file using the default English template drawing (acad.dwt). The set-up of this drawing is not important since it is not one that you will need to retain.

On the XY plane of the WCS, draw the three lines and one arc shown in Figure 1-1. Use AMPROFILE to turn the objects into a profile. The only geometric constraints the sketch is to have are for the long line to be con-

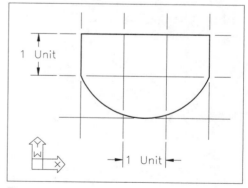

Figure 1-1

strained horizontally and for the two short lines to be constrained vertically. If the arc has tangent constraints with its adjoining lines, remove them. Also, do not add any dimensions to the sketch. Switch to a front-right isometric view point and, turn the sketch into a 3D feature with the AMEXTRUDE command, using a Blind termination, an extrusion Distance of 1.5 units, and a –10 degree Draft angle.

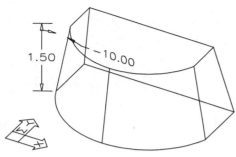

Figure 1-2

Invoke the Select Feature option of AMEDIT-FEAT, from either the command line or the feature's Desktop Browser menu. The **Extrusion** dialog box will reappear, with its parameters just as you set them in creating the feature. Change the Draft angle value from −10 to 0, and then click the OK button of the dialog box. Your 3D feature should look similar to the one shown in Figure 1-2, although your dimensions are likely to be in a different location. You will notice that the part has not been updated, and the draft angle has not changed.

Respond as follows to AMEDITFEAT's command line prompts:

```
Select object: (Pick the dimension for the extrusion's distance.)
Enter dimension value <1.5>: 1 (Enter)
Select object: (Enter)
```

You could have changed both the extrusion length and the draft angle from the dialog box, but for this exercise we elected to make one change from the dialog box and one from the command line to give you experience in both methods. The dimensions will disappear when you press Enter in response to the prompt to select an object, and your 3D feature will appear as it did before AMEDITFEAT. Invoke AMUPDATE and press Enter, and the changes will take effect. The 3D feature will now be shorter, and its sides will no longer taper.

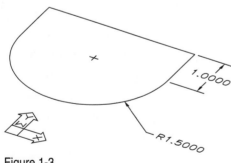

Figure 1-3

Initiate AMEDITFEAT again and choose the Sketch option, or right-click the name of the sketch in the Desktop Browser and select Edit Sketch from the shortcut menu.

The 3D feature will disappear, leaving just its profile sketch. Use the AMADDCON command to add tangent constraints between each vertical line and the arc. Then start AMPAR-DIM, and fully constrain the sketch with the two dimensions shown in Figure 1-3.

Invoke AMUPDATE again to put the changes to the sketch in effect. Your model, in wireframe form, should look similar to the one shown in Figure 1-4. That completes the exercise. We will do no further work with this model, so you do not need to save it. You may, though, want to experiment with modifying the feature on your own; perhaps, for example, using the Extrusion dialog box to change its extrusion height and draft angle and changing its termination from Blind to MidPlane.

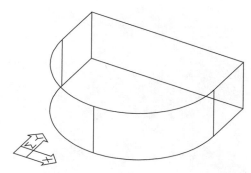

Figure 1-4

Utilizing Edges of Existing 3D Features

You can copy edges of existing 3D features with the AMPARTEDGE command. This is sometimes convenient when you want to base a profile on existing geometry. The copies are ordinary AutoCAD wireframe objects, such as lines and arcs, that you can modify and manipulate in any way you want. On the left in the following figure, a copy was made of the edges of a face on an existing 3D feature. The wireframe objects, which are shown highlighted in the figure, were left in place, turned into a profile, and a cut extrusion was made to remove material, as shown on the right.

AMPARTEDGE uses a command line prompt to offer two options. One is to individually select edges, and the other is to select a face. When you select a face, wireframe object copies will be made from the edges on the face. Even with the face option, though, you must make your selections by picking an edge. One of the two faces adjacent to the selected edge will be highlighted, and you can

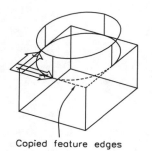

Copied feature edges

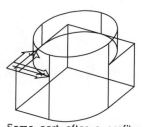

Same part after a profile
made from the copied
edges was extruded and
cut from the base feature.

accept it or switch to the next face. Both options will continue to prompt for selections, until you press Enter. The copies will be in the current layer, and they are coincident with the original edges.

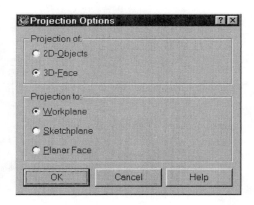

You can project the edges of a face onto a work plane, a sketch plane, or a planar face with the AMPROJECT2PLN command. When you initiate this command, the **Projection Options** dialog box will be displayed for you to use in specifying what type of object is to be projected and what type of object it is to be projected to.

In the cluster of buttons labeled Projection of, select 2D-Objects if the objects you want to project are AutoCAD wireframe objects, such as lines and arcs; select 3D-Face if you want to project the edges of a face on a 3D feature. The face to project does not have to be planar. In the cluster of buttons labeled Projection to, specify whether the objects are to be projected on to a work plane, the sketch plane, or the planar face of a 3D feature. The projected objects will be AutoCAD wireframe objects, such as lines and ellipses.

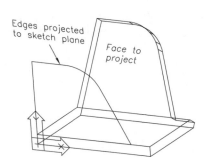

Making Copies of Sketches

You can make a copy of a sketch—regardless of whether it is a profile, path, or cutting line sketch—with the AMCOPYSKETCH command. You can even copy sketches that have been incorporated (consumed) into 3D features. You cannot, however, copy a sketch that has been closed by a 3D feature edge. The original sketch's internal constraints and dimensions, as well as any associated construction geometry objects are included in the copy. Dimensions and constraints that tie the original sketch to other features, however, will not be included in the copy. As shown in the next illustration, the copy will be placed on the current sketch plane, regardless of the location and orientation of the original sketch.

On the command line, AMCOPYSKETCH begins by offering two options.

```
Enter an option [Feature/Sketch]<Sketch>: (Enter an option or press Enter.)
```

Use the Sketch option to copy unconsumed sketches, and use the Feature option to make a copy of a sketch that has been consumed during the creation of a 3D feature. The feature may be a base feature or a sketched dependent feature. You will be prompted to select the feature that contains the sketch you want to copy. You can more directly make a copy of a consumed sketch by right-clicking the sketch's name in the Desktop Browser, and selecting Copy from the shortcut menu. Either way, if the feature was made by the AMSWEEP command, you will be asked if you want to copy the profile sketch or the path sketch.

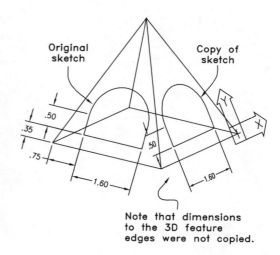

Once you have selected the sketch to be copied, AMCOPYSKETCH will ask you to specify the point at which the center of the copy will be located. As soon as you select a point, the copy will be displayed, and the prompt to pick the sketch center will be repeated. These prompts give you a preview of the sketch's location; they do not make multiple copies of the sketch. When the sketch is located as you want, press Enter to accept the location. The actual location of the copy is not critical, because you will use geometric and dimensional constraints to set and control the position of the sketch.

CHAPTER 10

Sweep Features

The geometry of a sweep feature is defined by moving a profile along a wireframe path. Unlike the extruded, revolved, and lofted 3D features described in Chapter 8, they are based on two different types of features—a profile feature and a path feature. Moreover, any of five different types of features can be used for the path. Because of these variations, this entire chapter is devoted to sweep features.

This chapter covers the following topics.

- Explains how to use the AMSWEEP command to create sweep features regardless of the path type.

- Describes how to sweep a profile along planar paths created from AutoCAD wireframe objects, such as lines, arcs, and 2D polylines, by the AM2DPATH command.

- Shows you how to make helix and spiral shaped features from paths made by the Helix option of AM3DPATH.

- Tells you how to transform AutoCAD spline objects into path features with AM3DPATH's Spline option.

- Explains how to use the Edge option of AM3DPATH to turn existing edges of 3D features into a sweep path.

- Shows how the Pipe option of AM3DPATH creates 3D paths from AutoCAD arcs, lines, and polylines. With these paths you can model piping, ducting, and other objects that typically extend along centerlines.

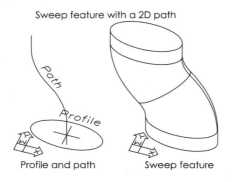

Sweep feature with a 2D path

Profile and path   Sweep feature

Creating Sweep Features

A sweep features is a sketched 3D feature that is made by pushing a profile along a path. The action is similar to extruding a profile, but since sweeping is not restricted to a straight line it is more versatile and can create more complex 3D geometry. In most cases the path is composed of AutoCAD wireframe objects, such as arcs and splines. Often the path is confined to a plane, and it is referred to as a 2D path. They are created by Mechanical Desktop's AM2DPATH command. But path objects can also twist and turn through space to make 3D paths. These are created by the AM3DPATH command.

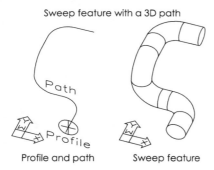

Sweep feature with a 3D path

Profile and path   Sweep feature

The object that is swept along the path is a closed profile feature created by AMPROFILE. Once you have both a path and a profile, you will use AMSWEEP create the 3D feature, whether the path is 2D or 3D. AMSWEEP displays a dialog box titled **Sweep** for you to use in specifying the sweep operation parameters. An image tile illustrates the effects of various combinations of sweep parameters. The options in this dialog box are as follows.

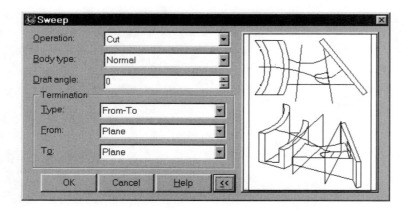

Operation This list box will be disabled when you are creating the base 3D feature, because only the Base operation type is allowed. When you are creating a dependent 3D feature; the Cut, Join, Intersect, and Split operation types are available.

Body Type   The two options in this category control the planar relationship between the profile and the path sketch.

Normal   The profile is always perpendicular (normal) to the path during the sweep operation, as shown on the left in the next figure.

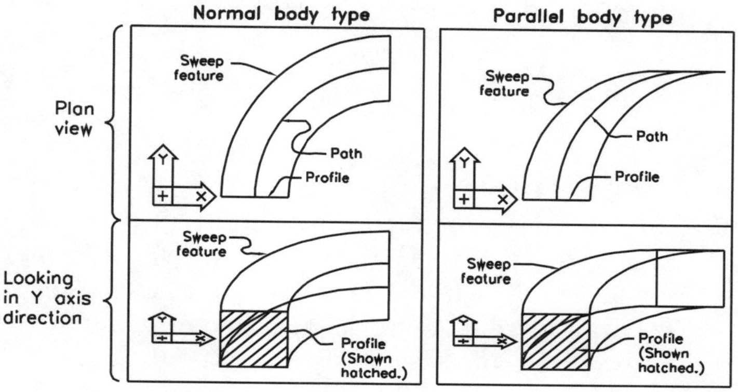

Parallel   The profile remains parallel with its original plane as it is swept along the path. This is shown on the right in the next figure. You cannot use parallel body types when the sweep path is closed.

Termination   The Path-Only, Face, Plane, Next, Extended Face, and From-To termination options are offered. See Chapter 8 for a description of these options. If the profile has an internal loop, Path-Only is the only termination option available.

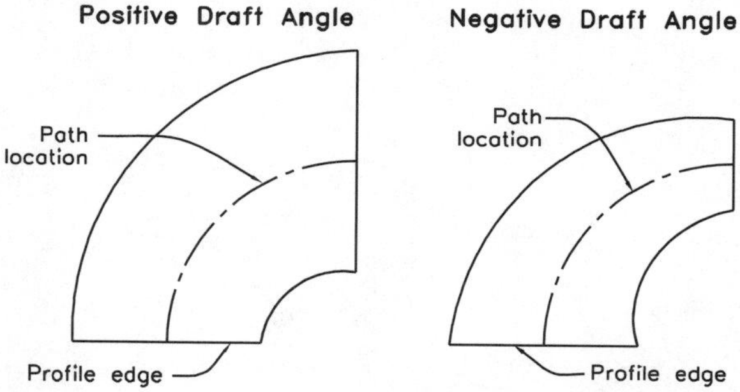

Draft Angle   The profile becomes larger as it is swept along the path when the draft angle is positive, and it becomes smaller when the draft angle is negative. Since draft angle is a dimension, you can enter the name of another dimension, an equation, or a design variable in the Draft Angle edit box. Also, shortcut menus for establishing angle values are displayed when you right-click within the edit box. This edit box will be grayed-out when Body type is set to parallel or the sweep path is closed.

After you have set the sweep feature parameters, click the OK button of the dialog box. Mechanical Desktop will dismiss the dialog box, prompt for termination planes if necessary, and make the sweep feature.

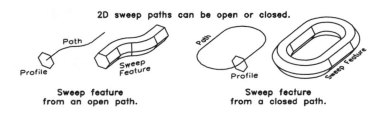

2D sweep paths can be open or closed.

Sweep feature from an open path.

Sweep feature from a closed path.

3D Features from 2D Sweep Paths

Two sketched features are needed to create a 3D feature from a 2D sweep path: a profile feature made by the AMPROFILE command and a path feature made by the AM2DPATH command. Usually you will make the path before you make the profile. Similar to profiles, the sketch for a path must lie on a sketch plane (and therefore be planar). The path can be open or closed. Any AutoCAD wireframe object, with the exception of a 3D polyline, can be used in drawing the path. Objects drawn in a linetype that is different than that of the path objects may be included as construction geometry to help constrain the path.

The rules established by the **amrulemode, amskangto, anskmode, pickbox,** and **amskstyle** system variables are applied when AMPATH transforms the AutoCAD objects into a sweep path feature. AMPATH uses the following command line prompts and input in creating a sweep path:

```
Command: AM2DPATH (Enter)
Select objects: (Use any AutoCAD method to select objects for the path.) (Enter)
Select start point of the path: (Pick a point on one of the path objects.)
Create a profile plane perpendicular to the path? [Yes/No] <Yes>: (Select an option or
    press Enter.)
```

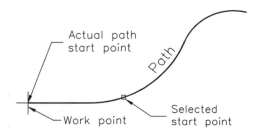

Actual path start point

Work point

Selected start point

On an open path, Mechanical Desktop will place the start point at the path end nearest the point selected as the start point. You do not need to use an object endpoint snap, or even to pick an end object in the path. On closed paths made from lines, arcs, and 2D polylines, the start point will be on the endpoint or vertex point nearest the point you picked. On closed elliptical paths, the start point will be at one end of the ellipse's major axis. Mechanical Desktop always places a work point on the path's start point.

Most of the time you will not accept the default option of the last prompt by AM2DPATH, which is to create a work plane perpendicular to the path. Instead, you will proceed with constraining and dimensioning the path before starting the profile. Geometric constraints and dimensions are applied with the same methods used in constraining a profile. If you do enter a positive response to the last prompt, the results are similar to those of the Normal to Start option of the AMWORKPLN command.

The profile that is to be swept must be located in the same plane as the path's start point. Generally, it will also be perpendicular to the sweep path's plane, but it doesn't have to be. Since dimensions and geometric constraints cannot be applied to objects within different sketches, you cannot directly tie a

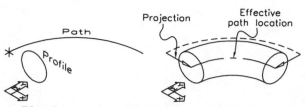

This path becomes smaller as it is projected to the profile.

profile to a sweep path. Nevertheless, their relative positional relationship is important, because the path is projected to the center of the profile in creating the sweep feature. This projection is similar to AutoCAD's OFFSET command, which means that path line lengths and arc radii may change as they are projected. Notice in the illustration above that the radius of the path becomes smaller as it is projected to the profile. To avoid such changes in the path, you should locate the geometric center of the profile precisely at the end of the path.

The easiest and surest way to correctly position the sketch plane for a sweep profile relative to the start point of its path is to first create the path with AM2DPATH. Then, after the path sketch is fully constrained, select the Normal to Start option of the AMWORKPLN command. This option places both a work plane and a sketch plane at the path's start point; each oriented so that it is perpendicular to the path.

Exercise 1

Experimenting with a Sweep Feature

Start a new Mechanical Desktop part file using the default English template (acad.dwt). You will not need to retain the results of this exercise, so its initial set-up is not important. On the WCS XY plane, draw one arc and two lines similar to those shown in Figure 1-1. The axes in this figure are to give you an idea as to the relative size and location of the three objects. Use a HIDDEN linetype for the two lines, so that they will be recognized as construction geometry objects.

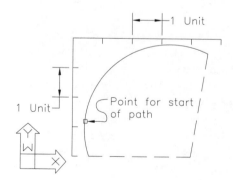

Figure 1-1

Invoke AM2DPATH, select the two lines and one arc, and pick a point near the lower left end of the arc for the path start point. Enter No to the prompt to create a work plane. Make certain that the horizontal construction line has a Horizontal constraint, and that the right-hand line does not have a Vertical constraint. Use AMADDCONS to add a Join constraint between the centerpoint of the arc and the right end of the horizontal line. Two dimensions are now needed to fully constraint the path.

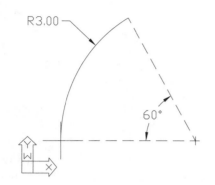

Figure 1-2

Start the AMPARDIM command; pick near the midpoints of the two construction geometry lines and assign a value of 60 degrees to the angle between the lines. Then, pick the arc, and give it a radius value of 3.0 inches. Your fully constrained path should appear similar to the one in Figure 1-2.

Set a front-right isometric view, and then initiate AMWORKPLN. In the **Work Plane Feature** dialog box select Normal to Start as the 1st Modifier, click the check box labeled Create Sketch Plane, and click the OK button. The dialog box will disappear and a work plane as well as a sketch plane will be positioned on the path starting point and will be perpendicular to the plane of the path. Also, an X-Y-Z axes tripod will be displayed on the end of the path, and command line prompts will be issued to establish the orientation of the sketch plane axes. Respond to these prompts as follows:

```
Select edge to align X axis or [Flip/Rotate/Origin] <accept>: R (Enter)
Select edge to align X axis or [Flip/Rotate/Origin] <accept>: R (Enter)
Select edge to align X axis or [Flip/Rotate/Origin] <accept>: (Enter)
```

Each time you use the Rotate option, the X and Y axes of the UCS icon will rotate 90 degrees. After the second rotation, the X axis will point to the right, while the Y axis will point vertically. (Actually, for this exercise the orientation of the sketch plane axes is not important, but that is an orientation that most people are accustomed to working in.)

The origin of the sketch plane (its 0,0,0 point) will be on the end of the path. Draw a circle having a radius of about 0.50 inches. Use AMPROFILE to transform the circle into a profile sketch. Use AMDELCON to delete the Fix constraint from the profile. Mechanical Desktop will report that 3 dimensions or constraints are needed to fully constrain the profile.

Use AMPARDIM to assign a diameter value of 1.0 to the profile, and 0.00 horizontal and vertical linear dimension values from the center of the circle to the work point. Your fully constrained profile and path sketches, the work plane, and the work point should appear similar to those in Figure 1-3.

Invoke the AMSWEEP command. In the **Sweep Feature** dialog box, set Body Type to Normal, Termination to Path –Only, Draft Angle to 0, and click the OK button. Your resulting sweep feature should appear similar to the one in Figure 1-4 when HIDE is on and the **dispsilh** system variable is set to 1. Notice that the path and profile sketches, as well as their dimensions and the work point, disappear as the sweep feature is created.

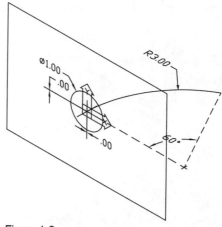

Figure 1-3

After inspecting the sweep feature, start the AMEDITFEAT command and select the sweep feature. In the Sweep dialog box keep the Normal Body Type and Path-Only termination, but change the setting of the draft angle to -5 degrees. Click the OK button of the dialog box and press Enter when you are prompted from the command line to select an object. Use AMUPDATE to initiate the changes. Your sweep feature should now look similar to the one in Figure 1-5.

Normal body type. No draft angle.

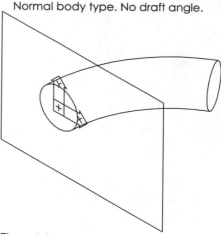

Figure 1-4

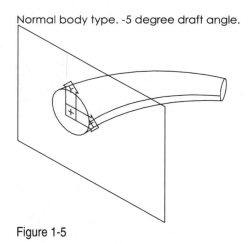

Normal body type. -5 degree draft angle.

Figure 1-5

Repeat the AMEDITFEAT command to change the sweep feature's Body Type to Parallel. Leave its Termination set to Path-Only. Notice that the Draft Angle option becomes grayed-out when the Parallel Body Type is selected. Your sweep feature should look similar to the one in Figure 1-6 after you update it.

That finishes this exercise. You do not need to save the file containing these objects. On the CD-ROM that accompanies this book, the sweep feature is in file md10e106.dwg.

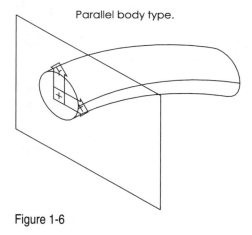

Parallel body type.

Figure 1-6

3D Features from 3D Sweep Paths

Unlike sweep paths made by the AMPATH command, those of the AM3DPATH command are not confined to a plane; they can twist and turn in three dimensions through space. AM3DPATH offers four options for making 3D sweep paths.

Helical   Makes helix and spiral shaped paths.

Spline   Creates a 3D path from an existing wireframe spline curve.

Edge   Transforms the edges of an existing 3D solid into a 3D path.

Pipe   Creates a 3D path from existing lines, arcs, and 2D or 3D polylines.

After you have used one of these options to create a 3D path, you will create a profile with AMPROFILE, and then sweep that profile along the path with AMSWEEP to make a 3D feature.

Helical Paths

You will use the Helical option of AM3DPATH to make helix and spiral shaped paths, and you can use those paths with AMSWEEP to make coil and spiral springs, screw threads, worm gears, and so forth. You do not draw any objects when you use this option. Instead, you specify the parameters of the path through a dialog box, and Mechanical Desktop draws the path for you.

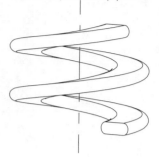

You can make coil springs from helix shaped sweep paths.

AM3DPATH starts with a command line prompt for you to pick a cylindrical 3D feature or a sketched work axis to serve as the centerline of the helix. These features must be perpendicular to the current sketch plane. You will select a sketched work axis if you are making the path for a base feature, and you will select a cylindrical feature if you are constructing a dependent feature.

Helical paths are based on a cylindrical 3D feature or on a sketched work axis. These features must be perpendicular to the current sketch plane.

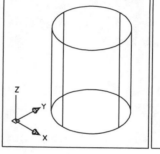
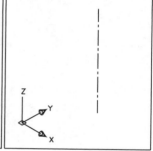

Once the axis of the helix has been established, AM3DPATH displays the **Helix** dialog box. The options in this dialog box are separated into four clusters—Type, Shape, Orientation, and Profile Plane.

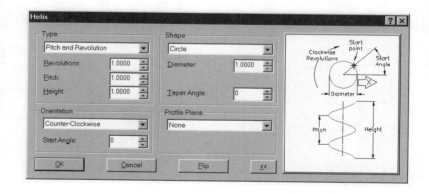

Type

This cluster of list and edit boxes controls the overall length of the helix and the spacing of its coils. A dropdown list box allows you to pick one of four options:

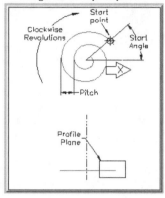

Image tile for spiral paths

Pitch and Revolution   You specify the helix's pitch (The distance between coils.) and the number of revolutions. (The number of coils.) The length of the helix will be the pitch distance times the number of revolutions.

Revolution and Height   You specify the number of revolutions and the overall length of the helix. Pitch will be height divided by the number of revolutions.

Height and Pitch   You specify the overall length of the helix and its pitch. The number of revolutions will be height divided by pitch.

Spiral   This option creates a 2D spiral. You specify the pitch (The distance that the spiral grows laterally with each revolution.) and the number of revolutions of the spiral.

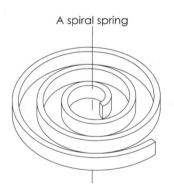

A spiral spring

Below the drop-down list box are three edit boxes for you to enter the helix's number of revolutions, its pitch, and its height. One of these edit boxes, depending upon the helix type you selected, will be disabled. A visual definition of these variables is shown in an image tile on the right side of the dialog box. The image tile used for all circular helix types is shown in the figure of the `Helix` dialog box, while the image tile for spirals is shown in the accompanying figure.

Orientation

A dropdown list box in this cluster allows you to control whether the helix will twist counterclockwise (when you are looking down on the sketch plane from the positive Z direction), or clockwise. The sketch plane's X axis direction is used as a reference for the start of the helix, with Start Angle being the angle between the X axis and a line extending from the center of the helix to its starting point. The direction of the starting angle—clockwise or counterclockwise—is dependent upon the specified helix twist direction.

Shape

You can specify that the cross section shape of the helix path is to be circular or elliptical. When the shape is circular, an edit box is displayed for you to enter the diameter of the helix. When the shape is elliptical, two edit boxes are displayed—one for the major diameter and one for the minor diameter of the helix.

When the value in the Taper Angle edit box is 0.0, each coil of the helix has the same diameter. If you enter a non-zero value in this edit box, the diameter of the helix becomes larger or smaller along its axis length. The result is that of a 3D spiral. When a positive taper angle has been entered, each coil will have a larger diameter than the previous coil; and when a negative taper angle has been entered, the coils will decrease in diame-

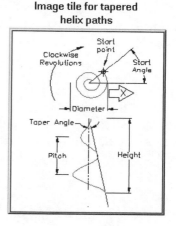

ter along the length of the helix. The taper angle value represents the angle between the centerline of the coil and a line drawn on the profile of the helix.

When an ellipse has been specified for the helix shape, the image tile in the **Helix** dialog box will change to show the parameters for the ellipse shaped helix. And, when a non-zero taper angle has been entered, the image tile will show the parameters for a tapered helix.

Profile Plane

The three options in this dropdown list box control whether or not Mechanical Desktop will place a work plane and sketch plane at the starting point of the helix, and the orientation of the two planes. The origin of the sketch plane will be on the starting point of the helix. The options are as follows.

None   No work plane or sketch plane will be created. Mechanical Desktop will, though, place a work point on the starting point of the helix.

Center Axis/Path   A work point, work plane, and sketch plane will be created and located at the start point of the helix. The plane of the work plane and sketch plane is defined by the centerline of the helix and the starting point of the helix; just as if the AMWORKPLN modifiers of On Edge/Axis and On Vertex were used to establish the work plane.

Normal to Path   A work point, work plane, and sketch plane will be created and located at the start of the helix. The work plane and the sketch plane are normal to the starting direction of the helix; as if the AMWORKPLN modifier of Normal to Start was used to establish the work plane.

As you select parameters and specify sizes in the dialog box, Mechanical Desktop will draw a preview version of the helix around the cylinder or work axis you selected at the start of the command. The Flip button in the dialog box reverses the direction of growth for the helix. When you have the helix parameters set as you want them, press the dialog box's OK button to end the 3DPATH command.

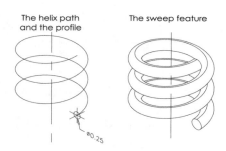

The helix path and the profile

The sweep feature

After the helix path has been created, you will draw the cross section of the helix 3D feature, turn it into a profile with AMPROFILE, constrain and dimension the profile, and use AMSWEEP to create a 3D feature. If a cylindrical feature was used as the center of the helix, you will use the Cut, Join, Intersect, or Split options of AMSWEEP to create a dependent 3D feature. In either case, the Body Type options of AMSWEEP are not available.

Profiles with multiple loops are acceptable. If the helix sweep feature is a dependent feature, interior profile loops of cut operations will be joined to the base feature while exterior loops will be cut. Conversely, interior loops of join operations are neutral (they neither cut nor join) and exterior loops are joined to the base feature.

Sweep features using helical paths require extremely complex computer computations, which can result in slow screen regens and large file sizes. Therefore, you should not use them indiscriminately. For instance, you should not create standard threads on screws, bolts, and nuts, even though they are fairly easy to make, unless you have a specific reason for doing so.

You can edit 3D paths with the AMEDITFEAT command, which can be implemented in any of the ways discussed in Chapter 9. The `Helix` dialog box will be displayed, and you can access all of its parameters, except Profile Plane. You must use AMUPDATE to implement your changes, even if the helix has not been incorporated in a 3D feature.

Exercise 2

Constructing a Worm Gear Model

In this exercise you will make a helix shaped groove around a cylinder, such as a worm gear might have. You will first make the cylinder; second, you will make a helix path on the cylinder; third, you will make and constrain a profile sketch for the groove; and lastly, you will sweep the profile about the helix path. Start a new Mechanical Desktop single part file using the default English template (acad.dwt). We will not do anything further with the model you will make in this exercise, so the initial set up of the drawing file is not important. We will though, reference some dimensions of the cylinder in the dimension of the helix path, so you should have AMDIMDSP display dimensions as equations.

On the WCS XY plane, draw a circle, and turn it into a profile feature with AMPROFILE. Use AMPARDIM to give the circle's diameter a value of 2.0. Then, use AMEXTRUDE to extrude the profile to a height of 3.0, and with no taper. Invoke AMEDITFEAT and make a note of the dimension names Mechanical Desktop has assigned to the diameter and extrusion height of the cylinder. The names of your dimensions may be different from those shown in Figure 2-1, but their values should be the same.

Now start AM3DPATH, and set the parameters of the `Helix` dialog box as follows.

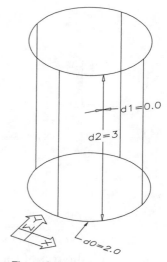

Figure 2-1

Type:	Height and Pitch
Pitch:	0.75
Height:	d2+0.5
Start Angle:	0
Shape:	Circle
Diameter:	d0
Taper Angle:	0
Profile Plane:	Normal to Path

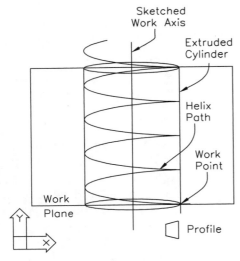

Figure 2-2

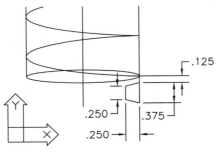

Figure 2-3

If your dimension names for the height of the cylinder and for its diameter are different, substitute your names for d2 and d0 in the edit boxes. We deliberately extended the helix path beyond the cylinder to ensure that the grooves will be cut through the cylinder's entire length. When you have the parameters established, press the OK button in the He lix dialog box. Mechanical Desktop will draw the helix, place a work point and a work plane at its starting point, and prompt for the X axis direction of the sketch plane. Rotate the sketch plane's X axis direction as necessary to have it point in the WCS X axis direction.

Establish a plan view of the sketch plane. Then draw two vertical and two slanted lines for a profile of the groove, as shown in Figure 2-2.

Set the **dispsilh** system variable to equal 1. You may also want to turn the visibility of the work plane to off, and set AMDIMDSP to display dimensions as numbers. Then, use AMPRO-FILE to turn the four lines into a profile. Make certain that the two vertical lines are constrained to be vertical. Then constrain the two slanted lines to have the same length, and constrain the long (right hand) vertical line to be collinear with the side profile of the cylinder. Mechanical Desktop will report that four dimensions are needed to fully constrain the profile. Use AMPARDIM to add the dimensions shown in Figure 2-3. The 0.125 dimension is from the top of the profile to the work point on the start of the helix curve.

To create the helix groove, start AMSWEEP, set Operation to Cut and Termination to Path Only. Then click the OK button. Your computer may take several seconds to process the calculations needed to create the groove in the cylinder. You will also notice that screen regens take considerably longer after the sweep feature has been created. Your model should look similar to the one in Figure 2-4 when hidden lines have been suppressed. Since we will not use this model in any other exercises, you do not need to save it. On the CD-ROM that accompanies this book, the model is in file md19e204.dwg.

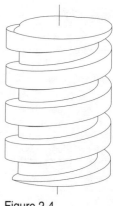

Figure 2-4

Spline Paths

Spline Objects

Splines are natural curves, such as those of a bent (but not kinked) hard rubber rod or hose. An AutoCAD spline is a multi-curved wireframe object that is made by the SPLINE command. The curves of a spline blend so smoothly between each other that you cannot tell where one curve ends and another begins. AutoCAD spline curves, unlike those of polylines, do not contain ordinary arcs and lines. Once a spline has been created, it can be edited by AutoCAD's SPLINEDIT command.

SPLINE will issue command line prompts for you to select the start point of the spline, the points that the spline is to pass through, the spline's end point, and the direction that each end of the spline is to point. Splines may be fully 3D; that is, the fit points are not confined to a plane. Most splines are open, but you can create closed splines, in which the ending point is the same as the beginning point. The points you select are referred to as the spline's *fit points*, and its specified end directions as the *tangent directions*.

When you specify a tangent direction, the effect is as if the end of the spline is clamped (and is, therefore, forced to point in the specified direction) and the spline assumes a shape to accommodate the direction while maintaining a perfectly smooth curve. When you do not specify a tangent direction, the spline swivels about the end point as it assumes its shape.

By default, splines pass through the fit points. You can, though, specify a *fit tolerance* to have the curve bypass the interior fit points. The higher the fit tolerance value, the further the spline will be from the fit points, and the straighter and less curvy the spline becomes. The endpoints of the spline, however, will always be exactly on their fit points. Although you can enter a fit tolerance each time you specify a fit point, only one fit tolerance value (the last one entered) is in effect for the entire spline. When you are creating splines for use in Mechanical Desktop, you will generally leave the fit tolerance to its default value of zero.

Spline Objects (Continued)

In addition to the user specified fit points, splines also have AutoCAD specified *control points*. The first and last control points are on the first and last fit points, but the interior control points are away from the fit points. Control points act as magnets that pull the spline into its shape. The number of control points is set by a property called *order*, which in turn, can be set by editing the spline. When you edit a spline, you can also assign a different weight to selected control points. The greater the control point weight, the closer the spline is pulled toward the control point. Although control points are normally invisible, they are displayed during SPLINEDIT's editing operations, as well as when the AutoCAD system variable **splframe** is set to 1. You will seldom need to modify a spline's control points when you are constructing Mechanical Desktop parametric solid models.

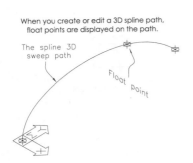

When you create or edit a 3D spline path, float points are displayed on the path.

The spline 3D sweep path

Float point

When you choose the Spline option of AM3DPATH, a command line prompt will ask you to select an object that was created by AutoCAD's SPLINE command. Next, a prompt will ask you to specify the starting end of the path by picking a point near one end of the spline. Mechanical Desktop replaces the spline with a 3D path feature that has the same color as that used for AutoCAD's grips (which, by default, is blue), and displays points on the spline path. Each of the points on the path is shown as three mutually perpendicular short lines and a circle. Mechanical Desktop refers to these points as *float points*.

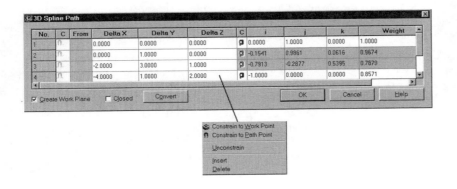

As it displays the path, Mechanical Desktop also displays a table-like dialog box titled `3D Spline Path`. Data pertaining to each of the float points is listed in the rows of the dialog box, and you can change this data by entering new values or by selecting an option from a right-click shortcut menu. Through options in this shortcut menu, you can delete points or add new ones, as well as change the constraints of the path.

By default, the float points on the path are constrained to point coordinates that are the same as those of the original spline's fit points. (Any fit tolerance the spline might have is ignored by Mechanical Desktop.) You can, though, constrain a float point to a work point by selecting an option in the shortcut menu. Moreover, if a work point coincides with a spline fit point, Mechanical Desktop automatically constrains the corresponding float point of the 3D path to the work point. An icon that is the same as the work point icon in the Work Features toolbar will appear in the dialog box column headed with the letter C. A gray magnet in this column indicates that the float point is constrained to the spline. The coordinates of the float points relative to the current sketch plane are given in the columns headed Delta X, Delta Y, and Delta Z.

The last five columns in the dialog box, which are labeled C, i, j, k, and Weight, apply to the direction of the 3D path at its start and end points. Mechanical Desktop often refers to this direction as the *tangency* of the path end points. Since the data in these five columns apply only to the end points of the spline path, the cells for the interior points are grayed-out. If the dialog box cell in the column labeled C contains a gray clamp, the tangency of end of the 3D path is not constrained, the path end will assume a natural spline shape, and the last four columns of the dialog box will be grayed-out.

If the cell in the C column contains a red clamp, though, the end of the 3D path is constrained to point in the direction defined by the columns labeled i, j, and k. The values in these three columns represent the X, Y, and Z directions of the end of the path. For example, the values of i=1, j=0, and k=0 mean that the end of the path is constrained to point in the X axis direction. You turn the tangency constraint on and off by pressing the pick button of your pointing device. You can also set the first or last point's tangent direction by constraining the point to a work point.

The values in the column labeled Weight control the relative distance at which each tangent direction is maintained before the spline curves toward the next fit point. (Note that the meaning of weight in this column is not the same as that of spline control point weight.) An example is shown in the following figure of a path made from a spline that, as shown on the

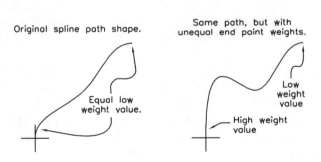

left, originally had equal and relatively low end weights. On the right side of this figure, the left end of the path was assigned a high weight value, while the right end retained the original low weight value.

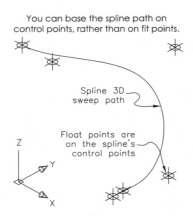

You can base the spline path on control points, rather than on fit points.

Spline 3D sweep path

Float points are on the spline's control points

Select the Convert button to base the spline path on control points, rather than fit points. Once you make this conversion, the spline's fit points are deleted and cannot be restored; although you can restore a close approximation of the original spline. The shape of the spline path is not changed by the conversion from fit points to control points, but the float points will now be on the spline's control points.

The dialog box for 3D spline paths based on control shows the coordinates of the control points. In this dialog box, the weight parameter now refers to control point weight, initially each control point has a weight of 1.0000. As you assign a higher weight to an individual control point, the spline path will pull closer to that control point.

3D Spline Path dialog box when the path is based on control points

No.	C	From	Delta X	Delta Y	Delta Z	C	i	j	k	Weight
1			0.0000	0.0000	0.0000		0.0000	1.0000	0.0000	1.0000
2			0.0000	0.3333	0.0000					1.0000
3			0.2151	1.6237	-0.0860					1.0000
4			-2.4194	4.4839	0.9677					1.0000
5			-3.0000	1.0000	2.0000					1.0000
6			-4.0000	1.0000	2.0000		-1.0000	0.0000	0.0000	1.0000

☑ Create Work Plane ☐ Closed Convert   OK   Cancel   Help

If you check the Create Work Plane option in the lower left corner of the `3D Spline Path` dialog box, Mechanical Desktop will place a work plane and the sketch plane on the starting point of the path. Mechanical Desktop will place a work point on the start point even if the Create Work Plane option is not selected. If you select the Closed option, Mechanical Desktop will close the spline and create a closed path, even if the selected spline was open.

Once you have set up the 3D spline path, you will create a profile feature and use the AMSWEEP command to create the 3D sweep feature. In the `Sweep` dialog box, you can choose Path Only, Plane, or From-To as the sweep feature's termination type, provided the profile does not contain multiple loops. If it does, only the Path Only termination is available. The Body type and Draft angle options in the Sweep dialog box will be grayed out.

Click the OK button of the Sweep dialog box to create the 3D feature. If you have trouble in wireframe views visualizing 3D features made from spline paths, increase the value of AutoCAD's **isolines** system variable from its default value of 4 to a value of 8 or more. A screen regeneration is required to put any changes to **isolines** in effect.

An example of what you can construct by using a spline sweep path is shown in a rendered view in the next figure. The part's flanges were created by extrusion after the curved tube-shape base feature was created.

The spline sweep path and the profile for the part are shown in the following figure. Notice that profiles having interior loops can be used in making sweep features from spline paths. This enables you to create both the inside and outside walls of the part in one step. Notice also that only two points and the end tangent directions define the spline.

A significant limitation in creating 3D features from 3D spline paths is that you cannot control the orientation, or twist, of the profile as it moves along the path. An example is shown in the next figure. Although the rectangular shaped profile of the feature has its sides parallel with the X and Y axes, the profile rotates during the sweep and the end of the feature is askew to the principle axes. Consequently you are basically restricted to sweeping circular shaped profiles when you use 3D spline paths.

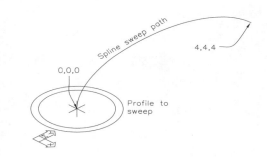

As with the other sketched 3D features, you can edit those that have been swept along a spline path by invoking the AMEDITFEAT command. The 3D **Spline Path** dialog box will reappear to allow you to make changes to the path, and then the **Sweep** dialog box will be displayed for you to make changes to the sweep operation. AMUPDATE must be invoked to initiate any changes you have made.

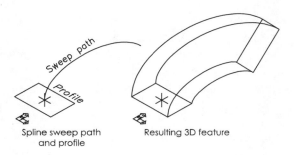

Spline sweep path   Resulting 3D feature
and profile

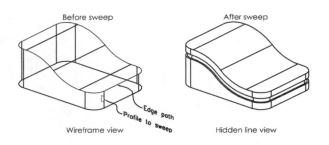

Before sweep · After sweep · Edge path · Profile to sweep · Wireframe view · Hidden line view

Edge Paths

The Edge option of AM3DPATH transforms existing edges on 3D features into sweep paths. Edge paths are especially useful when you want to make a feature, such as a groove, that is to follow an existing edge, as on the model shown in the accompanying figure.

When you choose this AM3DPATH option, Mechanical Desktop will issue command line prompts for you to select edges for the path. You must select each edge independently—window and crossing selection methods are not allowed. The selected edges must touch one another and each must be tangent to its adjacent selected edge. Thus the closed 3D path on the solid shown in the previous figure could not have been made if the four corners were not rounded. On the other hand, only some edges, such as those along one side of the two curved faces, can be selected to make an open path, as shown in the figure below.

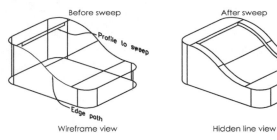

Before sweep · Profile to sweep · Edge path · Wireframe view

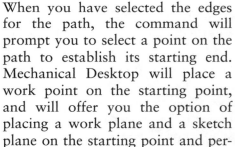

After sweep · Hidden line view

When you have selected the edges for the path, the command will prompt you to select a point on the path to establish its starting end. Mechanical Desktop will place a work point on the starting point, and will offer you the option of placing a work plane and a sketch plane on the starting point and perpendicular to the path. To help you identify the edge path, it takes the color of AutoCAD's grips. (Which, by default, is blue.)

After creating the edge path, you will create and constrain a profile to be swept along the path. Multiple looped profiles are accepted, but if the path is curved (as most of them are), the sweep operation will fail. You cannot edit an edge path directly, but the path automatically changes to match any changes that occur to the edges when the parent solid is edited.

Pipe Paths

This option of AM3DPATH creates a 3D sweep path from a set of connected lines and arcs. Mechanical Desktop will issue the following command line prompts.

```
Command: AM3DPATH (Enter)
Enter path type [Helical/Spline/Edge/Pipe] <Helical>: P (Enter)
Select polyline path source: (Select the path objects) (Enter)
```

Despite the wording of the last prompt, you can select lines and arcs as well as 2D and 3D polylines. You can select them individually or with window and crossing selection methods. Splines and other objects that are not suitable for path elements, are filtered out of the selection set. The objects must exactly touch one another—no gaps or overlaps are allowed. Also, arcs must be tangent to adjacent arcs or lines. Paths can have sharp corners, such as when two adjoining lines are pointed in different directions. The path can be a closed loop, but it cannot have branches.

When you finish selecting the objects for the path, Mechanical Desktop will prompt for a point to establish the starting end of the path. The AutoCAD objects will be transformed into a Mechanical Desktop path feature having the color of AutoCAD's grips. Also, Mechanical Desktop will place a float point at each path change-of-direction point and at the start and end of the path. (Mechanical Desktop's documentation sometimes refers to them

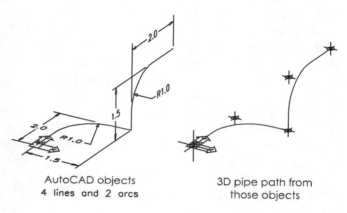

AutoCAD objects
4 lines and 2 arcs

3D pipe path from
those objects

as fit points.) Each float point is represented as three mutually perpendicular short lines and a horizontal circle. AutoCAD objects for a typical pipe path are shown on the left in the figure on this page. The dimensions in this figure are to help you visualize the objects; normally you will not place dimensions on path objects. The resulting 3D path and its float points are shown on the right.

Mechanical Desktop will also display a table-like dialog box titled **3D Pipe Path**. In this dialog box, data for each float point is shown in a row of cells. You can modify the data in the cells by entering new values or by selecting an option from the cell's right-click menu. A red magnet in the column labeled C, indicates that the float point is constrained to the path. This is the default condition. You can, through the right-click shortcut menu, constrain the float point to a work point instead. The following figure shows the dialog box for the path shown in the previous figure.

The values in the columns that are labeled Delta X, Delta Y, and Delta Z give the coordinates (based on the current sketch plane) of the float point relative to the float point whose number is listed in the column labeled From. The column labeled Length is the straight line distance to the next float point.

The column labeled Angle XY lists the angle in the XY plane to the next float point. Angles rotate counterclockwise with 0 degrees being in the X axis direction. The column labeled Angle Z lists the angle to the next float point from the XY plane. The last column in the dialog box, which is labeled Radius, gives the radius of the arc at the float point. If two straight lines meet at the float point, the radius will be zero.

If you check the Create Work Plane option in the lower left corner of the dialog box, Mechanical Desktop will place a work plane and the sketch plane on the starting point of the path. Mechanical Desktop will place a work point on the start point even if the Create Work Plane option is not selected. If you select the Close option, Mechanical Desktop will close the path by drawing a straight segment from the last point to the first point of the 3D path.

After you create a pipe path, you will create a profile that is to be swept along it, and then use AMSWEEP to create the 3D feature. The width of the profile cannot equal or exceed the radius of the smallest curve in the 3D pipe path. For instance, if the profile is a circle that has a one unit radius, the smallest arc in the 3D path must have a radius larger than one unit. When the path contains two adjacent lines that make a sharp bend, though, (such as two adjacent lines that are perpendicular to each other) the sweep solid forms a mitered corner at the bend.

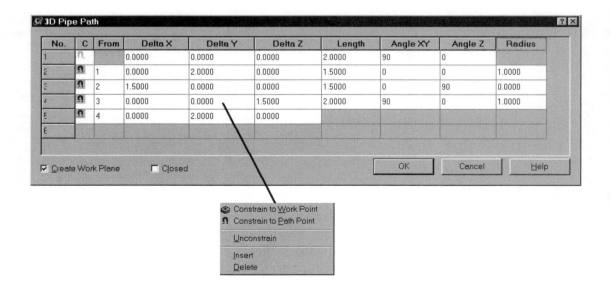

Profiles that have multiple loops are allowed, but they will cause the sweep operation to fail if the sweep path has any arcs or bends. As a result, you cannot directly model objects, such as pipes, that have a hole along their length, despite the option's name. You can, though, use AMSHELL to hollow out the swept 3D feature. Chapter 11 discusses the AMSHELL command in detail.

On the right side of the following figure is an example of a 3D solid feature made from the 3D pipe path and profile shown on the left. Only the normal body type of AMSWEEP is allowed with 3D pipe paths. When you edit a 3D pipe path, the **3D Pipe Path** dialog box is restored, and when you have finished editing the path, the **Sweep** dialog box is displayed for you to change the sweep parameters. AMUPDATE is required to initiate any changes you have made.

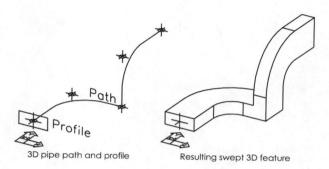

3D pipe path and profile   Resulting swept 3D feature

CHAPTER 11

Placed Features

Placed features are tools for modifying a part. As their name implies, they are not based on 2D profiles as are sketched features. Often, you will establish the parameters of a placed feature in a dialog box and then specify the location of the feature or select the feature that is to be modified. You will use some placed features—such as the one that makes round holes, and the one that rounds sharp edges and corners—often; but you will use others—such as the one that hollows-out a part, and the one that uses a Mechanical Desktop surface to shape a part—only occasionally.

This chapter covers the following topics.

- Describes how to make round holes, including those with counterbores and countersinks, in a part.

- Tells you how to bevel the sharp edges, both inside and outside, of a part.

- Explains how to round, or fillet, a part's sharp edges. Inside and outside edges, as well as corners, can be filleted. Also, the radius can be set to vary within a single fillet.

- Describes how you can hollow-out a part to leave a relatively thin shell. You can specify that selected faces will be left open, and you can specify that selected faces will have a different wall thickness than the other faces.

- Shows how you can use Mechanical Desktop surface objects to shape a part.

- Describes the placed features that are especially useful for designing parts that are to molded or cast. These placed features can create draft angles on specific faces, split a face into two faces, and even split a part into two parts.

Some typical placed features

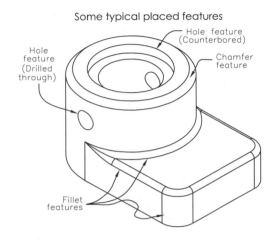

Unlike sketched features, *placed features* are not based on profiles. As their name implies, they are usually placed, or located, on existing features. Your most often use of placed features will be to make commonly occurring geometric shapes, such as round holes, beveled edges (chamfers), and rounded edges and corners (fillets).

You can also hollow-out a solid feature, to leave a shell having a specified wall thickness. A less often used, but powerful, placed feature enables you to make solid geometry having smooth sculpted surfaces by shaping a 3D solid with a Mechanical Desktop surface object. In addition to these general purpose placed features, Mechanical Desktop has some that are especially useful for creating parts that are to manufactured by molding and casting processes. Even though placed features serve a wide variety of uses and make a wide variety of 3D shapes, they are all constrained to the geometry of the feature on which they are placed; and as that feature is changed the placed features change accordingly. Also, if the parent feature is deleted, the placed feature will be deleted as well.

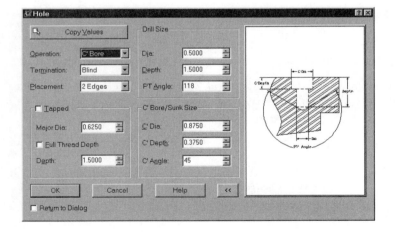

Hole Features

Because round holes occur so often in 3D models, Mechanical Desktop has a command that does nothing more than create round holes. This saves you the trouble of positioning a sketch plane, drawing and constraining a profile on it, and using a cut extrusion or revolution operation to make a hole. The command is AMHOLE, which displays a dialog box titled

Hole for you use in specifying the parameters of the hole. The options in the **Hole** dialog box are as follows.

Copy Values

When you click this button, you will prompted to select an existing hole feature. The parameters of that hole will then be entered in the current **Hole** dialog box.

Operation

Specify one of three styles for the start of the hole in this dropdown list box.

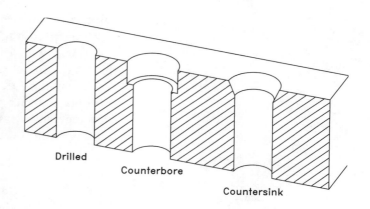

Drilled The diameter is the same throughout the length of the hole.

Counterbore These holes maintain a starting diameter that is larger than that of the main hole for a specified distance.

Countersink These holes have a bevel, or chamfer, around the starting edge of the hole.

Termination

This dropdown list box gives you three choices for ending the hole:

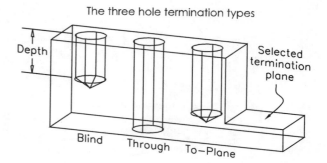

Through The hole passes completely through everything.

To-Plane The hole ends at a user specified plane.

Blind The hole has a user specified length, or depth.

In On-Plane terminations, the drill bit end extends beyond the termination plane.

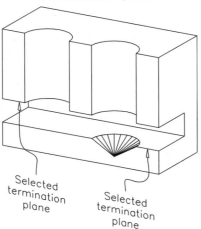

Selected termination plane

Selected termination plane

Mechanical Desktop treats holes as if they were made by a twist drill, and their length is to the point at which the straight sides of the hole end. Consequently in To-Plane terminations, the cone shaped drill bit end extends beyond the selected termination plane.

Placement

Choose one of the methods in this dropdown list box for specifying the hole's location. The method you select will depend largely on the geometry of the object in which the hole is to be made. After you press the OK button of the Hole dialog box, prompts that are appropriate for the selected hole placement method will be issued on the command line to position the hole.

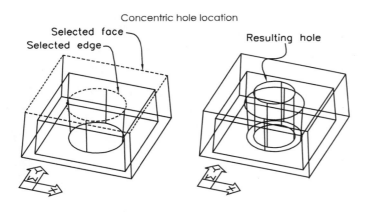

Concentric hole location

Selected face
Selected edge

Resulting hole

Concentric The hole will be on a planar face in the center of an existing arc or circular shaped edge. In locating the hole, command line prompts will ask you to first pick a plane or a face, and then to pick a curved edge. The curved edge does not have to be on the selected plane.

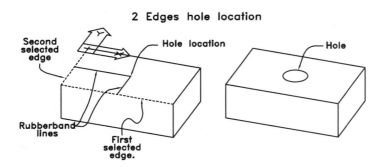

2 Edges hole location

Second selected edge

Hole location

Hole

Rubberband lines

First selected edge.

2 Edges The hole will be a user specified distance from two edges of a planar surface. Command line prompts will ask you to pick two edges. Although the edges must be straight and on the same plane, they do not have to be at right angles to one another. After picking the edges, you will be prompted to pick the hole location. Rubber-band lines will extend from the selected edges to help you visualize its position. Lastly, you will be prompted to enter the exact perpendicular distance of the hole from each edge.

On Point The hole will be centered on a work point and its axis will be perpendicular to the sketch plane of the work point. You will be prompted from the command line to select a work point, and then to specify the direction of the hole from the work point's sketch plane. The work point will be consumed when the hole is created. This method is useful in making holes in non-planar surfaces and when there are no edges suitable for the Concentric and 2 Edges methods.

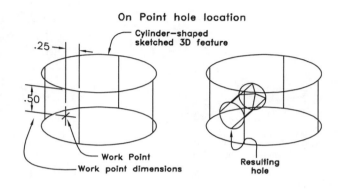

From Hole This method locates the hole relative to one or to two existing holes. You will be prompted from the command line to select a plane or a planar face on which the new hole is to be located, and then to establish the X and Y directions on this plane. Next you will be asked to select an X direction reference hole and a Y direction reference hole. These can be same hole. Then, you will be prompted to pick the

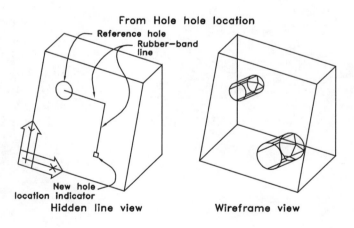

location of the new hole. As you move your pointing device, Mechanical Desktop will draw rubber-band lines from the reference hole, or holes, in the X and Y directions to help you locate the new hole. Lastly, you will be prompted to enter the exact X and Y distances of the new hole from the reference hole, or holes.

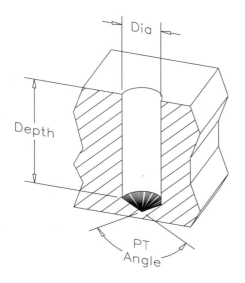

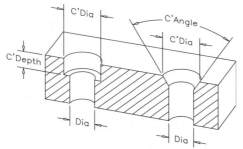

Counterbore & Countersink
dimensions

Drill Size

The drill specifications for the hole—depth, diameter, and point angle—are entered in this cluster of edit boxes If the hole termination is To Plane, the Depth edit box will be disabled; and if the hole termination is Through, both the Depth and PT Angle edit boxes will be disabled. If you want to create a flat bottomed hole, enter 180 degrees as the PT (point) angle.

C'Bore/Sink Size

Use this cluster of edit boxes to specify counterbore and countersink dimensions of the hole. When a counterbore hole operation has been specified, the edit boxes labeled C'Depth and C'Dia will be enabled. When a countersink hole operation has been specified, the C'Dia and C'Angle edit boxes will be available. The C'Dia must be larger than the hole diameter.

Tapped

When the check box labeled Tapped is selected, the hole will represent a threaded hole, and the options for specifying the major (nominal) diameter of the screw, and the length of the threaded portion of the hole are enabled. The major diameter you specify must be larger than the drill size diameter. The threads do not appear in the solid model. In fact, there is no difference in appearance between tapped holes and non-tapped holes in the model. Mechanical Desktop, however, does keep track of tapped holes, and shows the threads as dashed lines in drawing views.

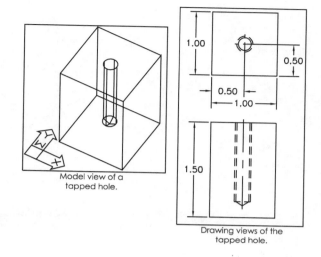

Model view of a tapped hole.

Drawing views of the tapped hole.

Click the dialog box's OK button when you have established the hole's parameters. Mechanical Desktop will dismiss the **Hole** dialog box and issue command line prompts for you to locate the hole, and, if you selected To Plane as the hole's termination, to specify a plane or face. As soon as you locate a hole, it will be created and AMHOLE will prompt for another hole's location. Press the enter key to end the command. Each hole you create is listed as a feature in the Desktop Browser, with a name such as Hole1.

You can modify an existing hole through the AMEDITFEAT command. The **Hole** dialog box will appear, with the current values of the hole in the edit boxes. You can modify most of the hole parameters in any way you want, including the hole style. For example, you can change a drilled hole to a counterbored hole. You cannot, however, change the placement method. When you press the OK button in this dialog box, the dimensions for locating the hole will be displayed, and can be modified. AMUPDATE must be invoked to put the changes into effect.

Chamfer features bevel sharp edges of 3D features.

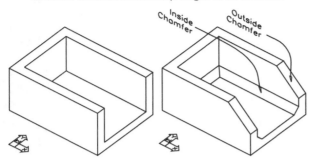

Chamfer Features

Chamfer features change sharp edges on 3D features into beveled edges. On outside edges, material is removed from the 3D feature in making the chamfered edge; while on inside edges, material is added to the 3D feature. The bevel can have equal or unequal offset distances from the original edge.

Chamfers are made by the AMCHAMFER command, which displays the **Chamfer** dialog box for you to use in establishing the characteristics and dimensions of the chamfer. The three options in the list box labeled Operation control whether the chamfer will have equal distances from the edge, unequal distances, or be based on a distance and an angle. The applicable parameters of the chamfer are depicted in the dialog box's image tile for the operation type you select.

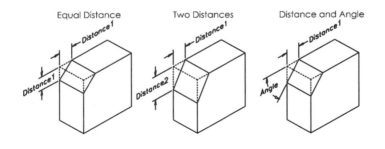

The cluster of three edit boxes labeled Parameters is for entering the dimensions of the chamfer. Which edit boxes are available depends on the operation type you selected.

• When the Equal Distances operation type has been selected, only the edit box labeled Distance1 is available. The edge of the resulting chamfer will be set back from the selected edge on both faces by the Distance1 length.

- When the Two Distances operation type has been selected, both the Distance 1 and Distance 2 edit boxes are available.

- When the Distance and Angle operation type has been selected, the Distance 1 and the Angle edit boxes are available.

When you press the OK button in this dialog box, Mechanical Desktop will issue a command line prompt for you to select an edge or face to chamfer. If you select a face, all sharp edges adjacent to that face and to faces tangent to it will be chamfered. The Distance 1 side of the chamfer is on the selected face.

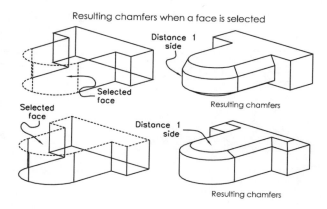

When you select an edge to be chamfered and the chamfer operation is Equal Distance, you will be prompted to select additional edges. Press the Enter key to stop the selection process and create the chamfers. The selected edges and all edges tangent to them will be chamfered.

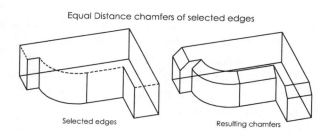

When you select an edge and the chamfer operation is based on Two Distances or on Distance and Angle, you are prompted to specify which of the faces adjacent to the selected edge is to serve as the Distance 1 face. Mechanical Desktop will chamfer the selected edge without giving you the opportunity to select other edges to chamfer.

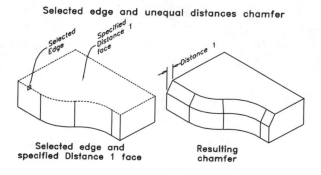

Chamfers are displayed in the Desktop Browser. You can edit them through AMEDIT-FEAT, which will restore the `Chamfer` dialog box so that you can change the dimensions of the chamfer. You cannot, however, change the chamfer's operation type. Thus, if the original chamfer was an Equal Distance type, you can only change the Distance 1 value—you cannot convert the chamfer to a Distance and Angle type. As with all editing operations on 3D features, you must invoke AMUPDATE to initiate the changes.

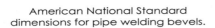

American National Standard
dimensions for pipe welding bevels.

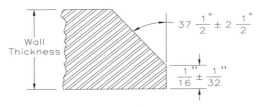

Figure 1-1

Exercise 1

Chamfering Edges

You will finish the model of a steel pipe eccentric reducer that you started in Exercise 3 of Chapter 8. In this exercise you will make a weld bevel on each end of the fitting. The American National Standard for welded pipe (ANSI B16.25) gives the dimensions shown in Figure 1-1 for butt weld bevels on the size of pipe our model pipe fitting represents—nominal 3 inch by 2 inch. Although these dimensions are backwards from those we need as input for AMCHAMFER, we can nevertheless use them to calculate the distance and angle parameters for the chamfer on each end of our model.

Open your drawing file of this model that you saved at the conclusion of Exercise 3 of Chapter 8, or file md08e305.dwg on the CD-ROM that comes with this book. We will first chamfer the small end of the fitting. Start AMCHAMFER, set the operation type to Distance and Angle, Distance 1 to 0.070, Angle to 52.5 degrees, and press the OK button. When you are prompted to select an edge, pick the outside edge (the larger circle) of the small end of the fitting, and specify the surface of the reducer as the face to apply the angle value. The chamfer will be created on the small end of the fitting.

Repeat the AMCHAFTER command. Select Distance and Angle as the Operation type, set distance to 0.118, Angle to 52.5 degrees, and click the OK button. As the edge to chamfer, pick the outside edge of the large end of the fitting, and specify the outside surface of the reducer as the face to apply the angle value.

This finishes our work on this part. Your model with the two chamfers, and with hidden line removal on, should look similar to the one in figure 1-2. We will do nothing further with this model. On the CD-ROM that accompanies this book, the model is in file md11e102.dwg.

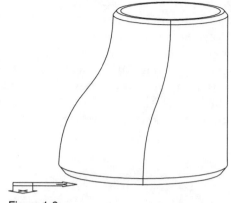

Figure 1-2

Fillet Features

Filleting operations convert sharp edges into rounded edges. Fillets can be on outside edges or on inside edges, and they can round corners where three edges meet. Fillets that round corners are often called ball fillets. A fillet can also have a radius that varies linearly, according to a cubic equation, or that varies as necessary to keep the width of the fillet constant. All of these configurations are made by the AMFILLET command.

Fillet features round sharp edges of 3D features.

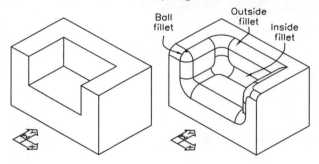

AMFILLET, displays a dialog box for you to enter the type and the dimensions of the fillet. On the left side of this dialog box is a column of four radio buttons for specifying the type of fillet—constant radius, fixed

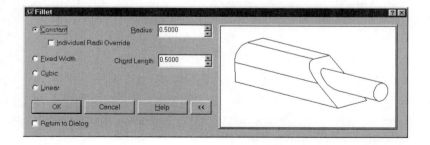

width, cubic, or linear. When you pick one of these buttons, the image tile of the dialog box will show an example of the fillet type. When you click the OK button, the dialog box will be dismissed and command line prompts will be issued for you to select the edges that are to be rounded, and if necessary, for you to enter additional fillet parameters. If you check the check box labeled Return to Dialog, the Fillet dialog box will reappear after you have created a fillet. Also, the button labeled OK will be labeled Apply when the Return to Dialog is checked. A characteristic of Mechanical Desktop fillets that you should keep in mind is that all edges tangent to a selected edge will also be filleted.

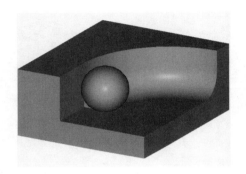

Constant Fillets

The radius of a fillet of this type remains the same throughout the length of the edge that is to be rounded. They are sometimes referred to as rolling ball fillets, because their surface can be defined as the imaginary surface formed by rolling a ball that has the radius of the fillet, along the selected edge. The points (the loci) at which the ball touches the faces adjacent to the edge define the tangents of the fillet. You specify the radius of the fillet by entering its value in the edit box labeled Radius. When the **Fillet** dialog box has been dismissed, command line prompts will ask you to pick the edges that are to be rounded. Press the Enter key to signal the end of the selection process and create the fillets.

If you activate the check box labeled Individual Radii Override you can specify that selected edges will have a fillet radius that is different than the value in the Radius edit box. After the **Fillet** dialog box has been dismissed, and you have picked the edges to be rounded, Mechanical Desktop will display the fillet radius of each selected edge next to the edge, and will ask you to select a radius. The current radius of the fillet you select will be displayed on the command line and you can enter a new value. The "Select a radius" prompt will be repeated until you press the Enter key to end the command and create the fillets.

Fixed Width Fillets

The width of these fillets remain the same throughout the length of the edge being rounded. If the angle between the adjoining faces varies, the radius of the fillet will vary as necessary to maintain a constant width. When you select the Fixed Width fillet type, the edit box labeled Chord Length will be activated for you to enter the size of the fillet. The value you enter in this dialog box represents the straight-line distance between the two endpoints of the fillet's arc. If the geometry of the edge being filleted is such that the angle between them does not vary, there will be no difference between a constant radius and a fixed width fillet, except for the manner in which their size is specified.

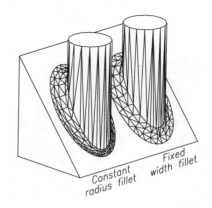

Cubic Fillets

The radius of cubic fillets vary along the length of the edge being rounded, as if the rolling ball that defines the fillet is continually changing size in accordance with a cubic equation as it moves. You do not specify the size of these fillets in the `Fillet` dialog box. Instead, after you have clicked the OK (or Apply) button of the `Fillet` dialog box and have picked an edge to be filleted, Mechanical Desktop will display the characters R=* on each end of the edge and issue the command line prompt:

```
Select radius or [Add vertex/Clear/Delete vertex]: (Select a radius or an option, or press
     Enter.)
```

The Add vertex option permits you to add points along the edge that are to have a specific radius. When you choose this option, you will be asked to pick a point on the edge. On the command line Mechanical Desktop will display the location of the point as a percentage of the edge's length:

```
Enter vertex placement <current>: (Enter a value between 5 and 95, or press Enter.)
```

Enter a percentage value to move the point, or press Enter to accept the current one. Once you have positioned a vertex point, the characters R=* will be displayed next to it. The asterisk represents a default radius value. When you pick a point on one of these characters, the current radius value for the fillet at that point will be displayed, and you can enter another value. The value must be greater than zero. The entered radius value will be displayed in place of the asterisk. You can eliminate a vertex (except for the ones on the ends of the edge) by choosing the Delete vertex option, and then selecting the vertex you want to delete. The Clear option returns the display of a selected radius back to an asterisk.

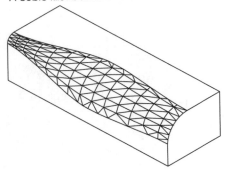

A cubic fillet based on three different radii.

When you press the Enter key in response to the main command line prompt, the fillets will be created. The radius and the tangent edges of the fillet are defined by a cubic equation.

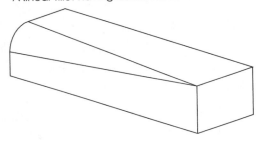

A linear fillet having a zero radius on one end.

Linear Fillets

Linear fillets have a radius value that changes linearly from one end of the selected edge to the other. You specify the radius value at each end of the fillet from the command line after you have pressed the OK (or Apply) button of the Fillet dialog box and have picked an edge to be filleted. Mechanical Desktop will display the equation $R=0$ at each end of the edge, and on the command line will ask you to select a radius. When you select one of the two radii, a default radius value will be displayed on the command line, and you press the Enter key to accept it or enter a new value. Pressing Enter in response to the prompt to select a radius will create the fillet and end the command.

Exercise 2

Adding Placed Features to a Sketched Feature

This exercise will demonstrate the steps for adding two fillets, two holes, and four chamfers to transform a simple sketched feature into a fairly complex part. Start a new part drawing file using the default English template file (acad.dwt). You will not need to retain this file, so its initial set up is not important. Set the viewpoint to a front-right isometric. Then start the AMSKPLN command, choose its worldYz option, and accept the default X axis alignment. Use six lines to draw the L-shaped object shown in Figure 2-1, turn it into a profile feature, and constrain and dimension the profile as shown in the figure.

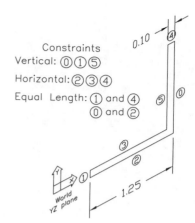

Figure 2-1

Extrude the profile 1.0 units in the positive Z axis direction. The resulting 3D feature will look similar to the one in Figure 2-2. In this figure, the viewpoint has been rotated slightly from a front-right isometric to avoid having the lines in the corner of the feature overlap.

Invoke AMFILLET to display the **Fillet** dialog box. Check the Cubic radio button and the Return to Dialog check box, and click the Apply button. Respond to the command line prompts as follows:

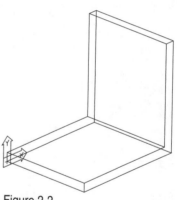

Figure 2-2

```
Select edge or [eXit]: (Pick a point on the edge forming
    the inside corner of the L-shaped feature.)
Select radius or [Add vertex/Clear/Delete vertex]: A
    (Enter)
Select location on edge: (Pick a point near the middle of
    the selected edge.)
Enter vertex placement <44.0525%>: 50 (Enter)
(The equation R=* is located on each end and in the middle of the edge.)
Select radius or [Add vertex/Clear/Delete vertex]: (Pick the equation on either end of the
    edge.)
Enter radius <0.5000>: 0.10 (Enter)
Select radius or [Add vertex/Clear/Delete vertex]: (Pick the equation on the other end of
    the edge.)
Enter radius <0.1000>: (Enter)
Select radius or [Add vertex/Clear/Delete vertex]: (Pick the equation in the middle of the
    edge.)
Enter radius or [Percentage] <0.1000>: 0.40 (Enter)
(The radius values on the selected edge will look similar to those in Figure 2-3)
Select radius or [Add vertex/Clear/Delete vertex]: (Enter)
```

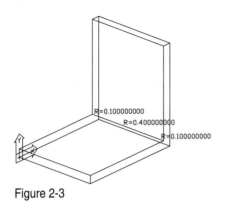

Figure 2-3

The inside corner surface of the L-shaped feature will be filleted, and the **Fillet** dialog box will reappear. Clear the Return to Dialog check box, and press the OK button to create a second fillet. Select the outside edge of the feature's corner as the edge to fillet, add a vertex to the middle of this edge, set the radius of each end to 0.20, and the radius of the middle vertex to 0.50. When you have set these radii, end the command by pressing Enter in response to Mechanical Desktop's prompt to select a radius. In the wireframe viewing mode, your part with its two fillets should look similar to the one in Figure 2-4.

You will next add two round holes to the part. Start the AMHOLE command. Set the parameters in the **Hole** dialog box as follows.

Operation:	Drilled
Termination:	Through
Placement:	2 Edges
Dia	0.25

Clear the Tapped and Return to Dialog check boxes. Check the OK button to dismiss the dialog box. The command line prompts and your input to position the hole are:

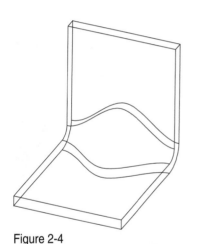

Figure 2-4

```
Select first edge: (Pick a point on the inside top edge
of the part, as shown in Figure 2-5.)
Select second edge: (Pick a point on the left vertical
edge of the part.)
Specify hole location: (Drag the screen cursor down and to the right from the selected
   edges and press the pick button.)
(The edge you selected first will be highlighted.)
Enter distance from first edge (highlighted) <current>: 0.375 (Enter)
(The edge you selected second will be highlighted.)
Enter distance from second edge (highlighted) <current>: 0.5 (Enter)
```

A hole through the vertical face of the part will appear. Actually, the order in which you select the edges is not important as long as long as you position the hole 0.375 from the top horizontal edge of the part and 0.5 from the vertical edge. Once you locate the first hole, Mechanical Desktop will issue prompts for you to position another hole. They will be the same as those used in positioning the first hole, and you will respond with similar input to locate the hole on the horizontal face of the part, 0.375 units from the end and 0.5 units from either side. Press Enter when you are prompted to select an edge for a third hole. Your part with the two holes should look similar to the one in Figure 2-6.

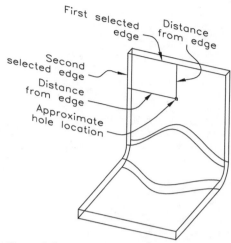

Figure 2-5

Lastly, you will chamfer the four sharp corners of the part. Start AMCHAMFER. In the **Chamfer Feature** dialog box, set Operation to Equal Distance, Distance 1 to 0.25, and clear Return to Dialog. Click the OK button to leave the dialog box. Each time you are prompted to select the edge to chamfer, pick one of the 0.10 long edges of the part. Press Enter when you are prompted to select a fifth edge.

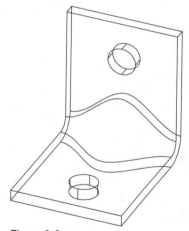

Figure 2-6

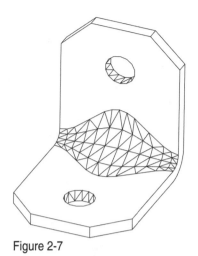

Figure 2-7

Your completed part, with the four chamfers, should look similar to the one in Figure 2-7 when hidden line removal is on. We will do nothing more with this part, and you do not need to save it. On the CD-ROM that comes with this book, though, the finished part is in file md11e207.dwg.

Shell Features

Similar to hole features, shell features always remove material from parts. They hollow out a part, leaving empty space under a relatively thin walled covering. Shell features work by offsetting the surfaces of the part a specified distance and then removing all of the part's material that is not between the original surfaces and the offset surfaces. The characteristics of shell features and the command—AMSHELL—that creates them are:

- An individual part can have only one shell feature.

- The entire part is shelled, except for selected faces. Those selected faces will be open.

- The wall thickness can vary between individual faces.

- The shell's wall can be offset to the inside of the part's surface, to the outside, or to both sides.

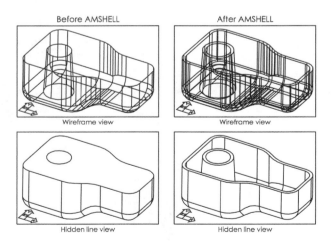

AMSHELL brings up the **Shell Feature** dialog box for you to use in specifying the parameters of the operation. In this dialog box, the types of shell wall offsets are listed as radio buttons, and the corresponding edit boxes are for you to enter the overall shell wall thickness. When you select Mid-plane, the part's surface is offset on both sides by a distance equal to one-half the specified wall thickness.

The cluster of two buttons labeled Excluded Faces are for specifying the part's faces that will not be shelled. When you press the Add button in this cluster, the dialog box will be temporarily dismissed for you to pick the faces that you want open. All faces that are tangent to a selected face will also be left open. Press Enter when you have finished selecting faces. The Reclaim button in the cluster is for de-selecting faces that have been picked to be open.

The cluster of buttons labeled Multiple Thickness Overrides is for assigning a shell wall thickness that is different than the default thickness to specific faces. You

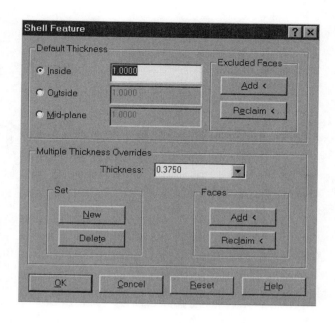

cannot access these buttons if Mid-plane has been selected as the shell wall offset type. Initially, all of its buttons will grayed-out, except for the one labeled New. The steps to specify an individual wall thickness are:

1. Click the New button.

2. Enter the desired wall thickness in the Thickness edit box.

3. Click the Add button. The Shell Feature dialog box will be temporarily dismissed for you to select the faces that are to have the specified wall thickness. The specified wall thickness will also be applied to faces that are tangent to the selected faces. Press Enter to restore the dialog box.

4. Repeat steps 1 though 3 for faces that are to have a different wall thickness

5. To globally remove a thickness override, highlight its value and press the Delete button.

6. To remove a thickness override from selected faces, highlight its value, press the Reclaim button, and select the faces that are to have the default wall thickness restored.

7. To restore the default wall thickness on all faces, click the button labeled Reset.

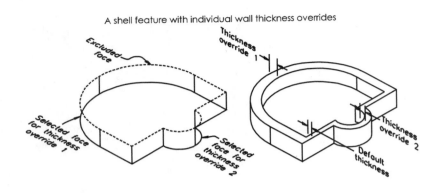

A shell feature with individual wall thickness overrides

When making a shell feature, you should give special attention to rounded edges on the part. First of all, your selection for a shell face exclusions or a wall thickness override will extend to faces tangent to the face you select. Also, when an inside offset is used, corners having radii that are smaller than the wall thickness will have a sharp-edged inside corner in the shelled feature. Sometimes, you will find it advantageous to postpone filleting operations until after a part has been shelled.

You can edit a shell feature by initiating the AMEDITFEAT command. The **Shell Feature** dialog box will be displayed with the current shell and wall parameters. If multiple wall thickness overrides are present, you can highlight a thickness value and the faces associated with that thickness will be highlighted. The Reset button in the dialog box will clear all wall thickness overrides. As with other 3D feature editing operations, you must use AMUPDATE to initiate the changes.

Exercise 3

Creating a Shell Feature

In this exercise you will create a shell feature during the construction of a part. Without the shell feature, constructing this part would be difficult; with it though, it is easy. Start a new part drawing file using the default acad.dwt English template. We will not use this part in later exercises, so its initial setup is not important.

On the XY plane of the World Coordinate System, draw the five lines and two arcs shown in Figure 3-1, and turn them into a profile feature. Constrain the two arcs to be tangent to each other and to their adjoining line. Constrain the lines to be either horizontal or vertical, whichever is appropriate. Then, add the parametric dimensions shown in Figure 3-1 to fully constrain the profile.

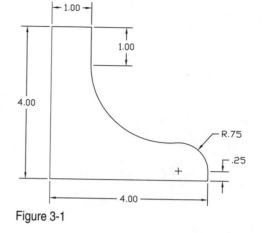

Figure 3-1

Change the viewpoint to that of an isometric-type view. Then extrude the profile to a height of 1.0 units. Your part should now look similar to the one shown in Figure 3-2. Start the AMHOLE command. Set Operation to drilled, Termination to Through, Placement to 2 Edges, and Drill Size Dia to 0.50. Click the OK button of the dialog box and place the hole as shown in Figure 3-2.

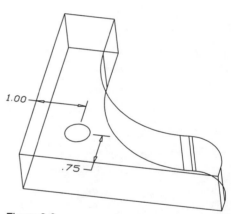

Figure 3-2

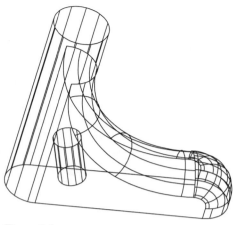

Figure 3-3

Start the AMFILLET command. Select Constant as the fillet type, set fillet Radius to 0.50, and click the OK button of the dialog box. Select the two straight edges on the left side of the part, and the two curved edges on the right side of the part as those to be rounded. Your filleted part should be similar to the one shown in Figure 3-3. (The file for this figure, though, has increased AutoCAD's **isolines** system variable from its default value of 4 to 12 to made the rounded surfaces on the part more apparent.)

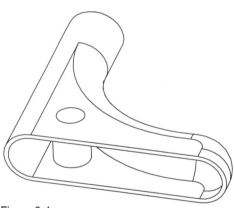

Figure 3-4

Invoke AMSHELL to bring up the **Shell Feature** dialog box. Set the offset to Inside, and the Default Thickness to 0.08. Click the Add button in the Excluded Faces cluster. The dialog box will be dismissed for you to select the faces that are to be open. Select the two end faces—one of them is round, and the other is oval-shaped. Press Enter to return to the dialog box, and click its OK button to create the shell feature. Your part should look similar to the one in Figure 3-4 when hidden line removal is on. Notice that the sides of the hole were also offset to form a tube through the part.

That finishes this exercise. Since we will not use this part in another exercise, you do not need to save it. On the CD-ROM supplied with this book, though, the part is in file md11e304.dwg.

Surfcut Features

If none of the other methods for creating 3D features are able to make the geometry you need, you will use the AMSURFCUT command. This command uses a Mechanical

Mechanical Desktop surface models can have smooth, sculpted shapes.

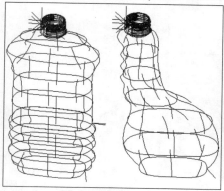

Wireframe viewing mode

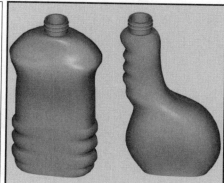

Rendered view

Desktop surface to shape an existing 3D feature. Virtually any shape can be made as a surface, including those that have continually changing radii to form smooth sculpted shapes. The price of this power is that surfaces are not parametric and that they can be difficult to work with. Almost all surfaces are based on wireframe boundary objects, which means you must visualize the surface you want to create, determine where wireframe objects must be placed to create that surface, and draw the wireframe objects in (often empty) 3D space. Unlike the wireframe objects used to create profile features, wireframe boundary objects for surfaces often twist and turn in 3D space.

Although the gap in geometry capabilities between parametric solid modeling and surface modeling decreases with each revision of Mechanical Desktop, you may sometimes need to create a part having a shape that cannot be made directly as a solid model. Then you will create a surface having the geometry you need, place it within the 3D feature you intend to shape, invoke AMSURFCUT, and specify which side of the surface is to be retained. The surface object and a portion of the 3D feature will disappear, leaving a sculpted surface on the remaining portion of the 3D feature. The resulting 3D feature,

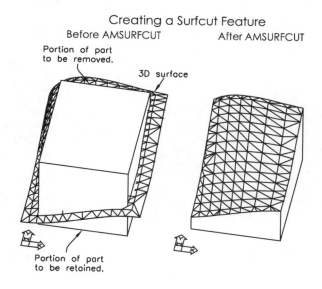

Creating a Surfcut Feature

Before AMSURFCUT

Portion of part to be removed.

3D surface

After AMSURFCUT

Portion of part to be retained.

which is often referred to as a *surfcut feature*, can subsequently be used and modified (including additional surface cuts) like any other 3D feature.

A valid surface for AMSURFCUT

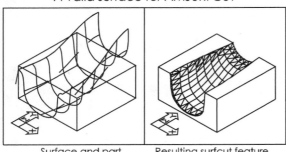

Surface and part | Resulting surfcut feature

The rules for using a surface to cut a part with AMSURFCUT are as follows.

• The surface must be a Mechanical Desktop surface. AutoCAD surfaces are not accepted.

• The surface be a single object. You cannot use two or more surfaces with a single call to AMSURFCUT.

A valid AMSURFCUT surface having multiple intersections with the part.

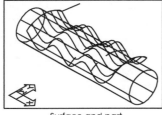

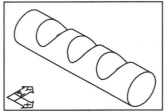

Surface and part | Resulting surfcut feature

• The surface must pass completely through the part, with the intersecting boundary between the part and the surface forming a closed loop. Multiple intersections of the surface with the part are allowed, provided a closed loop is formed with each intersection.

• The surface cannot contain a hole in the intersecting region of the part.

Invalid surfaces for AMSURFCUT

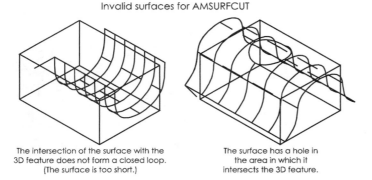

The intersection of the surface with the 3D feature does not form a closed loop. (The surface is too short.) | The surface has a hole in the area in which it intersects the 3D feature.

The AMSURFCUT command also has a mode, called *protrusion*, in which the space between the part and the surface is filled to become a 3D solid feature, while the rest of the part disappears. The surface must completely enclose a space outside the part.

Even though the surfcut feature cannot be fully dimensioned, you can control its location to some extent by tying the surface to a work point that has been constrained to the part by dimensions. Then, as the work point is moved relative

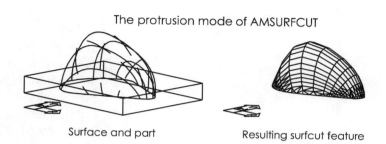

The protrusion mode of AMSURFCUT

Surface and part   Resulting surfcut feature

to the part, the surfcut feature will move with it. Furthermore, if the work point is on a work plane based on an angle or offset modifier, the surfcut feature will move as the work plane is moved.

You can also make changes to a surfcut feature through the Surfcut option of the AMEDITFEAT command. When you select this option, Mechanical Desktop will restore the surface used for the surfcut and roll back the 3D feature to its original condition.

Exercise 4

Experimenting with AMSURFCUT

This exercise will give you a hands-on feel for working with surfcut features. Begin a new Mechanical Desktop drawing using the default English template. The model you will make will not be one that you need to retain, so its initial set up is not important. Use the VPOINT command to set a view that has the direction coordinates of 1.0,-0.8,0.8. Then use the following command line input to draw a spline curve:

```
Command: SPLINE (Enter)
Specify first point or [Object]: 0,0,0.5 (Enter)
Specify next point: 0,1,0.5 (Enter)
Specify next point or [Close/Fit/Tolerance]<Start tangent>: 0,1.5,2.5 (Enter)
Specify next point or [Close/Fit/Tolerance]<Start tangent>: (Enter)
Specify start tangent: (Enter)
Specify end tangent: (Enter)
```

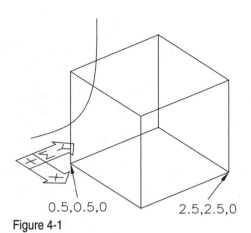

0.5,0.5,0   2.5,2.5,0

Figure 4-1

You will use this spline as the basis of a surface, but before making the surface you will make a parametric part. Use four lines to draw a 2 by 2 square, turn it into a profile, fully constrain it, and extrude it to a height of 2 units, using no draft angle. Move the resulting cube shaped part so that its base has opposite diagonal corners at the coordinates of 0.5,0.5,0 and 2.5, 2.5, 0. Your part and the spline curve should look similar to those in Figure 4-1.

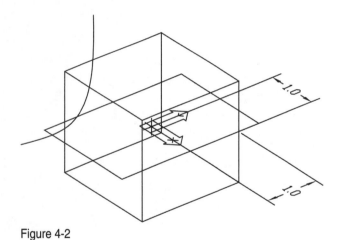

Figure 4-2

Next, create a work plane. Use the Planar Parallel and Offset modifiers with an offset distance of 1.0 units. Check the Create Sketch Plane box, and click the OK button of the Work Plane Feature dialog box. Select the lower surface of the cube as the planar face, and set the offset direction so that the work plane is inside the cube. Point the X axis of the sketch plane in the direction of the WCS X axis. Next, create a work point, and constrain it to any two edges of the 3D feature with two 1.0 linear dimensions. Your objects should look similar to those shown in Figure 4-2.

Now, use the following command line input to create a surface from the spline curve:

```
Command: AMEXTRUDESF (Enter)
Select wires to extrude: (Pick a point on the spline curve.)
Select wires to extrude: (Enter)
Define direction and length: (This is a message; not a prompt.)
Specify start point or [Viewdir/Wire/X/Y/Z]: X (Enter)
Enter length <1.0000>: 3.0 (Enter)
```

(An arrow pointing in the positive X direction will appear in the graphics area.)
```
Enter an option [Flip/Accept]<Accept>: (Enter)
Enter taper angle <0>: (Enter)
```

As shown in Figure 4-3, a surface that has the cross section shape of the spline, and passes through the part, has been created. Use the following command line input to create a surfcut feature:

```
Command: AMSURFCUT (Enter)
Type: Cut
Select surface or [Type]: (Pick a
    point on the surface.)
Select work point: (Pick the work
    point.)
Specify portion to remove [Flip/
    Accept]<Accept>: (If the blue
    arrow points in the general
    direction of the positive Y axis
    enter the letter F. Otherwise,
    press the Enter key.)
Specify portion to remove [Flip/
    Accept]<Accept>: (Enter)
```

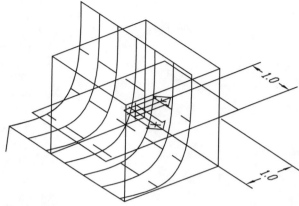

Figure 4-3

Your surfcut feature should look like the one in Figure 4-4. Notice that the surface was consumed when the surfcut was created. Also, Mechanical Desktop turned the visibility of the work point off.

Now invoke AMEDITFEAT, select the work plane. and change its offset dimension to move to move the work plane up or down to verify that the surfcut surface moves with it. Also, move the work point in the Y axis direction, through its dimensions, to verify that the surfcut surface is connected to the work point. You must turn the work point's visibility on, to access its dimensions, and you must invoke AMUPDATE to implement the changes you make.

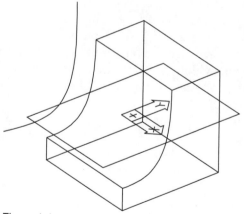

Figure 4-4

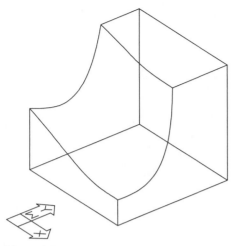

Figure 4-5

Next, invoke the AMEDITFEAT command, and experiment with its Surfcut option. This option will restore the surface used to make the surfcut. You can then use AutoCAD's STRETCH command to change the shape of the surface. When you update the 3D feature, the shape of the surfcut will conform to the new shape of the surface. Figure 4-5 shows one of many possible results.

That finishes this exercise. You do not need to save its file. On the CD-ROM that accompanies this book, though, the surfcut feature is in file md11e404.dwg.

Features Related to Molding and Casting Processes

Four of Mechanical Desktop's placed features are especially useful for designing parts that are to be manufactured by molding, casting, or forging processes, as well for designing the molds and dies that are used by these processes. Often the molds and dies have two sections, with the separation between the two sections being referred to as the *parting line*. Since the part must be pulled away from the parting line, it is often given a slight taper, which is called *face draft*, on both sides of the parting line. The four Mechanical Desktop commands we will discuss in this section are for creating face drafts and parting lines.

Creating Face Drafts

AMFACEDRAFT inclines, or tapers, the faces of a feature relative to the *normal* of a base plane. (The normal of a plane is the direction that is perpendicular to the plane.) Unlike the draft angles of the AMEXTRUDE, AMREVOLVE, and AMSWEEP commands, AMFACEDRAFT can set the draft angle of a 3D feature on a face by face basis. It also gives you more control over

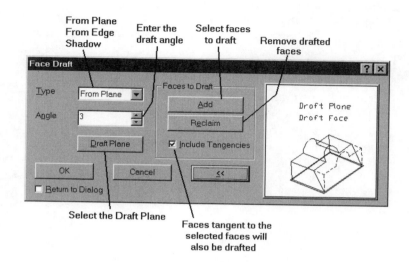

how the draft angle is based, and it allows you to add a draft angle to surfcut features.

AMFACEDRAFT displays a dialog box titled **Face Draft** for you to enter the parameters of the face draft feature. This dialog box gives you a choice of three different types of face drafts—From Plane, From Edge, and Shadow. The steps to create a From Plane face draft feature, which is the type you will most often use, are:

1. Click the Draft Plane button in the dialog box. The dialog box will be temporarily dismissed and a command line prompt will ask you to select one plane on the 3D feature to serve as the base of the draft angle. This plane can be either the planar face of a 3D feature or a work plane. As soon as you specify a plane, Mechanical Desktop will display the *direction arrow icon* on the plane. This icon points in the direction in which material will be removed when the face draft is created. As this icon is displayed, a command line prompt will allow you to switch the direction. When you have selected the face and the draft direction, press Enter to return to the **Face Draft** dialog box.

Note: You can change the relative size of the direction arrow icon by changing the value of Desktop Symbol Size in the Preferences tab of the Desktop Options dialog box displayed when the AMOPTIONS command is invoked.

2. In the **Face Draft** dialog box, select From Plane as the face draft type.

3. Enter the draft angle. This angle is measured from the normal of the selected draft plane to the inclined face. If the face is already inclined (such as a face on a extrusion having a draft angle will have), the draft angle is added to the existing angle.

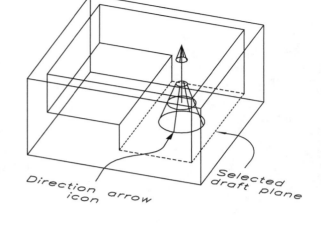

Direction arrow icon

Selected draft plane

4. Click the Add button of the dialog box. The dialog box will disappear to allow you to select the faces that are be drafted. The selected faces must be linear in the face draft direction established in step 1. Press the Enter key to end the selection and return to the dialog box. If you change your mind as to which faces are to be drafted, press the Reclaim button. The dialog box will disappear again, and all faces having a draft angle will be highlighted. Select the faces that are to have the draft angle removed, and press Enter to end the selection.

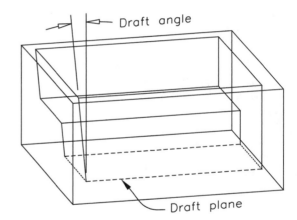

Draft angle

Draft plane

5. If Include Tangencies is checked, faces tangent to a selected face will also be drafted. Click the OK button of the dialog box to create the face drafts. The selected faces will become inclined to the draft plane, and a face draft feature icon will appear in the desktop browser.

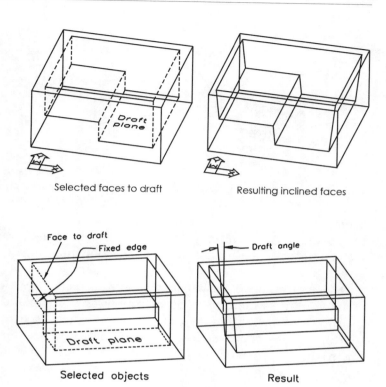

Selected faces to draft

Resulting inclined faces

From Edge face drafts are created in the same way, but after selecting the draft faces you will be asked to also select the edges that are to be fixed. Each face will pivot about their specified fixed edge. If the fixed edge is on the draft plane, there is no difference between a From Plane and a From Edge face draft.

Selected objects

Result

From Edge face drafts

Shadow face drafts are applicable only when the face to be drafted has a cylindrical, cone, or hemispherical shape. Material is added to make a linear surface between the draft plane and the drafted face. This linear surface is tangent to the draft face. and its angle to the normal of the draft plane is equal to the specified draft angle.

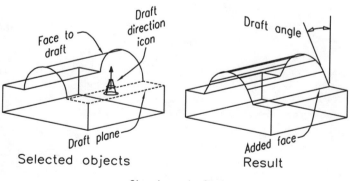

Selected objects

Result

Shadow draft

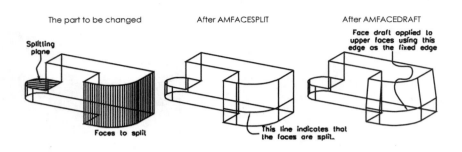

The part to be changed

Splitting plane

Foces to split

After AMFACESPLIT

This line indicates that the faces are split.

After AMFACEDRAFT

Face draft applied to upper faces using this edge as the fixed edge

Creating Faces

Sometimes the existing faces are not sufficient to create the drafts needed by a part that is to be molded or cast. You can create additional faces through the AMFACESPLIT command, which can then be given draft angles through AMFACEDRAFT. AMFACESPLIT, which operates from command line prompts, divides each selected face into two faces by projecting either wireframe objects or a plane onto the face. Whether you use wireframe objects or a plane will depend on the geometry of the part, as well as on your intentions for the geometry of the resulting faces.

The figure above shows an example of using AMFACESPLIT to split faces with a plane. The faces that are to be split along with the plane that is to be used to split them are shown on the left. In the center, the three faces have been split by the projection of the splitting plane's edge; the line across each face is an indication that they have been split. The part after AMFACEDRAFT has been used to give the top three faces a draft angle is shown on the right; the edge between the faces was used as the fixed edge of the draft angle.

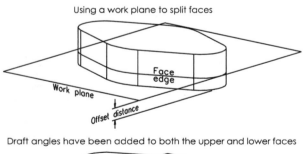

Using a work plane to split faces

Face edge

Work plane

Offset distance

Draft angles have been added to both the upper and lower faces

While this example used the planar face of a feature as a splitting plane, you can also use a work plane, as shown in the upper part of the next figure. The work plane has been positioned with Planar Parallel and Offset modifiers from the bottom face of the part. Then AMFAC-ESPLIT was used to create face edges completely around the part at its intersection with the work plane.

When you select faces that are to be divided by AMFACESPLIT, remember that all faces tangent to the selected face will be selected as well. Thus, only one of the vertical faces in the part shown in the previous figure needs to be selected. Once a face has been selected, though, you can remove it, even if it is tangent to faces that are to be split. The lower part of the previous figure shows the part after AMFACEDRAFT has been used to add draft angles to both the upper and lower faces, using the work plane as the draft plane. If you change the work plane's offset distance, the face edges will move accordingly.

Creating a split face having an edge that is not linear or is crooked can be done by projecting wireframe objects, rather than planes, onto the face with AMFACESPLIT. The wireframe objects are ordinary lines and arcs that have been transformed into a Mechanical Desktop feature called a *Splitline* through the AMSPLITLINE command. Splitlines are similar to 2D path sketches (made with AM2DPATH), in that they are drawn on the current sketch plane and they are to be constrained and dimensioned. They will always be open, but unlike path sketches, they do not have a start point.

An example illustrating how a splitline can be used to make face drafts on the part shown in Figure 11-1 is given in the next few paragraphs. This part models a blank for a wrench that is to be manufactured by forging.

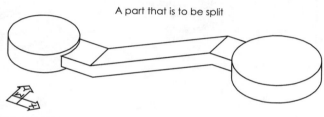

A part that is to be split

Figure 11-1

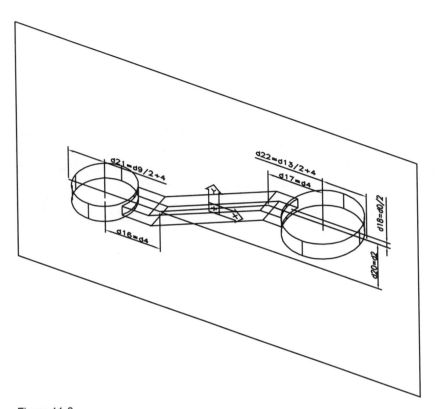

Figure 11-2

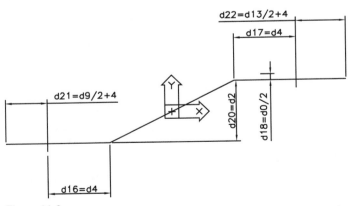

Figure 11-3

Figure 11-2 shows how a work plane and a sketch plane has been positioned in the middle of the part. On the sketch plane, three lines have been drawn, turned into a split-line by the AMSPLITLINE command, and fully constrained inter-nally as well as to the part. You will have to look closely in this figure to see the splitline. Notice that both of its ends extend beyond the part. AMFAC-ESPLIT requires that splitlines extend beyond the bound-aries of the faces they are to split.

Figure 11-3 shows just the splitline and its asso-ciated dimensions from a plan view of the sketch plane. The part itself has been frozen so that you can better see the splitline. All of its dimensions have been tied to the dimensions of the part through equations, so that any changes to the part will cause the splitline to change also.

Once the splitline has been constrained, splitting the faces on the part is easy. You invoke AMFAC-ESPLIT, select its Project option, and specify the faces that are to be split. The splitline will be consumed during the operation. Figure

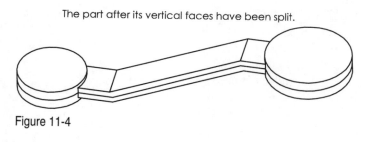

The part after its vertical faces have been split.

Figure 11-4

11-4 show the part with all of its vertical faces split. Hidden objects have been removed in this figure, and the work plane's visibility has been turned off.

Figure 11-5 shows a side view of the part after AMFACEDRAFT has created draft angles on all of the vertical faces. The interior face edges were used as a fixed edge for the draft angles. This part is in file md_1145.dwg on the CD-ROM that comes with

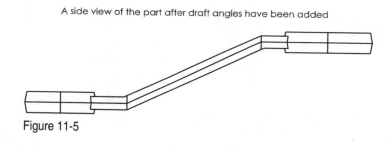

A side view of the part after draft angles have been added

Figure 11-5

this book. You will probably want to retrieve and open the file. You can use AMREPLAY (which is described in Chapter 13) to see the steps taken in constructing the part, and you can finish the part by adding hexagonal (or any other shape you desire) cutouts to the wrench ends.

Splitting Parts

Occasionally, especially when you are designing a mold or die that is to be used for manufacturing some item, you will want to split a part into two individual pieces. One piece will be for making one side of the mold or die, and the other piece will be used for the other side. While you could make these two pieces as two separate parts from the beginning, you will generally prefer to make them as one part and then split it into two parts with the AMPARTSPLIT command.

AMPARTSPLIT offers three command line options for specifying the object that is to be used to slice through the part.

1. You can use a work plane to divide the part, as shown in the adjacent figure. In this figure, the two parts have been moved away from each other. The original work plane remains with one part, and a new work plane is created for the other part.

2. You can use a planar face on a 3D feature to split the part.

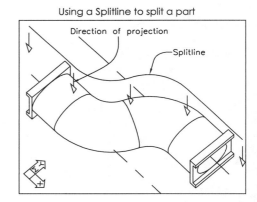

Using a Work Plane to split a part
(The two parts have been moved away from each other.)

3. You can use a splitline to slice through the part, as shown in the next two figures. The splitline is projected perpendicularly from its sketch plane through the part, and is then consumed. While the splitline in the first of the two figures is outside the part that is to be split (so that it can be easily seen in the figure), it would have worked just as well if it were in the center of the part.

Using a Splitline to split a part

Direction of projection

Splitline

Once you have specified the object that is to split the part, you will be asked to specify which side of the slice represents the original part and to name the new part. If you are working in Mechanical Desktop's single part environment, the new part will be called a toolbody. Initially the two parts will remain next to each other, but you can move them apart, as shown in the previous figures.

After AMPARTSPLIT
(The two parts have been moved away from each other.)

CHAPTER 12

3D Features from 3D Features

In its menus and toolbars, Mechanical Desktop groups most of the features we will discuss in this chapter with the placed features. But, unlike the placed features described in Chapter 11, these do not just modify existing features; they create new features from existing features.

This chapter covers the following topics.

- Explains how to make copies of existing features.

- Shows how to make copies of parts. The copy can be a mirror image of the original part, and you can choose to keep or discard the original part.

- Describes how to make multiple copies of a feature that are arranged in rectangular, circular, or spiral patterns.

- Tells you how to use Boolean operations as you combine two parts to make a single part.

Key Terms

Before discussing the commands that make features from existing parts and features, we will define some terms that often appear in their prompts, messages, and dialog boxes.

Part	A basic Mechanical Desktop object that represents a single real-world object that is typically manufactured as a single unit. If you want to construct more than one part within a Mechanical Desktop drawing file, invoke the AMNEW command, and begin creating the features of that part.
Toolbody	A part that you intend to combine with another part. The command that combines parts, AMCOMBINE, is discussed later in this chapter. When you are working within Mechanical Desktop's single part environment, any new part you start will have a name such as TOOLBODY1_1, rather than PART2_1.
Active Part	While you can have as many parts (and toolbodies) as you like within a file, you are allowed to work on just one of them at a time. The part you can work on is called the *active part*. The other parts are visible, but Mechanical Desktop does not recognize them for most operations. You cannot, for example, edit or add features to them. To have a part become the active part, invoke AMACTIVATE and select the part.
Definition	The Mechanical Desktop geometry and attribute data of a part.
Instance	The single occurrence of a part. Multiple instances of a part definition are allowed. When more than one instance exists, all of the instances are based on the same definition, and therefore, changes to one instance affects them all.

Making Copies

Copies of Features

You can make copies of most dependent 3D features. The command that does this is AMCOPYFEAT. The capabilities of this command are:

- You can copy a feature from an inactive part to the active part.
- The copy can be a mirror image of the original feature.
- You can have the dimensions of the copy change whenever the dimensions of the original are changed.

The restrictions of the command are:

- Only one feature can be selected with each use of AMCOPYFEAT.
- The location of the copy is always on the current sketch plane.
- Features having profiles that are closed by a feature edge cannot be copied.

- Sketched features that are dependent on the selected feature will not be included in the copy.

- Placed features on the selected feature will be copied, provided they are entirely dependent on the selected feature. Thus, fillets of edges on the selected feature will be included in the copy, but fillets of edges between the selected feature and another feature will not be included.

- You cannot copy the base feature.

- Features having Plane, Face, Extended Face, Next, or From-To terminations cannot be copied.

- You cannot copy features made from 3D paths.

- Lofted features cannot be copied.

- Except for hole features, placed feature types cannot be copied.

When you initiate AMCOPY-FEAT, a command line prompt will ask you to select the feature to be copied. This feature can be on an inactive part. As soon as you have identified the feature that is to be copied, the following command line message and prompt will be displayed:

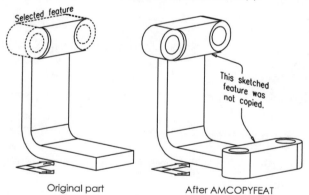

Sketched features dependent to the feature to be copied will not be included in the copy.

Selected feature

This sketched feature was not copied.

Original part   After AMCOPYFEAT

```
(Parameters = Independent)
Specify location on the active part
   or [Parameters]: (Enter a P or
   specify a point)
```

The parameters, which can be either independent or dependent, control how values in the dimensions of the copy are expressed. When they are independent, each dimension on the copy assumes the value of the corresponding dimension of the original feature. Conversely, when the parameters are dependent, each dimension of the copy assumes the dimension name of the original feature. Suppose, for instance, you copy a hole feature that has a diameter of 1.75 units and a dimension name of d8 for the diameter. If you use independent copy parameters, the diameter dimension of the copy will be 1.75. On the other hand, if you use dependent copy parameters, the diameter dimension will be d8. The message above the command line prompt shows the parameter type currently in effect. You can switch to the other type by entering the letter p.

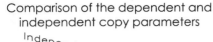

Comparison of the dependent and
independent copy parameters

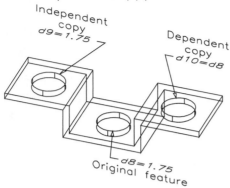

When you specify a point for the location of the copy, Mechanical Desktop will center an image of the feature on that point and issue the command line prompt:

```
(Parameters = Independent)
Specify location on the active part or
[Parameters/Rotate/Flip]: (Enter an option,
specify a point, or press Enter.)
```

Depending on the status of the Parameter option, the message preceding the prompt may be (Parameters = Dependent). When the feature being copied is from another part, the dimension parameters will always be independent, and references to them will not be included in the command line prompts and messages. Also, if the feature to be copied is a hole (made with the AMHOLE command), the Rotate and Flip options will not be offered. This prompt repeats until the Enter key is pressed to end the command with the copy in the specified location and condition. The effects of the options are:

Parameters   Displays a prompt for switching the treatment of dimension values on the copy.

Rotate   The image will rotate 90 degrees counterclockwise on the sketch plane.

Flip   The image will flip to become a mirror image of the original feature.

Select location   The center of the feature's image will move to the selected point.

The copy will be placed on the current sketch plane. It is not important to precisely position the copy, since you will use dimensions and, sometimes, geometric constraints to fix its location relative to other features. Often, you will even deliberately place the copy away from its intended position so that you can better see and select objects as you add dimensions and constrains. You will add these dimensions and constraints with the Sketch option of the AMEDITFEAT command.

The internal dimensions and constraints of the feature will be retained by the copy. You can change any of the internal dimensions, even if the dependent parameters setting was used during the copy. When a hole feature has been copied, Mechanical Desktop will include a work point with the copy.

Exercise 1

Copying a Feature

Retrieve file md12e101.dwg from the CD-ROM that comes with this book, and open it. In this exercise, you will make a copy of the slot in this sheet metal part. You will place the copy on the vertical section of the part. Therefore, your first step will be to move the sketch plane to the front of the vertical section, with the X axis of the sketch place pointed in the WCS X axis direction, as shown in Figure 1-1.

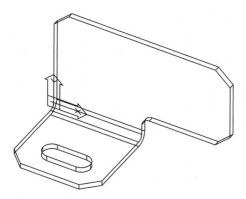

Figure 1-1

Start the AMCOPYFEAT command and select the slot as the feature to be copied. Set the copy's parameters to Dependent, pick a point somewhere on the right half of the vertical section, and rotate the image one time so that its location and orientation are similar to that in Figure 1-2.

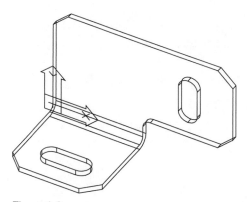

Figure 1-2

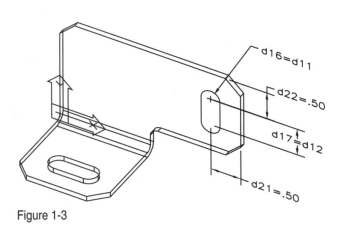

Figure 1-3

Once the copy is in its approximate location, use AMEDIT-FEAT to edit the sketch of the copy. The dimensions for the radius the arcs and their distance apart have been retained, but the dimensions tying the sketch to the 3D feature have not; you must add them manually. If you set the display of dimensions to the equation mode, the dimension for the radius of the arcs will be shown as d16=d11 and the dimension for the distance between their centers will be d17=d12. Add the two 0.50 linear dimensions shown in Figure 1-3 to fully constrain the sketch.

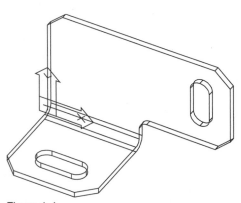

Figure 1-4

When you update the part, your model should look similar to the one in Figure 1-4. This finishes the exercise. On the accompanying CD-ROM, the model with the copied slot is in file md12e104.dwg. We will do nothing further with this model.

Copies of Parts

Copies of Part Definitions

Most of the time, you will need copies of a part only when you are making an assembly (Assemblies are discussed in Chapters 17–20 of this book). Occasionally, though, you may need a copy of an entire part, rather than a feature, during the construction of a single part; perhaps for instance, for use with the AMCOMBINE command. In Mechanical Desktop's single part environment, you can only copy toolbodies—you cannot copy the base part,

Copies of a part are made through the AMCATALOG command. When you invoke AMCATALOG, a dialog box titled Part Catalog will be displayed when the drawing file is in Mechanical Desktop's single part environment, and one titled Assembly Catalog will be displayed in the assembly environment. The contents of these two dialog boxes are virtually identical.

The steps to copy a part are:

1. Select the All tab of the dialog box..

2. In the right-hand list box (It will be labeled Local Assembly Definitions in the Assembly Catalog dialog box, and Local Toolbody Definitions in the Part Catalog dialog box.) right-click the name of the part (or toolbody) you want to copy. A pop-up menu will be displayed, in which you will select the Copy Definition option.

3. A dialog box titled Copy Definition will appear. Enter the name of the new part (or toolbody) in this dialog box, and click OK.

4. An image of the copy will appear on the screen and a command line prompt will instruct you to select an insertion point. A copy of the part will be centered on the point you select, and you will be prompted to select another insertion point. Press the Enter key to end the command.

If you were to select another insertion point, an instance of the copy would be inserted. The copies will be linked together, so that changes made in one will be made in the other as well. You can also create copies of parts with the Instance option of the pop-up menu. These copies will share the same data base as the original part, and any changes made in one instance of the part will be made in the other instance as well.

Mirror Image Copies

You can make a mirror image copy of a part with the AMMIRROR command. This can be useful, when coupled with AMCOMBINE, in creating a part that is symmetrical. Either an existing planar face or a line can be used to establish the mirroring plane. The command issues the following command line prompts:

```
Select part to mirror: (Pick a point on a part.)
Select a planar face to mirror about or [Line]: (Pick a point on a planar face or enter L)
```

If you select a planar face, it will used as the mirror plane. If you choose the Line option, you will be prompted to specify the endpoints of a line on the current sketch plane. The mirror plane will be perpendicular to the sketch plane, with this line representing one edge of the mirror. Once you have established the mirror plane, the following prompt will be displayed:

```
Enter an option [Create new part/Replace instances] <Create new part>: (Press Enter, or
    enter a R)
```

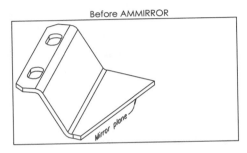

Before AMMIRROR

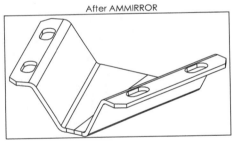

After AMMIRROR

The Create new part option leaves the original part as it is and creates a new part from its mirror image. You will be prompted from the command line to enter a name for the new part. The Replace instances option deletes the original part and uses its name for the new, mirror image part. AMMIRROR works the same in both the assembly and part environments, except that if you choose to create a new part from the mirror image, it will called a toolbody, rather than a part.

Pattern Features

A pattern feature is a set of copies of one or more features that are in a rectangular, polar, or axial arrangement. Copies in a rectangular pattern are arranged in rows and columns. Those of a polar pattern are arranged in a circle or arc, and those of an axial pattern are distributed around and along an axis. Pattern features came into existence in Mechanical Desktop Release 5, when array features became pattern features and the AMARRAY command was replaced by AMPATTERN. Also, the AMARRAY command could not make arrays having an axial arrangement.

The relationships between the original members of a pattern feature and the copies (Or, as Mechanical Desktop calls them, the instances of the pattern.) are:

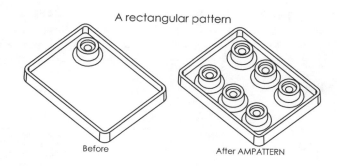

A rectangular pattern

Before   After AMPATTERN

- Modifications made to the size and shape of the original pattern members, such as changes to a profile sketch or to the radius of a fillet, will be made in all members of the pattern. You cannot, however, edit the size and shape of copied members of the pattern. Hence, if a fillet is included in a pattern, you cannot change the radius of that fillet on a copy member of the pattern.

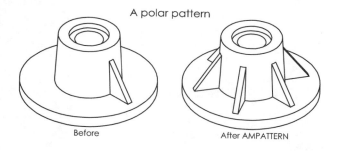

A polar pattern

Before   After AMPATTERN

- Feature additions to members of a pattern, either the original or the copied members, do not affect other members. For instance, if you created a pattern from a round hole and then chamfered the edge of the hole of either the original or a copy member of the pattern, the other members would not be chamfered.

- If an original member of a pattern is deleted, all copy members will be deleted as well. If you delete a single copy member of a pattern, the other copy members will also be deleted, but the original member of the pattern is not affected. (The deletion of features is discussed in Chapter 13.)

You can make a pattern feature from a pattern feature. Suppose, for example, a sheet metal part you are designing has a large

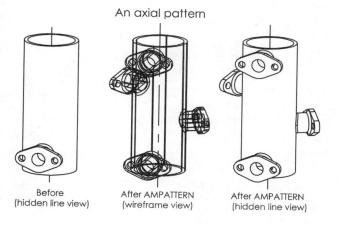

An axial pattern

Before   After AMPATTERN   After AMPATTERN
(hidden line view)   (wireframe view)   (hidden line view)

round hole with a keyway, and evenly spaced around that hole are four small holes for fasteners. The part is to have six sets of these holes arranged in two columns of three sets. You could make just one of the small holes, and then make a polar pattern of it around the large hole. Then you could make a rectangular pattern from the large hole and the polar pattern.

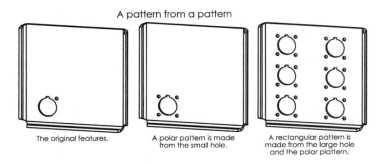

A pattern from a pattern

The original features.

A polar pattern is made from the small hole.

A rectangular pattern is made from the large hole and the polar plattern.

AMPATTERN uses a dialog box for you to enter the parameters of the pattern feature. This dialog box has a tab labeled Pattern Control whose contents vary according to the type of pattern you are creating. The options that the versions of this tab have in common are as follows.

Type   Use this list box to switch from one pattern type—rectangular, polar, or axial—to another.

Suppress Instance   This option allows you to control the display of individual pattern members, or instances. The dialog box will temporarily be dismissed and you will be prompted from the command line to select the pattern instances to suppress. The result is as if the selected instances were deleted; leaving empty spaces in the pattern. The instances are still there, though, and you can unsuppress them with this same option.

Preview   By default, Mechanical Desktop displays the results of the current pattern parameters on the part. For instance, as you specify the number of instances and their spacing in each row and column of a rectangular pattern, the instances are displayed on the part in the same color as AutoCAD's grips. When you select the small button to the right of the Preview button, a menu offering two options—True Preview and Dynamic Preview—is displayed. These options are toggles, with a check mark by their name indicating they are on.

When *True Preview* is on, all of the features of all instances are shown in their entirety in the preview to give a complete picture of the pattern. When True Preview is off, the outline of the instances is depicted in true size, but their edges and details are not shown. This setting controls the contents of the Mechanical Desktop **amtruepat** system variable.

Dynamic Preview controls whether or not preview images depicting the current pattern settings are displayed. The preview images are displayed when Dynamic Preview is on, and they are not displayed when Dynamic Preview is off. The value of Mechanical Desktop's **amdynpat** system variable is controlled by this option.

Selecting Features to Pattern

When you start AMPATTERN from the command line, the graphic area shortcut menus, or the screen pulldown menus, you will be prompted from the command line to select the features that are to be patterned. You can select as many features as you like. Press the Enter key when you have finished selecting features.

A more convenient way to select features and start AMPATTERN is from the Desktop Browser. Select the names of the features that are to be included in the pattern from the Browser as you hold down your keyboard's Ctrl key. Then right-click to display a shortcut menu; select Pattern and lastly select one of the three pattern feature types.

You can select multiple features for a pattern from the Desktop Browser by holding down the Ctrl key while making selections. Right-click to display a shortcut menu with options for creating one of the three types of pattern features.

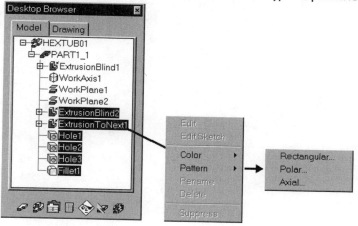

Limitations on feature types for patterns are:

- Fillet and chamfer features cannot be patterned by themselves, but they can be part of a selection set.

- Face drafts cannot be patterned. If a face draft is part of a feature that is patterned, it will not be included in the pattern.

- Shell features cannot be patterned.

- Features that use Split or Intersect as an operation type cannot be patterned.

- Work features cannot be patterned.

- Features using face and plane terminations are accepted, but they sometimes cause problems; especially in polar and axial patterns.

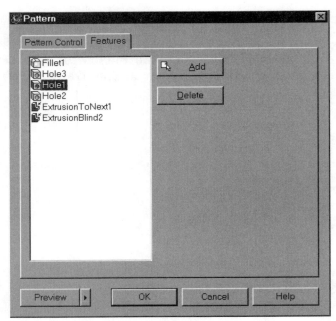

You can modify the pattern selection set from the Features tab of the **Pattern** dialog box that AMPATTERN displays. The names of all of the features that are currently selected are displayed in a list box. Click the Add button to add features to the selection set. The dialog box will temporarily disappear for you to select features from the graphics area; you cannot use the Browser to add features. To remove a feature, click on its name in the Features tab's list box and click the Delete button.

Rectangular Patterns

In rectangular patterns, the copies of the selected features are arranged on a plane in rows and columns, with the default distribution plane and directions being set by the current location and orientation of the sketch plane. The space between columns is in the X direction, while the space between rows is in the Y direction.

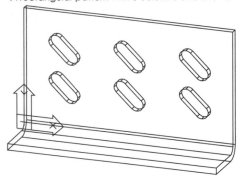

A rectangular pattern with 3 columns and 2 rows.

Use the Pattern Control tab for rectangular patterns of the **Pattern** dialog box to establish the number of pattern instances and their orientation. If the sketch plane is not located properly for the pattern you intend to create, select the Plane Orientation option. In effect, this option moves the sketch plane, and

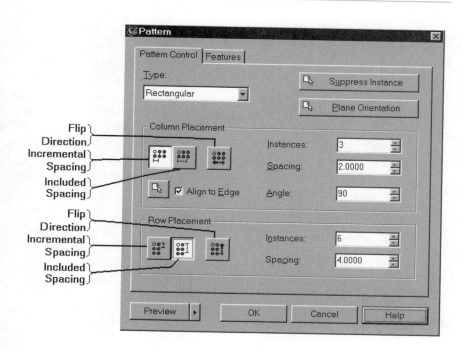

it works very much like the AMSKPLN command. The dialog box will temporarily disappear, and command line prompts similar to those AMSKPLN uses will lead you through the steps to select a distribution plane and the direction of the X axis on that plane.

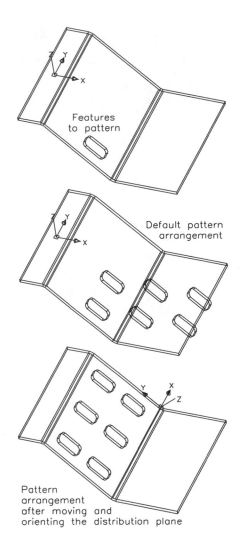

Features to pattern

Default pattern arrangement

Pattern arrangement after moving and orienting the distribution plane

Enter the pattern's number of row and column instances, along with their spacing, in the edit boxes that are provided. The selected features count as a pattern instance, so an entry of 1 for a row or column will make no copies in that direction. When you select the Incremental Spacing button, spacing represents the distance between each pattern instance, and when you select the Included Spacing button, spacing represents the distance between the first and last instance of the row or column. By default, the pattern grows in the positive X and Y direction, but you can reverse the direction by selecting the Flip Direction button for rows or columns.

Rows are always in the X axis direction, and by default columns are perpendicular (90 degrees) to the rows. However, when you select the Align to Edge check box and click the button to its left, the dialog box will be dismissed for you to select an edge that establishes the angle between rows and columns. You can also enter the angle between columns and rows in the Angle edit box.

Polar Patterns

In polar patterns the copies of the selected features are revolved about an axis for a full or partial circular distribution.

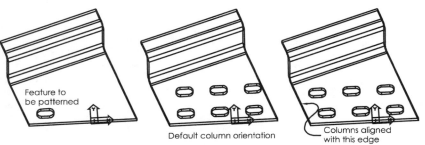

Feature to be patterned

Default column orientation

Columns aligned with this edge

Unless you start AMPATTERN from the command line, you will be asked from the command line to select the rotation axis before the **Pattern** dialog box appears. You can select a work point, a work axis, or a cylindrical face. When a work point is used as a center, the rotation axis is through the work point and perpendicular to the work point's sketch plane. Also,

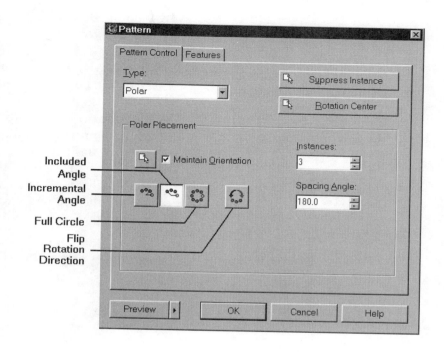

the work point will be consumed when the pattern is created. Once the Pattern dialog box is displayed, you can click Rotation Center to select or re-select the rotation axis.

Enter the total number of members that the pattern is to have in the edit box labeled Instances. The selected features count as one member, or instance, of the pattern. The edit box labeled Spacing Angle is for

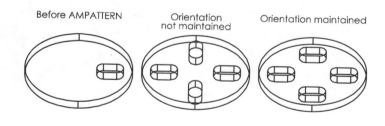

setting the rotation range of the pattern. Its value represents the angle between each instance when the Incremental Angle button is depressed. When the Included Angle button is selected, the instances will be evenly spaced through the angle specified in the Angle edit box. You can reverse the current rotation direction by clicking the Flip Rotation Direction button. The value in the Angle edit box should be less than 360 degrees; otherwise, the first and last instances will overlap or will occupy the same space. When the Full Circle button is depressed, the Spacing Angle edit box is disabled and the instances will be evenly spaced through a full 360 degree circle.

A polar pattern with 6 members

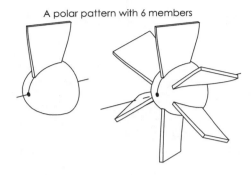

By default, the copies are rotated so that their orientation to the center of the pattern is the same as that of the original member. However, when the Maintain Orientation check box is selected, the copies will maintain the X and Y axes orientation of the original pattern member. This option requires a work point to serve as a reference point in maintaining a constant distance from the pattern center. Click the button to the left of the check box to select the work point. Usually you will have placed this work point near the geometric center of the feature to be patterned.

Axial Patterns

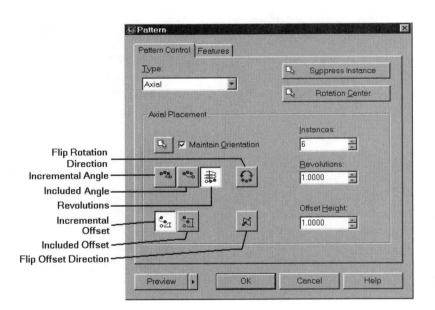

Similar to polar patterns, axial patterns revolve the copies about an axis; unlike polar patterns, though, axial patterns also spread the copies along the axis. Selecting the axis is the same as it is for polar patterns. In the **Pattern** dialog box you will enter the number of pattern members in the Instances edit box. Click one of the dialog box's radio buttons to specify whether the revolution of the instances about the axis is in terms of the revolution angle or the number of revolutions. You can also choose between having the number of degrees represent the angle between instances (incremental) or the cumulative (included) angle. An included angle of 360 degrees is equivalent to 1 revolution, 540 degrees is 1.5 revolutions, and so forth. Select the Flip Rotation Direction button to switch the current rotation direction.

The spacing of the pattern instances along the axis is set by the value you enter in the Offset Height edit box. Select the Incremental Offset radio button to specify that this value is the distance between instances, or select the Included Offset button to have the offset value represent the distance between the first and last instance. You must enter a value greater than zero for the offset height. You can reverse the offset direction by selecting the Flip Offset Direction button.

As the instances rotate about the axis, they revolve to keep their orientation with the axis the same as that of the base features. Select the Maintain Orientation check box to prevent the instances from revolving. Then click the button to the left to select a work point that is to serve as an orientation reference point.

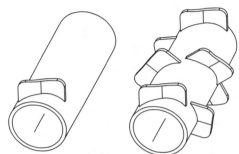

A two rotation axial pattern with 8 members

Editing Pattern Features

Each pattern feature is listed in the Desktop Browser with a name such as Rectangular Pattern3 or Polar Pattern1. Use the AMEDITFEAT command to edit a pattern. As in editing other features, the most conveniently way to initiate this command is by double-clicking the pattern's name in the Browser. This command displays the `Pattern` dialog box containing the settings of the pattern feature. You can change such things as the number of instances, their spacing, whether angles and distances represent incremental or included spacing, and you can flip directions. You can also add or remove features in the base pattern member by opening the dialog box's Features tab, and selecting the Add or Delete button. You cannot, however, add a feature that was created after the pattern.

As you would surmise, you cannot change from one pattern type to another. Also, you cannot change the pattern distribution plane in rectangular patterns, the axis of polar and axial patterns, or the rotational orientation of instances in polar and axial patterns. You must use AMUPDATE before any changes you have made to a pattern are incorporated.

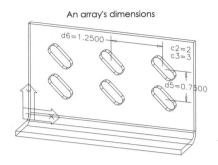

An array's dimensions

Array features created in versions of Mechanical Desktop earlier than Release 5 are not converted to patterns when the files they are in are opened in Release 5. In the Browser the arrays have names such as RectArray1 and PolarArray1. Editing these arrays works differently than it does for patterns. Instead of restoring a dialog box, all of the dimensions related to the array are displayed on the feature. The spacing between members of a rectangular array is displayed as linear dimensions. The names, or tags, of these dimensions begin with a lower case letter d, as do those for other parametric dimensions. The number of array elements is always displayed in equation form, and their dimension names begin with a lower case letter c. You can change the value of both the spacing dimensions and the row/column quantities.

The number of elements in a polar array is also displayed in equation form, with a name beginning with a lower case letter c, during editing operations. The included or incremental angle of the array will be displayed as an angular dimension. No angle will be displayed for a Full Circle array. You cannot change the type of angle specified for the array. For example, you cannot change an Included Angle array to a Full Circle array.

You can also release an instance from an array. The released array instance becomes a separate 3D feature, and its name will be listed in the Desktop Browser. The internal dimensions and constraints of the original member of the array will be incorporated in the new feature, but you must manually add any constraints and dimensions needed to tie the feature to external objects. If the array is based on a hole feature that was positioned on a work point, a work point is automatically created for the independent array instance. To release an array instance, select Independent Array Instance from the list of options in the command line version of AMEDITFEAT. You can also initiate this option by selecting Independent Instance from the right-click pop-up menu of the Browser. This option will ask you to select one array member, or instance. You cannot select the original member of the array. If both arrays and patterns are present in a file, this option is offered in the command line version of AMEDITFEAT, but you cannot release an instance from a pattern.

Exercise 2

Creating a Polar Pattern

In this exercise you will complete the model of
a pulley you worked on in Chapter 8. You created the pulley as a revolved feature in Exercise
2 of Chapter 8, and you added two rib features
to the model in Exercise 5 of Chapter 8. Open
your file of that model, or else retrieve and open
file md08503.dwg from the CD-ROM supplied
with this book. Zoom in close to the center of

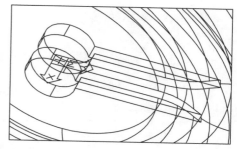

Figure 2-1

the pulley so that you are able to clearly see the edges of the rib features and the hub of
the pulley, as shown in Figure 2-1. The VPOINT rotation angles in this figure's view is 20
degrees in the XY plane from the X axis, and 45 degrees from the XY plane.

Start the AMFILLET command, and set the
fillet type to Constant and Radius to 0.05. Pick
the circular base of both hubs as the edges to
fillet. When hidden line removal is on, your
model should now be similar to the one in Figure 2-2.

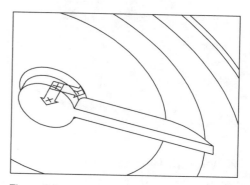

Figure 2-2

Start AMFILLET again. Leave the fillet type
to Constant and Radius at 0.05. Pick the edges
of the ribs that adjoin the hub. These edges
have a curve and there are two of them on each
rib. Now, when hidden line removal is on your
model should look similar to one shown in Figure 2-3. Notice that the edges between the hub
and the ribs is also filleted.

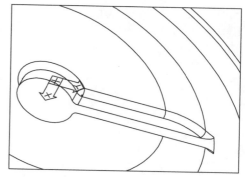

Figure 2-3

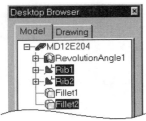

Figure 2-4

The Desktop Browser will list two fillet features. The first one you made, around the base of the hub is Fillet1; and the ones on the base of the ribs is Fillet2. As you hold down the Ctrl key, click on Fillet2's name in the Browser, and on the names of the two ribs. The names will be highlighted as shown in Figure 2-4.

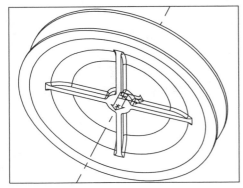

Figure 2-5

Right-click on one of the highlighted feature names in the Browser to display its shortcut menu; select Pattern, and then Polar. A command line prompt will ask you to specify the pattern's rotational center. Pick a point anywhere on the hub. The **Pattern** dialog box will appear. Click the Full Circle button, and set the number of instances to 4. Verify that the Maintain Orientation check box is cleared. Click the OK button to dismiss the dialog box and create the polar pattern.

After a few seconds, the pattern feature will appear on the part. Figure 2-5 shows the finished version of the part when hidden line removal is on. We will not do any further work on the model. You, though, may want to add more features to the pulley; perhaps a hole with a keyway through the hub and weight reducing holes between the ribs. You are acquainted with all of the commands needed to make such features. On the CD-ROM that accompanies this book, the finished part is in file md12e205.dwg.

Combining Parts

Boolean Operations

In non-parametric solid modelers, such as the one that is part of AutoCAD, complex models are typically constructed by combining basic geometric shapes through Boolean operations. The three Boolean operations are:

Operation	Description
Join	Combines two or more 3D solids into one solid. Volume common to the solids is absorbed into the combined solid. AutoCAD's solid modeler calls this operation *union*.
Cut	Subtracts the volume of one set of solids from the volume of a second set of solids. Volume of the subtracted set that is not within the base set is deleted. AutoCAD uses the word *subtract* for this operation.
Intersect	Creates a solid from the volume shared by a set of solids. Volume that is not common is deleted.

Mechanical Desktop also uses Boolean operations in constructing solid models, but their use is less obvious because the operations are performed simultaneously with the creation of each new 3D feature; whenever you transform a profile feature into a 3D feature—whether by extruding, sweeping, revolving, or lofting—you specify that the operation type will be either join, cut, or intersect.

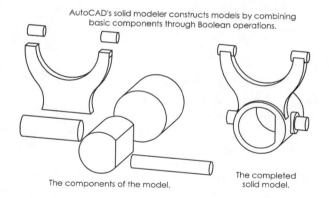

AutoCAD's solid modeler constructs models by combining basic components through Boolean operations.

The components of the model.

The completed solid model.

Although Mechanical Desktop's way of implementing Booleans has a couple of disadvantages—you can only operate on two solids at a time, and you must imagine what one of them looks like—most people do not have any trouble adapting to it. Also, in some circumstances Mechanical Desktop's Boolean operations work a little differently than those of other solid modelers. In AutoCAD for instance, when you subtract (or cut) solid A from solid B and there is no common volume between the two, solid A is deleted. In Mechanical Desktop, on the other hand, solid A remains even though you cannot see it, and if you move or create a solid within this space, the subtract operation takes effect.

Using AMCOMBINE

Mechanical Desktop does, though, have provisions for creating parts individually and combining them through Boolean operations similar to the methods of non-parametric solid modelers. You can even completely by-pass Mechanical Desktop's normal feature-by-feature approach by building a 3D model entirely by combining parts. For example, you can create all of the components shown on the left in the previous figure as separate parts, and then combine them with Boolean operations to create the part shown on the right in this figure.

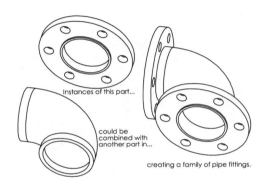

Instances of this part...

could be combined with another part in...

creating a family of pipe fittings.

Most of the time, though, you will combine parts only when you have created a mirror image part to be used in making a symmetrical part, and when you want to use the same geometry in a variety of parts. For example, if you were designing pipe fittings, you could create the pipe flange for a particular pipe diameter as a part, and use instances of that part to create ends for elbows, tees, and other fittings.

The Mechanical Desktop command that combines parts is AMCOMBINE. Two key restrictions of this command are that only parts, not features, can be combined, and that only two parts can be combined during one call to AMCOMBINE. The active part is called the *base* part, while the other part is referred to as the *toolbody*. The steps to combine two parts are:

1. Move the parts into a position relative to each other that will achieve the results you want. (You take this same step in non-parametric solid modelers to set up a Boolean operation.) Often you will use Mechanical Desktop's assembly constraints (which are sometimes referred to as 3D constraints) to do this. See Chapter 18 for information about assembly constraints. Assembly constraints are not a requirement for combining parts, though.

2. If necessary, use the AMACTIVATE command to establish which part is to be the base part for the combine operation. In Mechanical Desktop's assembly environment, any part can be the base part. In the single part environment, though, only the part that was first created in the file can be the base part, and it must be the active part.

3. Invoke AMCOMBINE. Choose Cut, Intersect, or Join as the Boolean operation from the command line prompt that AMCOMBINE issues.

4. Select the toolbody that is to interact with the base part. For Cut operations, the tool-body is subtracted from the base part.

Even though at least two parts must exist before you can use AMCOMBINE, you can combine parts in Mechanical Desktop's single part environment. In this environment, any new part you create in addition to the base part automatically receives a name such as TOOLBODY1_1 or TOOLBODY2_2, by Mechanical Desktop.

You can combine toolbodies to create a nested toolbody. And, you can create a pattern from a toolbody that has been combined, even if it is a nested toolbody, with the AMPATTERN command.

Creating Toolbodies

A variety of options for creating a toolbody that is to be combined with the base part are available to you. One is to select the Part option of the AMNEW command. Then, you will start from scratch in constructing a part, just as if you had opened a new drawing file. If you are working in the single part environment, the new part will be called a tool-body. When you have finished constructing the new part, it is ready to be combined with the original part.

In addition to constructing a toolbody in the current drawing file, you can import a part from another file for use as a toolbody. If the current file is in Mechanical Desktop's single part environment, the file of any part you import must also be in the single part environment. One way to import a toolbody from another file is with the AMCOPYIN command. This command displays a file-list type dialog box for you to use in locating the file of the part you want to import. The part in that file is inserted in the current file without additional prompts, and you can proceed to combine it with a part in the current file.

You can also import a part from an external file with AutoCAD's INSERT command. Although the imported part will be listed as an AutoCAD block, you do not have to explode it before combining it with another part. AutoCAD xRefs, on the other hand, are not recognized by Mechanical Desktop as either a part or a toolbody and cannot be combined with a part.

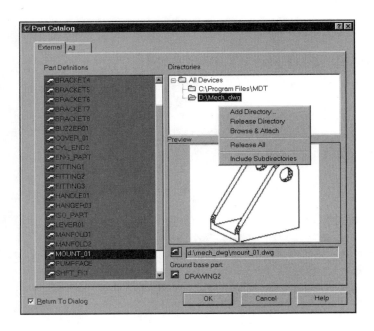

Even if xRefs worked, though, you probably would not use them for importing toolbodies since Mechanical Desktop's AMCATALOG command is a more powerful tool for working with external files. Like AutoCAD's XREF command, AMCATALOG allows you to insert a part from an external file into the current file, and that inserted part will change as the external file is changed. Unlike XREF, though, you can modify the inserted part, and you can choose to have that modification be made in the external file as well.

If you are working in Mechanical Desktop's assembly environment AMCATALOG displays a dialog box titled **Assembly Catalog**, and if you are in the single part environment it displays a dialog box titled **Part Catalog**. The contents of these two dialog boxes are virtually the same and you can use either to import parts that you intend to combine. The **Part Catalog** dialog box, though, is intended specifically for importing parts that are to be combined, rather than assembled. See Chapter 17 for more information about AMCATALOG.

The steps to import a part from an external file for use as a toolbody are:

1. Invoke AMCATALOG. If you are in the single part environment, a part must already exist.

2. Select the External tab of the **Part** (or **Assembly**) **Catalog** dialog box.

3. Right-click within the Directories pane to display its menu. Select Add Directory from this menu and browse to locate the directory that contains the file of the part you want to import.

4. The names of the drawing files in the directory you select will appear in the Part Definition pane. If you are working within the single part environment, only files in the single part environment will be displayed.

5. Locate the file you wish to import. When you click a filename, an image of its contents will appear in the Preview pane. Once you have located the file, either double click on it's name, or right-click it's name and select Attach from the resulting menu.

Converting a File from the Assembly Environment to the Single Part Environment

You may sometimes begin a new Mechanical Desktop drawing file in the assembly environment, and then decide that you should have started it in the single part environment. There is no direct way to convert a file from the assembly environment to the single part environment, but you can make the conversion from the Assembly Catalog. The steps are:

• Use the AMCATALOG command to open the `Assembly Catalog dialog` box.

• Click the All tab.

• In the Local Assembly Definitions list box, right-click the name of the part you want to convert. Select Externalize from the shortcut menu.

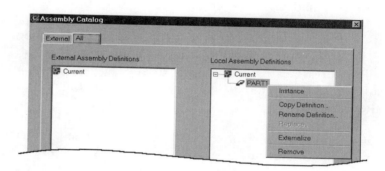

• A file management dialog box will appear. Select a name and location for the file, and click the Save button.

• The file you have created is in the single part environment.

Editing Combined Parts

Parts that have been combined do not lose their internal parametrics. However, there are no true parametric relationships between parts, because you cannot add parametric

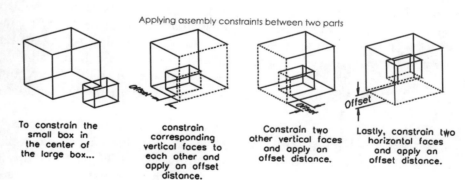

Applying assembly constraints between two parts

To constrain the small box in the center of the large box...

constrain corresponding vertical faces to each other and apply an offset distance.

Constrain two other vertical faces and apply an offset distance.

Lastly, constrain two horizontal faces and apply an offset distance.

dimensions between two separate parts. The best you can do in establishing editable spatial relationships between parts is to use assembly, or 3D, constraints. For example, to position a box-shaped part in the middle of a larger box-shaped part, you could use the

AMMATE command to constrain a face on one part with a face on the second part and then specify a distance, or offset, between the two faces. You would have to do this three times to completely establish the precise relative location between the two parts. You can edit 3D constraints by invoking the AMEDITCONS command. For more information on assembly constraints and these two commands, see Chapter 18.

You cannot edit the results of the AMCOMBINE command. For instance, you cannot change a cut combine operation to a join operation. You can, though, edit parts that have been combined, and edit the features of those parts. To edit a specific feature in a part that has been combined, whether the part is the base or the toolbody, invoke AMEDIT-FEAT and select the feature. The dialog box used in creating the 3D feature will reappear, and you can change the parameters within that dialog box just as if the feature was in a part that had not been combined. As with other modifications to features, you must invoke AMUPDATE before the changes take effect.

If you want to edit the profile sketch of a feature, choose the Sketch option of AMED-ITFEAT, and then select the feature you want to modify. The selected feature along with all features created after it will disappear, and the profile of the selected feature will appear for you to modify as you want. Update the part to initiate the changes and restore the features.

Even though two combined parts form one part, the parameter space of the two parts remains independent of each other. Thus, if one part has an equation based dimension that is d8=d7*2, Mechanical Desktop knows which of the combined parts the d7 dimension belongs to.

When you select the Toolbody option of AMEDITFEAT, Mechanical Desktop will prompt you to select the toolbody from a pair of parts that have been combined. The combined parts will then be restored to their condition before they were combined, and the toolbody will become the active part. Mechanical Desktop refers to this condition as the *rollback state*. In this state, you can freely edit the toolbody by invoking AMEDIT-FEAT again. You can also add features to the toolbody, and you can add or modify the 3D constraints between the toolbody and the base part. If you edit features of the tool-body part, you must either use the Part option of AMUPDATE to update the part and repeat AMUPDATE to update the combination, or use the Full option of AMUPDATE to perform both updates simultaneously.

You can edit an external part by invoking the AMACTIVATE command in the roll-back state. Mechanical Desktop will issue a message asking you to confirm the command, the part will be activated, and you can use AMEDITFEAT to modify it. After you have modified the part, you must update it, and then you must update the combination. When you update the combined parts, you can choose whether or not to change the part in the external file as well as in the open file.

Exercise 3

Combining Parts

In this exercise, you will finish the part you started in Exercise 1 of Chapter 8. Open your file that contains that part, or else retrieve file md08e110.dwg from the CD-ROM that accompanies this book,

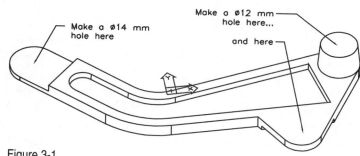

Figure 3-1

and open it. The part is shown in Figure 3-1. In finishing this part, you will add some fillets and holes to it, make a mirror image copy of it, and combine it with the mirror image copy.

Use the AMHOLE command to make one 14 mm and two 12 mm diameter holes in the locations shown in Figure 3-1. The Operation type for all three holes is Drilled, Termination is Through, and Placement is Concentric. Since you are now experienced in using AMHOLE, we will

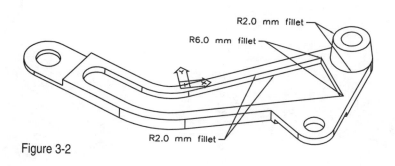

Figure 3-2

not describe the steps for making these holes. When you have made them, your model should look similar to the one in Figure 3-2.

Round the base and top edges of the boss that is located on the right side of the part with 2.0 mm radius fillets. Also, round the two sharp corners of the recessed area of the part with 6.0 mm radius fillets, and round the inside bottom and the top edges

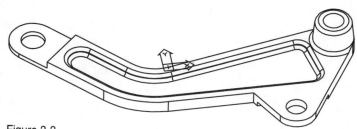

Figure 3-3

of the recessed area with 2.0 mm radius fillets. See Figure 3-2 for the locations of these fillets. All of the fillets have a constant radius. The 2.00 mm radius fillets around the top and bottom sides of the recessed area can each be made with a single pick, if you make them after the two 6.0 mm fillets. Other than that, we will not give you any instructions in making the fillets. When you have finished, your part should look similar to the one shown in Figure 3-3.

Next, you will make a part that is the mirror image of this part. The mirroring plane will be the lower, flat side of the part (corresponding to the sketch plane of the profile for the part's base feature). To more easily see and pick this face, you may want to rotate the viewing direction so that you are looking up toward the WCS XY plane. The command line sequence of prompts and input to create the new part is:

```
Command: AMMIRROR (Enter)
Select part to mirror: (Pick a point on the part.)
Select planar face to mirror about or [Line]: (Pick·a point on the bottom plane or its
    edge.)
(The edge of the face will be highlighted, and the animated cursor will appear.)
Enter an option [Next/Accept] <Accept>: (Enter)
Enter an option [Create new part/Replace instance] <Create new part>: (Enter)
Enter new part name <TOOLBODY1>: (Enter)
```

Figure 3-4

Your two parts should look similar to those in Figure 3-4. The viewpoint in this figure is 260 degrees from the World Coordinate System X axis and 25 degrees from the WCS XY plane. The AMMIRROR operation has left the two parts precisely aligned, so you could combine them as they are, but a good practice is to use assembly constraints to tie together any two parts you intend to combine. Although applying assembly constraints, or 3D constraints as Mechanical Desktop sometimes calls them, can be complicated, these two parts will be easy to constrain. This step will also serve as an introduction to assembly constraints. See Chapter 18 for more information about them.

Of the several types of assembly constraints we could use to tie these two parts together, we will use the insert constraint. This constraint connects two circular edges and their centerline. While the two circular edges do not have to have the same radius, the edges we will match in these parts do. To better see the objects that are to

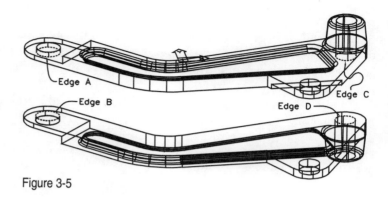

Figure 3-5

be matched, use AutoCAD's MOVE command to move the two parts away from each other, such as in Figure 3-5, and also switch to the wireframe viewing mode so that you can more easily see and select objects. Then use the following command line input to add an insert constraint between the two parts.

```
Command: AMINSERT (Enter)
Select first circular edge: (Select edge A in Figure 3-5)
(The circular edge will be highlighted, an arrow pointing away from the face will appear,
   and the animated cursor will appear.)
Enter an option [Clear/Flip] <accEpt>: (Enter)
Select second circular edge: (Select edge B in Figure 3-5)
(The Circular edge will be highlighted, an arrow pointing away from the face will appear,
   and the animated cursor will appear.)
Enter an option [Clear/Flip] <accEpt>: (Enter)
Enter offset <0>: (Enter)
```

The two parts will move together, and the two edges you selected will be aligned. The constraint you just added acts like a bolt that is inserted through the two holes and held with a nut. The nut is not tight, though, and consequently the two parts can revolve about the bolt. To prevent this rotation, you need to add an insert assembly constraint to a second pair of holes. In preparation for this, again move the two parts away from each other. Then, start AMINSERT and match the circular edges labeled C and D in Figure 3-5. It makes no difference which edge you select first. Accept the default offset of 0, and the two parts will once again move together. The spatial relationship between the two parts is now fully constrained. If the two parts become separated, you can invoke the AMUPDATE command, choose the Assembly option, and they will be rejoined.

In preparation for combining the base part with the toolbody, you need to activate the base part. From the command line, you can do that with the following input:

```
Command: AMACTIVATE (Enter)
Active part=TOOLBODY1_1: (This is a message that tells you which part is now the active
   part.)
```

```
Select part to activate or [?] <TOOLBODY1_1>: (Pick a point on the part that has the same
    name as the drawing file.)
```

Although it is good to know the basic command line for performing this operation, a more convenient method to activate the base part is to right-click its name and select Activate Part from the shortcut menu. If it is already the active part, this option will be grayed out.

Lastly, use the following command line input to combine the base part and the toolbody into one part:

```
Command: AMCOMBINE (Enter)
Enter parametric boolean operation [Cut/Intersection/Join] <Cut>: Join (Enter)
Select Part (Toolbody) to be joined: (Select the inactive part.)
```

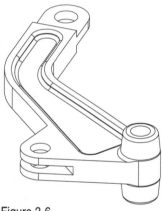

The edges that were between the two parts will disappear as evidence that just a single part now exists in the file. That completes this exercise and the part. Your finished part should look similar to the one in Figure 3-6. On the CD-ROM that comes with this book, the part is in file md12e306.

Figure 3-6

CHAPTER 13

Managing Features

This chapter, which is the last one devoted solely to part modeling, covers a variety of commands that will help you work with and manage features and parts.

This chapter covers the following topics.

- *Explains how to delete features and parts.*

- *Shows you how to examine the construction of a part, including a step-by-step graphic review of every operation.*

- *Explains how to suppress, or hide, specific features of a part, either manually or by a spreadsheet table. Suppressing features can make a complex part easier to work with, and enables you to create a family of parts from a base part.*

- *Describes how Mechanical Desktop reports data regarding the mass (weight), volume, and geometry of a part.*

- *Lists the commands for converting Mechanical Desktop part models into other formats.*

Deleting Objects

Features, whether they are sketched, placed, or work features, can be deleted with the AMDELFEAT command. This command will ask you to select one feature to be deleted. Then it will highlight the selected feature as well as all features dependent to the selected feature, and ask if you want to continue. If you respond positively, the highlighted feature, or features, will be deleted. All features dependent on the deleted feature will also be deleted. Saving the drawing file just prior to deleting a feature is a good practice, even though you can use AutoCAD's UNDO command to restore a deleted feature.

To delete an entire part, invoke the AMDELETE command. This command issues a command line prompt offering three options:

```
Enter an option [Definition/Instance/Scene]<Instance>:
```

The *definition* of a part is its Mechanical Desktop geometry and attribute data, and a part *instance* is a single occurrence of an object that is based on that data. If you delete an instance, only the instance you select is deleted. If you delete a part definition, all instances that use the definition are deleted. A *scene* is an exploded assembly of parts; they are described in Chapter 19. The Scene option will not be offered if the drawing file is in the single part environment.

Your usual method for initiating these two commands is most likely to be through the Desktop Browser, rather than from the command line. Highlight the name of the feature or part and select Delete from the right-click shortcut menu.

Reviewing the Construction of a Part

As you have been creating parts in the exercises of this book, you have seen how Mechanical Desktop builds an outline in the Desktop Browser that shows the sequence in which the features were created, their type, and their dependencies. You can obtain a command line list of the construction operations from the AMLISTPART command. The list, however, will simply show the sequence of operations—it will not show any details for the operations or show feature dependencies. AMLISTPART is an old Mechanical Desktop command that originated before the Browser existed, and it is a command you are not likely to need.

A more useful command for reviewing the construction sequence of a part, is AMRE-PLAY, which reconstructs the active part one step at a time in the Mechanical Desktop graphics window. At the start of the command, the part will disappear, and then each sketch plane, sketch (complete with its dimensions and constraints), work feature, and 3D feature will reappear in the order it was created. Moreover, the Desktop Browser will highlight the feature of the current step as you move through the construction steps. By seeing exactly how a part has been built you can sometimes discover the reason that a part you are having problems with does not behave as it should.

You cannot edit any of the features during this replay, but you can stop (truncate) the construction of the part at any step. Every feature that was created after that step will be deleted. You can also suppress all of the features that were created after a step. (We will discuss feature suppression later in this chapter.)

As each construction step is displayed in the graphics window, the command line displays the name of the operation or feature, followed by a prompt with options that vary according to the current feature type. If the feature is a sketch, the prompt is:

```
Enter an option [Display/Exit/Next/Size/Truncate]<Next>: (Enter an option or press Enter)
```

The Display option displays the geometric constraints of the sketch, while Size allows you to change the size of constraint symbols. Truncate deletes all features created after the current step and ends the command. Exit ends the command and restores the part, while Next advances to the next construction step.

For all other feature types the command line prompt is:

```
Enter an option [eXit/Next/Suppress/Truncate]<Next>: (Enter an option or press Enter)
```

The Truncate, Exit, and Next options produce the same results as those of the prompt for sketches. Suppress suppresses all features that follow the feature of the current step. If the part already has suppressed features, they will be listed as suppressed in REPLAY's command line message, and an Unsuppress option will be added to the prompt.

You can perform transparent zooms during AMREPLAY (by preceding ZOOM with an apostrophe), but you cannot change the viewpoint. Therefore, you will often find it helpful to have multiple viewports open, each showing the part from a different viewpoint, when you use AMREPLAY. This is likely to give you at least one unobstructed view of the part during each of the replay steps.

Although the Truncate option can be very useful, it is an option you should use with care, since it deletes all features, constraints, and dimensions that were created after the truncate step. Before you truncate your part, you should make certain that you have back-up copies of the drawing file.

Changing the Order of Construction

You can change the order in which the features of a part were created through the AMREORDFEAT command. This command will prompt you to select the feature that is to be reordered, and then to select a destination feature. The two selected features will switch positions in the construction sequence of the part. As you would surmise, the reorder must be physically possible. For instance, you cannot reorder a fillet so that would it be created before the edge it is on. If you select a destination feature that would result in an inappropriate order, Mechanical Desktop will report that your selection is invalid, and will prompt for another feature. Also, you cannot reorder the base feature of a part.

When you do need to reorder a feature, you will probably bypass the AMREORDFEAT command to use the Desktop Browser instead. You can simply highlight the feature's name in the Browser, hold down the pick button of your pointing device, and drag the feature to its new position in the assembly sequence. An image of the feature's name will move in accordance with your pointing device's movement, and if you drag the feature to an unacceptable location, a circle with a diagonal stripe will appear over the name's image.

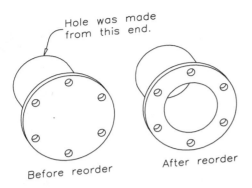

The figure to the left shows an example of reordering a feature. In this example, a cylinder was created as a base feature, and a hole feature using a Through termination was added to make a tube from the cylinder. Then a flange was added to the end of the tube. Since the flange was added after the hole, the hole no longer passes completely through the part. as shown on the left in the figure.

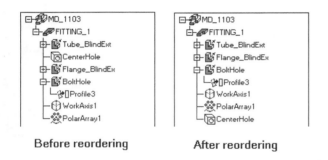

Before reordering   **After reordering**

You can reorder the hole by highlighting its name in the Browser and dragging it to a position below the flange. The part will automatically update itself, with the hole passing through the flange, as shown on the right in the previous figure. On the left, in the figure to the left, is the Browser for this part as it originally appeared, and on the right is the Browser as is it appears after the reordering.

Feature Suppression

Suppressed features, in effect, are temporarily removed from the part—they are no longer visible and Mechanical Desktop ignores them during recalculations. You have two very good reasons for sometimes suppressing features. One reason is to temporarily simplify a complicated part so that it will be easier to work with. The second reason is to create a family of parts in which some versions of the part have features that other versions do not have.

Any feature dependent to a suppressed feature will be suppressed as well. Therefore, the base feature of a part cannot be suppressed. Mechanical Desktop sometimes classifies the dependencies of features as being either a *hard dependency* or a *soft dependency*. A hard dependency is one that cannot be removed from the parent feature without removing the dependent feature. Fillets, for example, have a hard dependency with the feature edge they are on. Soft dependencies, on the other hand, can be removed or modified. Dimensions between a sketched dependent feature and its parent feature are examples of soft dependencies, because you can roll the feature back to its profile with AMEDIT-FEAT, and replace some or all of its dimensions with other dimensions and constraints. Mechanical Desktop displays soft dependency dimensions in a special color, which is set in the Part tab of the **Mechanical Options** dialog box, or by invoking the AMSUPPRCOLOR command.

Manually Suppressed Features

When you want to temporarily simplify a complicated part, you will suppress features manually. One way to do this is through AMSUPPRESSFEAT. The default option of this command is to select one feature to be suppressed. The selected feature, along with all of its dependent features, will be highlighted and you will be asked to confirm the suppression. When you do, the feature will disappear from the screen as if it had been erased. You can also initiate this option through the feature's right-click Browser menu.

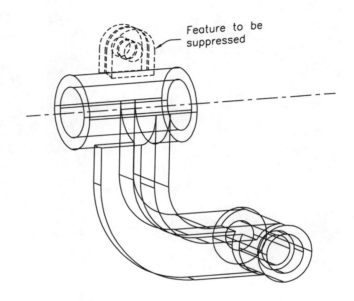

Feature to be suppressed

In the Desktop Browser, suppressed features are shown offset from the part's branch line and are connected to it by a dashed line with a circle-shaped node. Notice in the nearby figure of the Browser, which is for the part in the previous figure, that the feature named Hole1 has been suppressed along with the feature named ExtrusionMidplane2, because it is dependent to it. You can completely turn off the display of suppressed features in the Browser through the Browser Filter, which can be accessed through the right-click menu of the Browser's background.

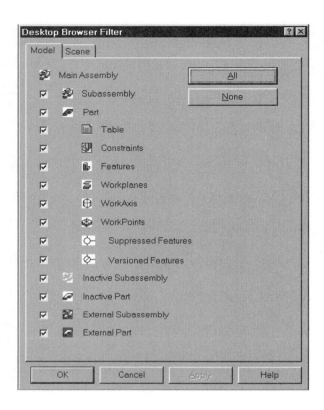

AMSUPPRESSFEAT also has an option to suppress features by their type. With this option, for instance, you can suppress all fillets on a part, and you can suppress all features that were created by extrusion. The option displays a dialog box containing check boxes for all Mechanical Desktop feature types within the drawing file. Feature types that are not in the drawing file are grayed out. You simply check the object types that you want suppressed. If you want to suppress all features that were created after a specific step in the construction of a part, you can do so through the AMREPLAY command we described earlier in this chapter.

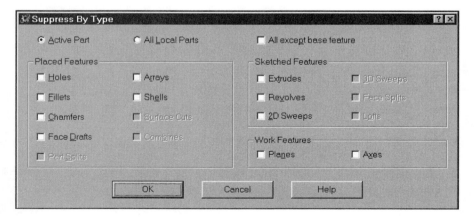

Features that have been manually suppressed can be unsuppressed through the AMUNSUPPRESSFEAT command. This command has two options. One—the All option—restores all features that have been suppressed. Its other option is to unsuppress features by their type. This option displays a dialog box similar to the one used for suppressing features, and you can clear its check boxes for various object types. Individual features can also be unsuppressed through the feature's right-click Browser menu. This menu offers two choices for unsuppressing features: Unsuppress and Unsuppress +. Unsuppress restores just the feature, while Unsuppress + restores the feature and its dependent features. Yet another way to unsuppress features is through AMREPLAY. When a suppressed feature is encountered during a step through the construction of a part, select Unsuppress from the command line prompt.

Version-Suppressed Features

If you want to have a family of parts in which different members of the family have different features, you will use version-suppressed features. You might, for instance, have a family of sheet metal parts. One version of the part will have all of the features, another version will be missing a particular flange, and another version will not have a particular hole.

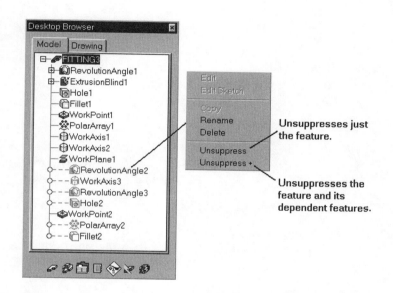

Unsuppresses just the feature.

Unsuppresses the feature and its dependent features.

Version-suppressed features are table driven: that is, they are both created and managed through Microsoft Excel spreadsheet files. Once a feature has been suppressed through a table, it cannot be manually unsuppressed.

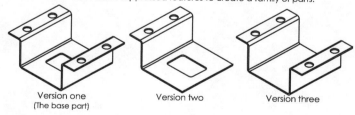

You can use version suppressed features to create a family of parts.

Version one
(The base part)

Version two

Version three

The part must be either unlinked from the spreadsheet, or else the spreadsheet contents must be modified. The steps to create a set of version-suppressed features are:

1. Create a base version of the part that has all of the features.

2. Open the **Table Driven Setup** dialog box. (See Chapter 6 for a description of this dialog box.) You can do this through the AMVARS command, or by selecting the Table option of the AMSUPPRESSFEAT command. In this dialog box, select Feature Suppression as the table Type, and click the Create button of the dialog box. Specify a name for the Excel spreadsheet file in the Create Table dialog box.

3. The Excel spreadsheet will open in a window over the Mechanical Desktop window. The dependent features of the part will be listed as column headings in the top row of the spreadsheet, beginning with the second column (Column B). Cell A2 will contain the word Generic, which represents the base version of the part. You can change the name if you like.

4. In the first column of the spreadsheet, beginning with row 3, enter a name for each version of the part. Enter the letter S in the columns across the row for the features you want suppressed for the version.

5. Save the spreadsheet file, and exit it.

6. In Mechanical Desktop's **Table Driven Setup** dialog box, click the button labeled Update link. Then click the OK button to exit the dialog box, and if necessary, another OK button to leave the Design Variables dialog box.

7. The names you assigned to the part versions will appear in the Desktop Browser.

8. You can make any version be the current version by double-clicking its name in the Browser, or by selecting Activate from its right-click menu.

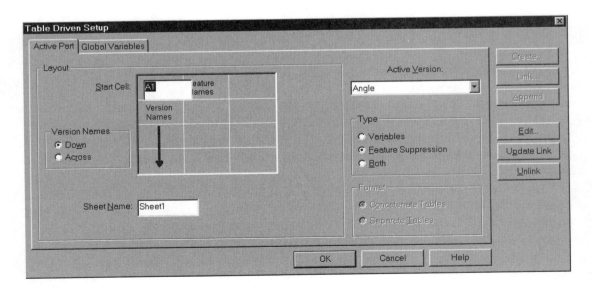

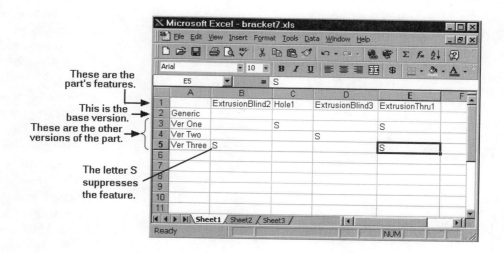

These are the part's features.

This is the base version.

These are the other versions of the part.

The letter S suppresses the feature.

If you have set the spreadsheet layout so that version names are down rather than across, the row and column descriptions in steps 3 and 4 will be reversed.

Version-suppressed features can also be used in conjunction with table driven variables. This allows you to have part versions that vary in size and proportion as well in the features they have. A convenient way to set up such a table is to first create the dimension variables and a spreadsheet for various values of the variables as described in Chapter 6. Then go to the **Table Driven Setup** dialog. There, check the button labeled Both for the Table type, and the button labeled Concatenate Tables for the Format type. Click the Append button to open the existing Excel spreadsheet file.

The names of all of the dependent sketched and placed features will automatically have been placed in the spreadsheet. They will be in consecutive cells following the variable names in the first row if you have set the table layout so that version names are down, and they will be in the first column if version names are across. The order in which the features are listed is the same as that of the Desktop Browser. You can delete the features you are not interested in, but since gaps between the feature names are not allowed, you will need to move the names of the remaining variables to other cells.

To suppress a feature for a specific part version, enter the letter S in the cell at the intersection of the row and column of the feature and version. The next figure shows a table in which version names are across the spreadsheet. There are three versions of the part, ten different variables, and two features that are to be suppressed. The feature named cutout_extr (in cell A13) is suppressed for the part version named 3.0x4.0, and Flange_extr (in cell A14) is suppressed for part version 2.5x3.0. No features are suppressed for version 5.0x6.0.

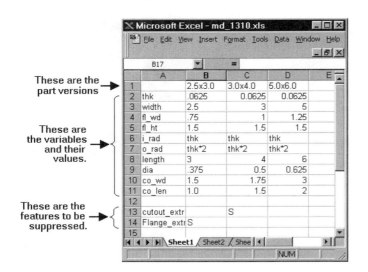

These are the part versions →

These are the variables and their values. →

These are the features to be suppressed. →

When you are satisfied with the spreadsheet, save and exit it to restore the **Table Driven Setup** dialog box. Click the Update Link button in this dialog box, and exit it to return to the Mechanical Desktop graphics window. Initially, there will be no difference in the appearance of the Browser, but when you activate versions of the part having suppressed features, features that are set to be suppressed by the spreadsheet will disappear and the Browser will show the features as suppressed. You activate a version by double-clicking its name in the Browser; or by right-clicking its name to bring up a menu, and selecting Activate from that menu (which is the only option in the menu).

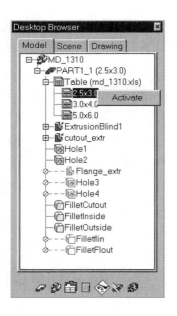

The part that goes with the spreadsheet shown previously is similar to the one at the first of this section that shows an example of version-suppressed features. On the CD-ROM that comes with this book, the part is in file md_1310.dwg and the Excel spreadsheet is in file md1310.xls. You should open these files and explore their relationships.

When you open md_1310.dwg, the spreadsheet table listed in the Browser may be shown with a red background. This is a signal that Mechanical Desktop cannot find the spreadsheet file. If this occurs, start the AMVARS command, select Setup, and then Update Link. A message box will tell you that the linked table could not be found, and will ask if you would like to resolve the error. Respond with a Yes, and dialog boxes to help you browse and locate the file will appear.

Exercise 1

Creating and Working with Version-Suppressed Features

This exercise will lead you through the steps in creating version-suppressed features. To complete this exercise, you must have Microsoft's Excel installed on your computer. Begin a new Mechanical Desktop single part environment file using the default metric template (acad-iso.dwt). With the sketch plane on the WCS XY plane, draw a rectangle that is 100 mm in the X direction and 10 mm in the Y direction. Turn it into a profile; constrain and dimension it; and, extrude it a distance of 100 mm.

On the left end of this base feature, draw a rectangle that is 10 mm in the X direction and 80 mm in the Y direction, as shown in Figure 1-1. Turn it into a profile, fully constrain it, and extrude it a distance of 100 mm using a Join operation. Create a profile and extrude a third 3D feature having the same geometry and dimensions on the right end of the base feature. See Figure 1-2.

Lastly, draw a rectangle having the same dimensions as the first one and located 90 mm from it in the Y direction. Transform the rectangle into a profile, constrain and dimension it, and extrude it to a height of 100 mm. Your part, as shown in Figure 1-3, should a 100x100x100 mm cube with an open top and bottom. Also, the feature names for your part should correspond to those shown in Figure 1-3.

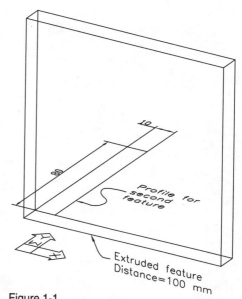

Figure 1-1

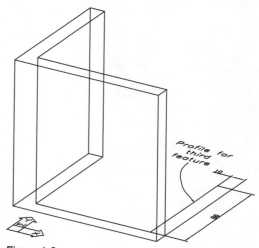

Figure 1-2

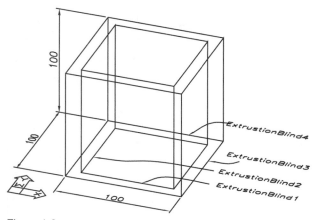

Figure 1-3

Although there are other, and easier, methods to create this part, it is important for this exercise that you construct it using the steps and order we have described. The Desktop Browser should show that your part consists of four extruded features. The base feature is named ExtrusionBlind1, and the dependent features are named ExtrusionBlind2, ExtrusionBlind3, and ExtrusionBlind4.

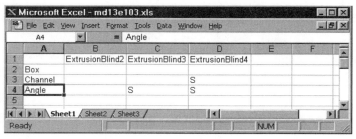

Figure 1-4

Start the AMSUPPRESS-FEAT command, and select its Table option to open the **Table Driven Setup** dialog box. Make certain that the Feature Suppression box is checked, and then click the Create button. The **Create Table** dialog box will appear. Assign a name to the spreadsheet file, specify a location for it, and click the Save button.

The Excel spreadsheet will open, you will see the names of the three dependent features in row 1, although you will probably need to increase the column widths to see their names in entirety. In cell A2, change the word Generic to Box. Enter the word Channel in cell A3, and the letter S in cell D3 (the column for the ExtrusionBlind4 feature). Enter the word Angle in cell A4, and the letter S in cells C4 and D4. Your spreadsheet should look similar to the one shown in Figure 1-4.

Save the spreadsheet file, and exit Excel to return to Mechanical Desktop's **Table Driven Setup** dialog box. Click the Update Link button. Then, exit the dialog box. The table will be shown as a feature in the Desktop Browser, with the Box, Channel, and Angle versions listed below it. See Figure 1-5.

In the Browser, double-click on the Angle version; or else highlight it, right-click to bring up its menu, and select Activate. Two of the extruded features will disappear, leaving an L-shaped part as shown in Figure 1-6. If you were to select Channel as the active version, just one of the extruded features would be suppressed, and the part would be U-shaped.

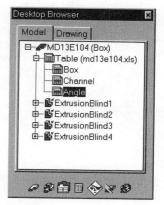

Figure 1-5

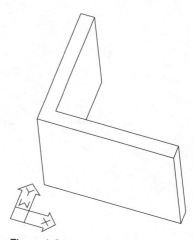

Figure 1-6

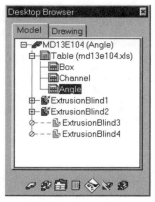

Figure 1-7

Notice that when Angle is selected as the version, the ExtrusionBlind3 and ExtrusionBlind4 features are shown as suppressed features in the Desktop Browser. Notice also that there is a diagonal line through the nodes of these features. This signifies that the features are version-suppressed, rather than manually suppressed. We are now finished with this exercise. You do not need to save either your Mechanical Desktop or your Excel file. On the CD-ROM that comes with this book, the part is in file md13e107.dwg and the feature suppression data is in file md13e107.xls.

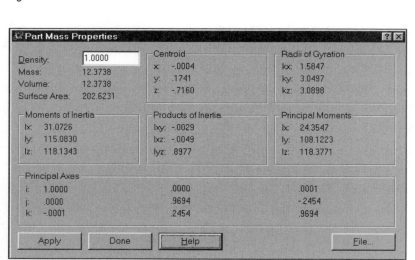

Mass Property Data

The AMPARTPROP command reports the active part's mass properties, which is a collection of data related to the part's mass (weight), volume, and geometry. The data is displayed in a dialog box, but you can output it to a text file that has a filename extension of ppr. Most of us are unlikely to ever use any of the mass property data other than mass, volume, centroid, and surface area. The other data is used primarily in complex calculations for speeds, accelerations, and forces of moving and rotating bodies.

The density of the part is used in the calculations for most of the mass property data. Density is the mass, or weight, per unit volume of the material that the part is to be made from. Mechanical Desktop uses a default density value of 1.0, which makes the mass of the part equal to its volume. You can enter another value in the edit box that is labeled Density, click the Apply button, and Mechanical Desktop will recalculate the mass property data to match the new value. You must be careful to enter a density value that corresponds to the dimension units of your part. Thus, if you used inches to dimension your part, you would use a density having units of pounds per cubic inch.

The centroid of the part is its center of gravity: the point at which the entire weight of the part appears to be concentrated. The X, Y, and Z coordinates of the centroid are based on the current location of the User Coordinate System.

Conversions

Mechanical Desktop recognizes three different 3D solid types.

Parametric Solid   A 3D solid composed of parametric features that can be fully edited. This is the type of 3D solid we have been discussing throughout this book.

Static Solid   A 3D solid that is not parametric, and cannot be edited. However, parametric features—sketched, placed, and work—can be added to a static solid, and those features can be edited. Sometimes Mechanical Desktop prompts refer to static solids as *base* solids. A base 3D solid is not the same as the base feature in a parametric solid.

AutoCAD 3D Solid   A 3D solid created through the AutoCAD commands of EXTRUDE, REVOLVE, CONE, WEDGE, and so forth. They are not parametric, and parametric features cannot be added to them. They are, however, based on the same ACIS geometric modeler kernel used for parametric solids. Sometimes they are referred to as AutoCAD *native* solids. When a parametric solid is exploded (with AutoCAD's EXPLODE command), it becomes an AutoCAD 3D solid.

Static solids can only be created indirectly. One way to create them is through the conversion of an AutoCAD 3D solid. This conversion is done by the AMNEW command. Select the Part option from AMNEW's command line prompt, and then pick a point on the AutoCAD solid.

Another way to create a static solid is by converting a parametric solid to a static solid. The command for this operation is AMMAKEBASE. Mechanical Desktop will highlight the active part, issue a warning on the command line that the ability to edit the part's existing features will be lost, and make the conversion—without giving you an opportunity to stop the command. All of the part's features will disappear from the Desktop Browser when the part becomes a static solid.

Your principal use of static solids will be for standard parts, such as fasteners, that you do not want modified. You can also use them to freeze a design for documentation purposes or in preparation for sending the model to an outside organization.

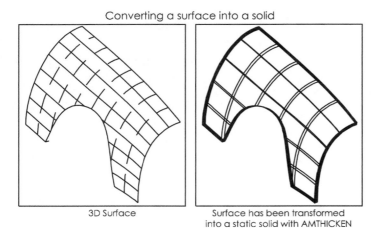

Converting a surface into a solid

3D Surface

Surface has been transformed into a static solid with AMTHICKEN

Beginning with Mechanical Desktop Release 5, you can convert a 3D surface object into a static solid. The command that does this is AMTHICKEN. Command line prompts will ask you to pick the surfaces to thicken, for the direction to thicken, and for the thickness. The thickened surface is shown in the Desktop Browswer as a base solid in a new part, or toolbody if the single part environment is in effect.

Some other commands that you may occasionally need in making conversions to and from non-Autodesk object types are:

AMSTLOUT   Converts parametric solids to STL (sterolithography) files. Sterolithography is a process for making physical models from computer data.

AMIDFIN   Converts printed circuit board data in the International Data Format (IDF) to Autodesk 3D objects.

AMVRMLOUT   Converts selected objects to Virtual Reality Modeling Language (VRML) for use in an Internet web page.

CHAPTER 14

2D Drawings from 3D Parts

You will leave the 3D space of Model mode in this chapter to begin working in the 2D space of Drawing mode. In Drawing mode, you can transform a 3D part into a detailed, multiview 2D drawing, complete with dimensions and notes, and if needed, section views, auxiliary views, and detail views. Furthermore, Mechanical Desktop will do virtually all of the drafting for you. Also, because the drawing is based on the same data used by the part model, you can make changes to the part in either Model mode or Drawing mode.

This chapter covers the following topics.

- *Describes the differences between Mechanical Desktop's Model and Drawing modes.*

- *Explains how to create, manage, and control the appearance of Drawing mode layouts.*

- *Explains the options and settings in the Drawing tab and the Standards tab of the Mechanical Options dialog box displayed by the AMOPTIONS command.*

- *Tells you how Mechanical Desktop uses layers in drawings.*

- *Introduces drawing views, and describes the data sets for creating the base view of a drawing.*

- *Lists the steps in making the base view of a drawing.*

Drawing Mode

The need for elaborate, multiview, two-dimensional drawings on paper is becoming less important as the transfer of data directly from computer models to production machines becomes more common. Still, a need for them does exist, and Mechanical Desktop has an extensive set of tools for creating 2D drawings from 3D models of parts, and from assemblies of parts. These drawings are created in Mechanical Desktop's *Drawing mode*. Unlike model mode, drawing mode is a 2D space. Working in Drawing mode is somewhat comparable to manual drafting, but Mechanical Desktop does almost all of the drafting for you. You simply specify the views that the drawing is to have, along with some other parameters, such as the scale of the views, and Mechanical Desktop creates them along with their dimensions for you.

Model Mode

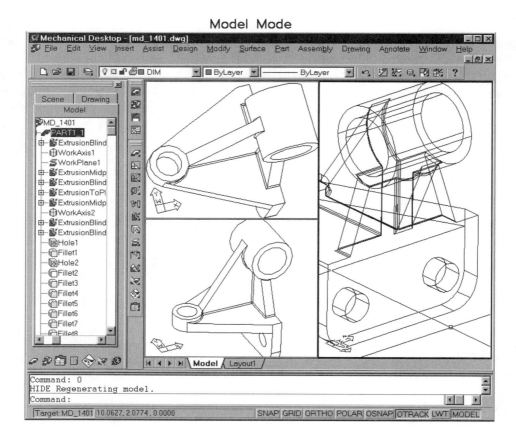

Although Mechanical Desktop's Drawing mode is virtually the same as AutoCAD's paper space (just as Model mode is virtually the same as AutoCAD's model space), and uses floating viewports as does AutoCAD, you will not use any of AutoCAD's commands for creating and working with floating viewports, or for adding dimensions and annotation.

Mechanical Desktop uses the same database for the drawing views of a part that it does for the part's 3D model. As a result of this database associatively, any changes you make in the values of dimensions in drawing views will also be made to the part, and any changes you make to the part will automatically be reflected in the drawing views.

You can switch between Drawing mode and Model mode through the AMMODE command, You will rarely use this command though, since an easier way to change

Drawing Mode

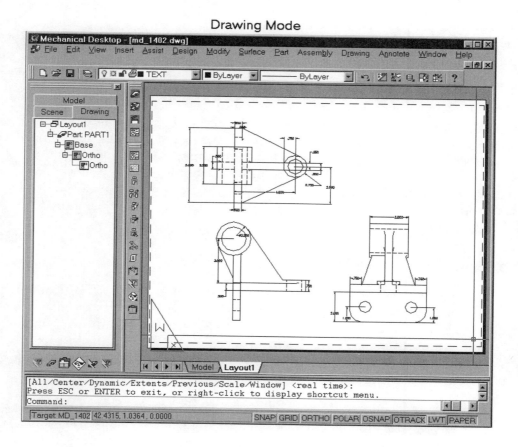

modes is to click either the Drawing or the Part tab of the Desktop Browser, or to click the Model or Layout tab on the bottom edge of the graphics window.

You can easily differentiate the two modes, even if the part is not shown, by the appearance of the UCS icon. In Drawing mode the icon is always a 30-60 degree triangle. Also, beginning with R4 of Mechanical Desktop, the default Drawing mode screen contains, by default, a simulated sheet of white paper.

Layouts

A layout is a named combination of plotting and Drawing mode parameters. At a minimum, a layout will designate the printing device and its settings, including the paper size that is to be used and its orientation (landscape or portrait). Typically, though, a layout will also include a particular arrangement of drawing views and a title block. You can have several layouts in a drawing file, which enables you to have layouts for different paper sizes, view arrangements, and even printers.

The names of layouts appear on tabs on the lower edge of the graphics window, as well as in the Desktop Browser. Their default names are Layout1, Layout2, and so forth. To activate any layout, either click on its tab or double-click on its name in the Browser.

The AutoCAD command LAYOUT establishes and manages layouts, but rather than invoking this command directly, you will generally right-click a layout tab and select an option from its shortcut menu. With this menu, you can change layout names, delete layouts, change the order of the layout tabs, copy layouts, and create a new layout from scratch, or import one from a template file. (You cannot delete, move, or rename the Model tab.) Layouts based on a template, include a border and title block, and set the paper size to accommodate the border. You can choose from about 24 pre-made templates in both inch and metric formats that are located in Mechanical Desktop's Template folder.

Establishing Page Parameters

Once a layout has been created, you will use AutoCAD's PAGESETUP command to establish, or modify, its page and printing parameters. By default, this command is automatically invoked the first time you switch from Model mode to drawing mode, and when you create a new layout. This command displays a dialog box titled `Page Setup` that is similar to the one used by AutoCAD's PLOT command. The steps to establish the page parameters of a layout are:

1. Select the Plot Device tab of the dialog box, and choose a printer.

2. Select the Layout Settings tab and select a paper size from the Paper size list box. Only those sizes that can be handled by the printer you specified will be listed. If you select

a paper size that is measured in millimeters, you should also select the mm button located just below the Paper size list box.

3. Specify Layout as the Plot area; and 1:1 as the Plot scale. This scale refers to paper space, not the scale of the drawing views you will eventually make.

4. Leave the other parameters at their default settings.

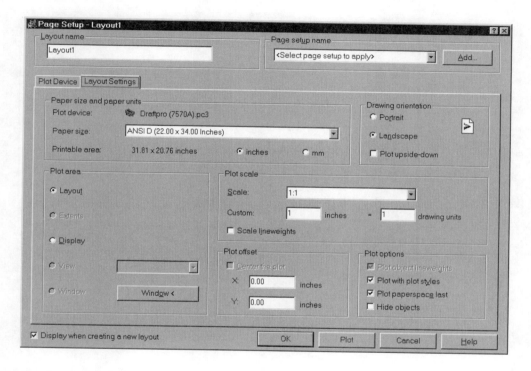

When you click the OK button of the dialog box, the simulated sheet of paper that is displayed on the screen will automatically adjust to match the size you specified. The dashed lines on the paper represent the printable limits of the printer you specified, and

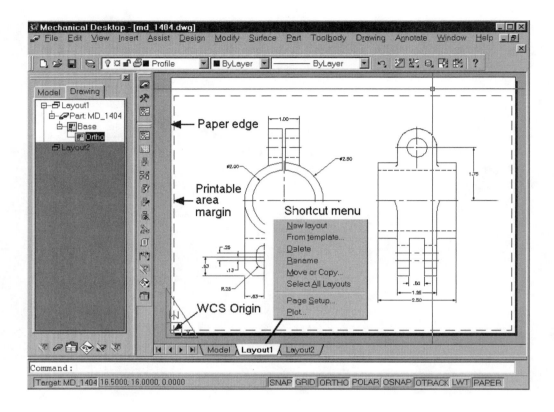

the Drawing mode World Coordinate System origin is in the lower left corner of the printable area.

Controlling Drawing Mode's Screen Appearance

You can change the appearance of the drawing mode screen by changing some settings in the Display tab of the **Options** dialog box that is opened by AutoCAD's OPTIONS command. Choose the check boxes in the "Layout elements" cluster to specify the layout elements you want. You should always, however, leave the "Create viewport in new layouts" option off. The "Colors" button opens a dialog box titled "Color Options" for establishing the color of the simulated paper (or, when the "Display paper background" option is off, the entire drawing mode graphics screen), as well as the color of the text on the layout tabs.

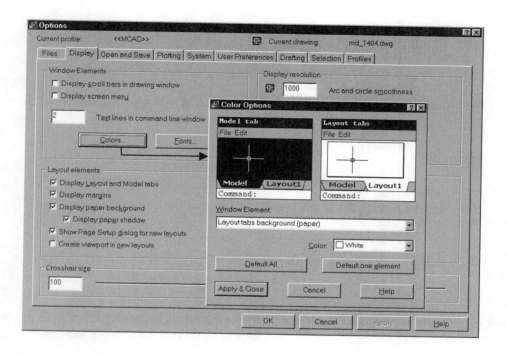

All layout elements displayed

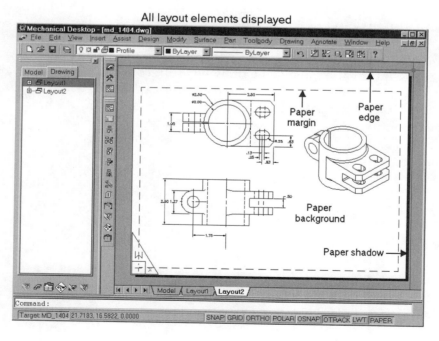

No layout elements displayed

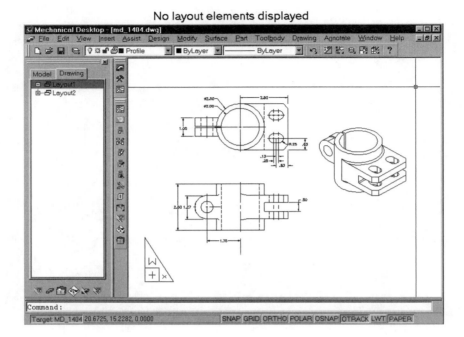

Borders and Title Blocks

Typically, 2D engineering drawings have a border around the edge of the paper and a title block containing information about the drawing; both of which conform to a company, industry, national, or international standard. These can be drawn in place using the AutoCAD commands for making lines, polylines and text within Mechanical Desktop's Drawing mode or, if you have a border and title block available, can be inserted as an AutoCAD block. Since Drawing mode is a one-to-one space, borders and title blocks will be drawn or inserted in full scale. Many people prefer to have a border and title block in

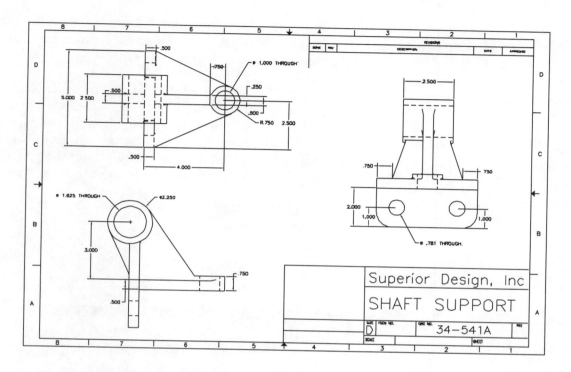

place before they create drawing views to help them judge their placement of views, but this is not a requirement.

As a service, Autodesk supplies some drawings of borders and title blocks that you can insert as blocks into your drawings. If you used the default Mechanical Desktop installation, they are located in the Program Files\Mdt\Template folder. Their filenames indicate the standard to which they conform and their size. For instance, the one conforming to US standards for C size drawings (nominal 22 by 17 inches) is ansi_c.dwg, and the one conforming to ISO standards for A2 size drawings (nominal 594 by 420 mm) is iso_a2.dwg. There are also border and title block drawings for German (DIN) and Japanese (JIS) standards. These files are also used when you select the Template option of the LAYOUT command to create a new layout, as described a few paragraphs ago.

If you select the Insert Title Block option from the menu displayed when you right-click the name of a layout in the Desktop Browser, a numbered list of title blocks in inch and metric sizes will appear. When you enter a number, the corresponding title block and border will appear in the layout, and you will be prompted to specify whether a drawing file of the title block is to be created. If you respond with a "yes," the title block and border will be an AutoCAD block; and if you respond with a "no," the title block and border will consist of AutoCAD lines, polylines, and text. (This method for inserting a title block uses an AutoLISP program named mvsetup.lsp.) The borders of these title blocks, as well as those of the files in the template folder, will not necessarily fit the paper size you have specified for the layout, and therefore, you will need to modify them after they are in place.

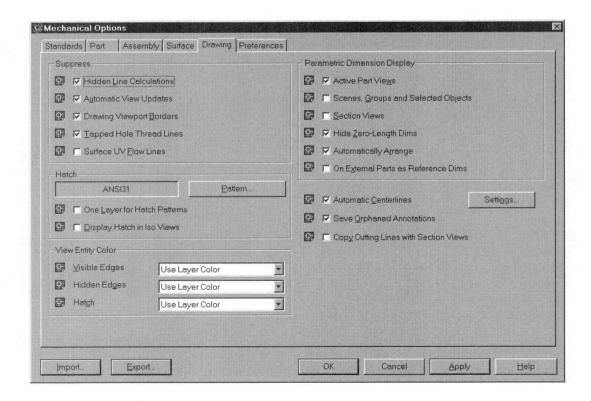

Setting Drawing Options

Many of the properties of your drawings are controlled by system variables. While you can set these variables one at a time from the command line, a more convenient way is through the Drawing tab of the `Mechanical Options` dialog box that is displayed by the AMOPTIONS command. The options in the Drawing tab are:

Suppress

The five check boxes in this cluster control whether certain operations that affect drawing views will or will not be performed.

Hidden Line Calculations   When this check box is cleared, calculations (which may be lengthy for complex models) to determine which edges of the model are hidden and which edges are visible are performed when a drawing view is created. When the check box is selected, these calculations are suppressed and the model is displayed in wireframe form in the drawing views. When you are ready to have hidden lines calculated and displayed, you can clear the check box and update the drawing views. The system variable **amhlcalc** is controlled by this check box. You can also control hidden line calculations on a view-by-view basis through a option of the AMDWGVIEW command.

Automatic View Updates   This check box controls whether or not drawing views are automatically updated after changes to the part have been made. When the check box is cleared, changes to the part will automatically be reflected in the drawing views. When it is checked, automatic view updates are suppressed and you must use the View option of AMUPDATE to force the views to display the part's changes. This check box sets the value of the **amviewrefresh** system variable.

Drawing Viewport Borders   All drawing views are created within a floating viewport. When this check box is checked, the borders of these viewports are hidden. The system variable **amvpborder** is controlled by this check box.

Tapped Hole Thread Lines   When this check box is cleared, the thread in tapped holes is displayed according to the drafting standard specified in the Standards tab of the `Mechanical Options` dialog box. (Tapped holes are created by selecting the Tapped option of the AMHOLE command, as described in Chapter 11.) When this check box is checked, the thread in tapped holes is not shown.

Surface UV Flow Lines   This option affects the display of Mechanical Desktop surface objects in drawing views. In Model mode, UV lines are displayed on surface objects to help you visualize the surface. When this check box is cleared, UV lines are also displayed in drawing views.

Hatch

The options in this cluster control the default settings for the hatch patterns that are used to indicate cuts through solids in section views.

Pattern When you click this button, the AutoCAD `Hatch Pattern` dialog box will appear for you to use in establishing the attributes of the hatch pattern. The hatch pattern you select from this dialog box will be offered as a default when you set up a Mechanical Desktop section view. The name of the current default hatch pattern appears to the left of this button.

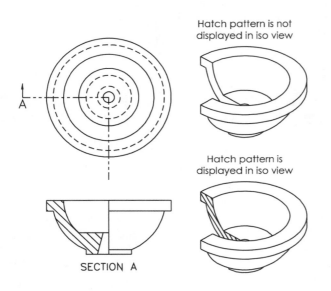

Hatch pattern is not displayed in iso view

Hatch pattern is displayed in iso view

SECTION A

One Layer for Hatch Patterns
When this option is selected, hatches are placed in a single layer, regardless of the hatch pattern they use. When this option is cleared, Mechanical Desktop will create and use a separate layer for each hatch pattern. Refer to the Layers in 3D Drawings section in this chapter for information about Mechanical Desktop's use of layers.

Display Hatch in Iso Views When this check box is cleared, the sliced surfaces in isometric views that are based on section views will not be hatched. When this check box is selected, isometric views based on section views will have hatch patterns on their sliced surfaces.

View Entity Color

The three list boxes in this cluster control the colors used for various object types in drawing views. The value of the **amdwgcolor** system variable is set by these check boxes.

Visible Edges You can set the color used in drawing visible edges within drawing views to either: Layer Color, Part Color, or Part and Feature Color.

Hidden Edges   You choices for setting the color used for drawing hidden edges in drawing views are: Layer Color, Part Color, and Part and Feature Color.

Hatch   You can set the color used for drawing hatch patterns in section views to: Layer Color or Part Color.

Parametric Dimension Display

The check boxes in this cluster control the conditions in which the parametric dimensions used in constraining the profiles of features are displayed in drawing views.

Active Part Views   The parametric dimensions used in constraining and creating 3D features are displayed in drawing views when this option is selected. It controls the contents of the **amreusedim** system variable. Dimensions are displayed when **amreusedim** is set to 1, and they are not displayed when it is set to 0.

Scenes, Groups and Selected Objects   Parametric dimensions are displayed in drawing views of scenes (exploded assemblies of parts), groups, and selected objects when this option is selected. Selecting this option also enables the On External Parts as Reference Dims option.

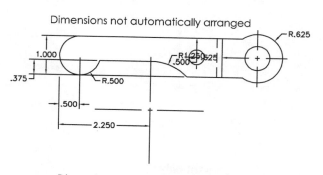
Dimensions not automatically arranged

Section Views   Select this option to have parametric dimensions displayed in section views. The system variable **amsectiondim** is set by this option.

Hide Zero-Length Dims   Occasionally zero-length dimensions are required to constrain a profile as you construct a part. Those dimensions are not displayed in drawing views when this option is selected.

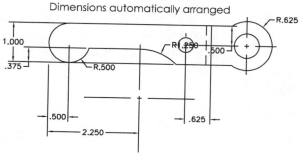
Dimensions automatically arranged

Automatically Arrange   When this option is selected, Mechanical Desktop will display parametric dimensions outside the part's envelope.

On External Parts as Reference Dims   This option is available only when the Scenes, Groups and Selected Objects option has been selected. When it is selected, parametric dimensions of external parts will be displayed in drawing views as reference dimensions. When this option is not selected, dimensions are not displayed in drawing views. (See Chapter 16 for information about reference dimensions, and Chapter 17 for information about external parts.)

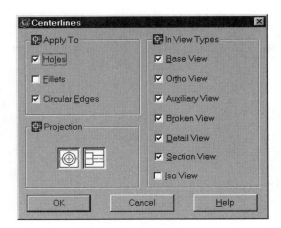

Automatic Centerlines

When you select this check box, Mechanical Desktop automatically draws centerlines on cylindrical objects and round holes in drawing views. If this check box is cleared, you must use the AMCENLINE command to add them. (Chapter 16 describes the AMCENLINE command.) Click the Settings button that is to the right of this check box to display the Centerlines dialog box for setting the centerline parameters. In this dialog box, the two buttons in the cluster labeled Projection control whether centerlines are drawn in views showing the cylindrical feature head-on or from the side, or both.

Save Orphaned Annotation

On rare occasions dimensions and other annotation do not update correctly. When this check box is on, the annotation will be saved in a group. The system variable **amannotepreserve** is set by this system variable.

Copy Cutting Lines with Section Views

When this check box is cleared, the copy of a section view uses the cutting objects as the original view. When this check box is selected, new cutting objects are created for the copied section view. This check box sets the value of the **amsectioncopy** system variable.

Setting Standards Options

The Standards tab of the `Desktop Options` dialog box, which is displayed by Mechanical Desktop's AMOPTIONS command, controls such things as the projection method for drawing views, the appearance of tapped holes, the symbols used for detail and section views, and the appearance of centerlines. The options in the Annotation tab are:

Standard   Select a drafting practices standards from this list box.

Measurement   In this list box, choose between the metric and English systems.

Scale   This list box contains ratios for establishing the default scale of the drawing layout. This list box does not set the scale used for drawing views.

Default Template   Click the Browse button to select a default template from a list of template files. The name and the path of the selected template file is displayed in a list box.

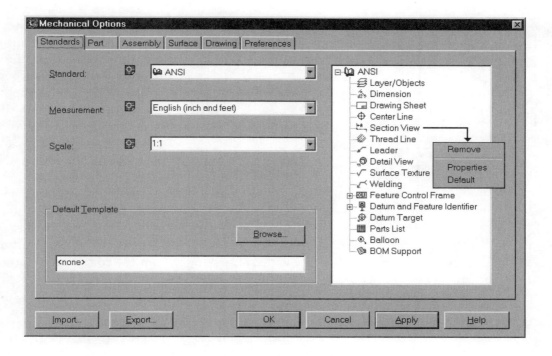

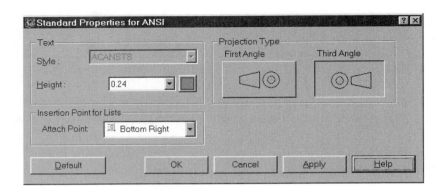

The pane on the right side of the Standards tab has a tree-like list of specific drawing and annotation objects. (You can also set these standards and their properties with the AMSYMSTD command. That command uses a dialog box containing the same a tree-like list of objects that is in the Standards tab.) When you right-click on one of these items, a shortcut menu containing a Properties option appears, and when you select that option, a dialog box for establishing the object's properties appears. The dialog boxes that control the properties of objects related to the overall appearance of drawings and to views are described in the following paragraphs. The dialog boxes controlling the properties of objects related to dimensions are described in Chapter 16, and those related to assembly drawings are described in Chapter 20.

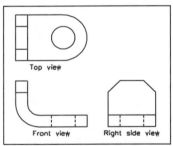

Third angle projection

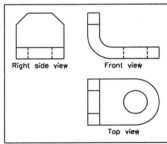

First angle projection

Drafting Standard The name of the current drafting standard is listed at the head of the list. When you select Properties from its right-click shortcut menu a dialog box is displayed containing options for establishing the height and color of the text used for section and detail view labels, the insertion point of lists (such as a Bill of Materials), and the projection type that is used in creating drawing views. Projection type can be set to First Angle, which is the type used in most of the world's countries; or Third angle, which is the projection type most commonly used in North America.

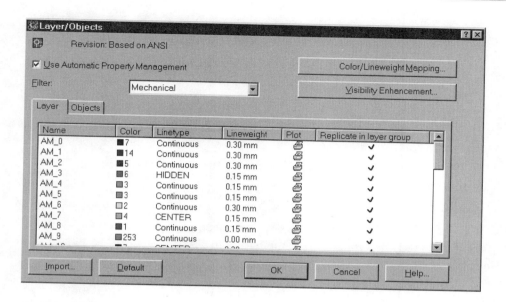

Layer/Objects   You can change layer and object colors, linetypes, and lineweights within this dialog box.

Center Line   Use this dialog box to control the parameters for the centerlines on round holes and cylindrical shaped objects in drawing views.

Centermark length is the length of the cross at the center of the object.

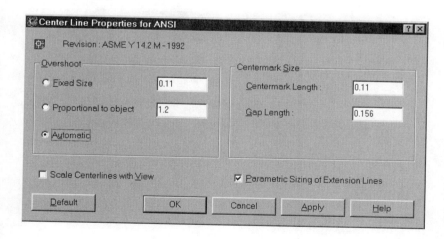

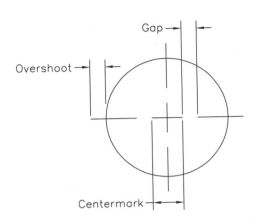

Gap length is the distance between the center-mark and the extension lines.

Overshoot is the distance the extension lines extend beyond the object. You can set overshoot to a fixed value or to a length that is proportional to the object of the centerline. When Automatic is selected, the overshoot will use either the fixed or the proportional value, whichever results in the best appearance.

Scale Centerlines with View   When this check box is selected, the centerline dimensions are scaled according to the scale of the view they are in.

Parametric Sizing of Extension Lines   Select this option to have the length of the centerline extensions automatically adjust to changes made to the part. The **amclpar** system variable is set by this option.

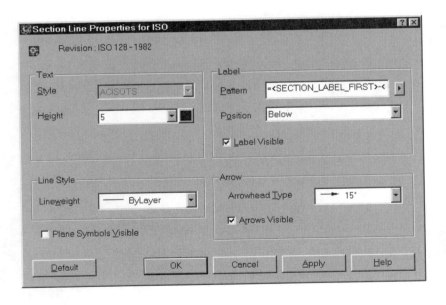

Section Line   The properties in this dialog box control the appearance of section lines. You can set the height and color of the text, the shape of the arrows on the end of the section line, the location of the section view labels, and the line style of the section line. Mechanical Desktop sets the text style of the labels to one that is appropriate to the specified standard, and does not permit you to change it. For example when ISO is the drafting standard, the text style is ACISO.

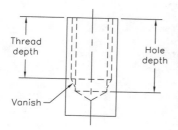

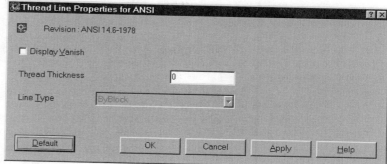

Thread Line   These properties control the appearance of thread representation of tapped (threaded) holes. When the ISO, GB, and DIN standards are selected as a drafting standard, threads are depicted as continuous lines in some views. You can set a width for those lines by entering a value in the Thread Thickness edit box. The value you enter is stored in the **amlinethick** system variable. If the thread depth of a tapped hole is less than the hole depth, a slanted line will be drawn from the end of the thread to the side of the hole in side views of the hole when the Display Vanish check box is selected. This option is available only when the ANSI drafting standard for holes is in effect. It sets value of the **amvanish** system variable.

Leader   Set the arrowhead size and style through the dialog box displayed for the leader property. These settings also control the size and appearance of section line arrowheads.

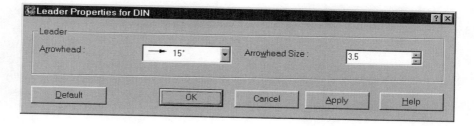

Detail View   The dialog box for setting the symbols for detail views controls such things as the size and color of the text, the line style of the detail border, and the content and position of the detail view labels. The text style for detail view labels is assigned by Mechanical Desktop. It varies by drafting standard, and you cannot change it.

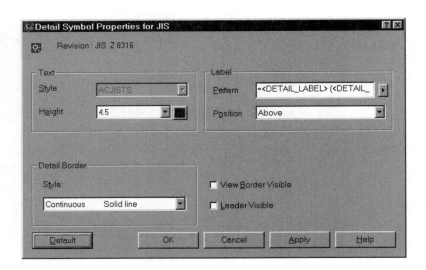

ANSI drafting standards for tapped holes, detail views, and section cutting lines.

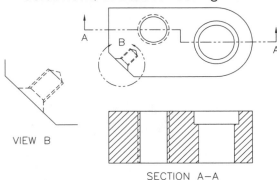

VIEW B

SECTION A–A

Layers in 2D Drawings

Mechanical Desktop relies extensively on layers to control the visibility of objects in drawing views, and it automatically places objects in their proper layer. The names of these layers and the drawing objects that use them are shown in Table 1. You should not use these layers since Mechanical Desktop routinely turns them on and off to fit the circumstances, and sometimes erases objects within the layers.

Table 1 Mechanical Desktop layers for drawing views

Layer Name	Objects using the layer
AM_4	Symbols for detail views
AM_6	Text for section and detail views
AM_7	Centerlines
AM_8	Hatch patterns in section views when one layer is used.
AM_10	Section cutting lines
AM_HID	Hidden edges in drawing views
AM_PARDIM	Parametric dimensions in drawing views
AM_REFDIM	Reference dimensions in drawing views
AM_VIEWS	Floating viewports for drawing views
AM_VIS	Visible edges in drawing views
AM_#_HATCH	Hatch patterns in section views; where # represents a Mechanical Desktop **assigned number.**

An Introduction to Drawing Views

All drawing views, whether they are orthogonal, auxiliary, section, detail, or even isometric, are created through one command—AMDWG-VIEW. At least one of the views in a layout will be called the *base* view, and the other views will, directly or indirectly, be based on and dependent to the base view. Usually, the base view represents the either the top view or the front view of the part.

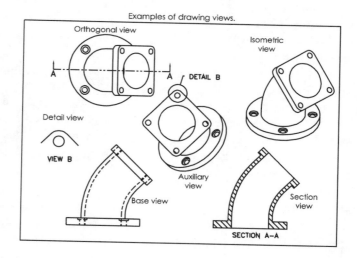

Examples of drawing views.

Mechanical Desktop allows you to have more than one base view, but as a rule you will have only one. The relationships between drawing views are shown in the Drawing mode Desktop Browser just as the Model mode Browser shows relationships between features.

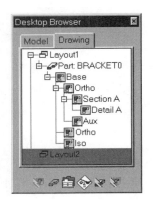

Mechanical Desktop's views are within floating viewports, which are AutoCAD objects that, in effect, are windows in Drawing mode that look into Model mode. You can go into a viewport by invoking AutoCAD's MSPACE command, and once you are within a viewport you can set the viewing direction and the relative size (zoom level) of the model. You can exit a floating viewport to return to drawing mode by invoking AutoCAD's PSPACE command. Each floating viewport resides in a layer and has a border that takes the color of the viewport's layer. You can change the size of the viewport by stretching its border, and you can move the viewport through AutoCAD's MOVE command. If the viewport's layer is turned off or frozen, its border disappears but the contents of the viewport remain. Another important property of floating viewports is that you can selectively freeze and thaw layers within a viewport so that some objects in the viewport will be visible, while others are invisible.

When Mechanical Desktop creates a view, it creates a floating viewport and it sets the viewpoint and the zoom level within the viewport to conform to the view direction and scale specified by the user in the Create Drawing View dialog box. The viewport is in the Am_views layer, which is turned off to make its border invisible. Within the viewport, Mechanical Desktop draws a 2D version of the part as it is seen in the viewport, and it freezes the layer of the part.

Since Mechanical Desktop does a good job in setting up and managing floating viewports, you are not likely to ever need to have any direct contact with them, or make any changes to them or within them. You should instead use Mechanical Desktop commands to relocate views, delete them, and change their scale and other properties. User drawn objects within a viewport are not updated when changes are made to the part, and changing the layer of objects within a viewport may cause the objects to not be visible when the view is updated.

Data Sets for Views

You can create drawing views of any 3D object within Mechanical Desktop's Model mode, regardless of whether the object is a single Mechanical Desktop part, an assembly of parts, a surface model, or an AutoCAD 3D solid. When you create the base view of the drawing, you can choose one of four options for specifying the objects that are to be included in the base view. These options, which are shown in a list box in the `Create Drawing View` dialog box of the AMDWGVIEW command, are described in Table 2.

Table 2 Data Set Options for Drawing Views

Option	Data Included in Base Drawing Views
Active Part	Just the active Mechanical Desktop part will be used for the drawing. No other parts may be added later. No prompts for specifying objects are used when this option is selected.
Scene	All of the parts in a selected assembly scene will be used for the drawing. (Scenes are discussed in Chapter 19.) When components are added or removed from the assembly, the drawing views adjust to reflect the changes.
Select	Selected objects will be used for the drawing. You will be prompted from the command line to select the objects that are to comprise the drawing. Objects cannot later be added to the drawing views.
Group	The objects to be included in the drawing will be members of an AutoCAD group (created by AutoCAD's GROUP command). A dialog box titled Select Group will be displayed for you to use in selecting the group. If no groups, exist this option will not be offered.

You can show multiple parts within one drawing by having more that one base view; with each part having its own set of dependent views. In this chapter, though, as well as in the next two, we will concentrate on creating drawings from the active part. Thus, there will be just one part per drawing. In design and manufacturing industries, such drawings, which provide a detailed description of a single part, are often referred to as *detail drawings*. In Chapter 20, we will discuss *assembly drawings* and *exploded pictorial drawings*.

Creating a Base View

Generally, the first view you create will be a base view, and your choice of parameters for that view are important because all of the subsequent views you create will be dependent to it. The steps to create a base view are:

1. Invoke the AMDWGVIEW command to display the `Create Drawing View` dialog box, and select either Base or Multiple from the View Type list box. The Multiple option creates a base view, and then goes on to create one or more orthogonal views from the base view. (Orthogonal views have a view direction that is ninety degrees to that of their parent view.) Broken views are discussed in Chapter 15.

2. Select the Data Set type that is to be within the view. Most of the time you will select Active Part.

3. Enter the scale of the view. Numbers larger than 1.0 cause the objects in the view to be drawn larger than their true size, while numbers less than 1.0 cause them to be drawn smaller than their true size.

4. Set the hidden line parameters. Hidden lines are representations of edges that are behind surfaces of the part, as seen from the viewing direction of the view.

   • If you clear the Calculate Hidden Lines check box, the other three check boxes in the cluster will be grayed out, and the Display As list box will be activated. In this list box, the Wireframe option causes only visible edges to be displayed, while the Wireframe with Silhouettes option causes all edges to be displayed in the CONTINUOUS linetype.

   • Usually, you will have hidden line calculations performed. If you want hidden lines to be calculated but not displayed in the view, clear the Display Hidden Lines check box.

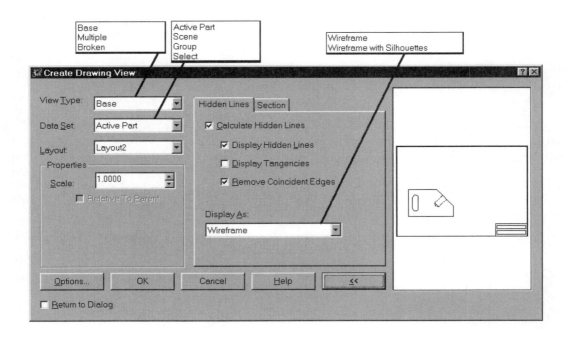

- A tangency represents the edge of a curved surface on a 3D feature at which it is tangent to an adjacent surface. The edges of fillets are an often encountered tangency. Tangencies will be shown when the check box labeled Display Tangencies is checked.

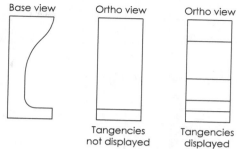

- In creating a view, Mechanical Desktop draws a wireframe version of the part. When the Remove Coincident Edges option is selected, edges that are directly behind other edges (such as the bottom four lines of a cube that is seen head on) are not drawn. The appearance of the part within the view is not affected by this parameter. Usually, you will have coincident edges removed.

5. The base view can be a section view. If it is to be a section view, you will set its section type and its hatch pattern parameters by selecting the dialog box tab labeled Section Views. Descriptions of the parameters for creating section views are in Chapter 15.

6. The button labeled Options opens the `Mechanical Options` dialog box. This allows you to establish some other parameters, such as to establish a drafting standard, on the fly.

7. When you have set the parameters for the base view, click the OK button to dismiss the Create Drawing View dialog box. Mechanical Desktop will switch to Model mode, and issue command line prompts for you to select a plane, and then to specify the direction of the X axis on that plane. (If the view data set is for anything other than Active Part, you will first be prompted to specify the data set objects.) The prompts and your input, which are similar to those for setting up a sketch plane, establish the viewing direction for the base view. The view will look perpendicularly toward the plane you specify, and the direction you specify for the X axis will be horizontal and point to the right in the drawing view. The actual location of the specified plane is not important, as long as it is perpendicular to the view direction you want to establish. You can also base the viewpoint of the base view on the current model mode view direction or on the direction that is perpendicular to the User Coordinate System XY plane.

3D part

Resulting Base view

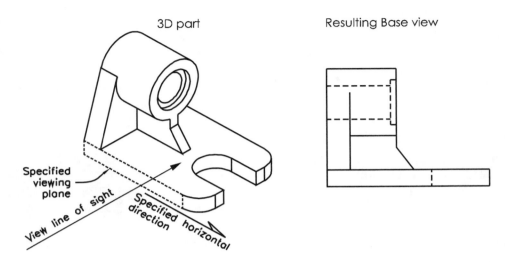

Specified viewing plane

View line of sight

Specified direction

Specified horizontal

8. Once you have established the view's viewing direction, Mechanical Desktop will return to Drawing mode and issue a command line prompt for you to pick a location for the view. The part will appear and will be centered on the point you specify. The prompt for the view's location will be repeated, so that you can try other locations, until you press the Enter key. If you selected Multiple as the view type, Mechanical Desktop will begin issuing prompts for you to create ortho views from the base view. Chapter 15 discusses ortho views.

CHAPTER 15

Working with Drawing
Views

The previous chapter introduced Mechanical Desktop's Drawing mode, layouts, and drawing views to you. This chapter concentrates on creating and managing drawing views.

This chapter covers the following topics.

- Describes how to create orthogonal and auxiliary views to show part surfaces in their true shape.

- Tells how to make isometric views for helping people better visualize the part.

- Shows how to create enlarged views from portions of other views to more clearly show small details.

- Describes the steps for making views of just the relevant areas of parts that are too long to fit within a drawing's borders with a scale that legibility shows the part.

- Explains how to show the interior portion of parts by making section views. You can make full section, half section, offset section, aligned section, and radial section views. You can also break out areas from a part's surface to reveal its interior.

- Tells how to update drawing views after changes have been made to them and to the part, as well as how to move, copy, and delete drawing views.

- Explains how to use Mechanical Desktop's tools for editing drawing views. These tools do more than just make changes and corrections—they can control the properties and visibility of objects in drawing views.

- *Describes how to retrieve information about drawing views and the objects in them, and how to export them to AutoCAD.*

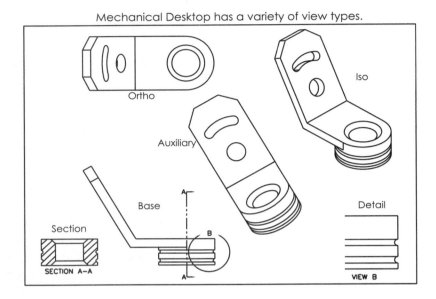

Mechanical Desktop has a variety of view types.

Creating Drawing Views

Drawings used for manufacturing parts consist of views that show the various surfaces of a part in their true shape. In each view the part is shown as if an image of it has been projected onto a screen. They are sometimes referred to as orthographic drawings, because the line of sight for a view is perpendicular to the projection screen. Generally, at least two views are required in a drawing, and as the complexity of a part increases, the number of views needed to fully depict it increases. Moreover, to clarify the internal geometry of a part, some views may show the part as if a section had been removed from it. Because of the wide spread use of drawings and their importance, national and international standards for controlling view selection, arrangement, and feature representation exist. Mechanical Desktop has tools for creating drawing views that conform to the most widely used standards, and we will describe those tools in this chapter.

Every Mechanical Desktop drawing layout contains a base view, and that will be the first view you create. Base views are described in Chapter 14, and you should review the steps listed in that chapter for creating base views if you are not familiar with them. Although you can have more than one base view in a layout, you will generally have just one. All of the other views in the layout will be an offspring of the base view, or an offspring of an offspring. Because of this linkage between views, changes you make to a parent view also affect the offspring of that view. For example, when you move a parent view all of its offspring move with it. Once you create a base view, you can create the following view types.

Ortho   Views that have a line of sight that is perpendicular to the line of sight of their parent view.

Auxiliary   Views having a line of sight that is perpendicular to a plane that is seen edge-on the parent view.

Detail   An (usually) enlarged view of a selected area in the parent view.

Iso   A pictorial view with a line of sight that has equal angles to the parent view's three principal planes.

Ortho and auxiliary views, as well as the base view, can be section views. And, an iso view based on a section view will be an isometric view of the section view.

Creating Ortho Views

Ortho, which stands for orthogonal, views have a view direction that is 90 degrees to that of their parent view. They are created by selecting Ortho from the View Type list box of AMDWGVIEW's `Create Drawing View` dialog box. Since the scale of an ortho view is always that of its parent, the Scale edit box will be grayed-out. The Data Set and Layout list box will also be grayed out. The parameters in the Hidden Lines tab are the same as those described in the discussion of base views in Chapter 14. The options in the Section tab are described later in this chapter.

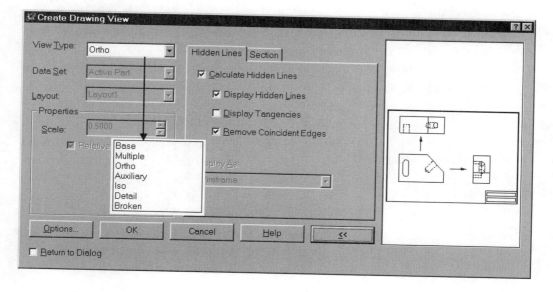

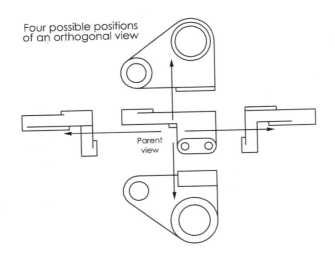

Four possible positions of an orthogonal view

Parent view

When you click the OK button of the **Create Drawing View** dialog box, Mechanical Desktop will issue a command line prompt for you to select the parent view. You select a view by picking a point anywhere within the view: the point does not have to be on an object. A rubber band line will be anchored in the center of the selected view, and you will be prompted to select a location for the orthogonal view. When you pick the location point, the part will be displayed with its center on the selected point, and the prompt to select a location will be repeated. Press the Enter key when you are satisfied with the location. For any parent view, there are four possible directions for locating the orthogonal view, as shown in the accompanying figure.

Creating Multiple Views

When you select Multiple as the view type, you can create more than one ortho view with one call to AMDWGVIEW. You can also create iso views with this option. When you

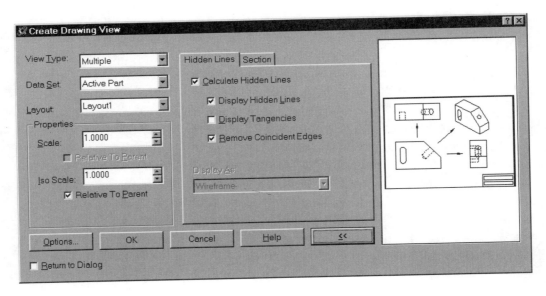

select Multiple, the Data Set and the Layout list boxes will be activated, but you will ignore them if you are creating dependent views. Also, the Scale and Iso Scale edit boxes will be activated. The Scale edit box is for establishing the scale of a base view and Mechanical Desktop will ignore its value when ortho views are based on an existing view. The value in the Iso Scale edit box always applies to iso views, though, even if they are based on an existing view.

When you click the OK button of the dialog box, Mechanical Desktop will issue a command line prompt for you to select an existing view to serve as the parent, or to create a base view. If you opt to create a base view, Mechanical Desktop will issue the prompts for establishing the view's line of sight and location we described in Chapter 14.

Once the base view has been created, or if you have selected an existing view, a command line prompt will ask you to specify the location of an offspring view. When you pick a point that is within approximately 10 degrees of a horizontal or vertical line from the center of the parent view, the offspring view will be an ortho view. Otherwise, the view will be an iso view. See the section on iso views later in this chapter for additional information. When the view type and its location is as you want it, press the Enter key. Mechanical Desktop will repeat the prompt for the location of an offspring view. Press the Enter key in response to the prompt to specify a view location when you have created all of the views you want.

Creating Auxiliary Views

The view direction of auxiliary views is perpendicular to a plane that is shown edge-on in an existing view. Objects on the plane are shown in their true form in the auxiliary view. When you select Auxiliary as the View Type in the **Create Drawing View** dialog box the Data Set and Layout list boxes, as well as the Scale edit box will be grayed out. Hidden lines and tangencies are handled just as they are for base and ortho views. We will discuss section views later in this chapter.

The plane of the auxiliary view must be seen edge-on in its parent view. When you press the **Create Drawing View** dialog box's OK button, Mechanical Desktop will issue command line prompts for you to establish the auxiliary view's plane. Often you will specify the plane by picking a point on its edge. The auxiliary view's line of sight will be perpendicular to this edge. Alternatively, you can specify the plane by selecting two points. And you can also use an existing work plane to define it.

After you dismiss the **Create Drawing View** dialog box, the initial command line prompt to establish the auxiliary view's plane is:

```
Select first point for projection direction or [Workplane]: (Enter W, or select an object
   in a view)
```

If you select an object, Mechanical Desktop will issue the prompt:

```
Select second point or <Enter> to use the selected point: (Select an object in the view or
   press Enter.)
```

If you are confident that the first point you picked defines the edge of the auxiliary plane, press the Enter key. Otherwise, select a second point on the edge of the auxiliary plane or on an edge that is perpendicular to the plane.

If you chose the option in the first prompt to select a work plane, Mechanical Desktop will ask you to select the parent view of the auxiliary view. The work planes that are parallel with the line of sight of the selected view will be displayed, and you will be prompted to select one.

Once you have identified the auxiliary view plane, regardless of whether you picked one point, two points, or a work plane, Mechanical Desktop will place a point near the edge of the auxiliary plane, anchor a rubber band line on it, rotate the coordinate system of the layout so that its X axis is parallel with the auxiliary plane, and issue the prompt:

`Specify location for view: (Pick a point.)`

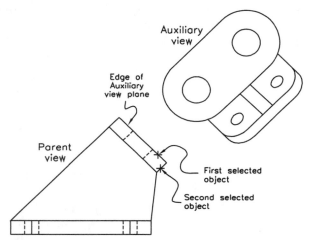

As soon as you pick a point the model will appear, and the prompt to select a location will be repeated. Press the Enter key to accept a location and end the AMDWGVIEW command.

Creating Isometric Views

Frequently, any view having a line of sight that is askew to the three principal projection planes is called an isometric view; often though, the view is actually an *axonometric* view. A *true isometric* view, which is a unique type of axonometric view, has a line of sight that is equally inclined to the three principal projection planes. Consequently, edges that are parallel to the principal projection planes are equally inclined in isometric views and are 81.65 percent of their true length. This equal inclination is where the view's name comes from: the prefix *iso* means equal, and *metric* means measure.

You can add an isometric view to a Mechanical Desktop drawing by selecting Iso from the View Type list box in the **Create Drawing View** dialog box. The only options available with isometric views are to set their scale and to control hidden line removal. Enter the scale of the isometric view in the Scale edit box. If the Relative to Parent check box is cleared, the scale is an absolute value; if it is checked, the scale of the isometric view is the product of the entered scale multiplied by the scale of the parent view. The hidden line options, are the same as for other view types, but unlike the other view types, the default setting is to not display hidden lines.

When you press the OK button of the **Create Drawing View** dialog box, Mechanical Desktop will issue a command line prompt for you to select the isometric view's parent. The isometric view will use the Y axis direction (which is vertical in 2D) of the parent view as its Z axis direction (which is vertical in 3D). Then you will be prompted to select the view's location. The isometric view's line

The four possible isometric views from a parent view

of sight depends on the location of the view relative to its parent view. If the location is above the parent view, the isometric view looks down toward the part; and if it is positioned below the parent view, the isometric view looks up toward the part. Also, if the isometric view is located to the right of the parent view, the viewpoint is from the right; and if it is located to the left of the parent view, the view point is from the left. As with the other view types, when you pick a location point the part will be displayed at that point and the prompt to select a location will be repeated until you press the Enter key.

Since the line of sight of an isometric view is dependent on its location relative to its parent view, you must sometimes place the view in an undesirable location. This is not really a problem, though, since you can use the AMMOVEVIEW command, which is discussed later in this chapter, to relocate the isometric view. If you want an isometric view to have a scale showing lines in their actual length (as in AutoCAD's isometric snap mode), set the view's scale to 1.2247 relative to the parent view. Also, although there are no options for creating an isometric section view, isometric views of section views show the sliced plane.

Creating Detail Views

Detail views are for showing the intricate details, and their dimensions, of a relatively small section of the parent view. Their scale is virtually always larger than that of their parent view. Unlike ortho, auxiliary, and iso views, detail views have the same view direction as the parent view, and can be placed in any location. They are created by selecting Detail as the View Type in the **Create Drawing View** dialog box.

You specify the scale of the detail view by entering a number in the Scale edit box. This number can represent the absolute scale of the detail view, or when the Relative to Parent check box is selected, its scale relative to the parent view. Mechanical Desktop outlines the detail's area in the parent view, and the character you enter in the Detail Symbol edit box is used to identify it. The characters in the Detail Symbol edit box are used to identify the detail view.

Although the options to display hidden lines and tangencies are active, they have no effect. Hidden lines and tangencies will be shown in the detail view if the parent view shows them, and they will not be shown if the parent view doesn't show them. All of the options in the Section tab are disabled.

When you press the OK button of the **Create Drawing View** edit box, you will be prompted from the command line to pick a vertex point in the parent view to serve as the center of the detail view. If you pick an arc or circle, the vertex will be at its centerpoint; if you pick a line, the vertex will be the closest endpoint of the line. You do not need to use object snaps to pick the vertex. Next, Mechanical Desktop will issue the following command line prompt you to specify the boundary of the detail view area:

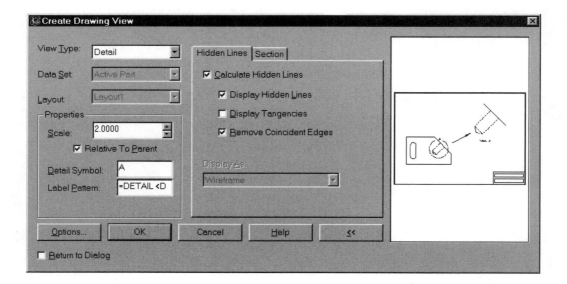

```
Specify center point for circular area or [Ellipse/Polygon/Rect/Select]: (Select a point or
   enter an option.)
```

The default response is to create a circular area for the detail view. After selecting its center, you will be prompted to specify its radius. As options, the detail view area's boundary can also be defined by an ellipse, a polygon, or a rectangle. When you choose one of these options, command line prompts lead you through the steps to draw the boundary object. The Select option is for using a pre-drawn closed polyline as a boundary. The viewport border of the detail view will take its shape from the boundary you define. (Because the layer Mechanical Desktop uses for drawing viewport boundaries is always turned off, the shape and size of the detail view's border is not evident, and usually it is not important.)

After specifying the detail view's boundary, you will be asked for the center location of the detail view. As with the other views, you can try any number of locations before you press the Enter key to signify acceptance.

Mechanical Desktop will label both the parent view and the detail view using the character, or characters you entered in the Create Drawing View dialog box and the drafting standards you specified in the Standards tab of the Mechanical Options dialog box, or with the AMSTMSTD command. The text style of the labels is set by Mechanical Desktop, and it varies according to which drafting standard you are using. If you move dimensions from the parent view to the detail view, they automatically adjust to any scale differences between the views. (Chapter 16 explains how to move dimensions from view to another.)

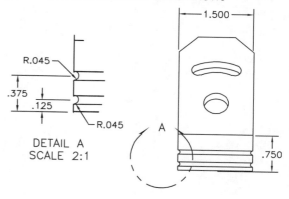

The ANSI standard for detail views

Creating Broken Views

When your part is too long to fit the on the drawing's paper in a scale that will clearly show its details, you can use broken views to display just the important areas of the part. Broken views are multiple sub-views that are aligned with one another, and have the same scale and view direction. When you move one sub-view the others move as well. Also, they do not require a parent view. Some other rules and characteristics of broken views are:

- At least two sub-views are required for each broken view.

- Broken views cannot be used as the parent of another view.

- Dimensions are not automatically added to broken views. They must be manually added as reference dimensions. (Chapter 16 discusses reference dimensions.)

- The alignment of sub-views is always in the X or Y directions. They cannot be aligned diagonally.

To create a set of broken views, select Broken as the View Type in the **Create Drawing View** dialog box of the AMDWGVIEW command. Enter the scale of the views and the Break Gap, which is the distance between the sub-views. When you press the OK button, Mechanical Desktop will switch to Model mode and prompt for a plane that the views are to look toward and for the horizontal direction of the view, just as it does for base views. These prompts are issued even if another view exists. The entire part will be displayed in Drawing mode for you to use in designating the sub-views. Command line prompts will be issued for you to select vertex points for aligning the sub-views, and to draw a rectangle around each sub-view to define its boundary.

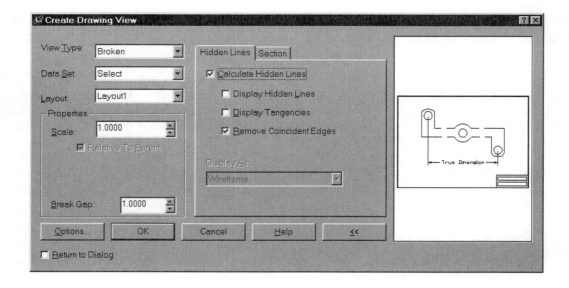

Exercise 1

Creating a Broken View

To give you a feel for broken views, this exercise will lead you through the steps to create broken views of the part shown in Figure 1-1 in an isometric wireframe view. Retrieve the file md15e101.dwg from the CD-ROM that comes with this book and open it.

Switch from Model mode to Drawing mode, and use the PAGESETUP

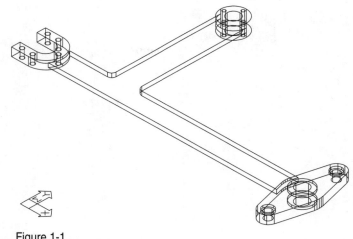

Figure 1-1

command to establish the parameters of a layout. In the Plot Device tab of the Page Setup dialog box, select a plot device of your choice; then move to the Layout Settings tab. Select a paper size that is approximately 11 by 8.5 inches. set the Plot area to Layout and Plot scale to 1:1. Leave the other settings at their defaults, and exit the dialog box.

Zoom back so that the horizontal distance across the graphics area is at least 24 units, because the initial view of the part will extend well beyond the borders of the paper size you specified. Start the AMDWGVIEW command to bring up the **Create Drawing View** dialog box. Select Broken as the View Type, Active Part for the Data Set, enter 0.5 in the Scale edit box, and enter 1.0 in the Break Gap edit box. The hidden line and tangencies settings are not important. Then press the OK button.

Mechanical Desktop will switch to Model mode. Enter X (for worldXy) when you are prompted to select a plane, and Enter X (for worldX) when you are prompted for an axis. Accept the displayed orientation of the X and Y axis. Mechanical Desktop will return to Drawing mode, and ask you to locate the broken view. Pick a point near the center of the simulated sheet of paper. A temporary image of the entire part will be displayed. Pick other points as necessary to move the image so that the left end of the part in is the lower left corner of the simulated sheet of paper, as shown in Figure 1-2. Press Enter to anchor the view position.

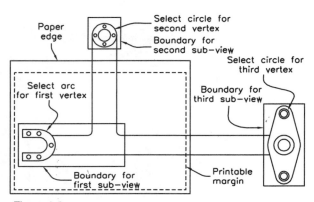

Figure 1-2

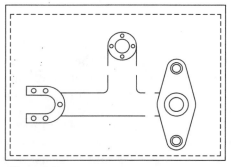

Figure 1-3

You will make three sub-views—one for each end of the part. The first sub-view, which will be on the left end of the part, will include the intersection of the vertical and horizontal bar. When you are prompted to select a vertex in the parent sub-view, pick one of the arcs on the left end of the part; and when you are prompted to define the boundary of the sub-view, draw a rectangle similar to the one in Figure 1-2.

The rectangle you drew will remain on the screen, and you will be asked to select a vertex for a second view. Pick a point on the largest circle at the end of the vertical bar, and draw a rectangle around that end of the part, as shown in Figure 1-2. When you are prompted to select another vertex, pick a point on one of the circles on the right end of the part, and then draw a rectangle around that end of the part, as shown in Figure 1-2. Press the Enter key when you are prompted to select another vertex. After performing some calculations, Mechanical Desktop will display the three broken views as shown in Figure 1-3.

Because the left end of the part was used to align both the vertical and horizontal bars, it was important that it be created first, and that it contain portions of both the vertical and horizontal bars. The order in which the other two views were created was not important. On the CD-ROM that accompanies this book, the broken views are in file md15e103.dwg.

Creating Section Views

Setting Section View Parameters

The View Type list box of AMDWGVIEW's **Create Drawing View** dialog box does not include a section view type. Instead, section is an option for base, ortho, auxiliary, and broken views. Although you can specify section options for a base view, the view will not be sectioned unless another view exists. You cannot make a section view of an isometric or detail view, but those views will be sectioned if the parent view is. To show dimensions in section views, open the Drawing tab of the Mechanical Options dialog box and select the check box labeled Section Views in the Parametric Dimension Display cluster; or set the system variable **amsectiondim** to 1 directly.

To set the parameters of a section view, select the tab labeled Section in the **Create Drawing View** dialog box. None is the default section Type, and all of the buttons and boxes in the tab will be grayed-out. Select Full, Half, Offset, Aligned, Breakout, or Radial as the section Type to activate the other options in the tab.

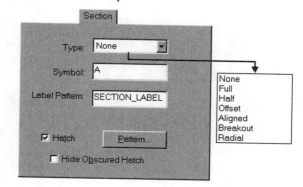

The entries in the Symbol and Label Pattern edit boxes are used to label the cutting line of the section in the parent view and to label the section view itself. The style used for the cutting line and the section view is according to the drafting standards you have specified in the Standards tab of the **Mechanical Options** dialog box, or with AMSYMSTD.

If you clear the check box labeled Hatch, the section view will contain no hatching. The button labeled Pattern opens a dialog box similar to the one used by AutoCAD's BHATCH command for you to choose a predefined hatch pattern and set its scale and angle.

When the check box labeled Hide Obscured Hatch is checked, hatches on faces that are partially hidden are trimmed back to the edges of surfaces that hide the hatch. If this check box is cleared, the entire hatch is shown. The need to obscure hatches is most likely to occur on isometric views with partial sections. The next figure shows two isometric views from the same half section orthographic view. In one of the isometric views the partially obscured hatch is not trimmed, while it is trimmed in the other isometric view.

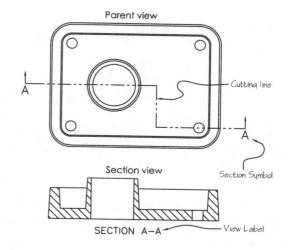

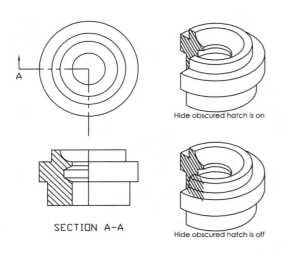

Hide obscured hatch is on

SECTION A-A

Hide obscured hatch is off

When you have set the parameters for the section view, press the OK button of the **Create Drawing View** dialog box. In addition to the command line prompts for locating the view, Mechanical Desktop will issue prompts, which vary according to the section view type, for defining the cutting plane, or planes, of the section view.

Full Section Views

Full section views have a straight slicing plane that extends completely through the part. After you have selected a location for the view, a command line prompt will ask you to define the section's cutting plane.

```
Enter section through type [Point/Work plane]<Work plane>: (Enter an option, or press
    Enter)
```

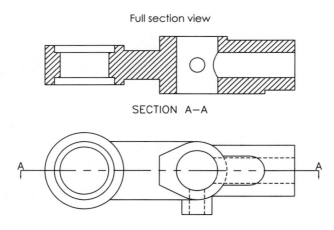

Full section view

SECTION A—A

When you select the Point option, you will be prompted to select a point in the parent view. You must select the point by picking an object in the parent view. When you pick a line, the nearest endpoint of the line will be used as the point; and when you pick an arc or a circle, its centerpoint will be used as the point. The cutting plane will pass through the point, and will be perpendicular to the line of sight of the section view. If you choose the Work plane option, which is the

default option, an existing work plane that is perpendicular to the line of sight of the section view will be used as a slicing plane. If more that one such work plane exists, you will be asked to select one of them.

Half Section Views

Half section views use two intersecting slicing planes. One is perpendicular to the line of sight of the section view, while the other is parallel with its line of sight. After you have selected the section view's location, Mechanical Desktop will display the command line prompt:

```
Enter section through type [Point/Work Plane]<Work plane>: (Enter an option, or press
      Enter)
```

If you choose the Point option, you will be prompted to select a point in the parent view to serve as the intersection of the two slicing planes. You select the point by picking an object. When the object is a line, the point will be on its endpoint nearest the pick point. When the object is an arc or circle, the point will be in its center. If you select the default Work plane option, Mechanical Desktop will display all of the work planes in the parent view that are perpendicular to the section view's line of sight, and will ask you to select one to serve as a slicing plane. Then it will display all of the work planes in the parent view that are parallel with the section view's line of sight, and prompt you to select one of them for the other slicing plane.

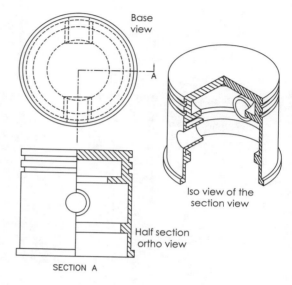

Once the intersection of the two slicing planes has been established, Mechanical Desktop will show you the quadrant that will be removed for the section by displaying the cutting lines in the parent view as two lines that are ninety degrees to each other, and issue the prompt:

```
Side of half section [Flip/Accept]<Accept>: (Enter an option, or press Enter)
```

If you choose the Flip option, the cutting line that is perpendicular to the section view's line of sight will flip to the other side.

Cutting Line Sketches

Cutting line sketches are a feature made by the AMCUTLINE command in Model mode for establishing the slicing planes for offset and aligned section views. They should be dimensioned and constrained to existing 3D geometry so they will change in accordance with changes to the part. Cutting lines must be created after a 3D feature exists, but before creating the section view they are used in. The rules for drawing a cutting line are:

- Cutting lines are drawn on the current sketch plane with a linetype defined by the **amskstyle** system variable (which is usually set to a continuous linetype).

- Either lines or 2D polylines having straight segments must be used in drawing a cutting line. No curves or arcs are permitted. Edges of 3D features cannot be part of the sketch.

- The lines cannot form a closed loop.

- The two ends of the cutting line must extend beyond the 3D part to be sectioned.

- If the sketch is to be used for offset section views, segments of the cutting line must be at right angles to one another, and the end segments must be parallel to each another.

- If the sketch is to be used for an aligned section view, only two segments are allowed. They do not have to be at right angles to one another, though.

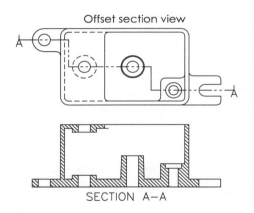

Offset section view

SECTION A–A

Offset Section Views

Offset section views are useful for making sections thorough a part having features that cannot be sliced by a single plane. When you have specified the location of the section view, Mechanical Desktop will temporarily switch to Model mode, and issue a command line prompt for you to select a cutting line sketch (made by the AMCUTLINE command). The segments of the cutting line sketch must be perpendicular to one another, their end segments must be parallel to each other, and the end segments must be perpendicular to the section view line of sight. The section view will then be created with no additional prompts. The cutting line sketch will disappear in Model mode when the section view is created, but you can use the Unhide option of AMVISIBLE to restore it.

Aligned Section Views

Like offset section views, aligned section views use cutting line sketches made by the AMCUT-LINE command to define their cutting planes. Unlike offset section views, though, the cutting line sketch for a aligned section view consists of just two segments, and the segments do not have to be perpendicular to each other. In fact, they seldom are. After you have positioned the aligned section view, Mechanical Desktop will temporarily switch to Model mode and issue a command line prompt for you to select the cutting line sketch. The Model mode visibility of the cutting line sketch will be turned off when the section view is created.

Radial Section Views

Radial section views are similar to full section views in that there is just a single slicing plane that extends completely through the part. Unlike full section views, though, the slicing plane is not perpendicular to the ortho view's line of sight. Moreover, in the section view, the sliced plane on the part is revolved so that it is perpendicular to the ortho view's line of sight.

In creating a radial section view you will be prompted, as soon as you set the location of the view, to select the work plane that is to serve as the slicing plane. Then, Mechanical Desktop will issue the prompt:

```
Select pivot point or <align with midpoint of
    section>: (Pick a point in the parent view or
    press Enter)
```

When you select a curved object in the parent view, Mechanical Desktop will rotate the sliced plane about the object's center point until it is perpendicular to the section view's line of sight. When you accept the default alignment option, Mechanical Desktop rotates

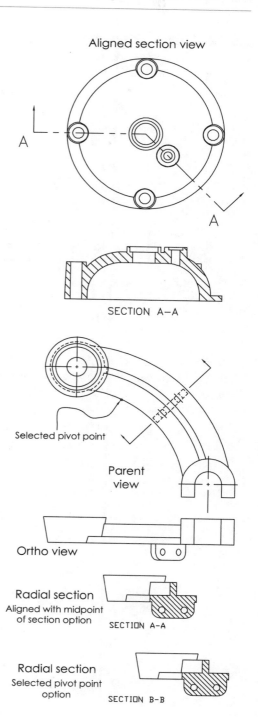

Aligned section view

SECTION A–A

Selected pivot point

Parent view

Ortho view

Radial section
Aligned with midpoint of section option   SECTION A–A

Radial section
Selected pivot point option   SECTION B–B

the sliced plane about its midpoint until it is perpendicular to the section view's line of sight. The accompanying figure shows three views based on the same parent view. One is a straight ortho view, the second is a radial section view aligned with the midpoint of the section, and the third is a radial section aligned with a pivot point.

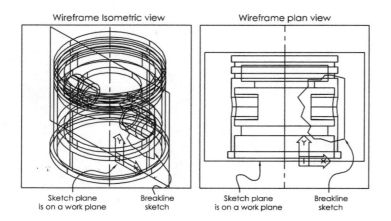

Wireframe Isometric view

Sketch plane is on a work plane — Breakline sketch

Wireframe plan view

Sketch plane is on a work plane — Breakline sketch

Breakout Sections

Breakout sections are used to expose a relatively small area of interior geometry when a larger section view is not necessary. Their appearance is that of a hole, or a broken out chunk, in the part; and often their edges are jagged to suggest broken sides in the section. Breakout sections are based on breakline sketches, which are created by the AMBREAKLINE command. Like the other Mechanical Desktop sketch features, breakline sketches are composed of AutoCAD wireframe objects that have been drawn on a sketch plane, and are subject to geometric and dimensional constraints. The sketch must form a closed profile.

To create a breakout section, select Breakout as the Section Type in the Section tab of the **Create Drawing View** dialog box. The Symbol and the Label Pattern edit boxes will be disabled, because cutting lines and section labels are not used with breakout sections.

When you have established the location of the view, Mechanical Desktop will switch to Model mode and prompt for the breakout sketch. Then, you will be prompted to select either the breakout sketch or a work plane to define the section depth. As soon as you specify the section depth plane, Mechanical Desktop will create a view containing the breakout section. Everything within the outline of the breakout sketch from this specified plane toward the viewer will be removed in the section view.

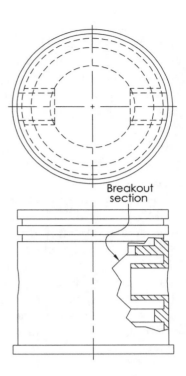

Breakout
section

Managing Drawing Views

Mechanical Desktop has a full complement of tools for managing the drawing views you create. You can move views, delete them, change their scale, change they way they display hidden edges, and even change the color and linetype used in drawing individual edges within a view.

Drawing Views and the Desktop Browser

Every view you create is listed in the Desktop Browser, in an outline format to indicate the dependencies of the views, and with each view having a name—such as Base, Ortho, or SectionA—corresponding to the view type. When you right-click the

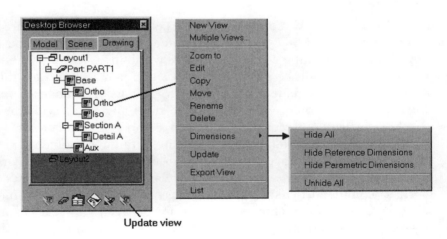

Update view

name of a view, a menu for editing and managing the view, including renaming the Browser's name for the view, will be displayed. You may want to give your views more meaningful names, such as Front, Top, or Half_SecA.

The Edit, Copy, Move, Delete, Update, Export View, and List items in the right-click view menus initiate Mechanical Desktop commands for managing views that we will discuss in this chapter. The options for hiding dimensions are discussed in Chapter 16. As you would surmise, the New View and Multiple View menu items initiate the AMDWG-VIEW command. The Zoom to option zooms in to the selected view so that it fills the graphics area.

Updating Drawing Views

Generally, when geometric changes are made to the 3D part, the drawing views are automatically updated. You can, though, turn off automatic drawing view updates through the Drawing tab of the Mechanical Options dialog box that is displayed by the AMOPTIONS command, as described in Chapter 14, or by setting the value of the system variable **amviewrefresh** to 0.

If you have turned off automatic updating, you must force view updates by invoking the AMUPDATE command, and selecting the View option. You will be asked to select a view to update, to update all of the views in the current layout, or to update all views in all layouts. If you select a view that has dependent views, you will receive a dialog box message asking if you want to update the dependent views as well. Changes to the 3D part must have been incorporated with AMUPDATE before you can update drawing views.

Moving Drawing Views

The AMMOVEVIEW command enables you to move and rearrange drawing views. From the command line you will prompted to select the view you intend to move. You select a view by picking a point anywhere within it—the point does not have to be on an object. Then you will be prompted to specify a new location for the view. Locations are always based on the center of the view. Movements of orthogonal and auxiliary views are restricted to positions that will preserve their alignment with their parent view. Conversely, whenever a parent view is moved, ortho and auxiliary views dependent to it will move as well to maintain their alignment. Detail and isometric views also move when their parent view is moved, even through they are not aligned with it. It is possible to modify and even remove the positional relationship between views through the AMEDITVIEW command, which we will discuss shortly. Although in most cases you do not want to remove the alignment relationship between views, it is sometimes useful to do so—such as repositioning a section view to better fit within the borders of the drawing.

Deleting Drawing Views

You can delete drawing views through the AMDELVIEW command. On the command line you will be asked to select the view you want to delete. Pick a point anywhere within a view to select it. If the view you select has one or more dependent views, a highlighted rectangle will be drawn around each dependent view and a message box will be displayed, asking if you would like to delete the dependent views also. You cannot have some dependent views deleted, while the others remain.

Making Copies of Drawing Views

You can copy a view with the AMCOPYVIEW command. From the command line, you will be prompted to select the view that is to be copied, and if the view you select has dependents, Mechanical Desktop will ask if you want them copied as well. Then, a prompt will ask you to pick a location for the copy.

If the view you have selected to copy is a base view, the location for the copy can be in another layout. To do this, enter the letter L (or the word layout) when you are prompted for the new view's location, and enter the name of the layout. Mechanical Desktop will open the layout you specified and prompt you to select a location for the copy.

Editing Individual Drawing Views

Use the AMEDITVIEW command to change the parameters of individual drawing views. If you start AMEDITVIEW from the command line, you will be prompted to select the view to be edited. You do so by picking a point anywhere within the view. Then the **Edit Drawing View** dialog box will be displayed. The view's type will be shown in the title bar of this dialog box, and buttons and edit boxes not applicable for that type of view will be grayed-out.

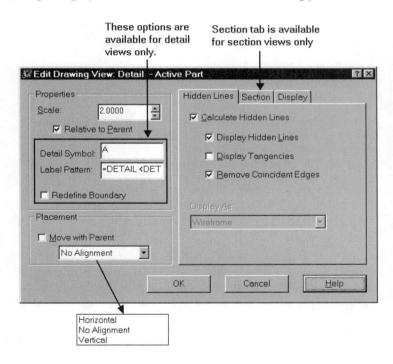

These options are available for detail views only.

Section tab is available for section views only

The Scale edit box allows you to change the scale of base, detail, and isometric views; while its associated Relative to Parent check box allows you to readjust the scale of detail and isometric views relative to their parent view. These options work the same as their counterparts in the **Create Drawing View** dialog box. Options for changing the symbol and label pattern, and for redefining the boundary are available when a detail view is being edited.

For all views other than detail views, the **Edit Drawing View** dialog box has a check box titled Parametric Viewport Sizing. This check box is turned off if you have stretched the viewport's border. When you turn it on, the viewport border is restored to its parametric size.

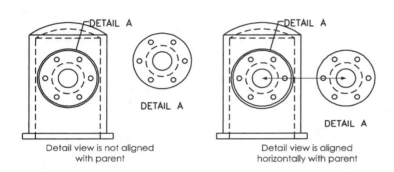

Detail view is not aligned with parent

Detail view is aligned horizontally with parent

When the Move with Parent check box is selected, which is the default setting for dependent views, the view being edited will move in accordance with movements of its parent view. When the Move with Parent button is cleared, the list box below it will be activated. There are three options in this list box—No Alignment, Align Horizontal, and Align Vertical.

- No Alignment removes all alignment constraints between the view being edited and its parent view. The view will not move when its parent is moved.

- The Align Horizontal and Align Vertical options assign an alignment constraint between two views that are normally independent, such as two base views; or between two views that are normally not aligned, such as a detail view and its parent. When you select one of these options, command line prompts will be issued (after you click the OK button of the **Edit Drawing View** dialog box) to select a point to be used for aligning the view. The point you select must be on an object within the view being edited. If the object you select is a line, its nearest endpoint will be used as the alignment point; and if it is an arc or a circle, its centerpoint will be used. Object snaps are not needed to specify these points. Then you will be asked to select the point in a second view that the first point is to be aligned with. The view being edited will move as necessary to align itself with the other view.

The dialog box's Tab that is labeled Hidden Lines contains the same options for hidden lines as those in the dialog box for creating views.

The Display tab of the **Edit Drawing View** dialog contains options for controlling the appearance and display of objects in the view. The four check boxes in this tab are equivalent to those with the same names in the Drawing tab of the **Mechanical Options** dialog box. (See Chapter 14 for a description of the Drawing tab.)

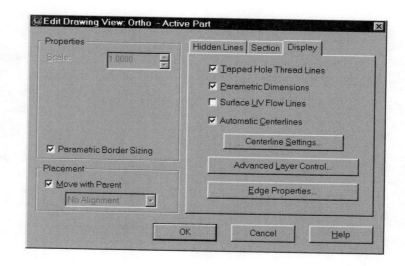

- The Tapped Holes check box determines whether the thread of tapped holes will or will not be displayed in the view.

- The dimensions used in Model mode to constrain profile features and to create 3D features will be displayed in the view being edited when the Parametric Dimensions check box is selected. This option displays dimension in the view even if Parametric Dimension Display for Active Part Views is turned off in the Drawings tab of the Mechanical Options dialog box.

- The UV lines on Mechanical Desktop surface objects are displayed in drawing views when this check box is active. It has no effect on 3D solid features.

- The display of automatically created centerlines is turned off when you clear the Automatic Centerlines check box. When this check box is on, automatic centerlines are displayed, even if Automatic Centerlines is turned off in the Drawing tab of the **Mechanical Options** dialog box.

- When you click the button labeled Centerline Settings, a dialog box titled Automatic Centerlines is displayed. In this dialog box you can select the type of objects that are to have centerlines, and you can individually turn the display of axial and profile centerlines on and off. The Standard Overrides button allows you to change properties, such as overshoot and gap dimensions, of the centerlines.

- The button labeled Advanced Layer Control opens a dialog box titled Layer Control. This dialog box consists of a list of the layers used by the view being edited and their freeze/thaw status in the viewport. You can toggle their status to cause objects in the viewport to appear or disappear.

- The Edge Properties option allows you to perform relatively low-level editing on objects within the view. When you click it, the **Edit Drawing View** dialog box will disappear, the screen cursor cross hairs will be within the view's floating viewport, and the following command line prompt will be displayed.

```
Enter an option (Edge Properties)[Remove all/Unhide all]/<Select>: (Enter an option or
    press Enter)
```

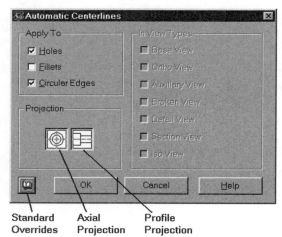

Standard   Axial   Profile
Overrides Projection Projection

If you choose the Unhide all option, objects previously hidden in the view will be restored; and if you choose the Remove all option, objects whose properties have been changed will be restored to their original condition. After entering either of these options, the **Edit Drawing View** dialog box will be restored.

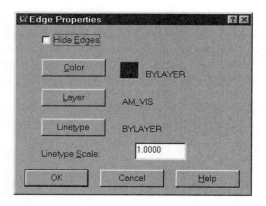

When you choose the Select option, you will be prompted to select the edges that are to be modified. You can use any AutoCAD selection method to do this. When you press Enter to signal the end of you selections, the **Edge Properties** dialog box will be displayed for you to specify how you want the selected edges modified.

With this dialog box, you can change the color, layer, and linetype properties of the selected objects. You can also hide the selected edges. This is sometimes useful for cleaning-up the appearance of auxiliary and detail views, as shown in the next figure.

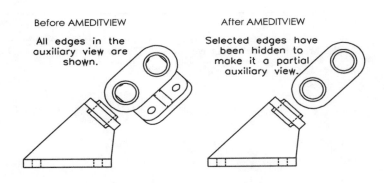

The Section tab lets you change the symbol and label used for the section view and the properties of the section's hatching. These options work in the same way as the corresponding options in the Section tab of the `Create Drawing View` dialog box. There is no provision for changing the section view's type.

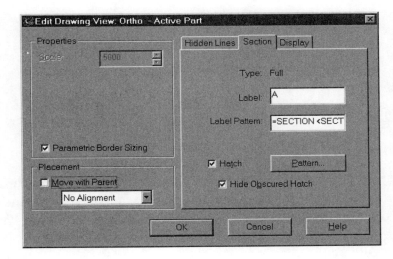

Information about Drawing Views

If you are uncertain about the properties of a view, or how you have set its parameters, you can obtain a report about it through the AMLISTVIEW command. You will be asked from the command line to select a view, and then Mechanical Desktop will display information in its text window about the selected view. Table 1 shows an example of the information displayed.

Table 1

Sample of View Information Displayed by AMLISTVIEW

```
Orthogonal Drawing View
id = 2
Name = Section A        view is ACTIVE and up to date
view scale    : 2.0000
view direction : 1.0000,0.0000,0.0000
center point      : 11.7500,7.8750       target point     : 0.0000,0.0000,0.0000
View is sectioned.     hatch layer: AMV_2_HATCH
Hidden lines are displayed.
Tangent edges are not displayed.
View has 1 descendants, 5 dimensions, 2 notes.
View is not aligned to any other view.
View has 0 views aligned to it.
One part represented
Third-angle projection
unfolded to the RIGHT a distance of 6.5000 from view 1
```

Exporting Mechanical Desktop Views

You can export Mechanical Desktop views to AutoCAD with the AMVIEWOUT command. The results are 2D objects in a specified file that are on the World Coordinate System's XY plane in AutoCAD's model space. Dimensions in the drawing views are not exported.

AMVIEWOUT first displays a dialog box titled **Export Drawing Views** to AutoCAD for you to use in naming the file that is to receive the drawing views, and in specifying its folder. Then AMVIEWOUT displays the borders of the Mechanical Desktop drawing views and issues a command line prompt for you to select the views that are to be exported. The views you select must have been created by AMDWGVIEW, and you must select them by picking a point on their border. The Mechanical Desktop drawing views are not affected by the export.

You can also export Mechanical Desktop views with the AMLEGIBLE command, although the main purpose of this command is to create 2D geometry to be used for analysis—such as to determine the area moments of inertial of a section. AMLEGIBLE creates 2D objects from edges in Mechanical Desktop views. The objects, which are typically lines, arcs, and circles, lie directly over the part edges in the drawing view. An option of AMLEGIBLE allows you to export the objects to another file, and dimensions and hatches can be included in the copy.

CHAPTER 16

Working with Drawing Dimensions and Annotation

The dimensions you created in Model mode to constrain sketches and features reappear in Drawing mode views to document the part. Generally, though, the dimensions need some work to change them into a format that meets the drafting standards you are using. You will also need to add notes to describe any round holes in the part, and to provide instructions for manufacturing the part.

This chapter covers the following topics.

- *Describes the database relationship between Model mode dimensions that constrain the sketches and features of a part and Drawing mode dimensions for documenting it.*

- *Explains how to control the appearance and visibility of dimensions.*

- *Tells how to create reference dimensions for fillets and other objects in drawing views that need dimensions.*

- *Shows how to move dimensions from one view to another, how to reattach their extension lines, and how to flip their text.*

- *Explains how to use AutoCAD Mechanical commands to manage extension and dimension lines, add geometric dimensions and tolerances symbols, add surface finish and welding symbols, and edit the appearance and content of dimension text.*

- *Shows how to use the Power Dimensioning commands to add special symbols and tolerances to dimensions.*

- *Describes how to determine the effect that dimension tolerances have on a part.*

- *Explains how to annotate holes features with notes, and how to create and manage hole note templates.*

- *Describes the components of centerlines for cylindrical features, and explains how to create them.*

- *Shows you how to create specialized annotation for a part and how to associate it with a view so that it moves with the view and as the part is modified.*

Database Associativity

Even though a 3D part resides in Model mode, while the 2D drawing of it is in Drawing mode, both modes use the same database of information about the part. Consequently, changes and additions you make to the part in Model mode are automatically reflected in the Drawing mode views of the part; and conversely dimension value changes you make in drawing mode causes the geometry of the part in Modeling mode to change. Thus, the creation a 2D drawing of a part does not make the geometry of the part static. Moreover, you can freely switch from Model mode to Drawing mode, and you can make changes to part in either mode.

If a drawing exists, Model mode changes to the part can be made in any of the ways described in Chapters 3–13 of this book, and when you return to Drawing mode those changes will have also been made in the drawing views. In Drawing mode, you can change the value of dimensions with the AMMODDIM command, just as you do with sketches. You must, though, use the AMUPDATE command to initiate the changes. Mechanical Desktop will automatically switch to Model mode to update the geometry of the model and return to Drawing mode with the part redrawn in the appropriate views to match the new dimensions.

Managing Dimensions

The parametric dimensions you added to the sketches of the part during its construction are automatically shown in the Drawing mode views of the part, provided the system variable **amreusedim** is set to 1. Dimensions that Mechanical Desktop created, such as those for extrusions and hole locations, are also displayed. Dimensions are placed in section views, however, only if the system variable **amsectiondim** is set to 1. Usually you will use the Drawing tab of AMOPTION's `Mechanical Options` dialog box to set these system variables.

Controlling Dimension Format

Unlike the objects—lines, arcs, circles, and so forth—used to depict the part's edges in drawing views, dimensions are not within floating viewports; they are in Drawing mode space within the AM_PARDIM layer. Many of AutoCAD's commands and techniques for working with dimensions can be used with dimensions in drawing views. Typically, prior to displaying the dimensions you will use AutoCAD's DDIM command to set the AutoCAD dimension variables that control the format of dimensions—text size, arrowhead size, number of digits to the right of the decimal point, tolerances, and so forth—and, you can use dimension styles and overrides just as you do in an AutoCAD 2D drawing. Refer to your AutoCAD User's Guide for information on dimension format and appearance.

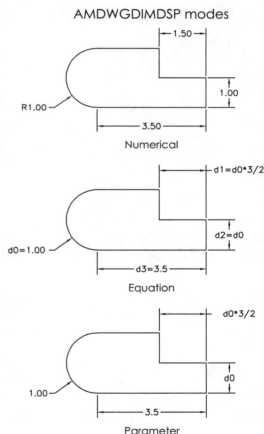

AMDWGDIMDSP modes

Since you can modify a 3D part by changing the value of the drawing view parametric dimensions, you will find it helpful to sometimes view the dimensions in their equation form. You can do this through the AMDWGDIMDSP command, which is the Drawing mode equivalent of the Model mode AMDIMDSP command.

AMDWGDIMDSP will ask you from the command line whether you want to view dimensions in their Numerical, Equation, or Parameter mode.

- The Numerical mode uses the AutoCAD dimension appearance properties to display the fully formatted dimensions.

- The Equation format shows the dimension's name to the left of an equal sign, while the source of the dimension's value—whether it is a mathematical expression, a variable name, a dimension name, or a numerical constant—is shown on the right side of the equal sign.

- The Parameter mode shows just the right side of the dimension equation.

This is unlike the Parameter mode of the AMDIMDSP command, which shows only the left side of the equation (the equation name).

If you want to view dimension names, you will have to use the Equation mode of AMDWGDIMDSP. After you specify the dimension display mode, AMDWGDIMDSP will give you three options for choosing the dimensions that are to be affected—all dimensions, just those in a certain view, or just the dimensions you select.

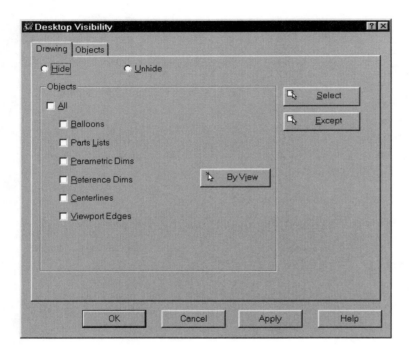

Often drawings will contain dimensions that are unnecessary for manufacturing purposes, due to the way the sketches for the part were constrained and dimensioned. Rather than erase those dimensions, you will hide them with the AMVISIBLE command. This command displays a dialog titled **Desktop Visibility** that has a Drawing tab for turning the visibility of various Drawing mode objects on and off. To hide specific parametric dimensions, you will click the Hide radio button, and then click the Select button. The dialog box will disappear and command line prompts will ask you to select the objects you want to hide. You can use any AutoCAD selection method. When you are finished, press the Enter key to restore the **Desktop Visibility** dialog box, and click its OK button to end the command. If you want to restore selected objects, click the Unhide button and then the Select button. Mechanical Desktop will temporarily display all hidden objects so that you can select the ones you want to be visible again.

The Drawing tab of the **Desktop Visibility** dialog box also has options for controlling the visibility of various types of drawing objects globally and by view. When you select the All button, when either hiding or unhiding objects, the Except button will be activated. Click this button to temporarily dismiss the dialog box so you can pick specific objects that you do not want hidden (or unhidden).

Sketches occasionally contain zero length dimensions, especially when they must be constrained to a work point. You can suppress these dimensions in drawing views by selecting Hide Zero-Length Dimensions in the Drawing tab of AMOPTION's `Mechanical Options` dialog box. You must select this option before the view they would appear in is created. Also, once the option is in effect, it cannot be reversed.

Reference Dimensions

Some dimensions needed for manufacturing a part may be missing from your drawing views. Even though Mechanical Desktop displays all of the parametric dimensions you used in constraining sketches, as well as extrusion lengths and the dimensions used to position holes, it does not show parametric dimensions for such features as fillets, chamfers, lofts, and 3D paths.

Missing dimensions can, though, be easily added as *reference dimensions*. Reference dimensions have a one way connection with the part: when changes are made to the geometry of the part, affected reference dimensions will automatically update to match the changes, but reference dimensions cannot be used to modify the part. For instance; if you added a reference dimension to a fillet, you could not change the radius of the fillet by changing the value of the dimension. However, if the radius of the fillet is changed in / Model mode by editing the part, the reference dimension's value will automatically change to reflect the new radius.

Reference dimensions are added by the AMREFDIM command. AMREFDIM works very similar to the AMPARTDIM command that is discussed extensively in Chapter 5. Thus, to dimension the fillet we mentioned in the previous paragraph, you would simply pick a point on the arc that represents the fillet and pick a second point to show the position of the dimension text. Mechanical Desktop will recognize the object as an arc, use a radius dimension, and supply the correct value for the dimension. Unlike dimensioning sketches, you cannot enter or modify reference dimension values. Reference dimensions are automatically placed in the AM_REFDIM layer.

Repositioning Parametric Dimensions

Often the position of a dimension will not be as you want it. It may obscure, or be obscured by, another dimension or by the part's edges. It may even be in, what you consider to be, the wrong view. You can reposition parametric dimensions with the AMMOVEDIM command. This command gives you three options in a command line prompt.

```
Enter an option [Flip/Reattach/Move]<Move>: (Enter an option or press the Enter key)
```

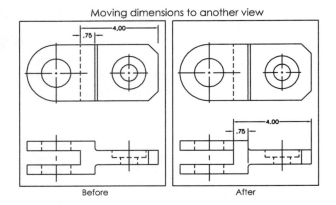

Moving dimensions to another view

Before   After

The default Move option is for moving a dimension either within its current view or to another view. You will be prompted to select the dimension to be moved and then for the view it is to be moved to. You must select a view by picking a point within it (you do not need to pick an object in a view) even if you want to relocate the dimension within its current view. Once you have specified the destination view, you will be prompted to pick a dimension location. You can pick various points to try out any number of locations until you press the Enter key to signal your acceptance of a location.

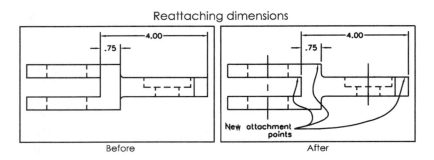

Reattaching dimensions

Before   After

Since the origin of dimension extension lines is based on Model mode sketches, they often overlap edges within drawing views. You should not use AutoCAD commands to move the origin of an extension line, instead you should use the Reattach option of AMMOVEDIM. A command line prompt will ask you to select an extension line, and then to select an attachment point. You select the attachment point by picking an edge that, preferably, is not collinear with the extension line, as shown in the accompanying figure. The endpoint of the edge will be used as the new attachment point.

When the space between extension lines is too small for the dimension text to fit, Mechanical Desktop places the text outside the extension lines. If this places the text in an inappropriate location, you can flip the text to the opposite side with the Flip option of AMMOVEDIM. You will be prompted to select a dimension, and the text of the dimension you pick will be flipped.

If AMMOVEDIM does not flip a dimension, try using its Move option to slightly move the dimension text, and then use the Flip option. You can also use AutoCAD's grip editing to move and flip dimension text. You should not, however, use AutoCAD commands to move a dimension to another viewport or move an extension line origin to another point.

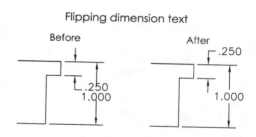

Using 2D Mechanical Drafting Commands

AutoCAD Mechanical is an Autodesk 2D drafting add-on product. Some of its commands for dimension arrangement, symbols, and format are included with Mechanical Desktop and can be used with drawing mode dimensions. These commands are divided into the following categories.

Dimension and Extension Lines

The commands in this category modify and control the placement of dimension lines and extension lines.

AMDIMALIGN   Aligns two or more linear or angular dimension lines.

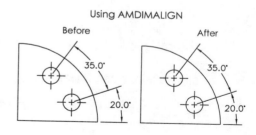

AMDIMARRANGE Moves and aligns selected dimensions. You can pick specific dimensions, or use a window selection to arrange multiple dimensions.

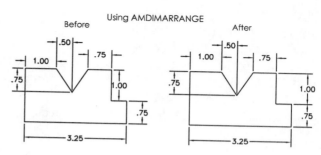

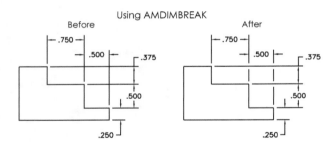

AMDIMBREAK   Creates a gap in a dimension's extension line. This command is useful when two extension lines intersect.

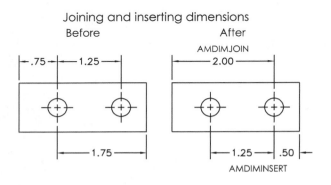

AMDIMINSERT   Divides an existing linear dimension into two separate dimensions. When this command is used on a parametric dimension, it creates reference dimensions and hides the parametric dimension.

AMDIMJOIN   Combines two or more linear or angular dimensions to form a single dimension. The resulting dimension is a Mechanical Desktop reference dimension, with the original parametric dimensions being hidden.

Geometric Dimensions and Tolerances

These commands are especially useful in drawings that use geometric dimensions and tolerances (GD&T).

AMSYMSTD   Defines and edits drafting standards to be used with symbols for datum and feature control, surface texture, and so forth. This command displays a dialog box titled **Symbol Standards**. The contents of this dialog box are similar to those in the right-hand pane in the Standards tab of the **Mechanical Options** dialog box of the AMOPTIONS command. Although Mechanical Desktop Release 5 supports this command, it is no longer documented. Therefore, you should now select drafting standards and set their properties though the Standards tab of the Mechanical Options dialog box.

AMDATUMID Creates a frame, or box, for a datum dimension identifier.

AMDATUMTGT Creates a datum target symbols.

AMFCFRAME Creates a feature control frame. This command is an enhanced version of AutoCAD's TOLERANCE command.

AMFEATID Creates a feature identifying symbol. This command is not functional when the drafting standards style is ANSI.

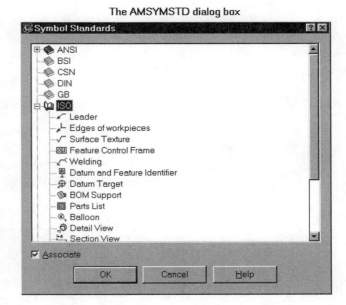

The AMSYMSTD dialog box

Manufacturing Symbols

The symbols these commands create instruct machinists and fabricators to perform specified operations.

AMEDGESYM Creates a symbol for specifying production treatments for edges. This command is not functional when the drafting standards style is ANSI.

AMSURFSYM Creates a surface texture symbol.

AMWELDSYM Creates a welding symbol.

Editing Dimensions and Symbols

These commands edit dimensions and symbols that have been created by AutoCAD Mechanical commands.

AMDIMFORMAT Opens a dialog box for editing a selected dimension. Tabs within the dialog box lead to options for controlling arrowhead and dimension line properties, placement and fit of text, format for tolerances, and numerical format of the dimension text.

AMEDIT Edits symbols for welding, surface textures, feature control frames, datum targets, and datum and feature identifiers.

AMSYMLEADER Adds or removes leaders from existing symbols.

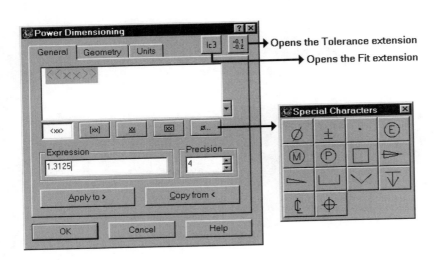

→ Opens the Tolerance extension
→ Opens the Fit extension

Using Power Dimensioning

Power dimensioning is another set of commands from AutoCAD Mechanical that work in Mechanical Desktop. In this set, AMPOWERDIM creates dimensions. It starts with a command line prompt for you to select a point to serve as the first extension line's origin, and then for the second extension line's origin. Similar to the action of the AMPARDIM command we discussed extensively in Chapter 5, you then move the cursor away from those two points to locate the dimension line and its text. Unlike AMPARDIM, though, a dialog box will appear as soon as you have established the location of the dimension line. This dialog box displays the dimension's value, and has an options for changing the value, as well as options for setting the number of digits to the right of the dimension's decimal point, copying dimension values from other dimensions, setting tolerance or limit conditions to the dimension, and so forth. You can also add symbols to the dimension text to indicate slope, diameter, depth, counterbore, and so forth. These symbols are premade, and are selected from a secondary dialog box titled `Special Characters` that is opened by clicking the Special Characters button. The dimensions created by AMPOWERDIM are fully parametric and are completely interchangeable with those created by AMPARDIM.

When you click the Fit button, which is located at the top of the **Power Dimensioning** dialog box, an extension to the dialog box is opened for establishing the fit dimensions between a hole and shaft.

Many Mechanical Desktop users prefer to use AMPARDIM when they are creating dimensions for constraining sketches

Power Dimensioning dialog box Fit extension

in Model mode (as we have done throughout this book), because the command is less involved than AMPOWERDIM and the power dimensioning options for controlling dimension appearance are not important during the construction of part. However, the power dimensioning tools for editing dimensions are very useful in Drawing mode views.

The power dimensioning command for editing dimensions, AMPOWEREDIT, will prompt you from the command line to select one dimension to be edited. As soon as you pick a point on a dimension, a dialog box titled **Power Dimensioning** is displayed. This is the same dialog box that is displayed by the AMPOWERDIM command in creating dimensions. With this dialog box you can change the number of digits to the right of the decimal point in the dimension text, and you can even change the value of the dimension. As with AMMODDIM, you must perform an update for the change to take effect.

Power Dimensioning dialog box Tolerance extension

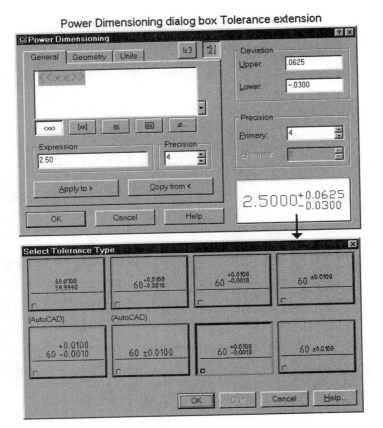

The **Power Dimensioning** dialog box is especially useful for adding tolerances to dimensions. Click the Add Tolerance button, located in the upper right corner of the dialog box to open the Tolerance extension of the dialog box. Then, you can enter values in the Upper deviation and Lower deviation edit boxes. The dimension and the tolerance values are displayed in a window in the lower right corner of the dialog box. When you click within that window a secondary dialog box is displayed for you to choose one eight different styles for displaying dimensions and tolerances.

Modifying dimensions with POWEREDIT

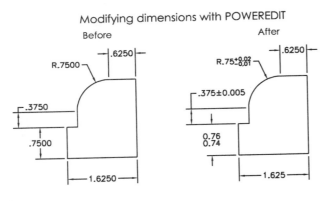

An especially convenient way to initiate AMPOWEREDIT is by double-clicking a dimension. The power dimensioning command AMDIMMEDIT performs the same editing functions and uses the same dialog box as AMPOWERDIM. However, its command line prompt allows you to select more than one dimension, and the modifications you make in the **Power Dimensioning** dialog box affect all of the selected dimensions. If the selected dimensions have different dimension values, the Expression edit box will be disabled.

Tolerance Modeling

You can study the effect that dimension tolerances have on a part with the AMTOLCONITION command. With this command, which works only with dimensions that have tolerances, you can change a dimensioned size on a part so that it represents one of three conditions: (1) the minimum value allowed by the dimension tolerance, (2) the maximum value allowed by the tolerance,

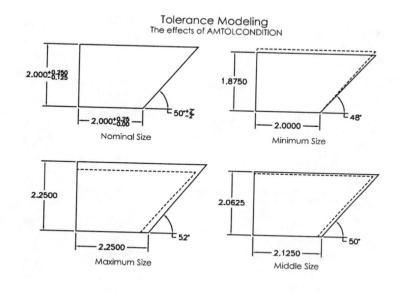

Tolerance Modeling
The effects of AMTOLCONDITION

Nominal Size

Minimum Size

Maximum Size

Middle Size

or (3) the value midway between the minimum and maximum sizes allowed by the tolerance values. Not only is the dimension value changed, the part itself is changed to match the new value. For example: Suppose a straight edge on a part is 2.000 inches long, and its dimension tolerances allow it to be up to 0.25 inches longer or 0.125 inches shorter. When you put the AMTOLCONDITION minimum tolerance in effect, and the edge shrinks to 1.875 inches long. When you put the maximum tolerance in effect, the edge lengthens to 2.25 inches, and when you put the middle tolerance in effect the edge becomes 2.0625 inches long (which is the average of 2.25 and 1.875).

When you invoke AMTOLCONDITION, a dialog box titled `Transformation of Model` appears. In this dialog box, the Nominal Size check box returns dimensions to their original condition. You will use this option after you have finished studying the effects of tolerances. If you do not want all of the toleranced dimensions of a part affected, select the Manual Selection of Dimensions check box and pick just those dimensions you want changed. When you select the Real Size check box, the two check boxes just below it will be opened. Select Dimensions to Middle of Tolerance Field to have dimension values assume the value midway between the maximum and minimum tolerances. When you select Dimensions with Control for Each Tolerance, a dialog box titled Manual Control of Dimensions appears. In this dialog box you can set the dimension to its minimum, maximum, or middle tolerance values. You can also even enter an entirely new dimension value.

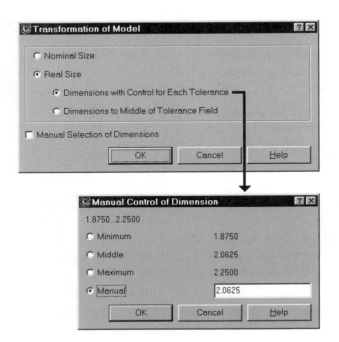

Most of the time you will use tolerance modeling to check the fit and spatial relationship between two or more parts. The parts should be constrained to their assembly positions, and they will be in an assembly drawing. Also, you will use the AMINTERFERE command to determine if more than one part occupies the same space when certain tolerance conditions are in effect. Assembly constraints are discussed in Chapter 18, assembly drawings in Chapter 20, and interference checking in Chapter 19.

Drawing Annotation

Hole Annotation

Hole Notes

Round holes that you have made with the AMHOLE command are not automatically dimensioned in Mechanical Desktop drawings. You must add them through the AMHOLENOTE command in the form of a note that has a leader pointing to the hole. The diameter, depth, and angle values within the notes are taken from the AMHOLE parameters, and they change whenever the hole parameters are changed in Model mode. You cannot, however, change the Model mode hole parameters by editing hole notes in Drawing mode. In this respect they are similar to reference dimensions.

AMHOLENOTE, which is used for both creating and editing hole notes, is straightforward to use. After specifying that you want to create a hole note, you will be prompted from the command line to select a hole feature. You select the hole by picking a point on its circumference—not on its side. The point you select will be used as the arrow end of the leader. Then a dialog box titled `Create Holenote` (or `Edit Holenote` if you are editing an existing hole note) will be displayed.

The text and symbols within hole notes are based on named templates (which we will discuss shortly), and you must select one from a list of templates shown in the dialog box. The three radio buttons in the cluster labeled Leader Justification determine the end location of the note's leader relative to the note's text, as shown in the figure illustrating examples of hole notes shown earlier.

Examples of hole notes

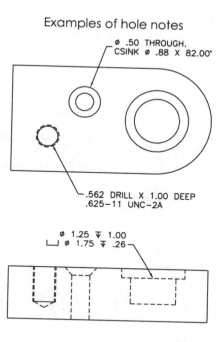

The button labeled Edit Template, which allows you to override the contents of the selected template, opens the same `Multiline Text Editor` dialog box used by AutoCAD's MTEXT command. We will describe the typical contents of this dialog box when we discuss hole note templates. The appearance characteristics of the note, such as the size of the leader arrow and

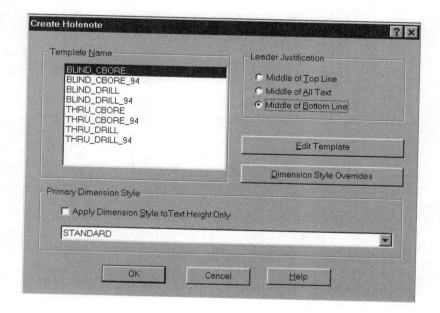

the text, are controlled by AutoCAD dimension variables and styles. You can apply a specific dimension style through the cluster of buttons labeled Primary Dimension Style, or you can override selected components of the dimension style by pressing the Dimension Style Overrides button. This button displays a dialog box titled `HoleNote Dimension Style Overrides` that lists the note's dimension parameters and allows you to individually change certain of their appearance settings.

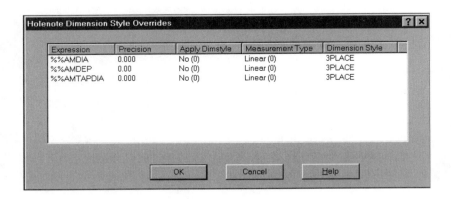

Hole Note Templates

Mechanical Desktop bases the contents of hole notes on templates that are created and managed by the AMTEMPLATE command. This command uses a dialog box titled `Hole Templates` for managing templates. In this dialog box, the names of existing templates are shown in a dropdown list box. Six standard hole note templates are always listed: BLIND_CBORE, BLIND_CSINK, BLIND_DRILL, THRU_CBORE, THRU_CSINK, and THRU_DRILL. You cannot edit, delete, or rename those standard templates, but since you can copy a template by entering another name for it, you can use them as the basis of other templates. The Edit Template button opens the same Multiline Text Editor used by AutoCAD's MTEST command.

The ANSI depth and counterbore symbols in the template (BLIND_CBORE_94) shown in the Multiline Text Editor in the following figure are from the AutoCAD shape file named GTD.SHX. The results of this template, which is for a counterbored hole, are shown in the earlier figure of examples of hole notes. Not all templates use this shape file, or any shape file. All templates do contain, however, special hole note parameters that represent the dimension values from the AMHOLE command. Seven parameters, representing all possible hole dimensions, are available.

Parameter	Dimension
%%AMDEP	Hole depth
%%AMDIA	Hole diameter
%%AMCBDEP	Counterbore depth

Parameter	Dimension
%%AMCDIA	Counterbore and countersink diameter
%%AMCSANG	Countersink angle
%%AMTAPDEP	Tapped hole depth
%%AMTAPDIA	Tapped hole major diameter

Hole templates are saved on a file-by-file basis. Therefore, you may want to include the hole templates you regularly use in prototype, or template, drawings. Also, Mechanical Desktop does not have a ready-made template for tapped holes. You will need to make them yourself to conform to the drafting standards you use.

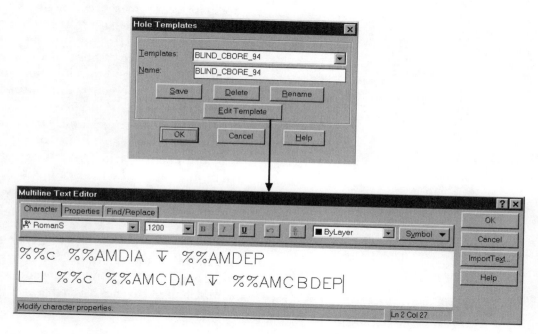

Centerlines

Centerlines in drawing views indicate the center of objects having cylindrical, spherical, or conical geometries. In plan views of the object, centerlines are drawn as crosshairs, while in side views they are drawn along the axis of the object. To have Mechanical Desktop automatically draw centerlines for you:

1. Invoke AMOPTIONS to open the **Mechanical Options** dialog box, and select the Drawing tab.

2. Select the Automatic Centerlines checkbox.

3. Click the Settings button to bring up the Centerlines dialog box.

4. Select the type of geometry—holes, fillets, and circular edges—that are to have centerlines.

5. Select the drawing view types—base, ortho, section, and so forth—that are to have centerlines.

6. To create centerlines in views showing the object as a circle or arc select the Axial toggle button, and to create them in views showing the object as two lines select the Profile toggle button.

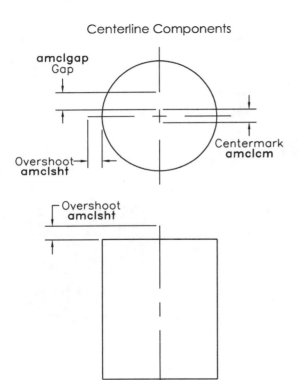

Centerline Components

Crosshair centerlines are drawn as six separate lines. The length of the two centermark lines is set by the **amclcm** system variable; the overshoot of the four extension lines beyond the circumference of the circle or arc is set by **amclsht**; and the gap between the centermark and extension lines is set by **amclgap** If the **amclpar** system variable is set to a value of 1, the extension line overshoot will remain the same when the radius or the length of the feature changes. You can set these system variables directly, or more conveniently, through the Standards tab of the **Mechanical Options** dialog box by selecting Properties from the Center Line shortcut menu. Changes to these system variables do not effect existing centerlines.

Centerlines can be made manually by the AMCENLINE command, which uses the following command line prompts and input:

```
Select Edge: (Pick a point on an arc or a circle, or on a straight edge that represents the
    side of a cylindrical or cone shaped feature.)

Select mirrored edge or <Enter>: (If you selected an arc or circle at the first prompt,
    press the Enter key. If you selected a straight line, pick a point on a second straight
    line that represents the opposite side of the feature.)
```

If you press the Enter key, the centerline will be drawn with no user input as a cross-hair with two centermark lines and four extension lines. If you pick a second edge, a centerline will be drawn along the axis of the feature and you will be prompted to specify the ends of the centerline.

```
Specify first trim point: (Pick a point on the centerline to represent one of its
    endpoints.)
Specify second trim point: (Pick the opposite endpoint of the centerline.)
```

Centerlines along the axis that are created by AMCENLINE do not automatically become longer or shorter as the length of the cylindrical feature is changed, regardless of the **amclpar**'s setting. You can, though, use AutoCAD commands to lengthen, extend, or trim centerlines.

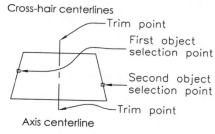

Using AMCENLINE to create centerlines

Specialized Annotation

Specialized annotation, such as those used for manufacturing instructions, that move as the part changes size and when the view is relocated can be added to objects in drawing views. There are two commands for doing this: AMANNOTE attaches a wide variety of annotation objects to a part within a drawing view, while AMNOTE is for attaching textual notes.

With AMANNOTE, you first create the annotation within Mechanical Desktop's drawing mode using the appropriate AutoCAD commands for drawing objects and creating text. These objects should be in the exact location you want them relative to the objects in the drawing view. Then you will associate, or attach, the annotation within a view through the AMANNOTE command.

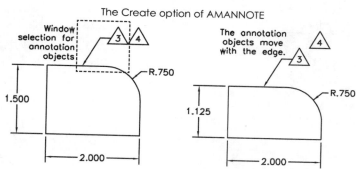

The Create option of AMANNOTE

AMANNOTE uses command line options for creating and managing the annotation.

```
Enter an option [Add/Remove/Delete/deTach/Move/Create]<Create>: (Enter an option or press
    Enter.)
```

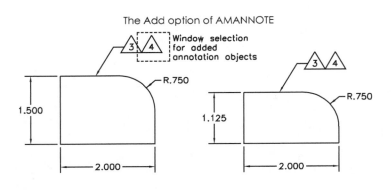

The Add option of AMANNOTE

When you choose the Create option, you will be prompted to select the objects that are to be included in the annotation, and then you will be prompted to pick a point in the view that the annotation objects are to be attached to. The deTach option removes the association between the annotation and the view. You can add objects to attached annotation with the Add option, and you can remove selected objects from attached annotation with the Remove option. The Delete option removes annotation from the Mechanical Desktop data base. You will be asked to specify the annotation that is to be deleted by picking a point on any of its objects: All objects in the selected annotation will then disappear.

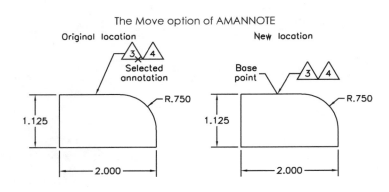

The Move option of AMANNOTE

The Move option moves selected annotation while maintaining its base point. You will be prompted to select the annotation to be moved, and then to select a new location for the annotation. You can try any number of locations until you press the Enter key to specify the location you want.

The AMNOTE command creates and attaches a leader and text to an object within a drawing view. You will be prompted from the command line to select an object. Next, you will be prompted to select the starting point for the leader's arrow, and then for points along the leader. This enables you to create multi-segmented leaders that have dogleg bends. You cannot create curved leaders. Press the Enter key to signal the end of the leader, and open the `Note Symbol` dialog box.

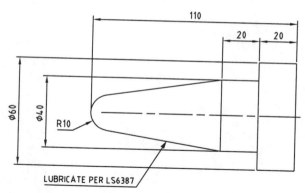

Example of an AMNOTE text and leader

In the `Note Symbol` dialog box, enter the text for the note in the list box, or alternately pick the Edit Mtext button to open AutoCAD's `Multiline Text Editor` dialog box for entering the text. When the check box labeled Landing is selected, the text will be underlined. The text of the note assumes the properties of the current drafting standard. By default, the leader's arrowhead also assumes the properties of the current drafting standard, but you can change the arrowhead appearance by clicking the Arrowhead Style button. When you click the Detach button, the note is no longer associated with the drawing object. Click the

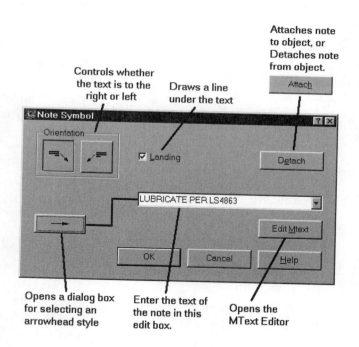

Attach button to associate an existing note with a drawing object. You can edit the note with the AMPOWEREDIT command, or more conveniently, by double-clicking the note.

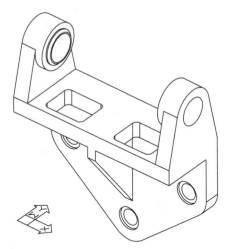

Figure 1-1

Exercise 1

Creating a Drawing

In this exercise, you will create a multiview 2D drawing of the part shown in Figure 1-1. Millimeters have been used in constructing and constraining this part. The drawing will have four views—a front view, a top view, a side view, and a detail view. The side view will be an offset section view to more clearly show the counterbored holes and the rectangular holes. The overall scale of the drawing will be 1:2, with the detail view being 1:1.

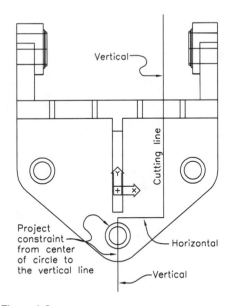

Figure 1-2

Retrieve md16e101.dwg from the CD-ROM that comes with this book, and open it. Before you begin making drawing views, you will make a cutting line sketch for the section view. In Model mode, place the sketch plane on either the front or back surface of the triangular shaped section of the part. Switch to a plan view of the sketch plane, and draw three lines similar to those shown with thick lines in Figure 1-2.

Use the AMCUTLINE command to turn the three lines into a cutting line sketch. Mechanical Desktop will report that 5 dimensions or constraints are needed to fully constrain the sketch. Make certain that the two end lines are vertical and that the middle line is horizontal. Then add a project constraint from the center of the bottom counterbored hole to its neighboring vertical line as shown in Figure 1-2. Mechanical Desktop will now report that 4 dimensions or constraints are needed to fully constrain the sketch. They will all be dimensions.

Add the four dimensions to the cutting line sketch that are shown in Figure 1-3 to fully constrain the sketch. The values of these dimensions, which are in millimeters, are not critical as long as the cutting line goes through the center hole, is to the right of the center web, goes through the right rectangular hole, and extends beyond the part at both ends. The dimensions are to hold the cutting line in place if the part is ever changed—they will not appear in the drawing.

Change the viewpoint to that of a front-right isometric and set the sketch plane to coincide with the WCS, so that it will be easier to visualize and set directions for the base view of the part. Then click either the Drawing tab of the Desktop Browser or the Layout1 tab to go into Drawing mode. If a floating viewport exists, erase it.

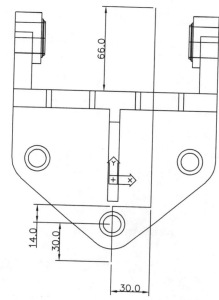

Figure 1-3

If the Page Setup dialog box does not automatically appear, invoke the PAGESETUP command. In the Plot Device tab, select a plotter that will handle ISO A3 (nominal 420 by 297 mm) paper. In the Layout Settings tab, set the paper size to ISO A3 (420x297 mm), and make certain that the mm check box is active. Select Layout as the plot area, and 1:1 as the Plot Scale. Then exit the Page Setup dialog box.

If you do not have a suitable border and title block, you can use one of these two alternatives:

1. Use AutoCAD's INSERT command to locate and insert Autodesk's iso_a3.dwg as a block into this drawing. If you used the default Mechanical Desktop installation, this file will be in the Program Files\Mdt\Template folder. Use 0,0,0 as the insert point, 1.0 as the X and Y scale factors, and 0 for the rotation angle.

2. If the border of the Autodesk file is too large for the paper size your plotter can handle, you can use the title block and border in file iso_a3bd.dwg on the CD-ROM that accompanies this book. It will fit within a 404 by 254 mm space. That border and title block, which is shown in Figure 1-4, is the one we used in this exercise.

Invoke AMOPTIONS to open the `Mechanical Options` dialog box. Select the Drawing Tab. In that tab:

- Select the Active Part and Section View check boxes in the Parametric Dimension Display cluster.
- Select Automatic Centerlines Settings.
- Leave the other options in the Drawing tab at their default settings.

Select the Standards tab of the Mechanical Options dialog box. In that tab:

- Verify that ISO is the Standard, and that in its `Properties` dialog box First Angle is the Projection Type.
- In the `Section Line Properties` dialog box, enter 7 for the Text Height, select 30 degrees as the Arrowhead Style, and verify that the Label Visible and Arrows Visible checkboxes are active.

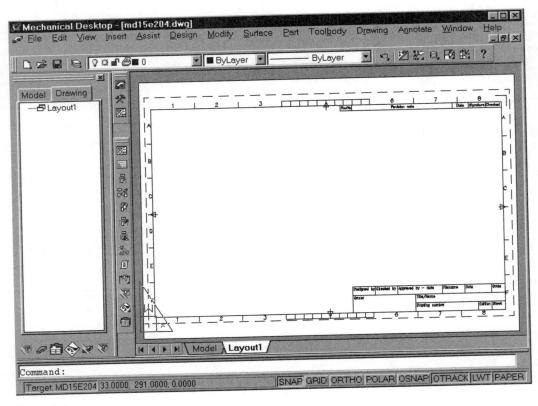

Figure 1-4

- In the **Leader Properties** dialog box and set Arrowhead Size to 5.

- In the **Detail Symbol Properties** dialog box, set text height to 7 and leave the other settings at their defaults.

- In the **Center Line Properties** dialog box, set Overshoot to a fixed size of 3.

Start AutoCAD's DDIM command to set the dimension style parameters for the drawing.

- In the Lines and Arrows tab set Baseline spacing to 4, Extend beyond dim lines to 3, Offset from origin to 1.5, Arrow size to 3, and Center mark for circles to None.

- In the Text tab set Text Style to that of a Romans.shx font, Text height to 2.5, Vertical Text placement to above and Horizontal Text placement to Centered, Offset from dim line to 1, and Text to be Aligned with dimension line.

- In the Primary Units tab set Unit format to Decimal, Precision to 0.0, and Decimal separator to Comma. Verify that the Scale factor is 1.0.

- Leave the settings in the Fit, Alternate Units, and Tolerance tabs as they are.

Close the **Dimension Style Manager** dialog box.

Now, you will begin creating the four views for the drawing. Start the AMDWGVIEW command. Select Base as the View Type, Active Part as the Data Set, and specify the Layout you are using (which is probably Layout1). Verify that Display Hidden Lines is checked and Display Tangencies is cleared. Enter 0.50 in the Scale edit box. Then click the OK button.

The **Create Drawing View** dialog box will be dismissed; Mechanical Desktop will switch to Model mode, and you will be prompted to select a plane. The line of sight of the view you create will be directly toward this plane. This first view will be the top view, so you should either enter X (for worldXy) or select the upper flat face of the part as the plane. Next, you will be prompted to specify the positive X direction of the view by selecting an axis or a straight edge. Enter X (for worldX) or select one of the long edges of the part to specify this direction. The UCS icon will move to the plane, with its X axis pointing in the direction you specified, and you will be prompted to accept it or rotate it. Press Enter to accept the viewing plane and the axis direction.

Mechanical Desktop will switch back to Drawing mode and prompt for a location of the view. Pick a point at the approximate X and Y coordinates of 170, 60 as the center of the view. Your drawing, with its border and the one view should look similar to the one in Figure 1-5. AutoCAD's general linetype scale has been set to 0.375.

The view you just created, represents the top view of the part. Since first angle projection is being used, the front view of the part, which you will make next, is above the top view. Start AMDWGVIEW again. Select Ortho as the View Type. Verify that hidden lines are displayed and that tangencies are not. Notice that the Scale edit box is grayed-out. Click the OK button to dismiss the dialog box. Depending on how you invoked AMDWGVIEW, you may be asked from the command line to select the parent view. If you are, pick a point near the center of the existing view. Then you will be asked for the view's location. Place the center of the view about 110 mm above the first view.

Repeat AMDWGVIEW. Again select Ortho as the View Type. Click the Section tab, and select Offset as the section Type. Accept the default section Symbol and View Label. Verify that the Hatch check box is active. Click the Pattern button to display the Hatch Pattern dialog box. Select ANSI31 as the hatch pattern, set its Scale to 1.0 and its Angle to 0.0. Click OK to return to the **Create Drawing View** dialog box. Clear the Display

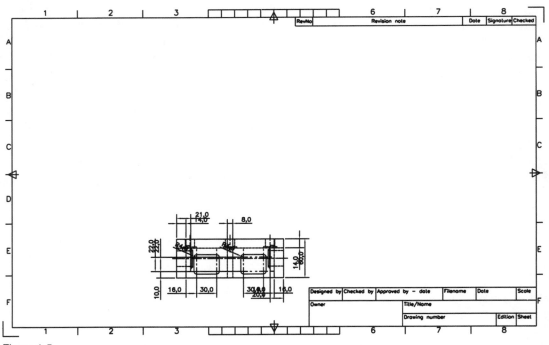

Figure 1-5

Hidden Lines check box, because most drafting standards do not display hidden lines in section views. Click OK to leave the dialog boxes.

Select the front view if you are asked for the parent view, and center the section view about 110 mm to the left of it. When you press the Enter key to signal your acceptance of the view's location, Mechanical Desktop will switch to Model mode and ask you to select the cutting line sketch. Pick a point anywhere on the cutting line sketch. Mechanical Desktop will return to Drawing mode, add the section view and draw the cutting line of the section in the front view. Your drawing, with its three views, should now look similar to the one in Figure 1-6. Do not be concerned at this time about the placement or location of the dimensions.

The final view you will create will be a detail view of the profile of one of the rings around the two concentric holes. You may want to zoom in toward the upper right quadrant of the drawing. Start AMDWGVIEW. Set the View Type to Detail. Enter 2.0 as the Scale, and select the Relative to Parent check box. Enter the upper case letter B as the Detail View Symbol. Verify that hidden lines will be displayed, and then click the OK button of the dialog box.

From the command line you will be prompted to select a vertex to serve as an attachment for the detail view. Pick the edge shown in Figure 1-7. Select Rect as the method for establishing the extent of the detail view, and draw a rectangle approximately as shown in Figure 1-7.

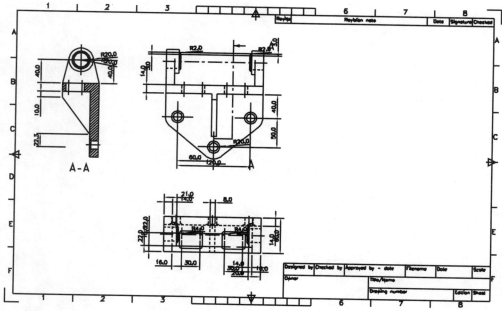

Figure 1-6

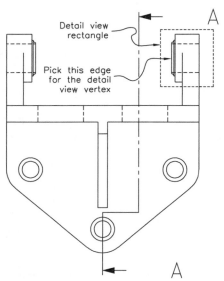

Figure 1-7

Lastly, you will be prompted to select the location of the detail view. Pick a point having the approximate X and Y coordinates of 280,180. Mechanical Desktop will draw the detail view with a scale that is twice that of its parent view, and draw a rectangle in the parent view to indicate the source of the detail view. At this stage, your drawing should look similar to the one in Figure 1-8.

Now that all of the views have been created, you will work on the dimensions of the part. This work will require numerous steps, but generally each step will take just a few seconds. You will begin with the dimensions in the section view.

• Use the AMVISIBLE command to hide the 40.0 dimension on the right side of the part and one of the R20.0 dimensions.

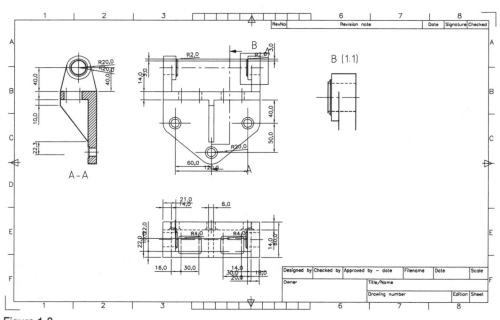

Figure 1-8

- Then use the Reattach option of AMMOVEDIM to attach the lower extension line of the 18.0 dimension to the end of the centerline of the counterbored hole.

- Add a reference dimension from the center of the 20.0 mm cylinder to the back end of the part. Although Mechanical Desktop does not need this dimension because of the way the profile was constrained, most people using the drawing will want to know this distance. To add this dimension, start the AMREFDIM command. In response to its prompt to select an object, pick any of the circles; and when you are prompted for a second object, pick the right-hand vertical edge of the part.

- Use AMMOVEDIM to move the 14.0 dimension, which is for the thickness of the back plate, from the right side of the top view to the bottom of the section view. Then use the Flip and the Reattach options of AMMOVEDIM to position the text and the extension lines of the dimension.

- If necessary, use AMMOVEDIM, AutoCAD's STRETCH command, and AutoCAD grip editing to move extension lines and dimension lines or their text to obtain better visibility.

The before and after dimensions of the section are shown in Figure 1-9.

Next, you will move some dimensions from the front and top views to the detail view.

- Use AMMOVEDIM to move the 3.0 dimension on the right side of the front view to the detail view. Notice that when you move dimensions to a view having a different scale, the dimension and extension lines automatically adjust to accommodate the other scale.

- Use AMMOVEDIM again to move the R2.0 dimension on the right side of the front view to the detail view.

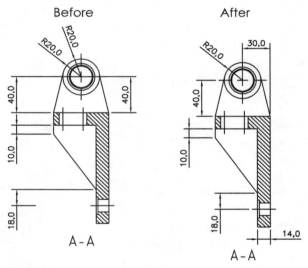

Figure 1-9

- Move the 20.0 dimension in the lower right side of the top view (You may have to look close to find it.) to the detail view.

- Use the Reattach option of AMMOVEDIM to attach the extension lines of the 20.0 dimension to the top edge in the detail view.

- Use the grips on the dimensions to stretch the extension lines and position the text of the 3.0 and R2.0 dimensions so that they are clearly legible.

The detail view in your drawing should now look similar to the one in Figure 1-10.

You will now work on the dimensions in the front view.

- Use AMVISIBLE to hide the 3.0 and R2.0 dimensions on the left side of the front view.

- Use AMMOVEDIM to move the 8.0 dimension of the rib thickness in the top view to the front view, flip its text so that it is away from the section cutting line, and reattach its extension lines to the top of the web.

- Use AMMOVEDIM's Reattach option to attach the extension lines of the linear dimensions to the ends of the centerlines or to part edges.

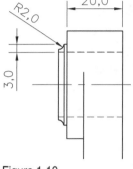

Figure 1-10

- Use grip editing and AMMOVEDIM to position the dimension lines and text of the linear dimensions and the R20.0 dimension so that they are legible.

The before and after dimensions in the front view are shown in figure 1-11.

Next, move your attention to the top view of the drawing.

- Invoke AMVISIBLE. In the Drawing tab select Centerlines as the object to hide, and click the By View button. When you are prompted to select a view, pick a point within the top view.

Before

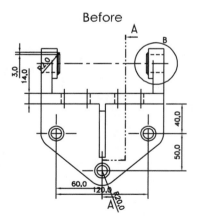

After

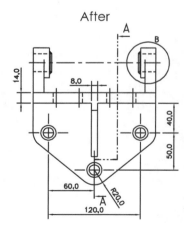

Figure 1-11

- The hidden lines in this view are, as were the centerlines, more confusing than they are helpful, so start the AMEDITVIEW command and clear the Display Hidden Lines check box.

- Use AMVISIBLE to hide the 14.0, 16.0, 30.0, and R4.0 dimensions that are on the right side of the part. Also hide the 22.0 dimension that belongs to the cutout on the right side of the part.

- Use the Move, Reattach, and Flip options of AMMOVEDIM to position the dimension and extension lines, and the text, of the dimensions that are still visible.

The before and after dimensions in the top view are shown in figure 1-12.

Now that you have finished working on the dimensions, you will add hole notes to the drawing.

- Start the AMHOLENOTE command, and press the Enter key to accept the command's default option of New. When you are prompted to select a hole feature, select the large hole in the upper part of the section view. A dialog box titled **Create Hole Note** will be displayed. Verify that the hole Template Name is THRU_DRILL, and click the dialog box's OK button. Locate the hole note to the left of the section view.

- The prompt to select a hole feature will be repeated. This time, select the leftmost counterbored hole in the front view; verify that THRU_CBORE is the template name, and locate the note below and to the left of the hole.

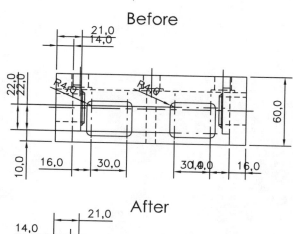

Before

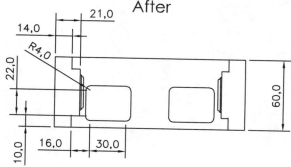

After

Figure 1-12

That finishes this exercise. Your drawing should look similar to the one in Figure 1-13. We have added a first angle projection note since that projection type is not common in North America. We have also partially filled in the title block. The finished drawing is in file md16e113.dwg on the CD-ROM that comes with this book.

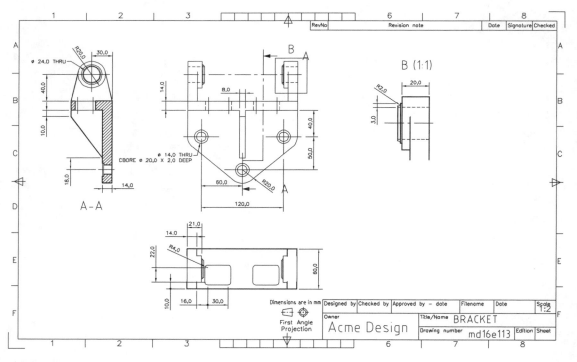

Figure 1-13

CHAPTER 17

Working with Multiple Parts

Because a single part is usually connected in some way to other parts to form an assembly, Mechanical Desktop has a full set of tools for working with multiple parts and for making models of assemblies. You will make the transition from single part modeling to assembly modeling in this chapter as you learn some of the basic concepts and commands for working with multiple parts.

This chapter covers the following topics.

- *Summarizes the key features of Mechanical Desktop's assembly modeling module.*
- *Defines the often used important terms for assembly models.*
- *Explains how to set Mechanical Desktop's options for assembly modeling.*
- *Describes the commands for working with multiple parts.*
- *Tells you how to simplify an assembly by dividing it into subassemblies.*
- *Explains how to use parts and subassemblies from other files in the file of an assembly.*

Assembly Modeling

Since a single part is seldom used alone, Mechanical Desktop contains a module that has tools for modeling assemblies of parts. Some of the key features of the assembly modeling module are:

External Component Management   Even though you can create all of the parts you intend to use in an assembly within the file of the assembly, Mechanical Desktop has tools that allow you to import parts from other drawing files into the assembly file. This not only simplifies the assembly file, it allows parts to be used in more than one assembly. For instance, if you have a special fastener that you use in a variety of assemblies, you can create it just once in its own drawing file and insert it in the file of every assembly that needs it. Furthermore, when an external part is modified in its file, those part changes will be reflected in the assembly file. Beginning with Mechanical Desktop R4, the converse is also permitted; you can modify external parts in an assembly file, and have those modifications incorporated in the external files.

Component Constraints The individual components, or parts, of an assembly must fit together in specific ways. A nut, for example, must fit on a similarly sized bolt or stud. Therefore, Mechanical Desktop has a set of commands that constrain two individual parts into a specified spatial relationship. These assembly constraints, which are sometimes called 3D constraints, are not the same as the sketch and feature constraints that were discussed in Chapters 3–13 of this book. Assembly constraints are discussed in Chapter 18.

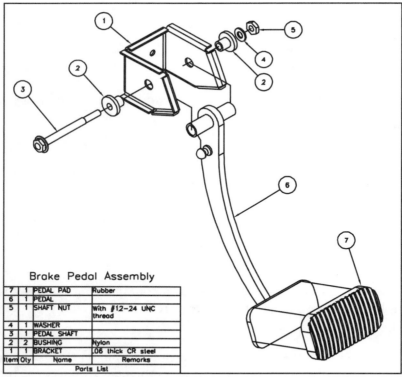

Mass Property and Interference Determination
Once the parts of an assembly have been constrained, Mechanical Desktop can determine the mass properties—such as weight and center of gravity—of the assembly. Mechanical Desktop can also detect the interference, or overlap, between two or more parts of an assembly. Assembly mass properties and interference checking are discussed in Chapter 19.

Brake Pedal Assembly

Item	Qty	Name	Remarks
7	1	PEDAL PAD	Rubber
6	1	PEDAL	
5	1	SHAFT NUT	With #12–24 UNC thread
4	1	WASHER	
3	1	PEDAL SHAFT	
2	2	BUSHING	Nylon
1	1	BRACKET	.06 thick CR steel
Item	Qty	Name	Remarks

Parts List

Exploded view drawings, complete with a parts list and part number balloons, can be made of assemblies.

Exploded Views   Exploded views, in which the individual parts of an assembly are spread apart to show their form and their positional relationships, are often used in manuals and documentation for assemblies. Usually they are shown as isometric type views. Mechanical Desktop can easily make exploded views. They are referred to as *scenes*, and you can create more than one scene for an assembly. Scenes are discussed in Chapter 19.

Assembly Drawings   Just as with individual parts, 2D drawings can be made of assemblies. These drawings can show orthographic views, section views, isometric views, and exploded views. They can have a Bill of Materials (BOM) that lists the individual components of the assembly, and the components can be identified by part numbers within balloons. Assembly drawings, BOM's, and balloons are discussed in Chapter 20.

Key Terms for Assembly Models

To successfully work with multiple parts, you need to understand the meaning of the terms that are commonly used with the Mechanical Desktop commands and dialog boxes.

Assembly	A collection of two or more components that are spatially related.
Attach	The insertion of an external part or subassembly into the current file.
Component	One unit of an assembly. It can be a single part or a subassembly.
Component, Root	The fundamental basis of an assembly that is automatically created when a new assembly drawing file is opened. It will be the first item listed in the Desktop Browser, and it will be initially listed as the target.
Component, Grounded	The component that all other assembly components are spatially related to. When constraints are added, and scenes are created, the location of the grounded component remains fixed. By default, the first part created in a multiple part file, or the first component that is attached to the current file is the grounded component.
Definition	The Mechanical Desktop data of the geometry and attributes of an instance.
Instance	The single occurrence of a part. Multiple instances of a part share the same definition, so that changes to one instance affect all of them.
External	A component of the current file whose definition is in another file.
Local	A component of the current file whose definition is in the current file.
Part	A parametric 3D solid object.
Subassembly	Two or more spatially related components that act as a unit and is a component of an assembly. Subassemblies can be nested.
Target	The root component, subassembly, or scene that is active. Only one target is active at one time.

Establishing Assembly Options

You can conveniently set some of the parameters for assemblies through the Assemblies Tab of the **Mechanical Options** dialog box that is displayed by the AMOPTIONS command. This tab is divided into two areas—one for Assembly options and another for Scene options. The Scene options are described in Chapter 19, The Assembly options of this tab are as follows.

View Restore with Assembly Activation   When you activate a subassembly, components that are not part of the subassembly disappear from the screen, leaving just the active subassembly. When the View Restore with Assembly Activation option is selected, the last zoom level and viewing direction used with the subassembly is also restored when the subassembly is activated. This option controls the **amviewrestore** system variable. When the option is selected, **amviewrestore** is set to 1; and when it is cleared, **amviewrestore** is set to 0. Subassemblies and their related commands, as well as the steps to activate a subassembly, are discussed later in this chapter.

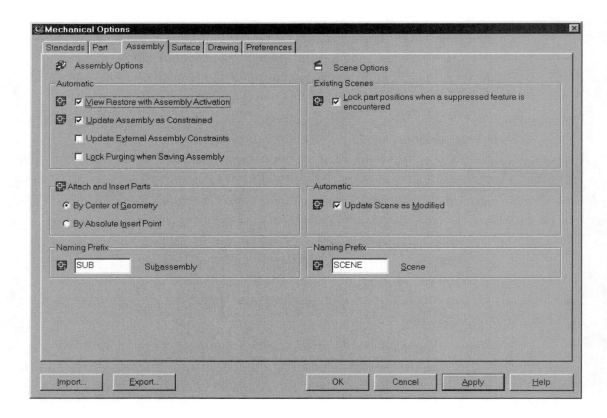

Update Assembly as Constrained When this option is selected, parts automatically move to their constrained position as each assembly constraint is applied. When this option is cleared, parts will not move to their constrained positions until the AMASSEMBLE command is issued. The **amautoassemble** system variable is assigned a value of 1 when this option is selected, and a value of 0 when this option is cleared. Assembly constraints are discussed in Chapter 18.

Update External Assembly Constraints Changes to an external part in the external part's file can affect the assembly constraints between that part and other components of the assembly. Select this option to avoid losing those assembly constraints. When this option is selected, the **amxassemble** system variable is set to 1; when it is cleared, **amxassemble** is set to 0.

Lock Purging when Saving Assembly When this check box is active, locked files are automatically purged when you save an assembly file. Locked files are most likely to occur when Mechanical Desktop is running within a network.

Attach and Insert Parts These two radio buttons control the insertion point for attached components within the current drawing. When the By Center of Geometry option is selected, the insertion point for attaching components is based on their geometric center; and when the By Absolute Insert Point is selected, the insertion point is based on the origin of the coordinate system of the attached component. The value of the **aminsertabs** system variable is controlled by these two radio buttons. **Aminsertabs** is set to 0 when By Center of Geometry is in effect, and it is set to 1 when By Absolute Insert Point is selected. Attached components are discussed later in this chapter.

Naming Prefixes The name you enter in the edit box labeled Subassembly determines the default prefix offered by the AMNEW command for assigning subassembly names to the Desktop Browser. If you accept the default name of SUB, the default browser names of subassemblies will be SUB1_1, SUB2_1, and so forth. The use of the AMNEW command to create subassemblies is discussed later in this chapter.

Managing Multiple Parts

Parts and Instances

Creating New Parts

When Mechanical Desktop is in its Assembly Environment, as described in Chapter 2, you can create an additional part through the AMNEW command, regardless of how many parts are already in the drawing file. AMNEW will ask if the object you want to create is to be a new part, a subassembly, a scene, or an instance. (As explained in the discussion on combining parts in Chapter 12, you can also have multiple parts in Mechanical Desktop's Single Part environment. Additional parts in that environment, though, are intended to be used as toolbodies, rather than for creating assemblies, and are called toolbodies instead of parts.) We will discuss the Subassembly option later in this chapter, and we will discuss the Scene option in Chapter 19.

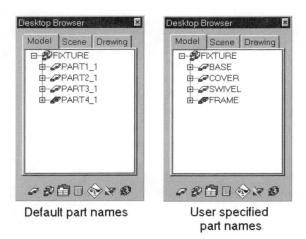

Default part names   User specified part names

When you specify that the new object is to be a part, Mechanical Desktop will prompt for the name of the new part, and will offer a default name that is based on the Naming Prefix specified in the Parts tab of the **Mechanical Options** dialog box of the AMOPTIONS command. Enter a new prefix in response to the prompt, if you want the part to have a more descriptive name. The part's name will appear in the Desktop Browser and the next profile sketch you create will be the basis of the new part.

Activating and Viewing Parts

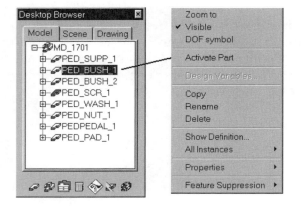

Although you can have as many parts as you like in one drawing file, you can add-to and edit only one part— the *active part*—at a time. To activate a part, select the Part option of the AMACTIVATE command, and pick a point on the part you want to be the active part. A more convenient way to activate a part, though, is to select Activate Part from the right-click menu for the part's name in the Desktop Browser. This menu option will be grayed out when the selected part is the active part. An even more convenient way to activate a part is to double-click its name.

The Part option of the AMSHOWACT command identifies the active part for you by highlighting it. The active part will remain highlighted until you press the Enter key to end the command. If the screen is too cluttered, you can use the Assembly tab of the AMVISIBLE command to hide the parts that you are not working with. You can also use the Visible option in the right-click menu of a part's name in the Browser to turn the visibility of parts on and off.

Creating Instances

When you choose the Instance option of the AMNEW command, you will be prompted to select the part that the instances are to be based on, with the default being the active part. You can choose another part, though, by picking a point on it. As soon as you select a part, an image of it will appear. The image will move as you move your pointing device, and an instance will be created every time you press the pick button. Press the Enter key to end the command. The insertion point of instances created in this manner is always based on the geometric center of the part.

In the Browser, the name of each instance will be the same as the default part name plus a consecutive number. For example, three instances of PART2_1 will be named PART2_2, PART2_3, and PART2_4. You can make any instance be the active part; and, once it becomes the active part, you can edit and add features to it. Any changes and additions to one instance, even if it is not the defining part, are made in all of the other instances as well.

Multiple instances of a part are very useful when your assembly needs several components, such as a screw, that are exactly the same. They not only require less overhead in the computer file, you are ensured that the parts are exactly alike. If you want to make a copy of a part that is not an instance of the original, you must use the AMCATALOG command to make a copy of its definition, as described in Chapter 12.

Identifying Parts and Instances

As the number of parts in an assembly increases, your computer screen will become more cluttered and you may occasionally have trouble identifying parts and even finding a particular part. The AMSHOWINST command can be helpful in identifying parts. When you invoke AMSHOWINST, each part's name will appear beside it in the graphics area when you move the screen pickbox over the part or instance. You do not need to pick a point on a part. The edges of the part will be highlighted also.

The Browser is also useful in identifying parts. When you highlight the name of a part in the Browser, the part itself will be highlighted. Also, the Zoom to option of a part's right-click menu zooms in to the part.

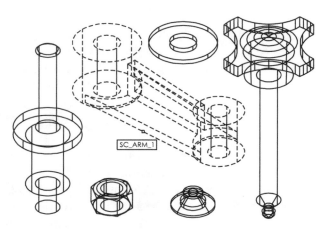

AMSHOWINST helps you identify parts

AMWHEREUSED is yet another way to locate parts. The command displays a dialog box listing all of the parts in an assembly. You can select a name in the dialog box to have the part highlighted in the graphics area and to receive a command line list of the subassemblies the part is used in. AMWHEREUSED, however, is a command that predates the Desktop Browser, and you will seldom use it.

Deleting Parts and Instances

Parts can be deleted by the AMDELETE command. From the command line, AMDELETE will ask if you want to delete a part definition, a part instance, or a scene. If you choose to delete an instance or a definition, you will be prompted to select one object. As soon as you pick a point on an instance or a part, it will be instantly deleted. If you choose the option to delete an instance, other instances of the part will remain, even if you pick the defining part. However, if you choose the option to delete a definition, all instances and the defining part will be deleted, regardless of whether you pick an instance or the defining part.

Exporting and Importing Parts

Just as you can use AutoCAD's WBLOCK command to export the definition of a block to a file, you can use Mechanical Desktop's AMCOPYOUT command to export the definition of a part or subassembly to a file. This command will display a dialog box for you to use in selecting the object to be exported, and to specify the name and the location of the file. You can select only one part or one subassembly. Unlike AutoCAD's WBLOCK command, AMCOPYOUT leaves the exported component as it was in the current drawing file.

The reverse of AMCOPYOUT is AMCOPYIN. This command imports the definition of one or more parts from another drawing file to the current drawing file. A dialog box titled File to Load will appear for you to use in locating and specifying the file to import. If multiple parts exist in the file, they will be inserted as a subassembly. While AMCOPYIN is sometimes a convenient way to import a part, most of the time you will use AMCATALOG, which is discussed later in this chapter, to import parts and subassemblies into the current assembly drawing.

Replacing Instances

You can replace a part with another part through the AMRE-PLACE command. This enables you, for example, to replace bolts that are too short in an assembly with longer bolts. AMREPLACE displays a dialog box that has two list boxes. The list box on the left, which is

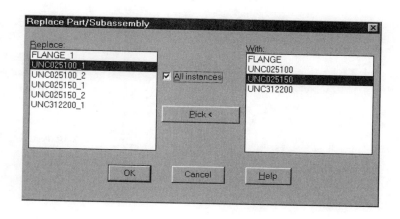

labeled Replace, contains the names of all instances in the assembly; and the list box on the right, which is labeled With, contains the names of all part definitions in the assembly. You can specify the instances to be replaced by either:

- Clicking their names in the Replace list box.

- Clicking the button labeled Pick, and then picking a point on each instance you want replaced. As an instance is selected, its name is highlighted in the Replace list box.

- Clicking the name of one instance and selecting the All instances check box. All other instances of the specified instance will be replaced, even though their names will not be highlighted.

After you have specified the instances to be replaced, select one part definition in the With list box as the replacement. If you have selected all of the instances of a part, a message box will ask if you want to delete the definition of the part. While the new instances will be in the same location as those they replaced, the assembly constrains of the old instances will not be transferred to the new ones.

Renaming Parts

You can change the names that Mechanical Desktop assigns to parts with AMRENAME. On the command line, you will be asked if you want to rename a part definition, a part instance, or a scene. When you choose to rename a part instance, you will be prompted from the command line to select an instance and then to enter a new name for it.

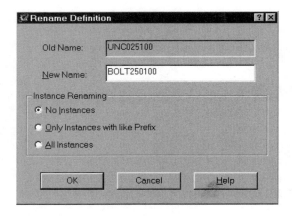

When you choose to rename a part definition, you will be asked to select a part. When you do, a dialog box titled **Rename Definition** will appear. The current name of the part will be displayed, and you will enter a new name in the edit box labeled New Name.

The cluster of three radio buttons labeled Instance Renaming control how the new part name is applied to instances of the part.

No Instances   When you select this radio button, the part definition will change but no name changes will occur in the part instances or in the Browser. You will sometimes select this option to change the name of parts in Bills of Materials (BOM) and in parts list. See Chapter 20 for discussions on the BOM and on parts lists.

Only Instances with Like Prefix   All instances of the selected part definition having a prefix that is the same as the old one will use the new name as a prefix. Thus, if the old prefix for a set of part instances was SCREW, and the new prefix is BOLT; the instance names will change from SCREW_1, SCREW_2, and so forth to BOLT_1, BOLT_2, and so forth.

All Instances   All instances of the selected part definition will use the new name as a prefix, regardless of their current prefix.

With the Browser, you can use either of two methods to change the names of individual parts. One way is by selecting Rename from the right-click menu of the part's name. The cursor will move to the part's name, and you can delete and add characters. Press Enter or move the cursor from the name and click the pick button of your pointing device to end the renaming operation. The second way is to by-pass the menu by highlighting the name, and then clicking it again to begin editing the name.

Exercise 1

Working with Multiple Parts

This exercise will give you experience in working with multiple parts and with multiple instances of a part. Retrieve and open file md17e101.dwg from the CD-ROM that accompanies this book. The three parts, which are named BASE, COVER, and SCREW, that are in this file are shown in Figure 1-1. The parts are all local—that is, they are completely defined in the file. Click the names in the Desktop Browser as necessary to expand the information listed for each of the three parts. Then experiment with the AMSHOWACT, AMACTIVATE, and AMSHOWINST commands, both in their command line and Browser forms, to see how they work.

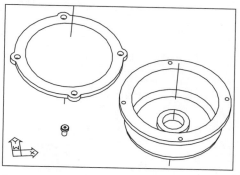

Figure 1-1

Make certain that SCREW is the active part, and then use the AMNEW command's Instance option to make two additional instances of the screw. See Figure 1-2. The locations of the two new instances are not important. Notice in the Browser that Mechanical Desktop assigned the names PART3_1 and PART3_2 to the instances. Use the AMRENAME command, or the Browser, to change their prefix to SCREW.

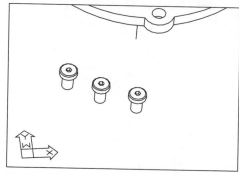

Figure 1-2

Note: Although it is not relevant to the exercise, you may be curious about the screws. They model a #4-40 UNC low head hex socket, cap screw. As is typically done with threaded fasteners, the threads are not modeled. Instead, the threaded portion of the screw is modeled as a cylinder that has the same diameter as the basic diameter of the screw, which in this case is 0.112 inches.

To improve your visibility for this step, you may want to use any of the methods we have described in this chapter to hide the BASE and COVER parts. The flanges on the base and the cover are each 0.125 inches thick, while the screws are only 0.1875 inches long. Therefore, you need to lengthen the screws to 0.25 inches, so that they will extend completely through both flanges. You will use the commands for editing features you learned in Chapter 9 to modify one instance of the screw. In preparation for this, make any one of the screw instances the active part.

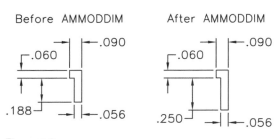

Figure 1-3

Start the AMEDITFEAT command, choose the Sketch option, and pick the active part when you prompted to select a sketched feature. The solid feature will disappear, leaving just the dimensioned profile sketch for the screw, as shown on the left in Figure1-3. Invoke the AMMODDIM command, and select the 0.188 dimension when you are prompted to select a dimension to change. Enter 0.25 in response to the prompt for a new value. Your edited sketch will look similar to the one on the right in Figure 1-3. Lastly, invoke AMUPDATE to initiate the changes.

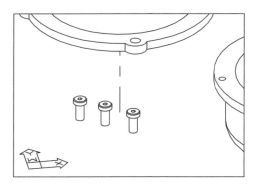

Figure 1-4

Notice, as shown in Figure 1-4 that all three instances of the screw are now longer, even though only one of them was changed. That finishes this exercise. On the accompanying CD-ROM, the edited assembly is in file md17e104.dwg

Working with Subassemblies

A subassembly is an assembly within an assembly. Typically, subassemblies are used to organize manufacturing and assembly operations; and what constitutes a particular subassembly depends on the relationships between the parts, as well as on the manufacturing and assembly techniques to be used. In complex assemblies, subassemblies will often have subassemblies of their own. The components of a subassembly are entirely up to you— Mechanical Desktop makes no judgement as to the suitability of subassembly components. In your subassemblies, though, you will want to include only components that are spatially related, and could physically be assembled and installed in a higher level assembly as a unit.

As a rule, you will use subassemblies whenever you can, because they divide a complicated assembly into more easily managed units, as illustrated in the accompanying figure of an air cylinder, Even a relatively simple assembly such as this can present problems in visualizing, manipulating, and keeping track of parts. When the assembly is divided into these three subassemblies, though, the main, or top level, assembly is easy to work with.

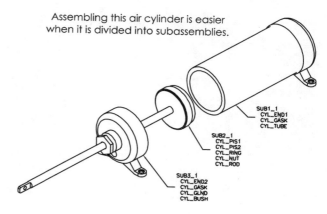

Assembling this air cylinder is easier when it is divided into subassemblies.

SUB1_1
CYL_END1
CYL_GASK
CYL_TUBE

SUB2_1
CYL_PIS1
CYL_PIS2
CYL_RING
CYL_NUT
CYL_ROD

SUB3_1
CYL_END2
CYL_GASK
CYL_GLND
CYL_BUSH

Each subassembly acts very much like an individual part. They each move as a unit, are fixed in position (constrained) to other components as a unit, are activated as a unit, and their visibility is controlled as a unit. You can even create a subassembly in its own computer file, to be inserted into a higher level assembly. In the Browser, each subassembly has a node on the main branch of the assembly tree, and their parts are listed in a branch from the subassembly node.

Use the following steps to create a subassembly.

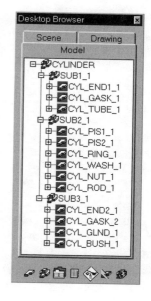

1. Use AMACTIVATE to activate the component that the subassembly is to be based on. This could be the root component, or a subassembly that already exists.

2. Invoke the AMNEW command, and select its Subassembly option.

3. Accept the default subassembly name prefix, or enter one of your choice. The subassembly's name will appear in the Browser.

4. Use AMACTIVATE to activate the subassembly. The parts and subassemblies that do not belong to the activated subassembly will disappear from the computer screen, and their names will be shaded in the Browser.

5. Create, or attach, the parts that are to be in the subassembly. AMCOPYIN cannot be used to add parts to subassemblies. Attaching parts is explained in this chapter during the discussion of the assembly catalog.

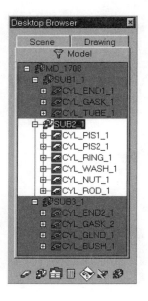

When you activate a subassembly, other parts and subassemblies are no longer accessible and their names in the Browser are shaded. Also, in Mechanical Desktop versions prior to Release 5, the components of non-active subassemblies disappear from the graphics area to leave only the components of the active subassembly; and these components appear just as they were the last time you worked with them—including the zoom level and viewpoint (provided the Assembly Preferences View Restore option has been selected).

Using External Files

The definitions of the components of an assembly can reside in another computer file. These are referred to as external components. While most external components are an individual part, they can be an assembly of parts that are suitable for use as a subassembly within a more complex assembly. One advantage in using external files is that the assembly file will be much smaller and more easily managed. A second advantage is that, similar to having real parts available on a shelf, a component definition can be used in a variety of assemblies. You will prefer to use external components rather than create the components of an assembly within the assembly file, except for very simple and very unique assemblies,

Mechanical Desktop maintains a link between the external component's file and the assembly file, so that changes made to the component are automatically made in the assembly file. Beginning with Mechanical Desktop Release 4, you make changes to an external component within an assembly file, and the changes you make are reflected in the file of the external component. Autodesk refers to this as *editing in place*. If, within an assembly, you want to modify an external component without affecting its file, you can localize the external component, and then change it. Once a component is localized, it no longer has any connection with an external file.

Working with the Assembly Catalog

External files are attached and managed by the AMCATALOG command. This command displays a dialog box titled **Assembly Catalog** that has two tabs—External and All. Most actions within either tab are initiated through right-click pop-up menus. When you are attaching external files to an assembly file, you will begin with the External tab.

External Tab

Your first step in attaching a component is to locate and open the directory that contain your part definitions. You will do this through the right-click menus of the Directories window.

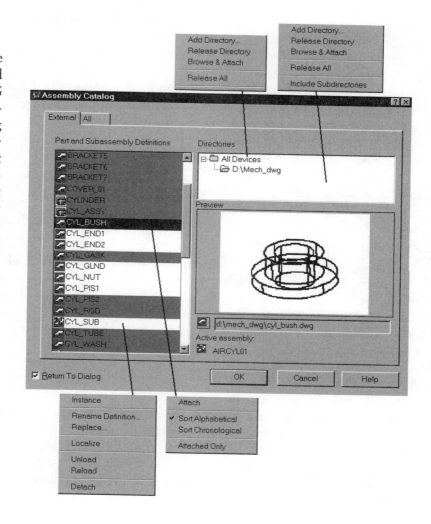

Add Directory A window titled Browse for Folder will be displayed for you to locate the directory that contains the files for your component definitions. This window shows, in an outline or tree-like format, all of the directories in your computer. Highlight the directory folder you want, and click the OK button of the window. The selected directory will be listed in the Directories window of the External tab, and the files in the directory will be listed in the External tab's Part and Subassembly Definitions list box.

Release Directory   Use this option to remove the directory that is highlighted in the Directories window.

Browse and Attach   This option is for locating a single external file and attaching the component in it to the current assembly file. A window titled External file to attach will be displayed for you to locate the file. You will then be prompted to select the position of the selected component instance in the assembly file.

Release All   All displayed directories will be removed when you select this option.

Include Subdirectories   This option, which is available only when you right-click the background area of the Directories window, will display the subdirectories of the directory selected by the Add Directories option. When you highlight a subdirectory, all of its files will be displayed in the External tab's Part and Subassembly Definitions list box.

Once you have associated a directory with your assembly file, you will switch your attention to the Part and Subassembly Definitions list box on the left side of the External tab. Initially all of the drawing files in the selected directory will be displayed with a gray background to signify that they are not attached. When the name of a file is highlighted, an image of the component will be displayed in the preview window, and you can access the following right-click menu options.

Attach   This option, which will be your most often used option, attaches the component in the external file to the current assembly file. The Assembly Catalog dialog box will be temporarily dismissed, and you will be prompted to select an insertion point for the component. You can insert as many copies, or instances, of the component as you like. Press the Enter key to quit attaching instances. In the Part and Subassembly Definitions list box, the background for name of the attached file will become white. You can bypass the right-click menu to select the Attach option directly by double-clicking the name of the part that is to be attached.

Sort Alphabetical   The files in the Part and Subassembly Definitions list box will be ordered alphabetically when this option is selected.

Sort Chronological   When you select this option, the files in the Part and Subassembly Definitions list box will be shown in the order of their creation.

Attached Only   Only files that are currently attached to the current assembly file will be shown in the Part and Subassembly Definitions list box when you select this option.

When a file that is attached to the current assembly file is highlighted, the following right-click menu options are available.

Instance You can add instances to the assembly file with this option. Its action is the same as that of the Attach option.

Rename Definition Use this option to rename components that have been attached. It uses the same dialog box that is used by the AMRENAME command.

Replace This option replaces all instances of the highlighted file with another attached file. A dialog box titled `Replace Definition` will be displayed. The name of the component that is to be replaced will be shown, and you can select its replacement from a dropdown list box. All instances of the highlighted file will be replaced by the selected file. After the replacement has occurred, a message box will ask if you want to remove the definition of the replaced file. If you answer Yes, all traces of the component as well as its connection to an external file will be removed. If you answer No, the file will remain attached even though no instances of it are in the assembly.

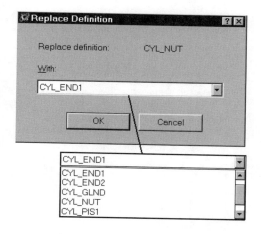

Localize When a component is localized, a copy of its definition is inserted into the assembly file, and the component's attachment to the external file is severed. The result is as if the component had been created within the assembly file.

Unload When you are working with an assembly that has numerous components, which make it difficult to work with, you can use this option to temporarily remove an attached file from the assembly. The component will disappear from the assembly, but its assembly and scene constraints will remain. In both the Browser and the assembly catalog's list of part and subassembly definitions, the name of the unloaded file is offset to the right and preceded with dashed lines.

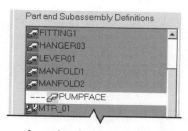

An unloaded component

Reload An file that has been unloaded is reloaded into the current assembly with this option.

Detach This option removes all instances of an attached component from the assembly and severs the link between the component file and the assembly file.

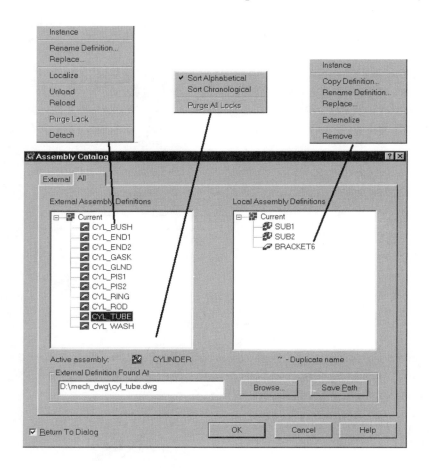

The All Tab

The All tab of the **Assembly Catalog** dialog box is for managing the components in the current assembly file. The left-hand list box, which is labeled Referenced External Definitions, contains the names of all components that are attached to the assembly file and have their definitions in an external file. The right-click menus for this list box are the same as those for the Part and Subassembly Definitions list box of the External tab, except there is no Attach option, because these components are already attached; and there may be options for purging locked files. Locked files, which are most likely to occur in networked Mechanical Desktop installations, are indicated by a red lock icon in front of the names of the locked components. If any of the attached files are open in Mechanical Desktop's multiple document interface, a gray lock icon will appear before their names. You cannot purge these locks. If there are no files with red locks, the options to purge locks are grayed out.

The list box on the right, which is labeled Local Assembly Definitions, shows the names of the components that have been either created within the assembly file or have been localized from an external file. The following right-click menu options are available for the items in this list box.

Instance   You can create one or more copies of the selected component with this option. The `Assembly Catalog` dialog box will temporarily disappear, and you will be prompted to select an insertion point. You can insert as many instances as you like. Press the Enter key to stop inserting instances and restore the dialog box. All of the instances will share the same definition. Therefore, any changes made to one instance will occur in the others as well.

Copy Definition   This option also creates one or more copies of the selected part. Unlike instance copies, the copies will be completely independent from the original. You will be prompted to specify a name for the new part, and then you will be prompted to specify the insert points for the copies. You can create any number of copies until you press the Enter key. All of the copies will share the same definition. The Copy Definition option is not available for subassembly components.

Rename Definition   This is a duplicate of the option with the same name in the External Tab.

Replace   This option is the same as the Replace option in the External Tab.

Externalize   This option is the reverse of the Localize option. You will be prompted for a file name and location for the component. A file will be created for the component, if a file does not exist, and the component's name will move to the Referenced External Definitions list box. The component will not be deleted from the assembly.

Remove   Components are deleted from the assembly with this option. A message box will appear for you to confirm the operation before the components are removed. All instances of the component will be removed.

Managing Links with External Files

By default, Mechanical Desktop automatically audits the files of referenced assembly components whenever an assembly file is opened, and incorporates any changes that have occurred in those files. You can use the AMAUDIT command to determine if any external files have changed after the current file has been opened. AMAUDIT, however, only lists the files that have changed; it does not update the current file, You must use AMRE-FRESH to incorporate changes to external files. AMREFRESH displays a dialog box showing the external files that have been changed, and asks you to specify the ones that are to be updated in the current assembly file.

To modify an external part in an assembly file, activate the part and then make the changes you desire. Update the part, and activate the assembly. Mechanical Desktop will ask if you want to update the external file to reflect the changes you have just made. If you choose not to update the external file at that time, another dialog box for updating the external file will appear when you save or exit the assembly file.

Assembly Restructuring

Beginning with Release 5, you can change the part structure of a Mechanical Desktop assembly. While there is a command for doing this, AMRESTRUCTURE, you will probably use the Browser instead. You can change the order of the parts in the assembly, and you can move parts into a subassembly.

To change the order of a part in an assembly: highlight the part's name in the Browser, hold down the Shift key and drag the part to its new location. Your main reason for doing this will be to change which part is the grounded component of the assembly.

To move parts into a subassembly: create the subassembly, select the components that you want to be within the subassembly, and drag them to the subassembly name without holding down the Shift key. You can select multiple components by holing down the Ctrl key as you pick their names.

Exercise 2

Working with External Files

bolt3-8.dwg	va_gask.dwg
flatscr4.dwg	va_hang.dwg
nut_1-4.dwg	va_pin.dwg
nut_3-8.dwg	va_seal.dwg
va_body.dwg	va_seat.dwg
va_cover.dwg	wash_3-8.dwg
va_disk.dwg	

In this exercise you will place all of the parts of a four inch flanged check valve into an assembly file. In the next chapter, you will assemble the check valve. Before you begin the exercise, locate the 13 files listed on the left on the CD-ROM that comes with this book and copy them to a directory of your choice in your computer.

Start a new assembly file, assigning any name you like to it. Set the viewpoint of the graphics area to that of a front-right isometric view. (Or, a SE isometric view, depending on which Mechanical Desktop method you use in establishing the preset view.) Invoke the AMNEW command to create a subassembly. Name this subassembly BODY. Then create a second subassembly named DISK, and a third one named COVER.

Make the BODY subassembly the active assembly. Start the AMCATALOG command, and open the External tab. In the Directories window, add the directory you used to store the files for the check valve. Then, in the Part and Subassembly Definitions list box locate VA_BODY and display its right-click menu. Select Attach from this menu, and insert one instance of the part. Its location is not important, but it is important that the valve body be first part inserted, because it is to serve as the grounded component of the assembly.

Locate VA_SEAT in the Part and Subassembly Definitions list box, and insert one instance of it somewhere near the valve body. Lastly for this subassembly, insert four instances of FLATSCR4 near the valve body. End the AMCATALOG command. Your subassembly and the Desktop Browser should look similar to the one in Figure 2-1.

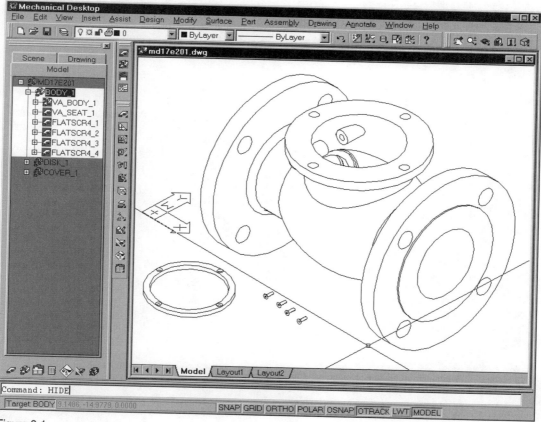

Figure 2-1

Activate the DISK subassembly. Start the AMCATALOG command again, and insert one instance of each of the following parts: VA_DISK, VA_HANG, and NUT_1-4. While the parts should be located near each other, their actual location is not important. Your DISK subassembly should look similar to the one in Figure 2-2.

Activate the COVER subassembly. Start AMCATALOG and insert one instance of VA_COVER, one instance of VA_GASK, and four instances of BOLT3-8. Your version of this subassembly should look similar to the one in Figure 2-3.

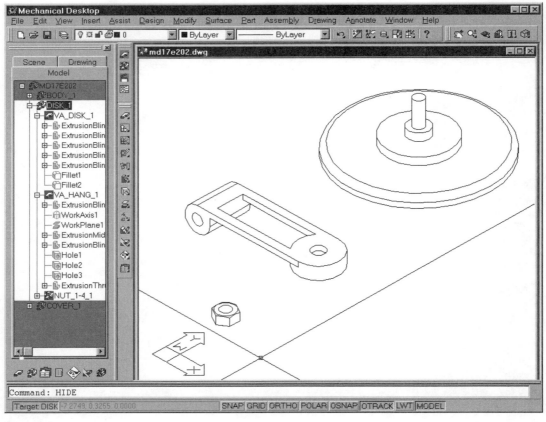

Figure 2-2

Activate the top level assembly. You can use AutoCAD's MOVE command to separate the subassemblies. You will notice that all of the components of a subassembly move as one unit. You will attach the remaining four parts to the top level assembly, because they do not logically fit in a subassembly. Start AMCATALOG and insert one instance of VA_PIN, one instance of VA_SEAL, four instances of WASH_3-8, and four instances of NUT3-8. Here too, the locations of the parts is not important, but you may want to keep them close together. Your assembly should look similar to the one in Figure 2-4.

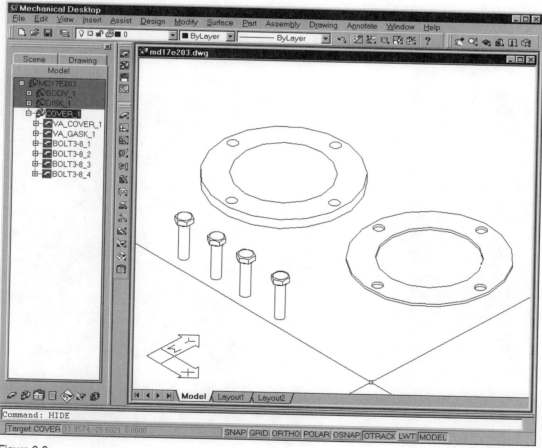

Figure 2-3

That finishes this exercise. You should save your file, because you will use it to assemble the check valve in the next chapter. On the CD-ROM that comes with this book, the valve assembly as this stage is in file md17e204.dwg. All of the parts in this file have been localized to avoid any problems that Mechanical Desktop might have in locating external files in your computer.

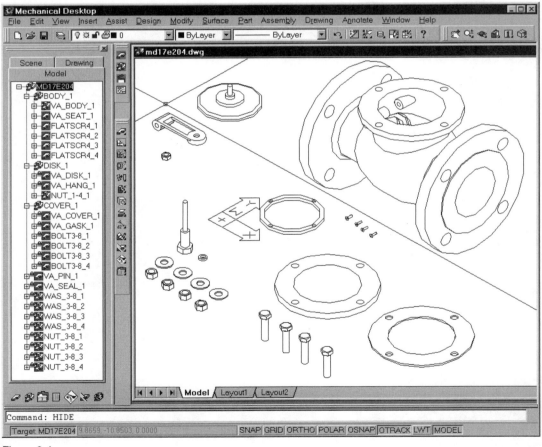

Figure 2-4

CHAPTER 18

Working with Assembly Constraints

Most products, from automobile engines to office staplers, are an assembly of individual components, or parts, that are held together with threads, bolts and other fasteners, welds, press fits, and so forth. Parts in Mechanical Desktop models of assemblies are held together with assembly constraints, or as they are sometimes called, 3D constraints. Unlike the geometric constraints that control the relationships between lines, arcs, and circles in 2D sketches, assembly constraints control the relationships of surfaces, edges, axes, and points between parts.

This chapter covers the following topics.

- Describes the uses of assembly constraints.

- Introduces you to the concept of Degrees of Freedom.

- Describes the geometric shapes that are used for constraints.

- Explains how to select constraint geometry objects.

- Tells how to use the commands that apply constraints (i.e., AMMATE, AMINSERT, AMFLUSH, and AMANGLE).

- Tells how to manage, edit, and update assembly constraints with AMUPDATE, AMEDITCONST, and AMLISTASSM.

- Explains how to move, rotate, and copy parts with the AM3DMINIPULATOR command.

Assembly Constraints

Mechanical Desktop's assembly constraints, or 3D constraints as they are often called, control positional relationships between individual parts. For example, the model of a screw is held within its tapped hole by assembly constraints, as is a ball bearing within its race, and a shaft key in its keyway. Assembly constraints should not be confused with the geometric constraints of sketched features. Although you can simply move parts into their relative positions with AutoCAD commands, this does not give you the control, flexibility, and information that is provided by assembly constraints. When you use assembly constraints:

- The constrained parts automatically move into their relative locations and orientations. Moreover, if the parts are ever moved out of position, you can restore their constrained configuration with the click of a button.

- You can easily create exploded view drawings of assemblies. Mechanical Desktop refers to exploded assemblies as scenes.

- You can check assemblies for interference (where more than one part occupies the same space).

- You can find the mass properties of an entire assembly—its weight, volume, center of gravity, and so forth.

- Third party programs for simulating motions and dynamics in 3D models base their speed and force calculations on Mechanical Desktop's assembly constraints.

You will also use assembly constraints during the construction of a part whenever you use the Boolean union, subtract, and intersect operations of the AMCOMBINE command, which is discussed in Chapter 12, to modify one part (the active part) with a second part (the toolbody). Here too, you can just move the two parts into their relative positions and perform the Boolean operation, but to ensure that the combined part's parametric properties remain intact, you should tie them together with assembly constraints.

Degrees of Freedom

The term *degrees of freedom* (DOF) is used to indicate the possible movements of an individual part. A completely unconstrained part, such as a cube, in model space (where there is no gravity to contend with) has six degrees of freedom, because it can move simultaneously in the X, Y, and Z directions as well as rotate simultaneously about the X, Y, and Z axes. Movements in the X, Y, and Z directions are referred to a *translational degrees* of freedom, while rotations about the axes are referred to as *rotational degrees* of freedom. If you were to constrain the bottom surface of the cube we mentioned to the top surface of a second cube, it would have just three degrees of freedom, because it can move only in the X and Y directions, and rotate only about the Z axis.

Mechanical Desktop has a symbol that can be displayed within a part to let you know which movements of the part are possible. In this symbol, cone tipped arrows indicate possible translational movement while arc-shaped arrows indicate possible rotational movement. The DOF symbol for the unconstrained cube mentioned in the previous paragraph is shown on the left in the following figure, while its DOF symbol when it is constrained to the top surface of a second cube is shown on the right.

Unconstrained cube.
Six degrees of freedom.

Partially constrained cube.
Three degrees of freedom.

You can display this symbol for one part by right-clicking the part's name in the Desktop Browser, and select DOF Symbol from the resulting shortcut menu. You can globally display the DOF symbol by invoking the AMVISIBLE command and selecting both the Degrees of Freedom and Unhide options from the Assembly tab of the **Desktop Visibility** dialog box. The relative size of the DOF symbol is controlled by the Desktop Symbol Size option in the Preferences tab of the AMOPTIONS command's **Mechanical Options** dialog box.

The number within the circle of the DOF symbol is the order in which the part was instanced. In the example we have been using, the instance number of the cube is 2, which means that it was the second part created within the assembly drawing file or else it was the second part attached to the file. When a part becomes completely restrained, its DOF symbol will consist of just the part's instance number. The *grounded component* of an assembly always has zero degrees of freedom. Also, parts move to the grounded component as they are constrained to the grounded component.

Examples of assembly constraints

A planar surface on one part constrained to a planar suface on another part.

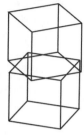

The centerline of a cylinder constrained to the centerline of a hole.

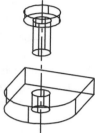

The surface of a sphere constrained to the inside surface of a ring.

Constraint Geometry Objects

Even though four different commands are used to implement assembly constraints—AMANGLE, AMFLUSH, AMINSERT, and AMMATE—these commands have similar command line prompts and object selection methods for specifying constraint geometry objects. Therefore, we will describe constraint geometry objects and the methods for selecting them before discussing the individual assembly constraint commands.

Assembly constraints are always applied between just two parts. The first step in creating a constraint is to decide what geometry on each part you want constrained. You may, for example, want a planar surface on one part to be placed on a planar surface of another part, the centerline of a cylinder aligned with the centerline of a hole, or the surface of a sphere to touch the inside surface of a ring. These three examples represent different types of constraint geometry objects. The four geometry object types you can use for assembly constraints are:

Points as found at the end of a line, the end of an edge on a solid; the center of an arc, sphere, or torus; or a Mechanical Desktop work point.

Axes which may be a line, a straight edge on a solid, a work axis; or the axis of an arc, cylinder, cone, or torus. You can also specify an axis by selecting two points. (Note that this use of the word axis does imply revolution.)

Planes as defined by the planar face of a solid or by a work plane. You can also use two coplanar axes, an axis and a point, or three points to define a plane.

Non-planar Faces as found on the surface of a sphere or torus, or on the side of a cylinder or cone. Surface cut faces, however, cannot be used as constraint geometry. (Surface cut faces, which are made by the AMSURFCUT command, are described in Chapter 11.)

Selecting Geometry Objects

Geometry Type Icons

When you invoke an assembly constraint command, you will be prompted to select a geometry object on each of the two parts that you intend to constrain. For example: if you want to place a sphere on the surface of a cube, you will select the sphere's surface as one geometry object and a flat face on the cube as the second geometry object. The order in which you select the two geometry objects is not important, because the part having the larger instance number will move into its constrained position, regardless of whether it is selected first or second.

Mechanical Desktop displays icons to help you verify the geometry object type you have selected. For instance, when you select either a plane or a non-planar face, Mechanical Desktop displays an arrow that is on and perpendicular (normal) to the solid's surface.

When the geometry object is a point, an icon in the shape of a globe is shown on the point; and when the geometry object is an axis, the icon is a line drawn along the axis.

Examples of these two icons are shown on the left in the accompanying figure, and the two parts are shown on the right in their constrained positions. In this figure, the bottom face of the smaller part was previously constrained to the top face of the larger part. Notice from the DOF symbols that part number two went from three degrees of freedom to one degree of freedom—it is still able to revolve about one axis.

An arrow icon is used to indicate a surface.

Second geometry object:
A face on the cube

First geometry object:
Surface of sphere

Resulting assembly
constraint

A globe icon indicates a point and
a line icon indicates an axis.

Point I

Axis

The bottom face of
the small part is
constrained to the
top face of the
large part.

Resulting new point/axis
assembly constraint

Options for Selecting Geometry Objects

The geometry object type and the constraint geometry location depends not only on the shape of the part that is selected, but also on the location of your object selection point. Furthermore, the command line prompts of the commands that create assembly constraints offer options that allow you to change geometry object types as well as constraint locations. For example, if you pick a point on the straight edge of a plane as a constraint object, Mechanical Desktop will interpret the selection as an axis, but you can change the geometry type to either a plane or a point through command line options. Moreover, you can specify which of the two planes that are adjacent to the selected edge is to be used as the plane constraint geometry, and whether the constraint point is to be on one of the two ends of the edge or in its middle.

The command line prompts for the commands that create assembly constraints vary according to the geometry of your object selection point, but they always contain an option called Cycle that steps through appropriate constraint geometry object types and locations. The following descriptions give the command line options for an assortment of geometry object types and selection points, and illustrate the results of the options, including Cycle. All of the prompts also offer two options that are not described in the following paragraphs: Clear, which clears the selection set and prompts you to select another object; and Accept, which accepts the current selection.

Object Selection Geometry Type: Plane	
Options:	Next/Flip/Cycle

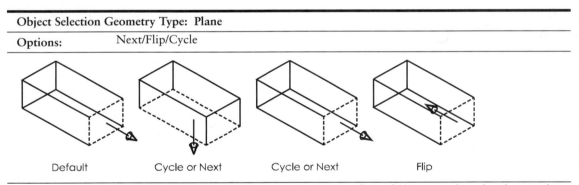

| | Default | Cycle or Next | Cycle or Next | Flip |

| **Note:** | You select a plane by picking a point on its surface. If planes overlap, the plane in the foreground will be the one selected. |

Object Selection Geometry Type: **Straight Edge**

Options:	Face/Point/Cycle

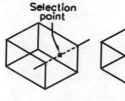   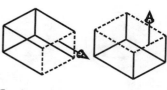

Default   Cycle or Point   Cycle   Cycle   Cycle or Face   Cycle

Note: When the selection object type becomes a face, Next and Flip options are offered, similar to a plane selection. Also, if the object selection point is near a face corner, the point option and the first cycle will locate the point at an edge end, rather than in the middle of the edge.

Object Selection Geometry Type: **Curved Edge**

Options:	Face/Point/Cycle

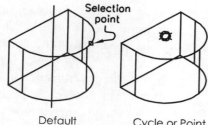  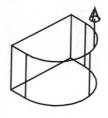 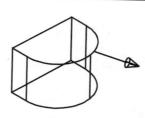

Default   Cycle or Point   Cycle or Face   Cycle or Next

Note: The default option is the centerline axis of the curved edge. When the selection object becomes either a planar or non-planar face, Next and Flip options are also offered.

Object Selection Geometry Type: Non-planar Face

Options:	Face/Cycle

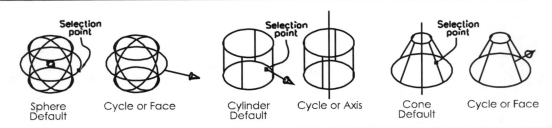

| Sphere Default | Cycle or Face | Cylinder Default | Cycle or Axis | Cone Default | Cycle or Face |

Note:	The face can be selected by picking a point anywhere on its surface. A Flip option is offered when the object type becomes a face.

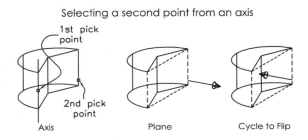

Selecting a second point from an axis

1st pick point

2nd pick point

Axis   Plane   Cycle to Flip

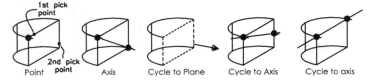

Selecting a second point from a point

1st pick point

2nd pick point

Point   Axis   Cycle to Plane   Cycle to Axis   Cycle to axis

Multiple Object Selections

For axis and point geometry types, you can also select a second point in response to the command line options for constraint geometry. When the geometry type is an axis, for example, selecting a second point causes the geometry type to become a plane.

If the current object type is a point, a second point causes the geometry type to become an axis that passes through the two points. The rules for the second point's location are the same as those for the first point. For instance, if the pick location of the second selection is near the end of a straight edge, a point is located on the end of the edge and an axis is drawn between the first and second points. The constraint geometry cycles to a plane, and then back to an axis but with the second point moved to the midpoint of the edge, and again to a axis with the second point moved to the opposite end of the edge.

If the constraint geometry type is a point, you can select two additional points in response to the command line options to define an assembly constraint plane.

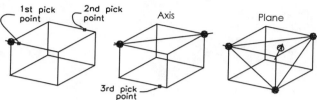

Three points define a plane.

1st pick point   2nd pick point   Axis   Plane

3rd pick point

Object Cycling

You can eventually reach all of the available constraint geometry types by repeatedly selecting the Cycle option. (To reverse the normal of a face, though, you must use the Flip option.) Because this is such a helpful and often used option, the assembly constraint commands have an animated cursor similar to the one used in the AMSKPLN command. This cursor, which is displayed during the prompts for object selections when you move the pickbox away from objects, looks like a cylinder encircled by a rotating arrow. This cursor is a signal that you can press the pick button of your pointing device to cycle to the next constraint geometry type. The method is offered as a convenience to reduce keyboard usage. When you press the Enter button of your pointing device, the current constraint geometry type and location is accepted.

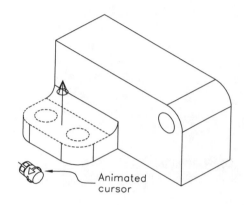

Animated cursor

Using Assembly Constraint Commands

The four commands for applying assembly constraints are as follows.

AMMATE   This is a general-purpose constraint command that allows you to constrain parts that have a wide variety of geometric shapes.

AMANGLE   This constraint command controls the angle between a plane and another plane or an axis.

AMFLUSH   You will use this constraint command to make two planes coplanar, with their normals pointed in the same direction.

AMINSERT   This constraint command makes two planes that have circular or arc-shaped edges coplanar, with the centers of their edges coinciding and their normals pointed in opposite directions.

Assembly constraints are always between just two parts, or components. As a rule, your goal in applying them is to reduce the degrees of freedom of all components, except the grounded component, to zero. Usually, more than one constraint for each component is required to do this. Occasionally, though, you will not want to fully constrain a part. For instance, you may want to allow a shaft to rotate or a bar to slide within a groove.

By default, Mechanical Desktop automatically moves the two parts into their constrained positions as soon as an assembly constraint is created. If you set the system variable **amautoassemble** to 0 or clear the Update Assembly as Constrained check box in the Assemblies Tab of the `Mechanical Options` dialog box, though, the two parts will not move as they are constrained. Most people prefer to have the parts automatically move into their constrained positions so that they can verify that the assembly constraint is correctly applied. Once two parts have been constrained, you can use AutoCAD's MOVE command or Mechanical Desktop's AMMANIPULATOR command to move the parts away from each other to give you better visibility for adding another constraint. Invoke the AMUPDATE command and select the Assembly option to force parts into their constrained positions.

Applying Mate Constraints

AMMATE is a versatile constraint command, covering a wide range of geometric shapes, as shown in Table 1. In this table, the labels Sphere, Cylinder, and Cone refer to the surface of those geometric shapes. As shown in this table, you can constrain an axis to a point, a point to a plane, the surface of a sphere to a plane, and the surface of a cylinder to the surface of another cylinder. You cannot, though, constrain the surface of a sphere to a point, or the surface of a cone to an axis or to the surface of a cylinder.

Table 1 Allowable Mate Geometry Pairs

First Geometry Selection	Second Geometry Selection					
	Point	Axis	Plane	Sphere	Cylinder	Cone
Point	Yes	Yes	Yes	No	No	No
Axis	Yes	Yes	Yes	No	No	No
Plane	Yes	Yes	Yes	Yes	Yes	Yes
Sphere	No	No	Yes	Yes	Yes	Tangent
Cylinder	No	No	Yes	Yes	Yes	No
Cone	No	No	Yes	Tangent	No	No

A few examples of the many possible Mate constraint geometry pairs are:

• A sphere is tangent with a cylinder, plane, cone, or another sphere,

- Two planes are coplanar and their normal vectors are pointed in opposite directions.
- Two edges are coincident.
- A point on one part is constrained to a plane on another part.
- The axis of a cone is coincident with the axis of another cone.

You will notice in this table that there are not many choices for constraining cones. When the two geometry selections are a cone and a sphere, the sphere is located at the point along the axis of the cone where it touches the surface of the cone, or would touch the cone if the cone's surface was extended. Consequently, when a sphere is larger than the largest diameter of a cone, or is smaller that the cone's smallest diameter; it will positioned outside the cone and will be tangent to the projected surface of the cone.

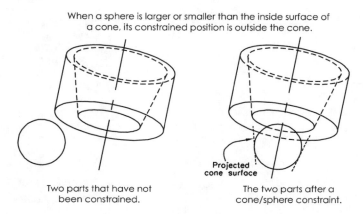

When a sphere is larger or smaller than the inside surface of a cone, its constrained position is outside the cone.

Projected cone surface

Two parts that have not been constrained.

The two parts after a cone/sphere constraint.

When you invoke AMMATE, a command line prompt will ask you to select the first set of constraint geometry. It will then report the geometry type that was selected—such as point, plane, or axis—and issue a command line prompt with wording that varies as described earlier in this chapter in the section headed Options for Selecting Geometry Objects. Once you have specified the first set of geometry, AMMATE will prompt you to specify the second set of geometry. Lastly, you will be prompted to specify the offset distance between the two geometry objects. Then, the part that was instanced last will move to the other part, regardless of which geometry set was selected first in AMMATE.

To give you a feel for how AMMATE works, the following example will show how you would constrain a box shaped part to the top surface of a cylinder. The cylinder is the grounded part.

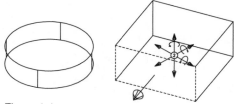

Figure 1-1

```
Command: AMMATE (Enter)
Select first set of geometry: (Pick a point on
    the side surface of the box as shown in
    Figure 1-1.)
(A normal direction vector will point away from
    the side surface.)
```

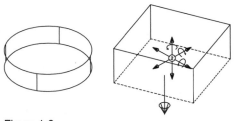

Figure 1-2

```
First set = Plane
Enter an option [Clear/Next/Flip/cYcle]
<accEpt>: Next (Enter)
(The normal direction vector will move to the
bottom surface and point away from it. See
Figure 1-2.)
First set = Plane
Enter an option [Clear/Next/Flip/cYcle]
<accEpt>: (Enter)
Select second set of geometry: (Pick a point on
the top surface of the cylinder.)
(A normal direction vector will point away from
the surface. See Figure 1-3.)
Second set = Plane
Enter an option [Clear/Next/Flip/cYcle]
<accEpt>: (Enter)
```

```
Enter offset <0.0000>: (Enter)
(The bottom surface of the box will move to the top surface of the cylinder, as shown in
    Figure 1-4.)
```

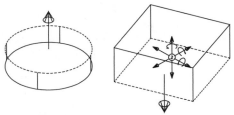

Figure 1-3

Notice that the DOF symbol for the box indicates that it still has three degrees of freedom—two translational and one rotational. Furthermore, the plane/plane constraint just constrains the plane of the bottom surface of the box to the plane of the top surface of the cylinder. The box does not necessarily sit on top of the cylinder. You would have to apply other constraints, such as constraining the side surface of the cylinder to be in the same plane as one face of the box, to insure that it would do that.

You can use global variables in specifying an offset. You cannot, however, use active part variables or dimension names, because more that one part is involved. An example of a situation in which you might use an offset is in constraining a tapered roller bearing to be tangent to the inside of a tapered bearing race. Since both parts are cones, you will have to constrain their axes, and then specify an offset distance based on the radius of the bearing and of the race. You would probably also add a flush constraint to keep the faces of the two parts matched.

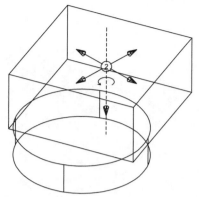

Figure 1-4

Applying Insert Constraints

Insert constraints align the axes of two circular or arc shaped features, and also match a planar surface on each part. The selection points must be on the rounded edges of the planar surfaces you want matched.

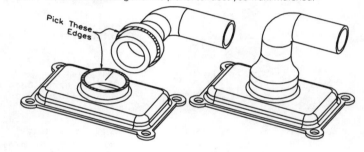

Insert constraints, which are applied through the AMINSERT command, are for aligning the axis of two cylindrical or conical features. You will use this constraint to insert bolts and screws into holes, nuts onto bolts, bearings onto shafts, and so forth.

It works by aligning a planar surface on each part, as well as aligning their axes, and the command requires that you select the constraint geometry for each part by picking a circular edge. You are not allowed to pick an axis or the surface of a plane. The part does not need to be a complete cylinder or cone, though. It can be arc shaped in cross section, or an arc shaped portion of a part. As soon as you pick a point, Mechanical Desktop will display a surface normal vector, and you can reverse its direction through command line input or through object cycling.

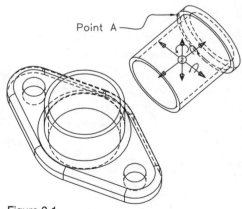

Figure 2-1

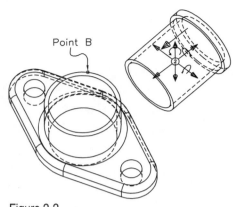

Figure 2-2

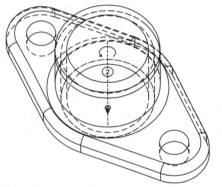

Figure 2-3

After specifying the constraint geometry, you can specify an offset distance between the two planes. The inserted part will lose two rotational and all of its translational degrees of freedom.

As shown in the following example, the command line prompts and your input for AMINSERT are not as involved as that of AMMATE. In this example, the part with the diamond shaped base is the grounded part.

Command: AMINSERT (Enter)

Select first circular edge: (Pick point A in Figure 2-1.)

(A normal direction arrow appears on the plane of the surface you selected.)

Enter an option [Clear\Flip] <accEpt>: (Press Enter if the arrow points toward the side you want constrained. Otherwise, enter an F and then accept the direction.)

Select second circular edge: (Pick point B in Figure 2-2.)

(A normal direction arrow appears on the surface you selected.)

Enter an option [Clear\Flip] <accEpt>: (Press Enter if the arrow points toward the side you want constrained. Otherwise, enter an F and then accept the direction.)

Enter offset <0.0000>: (Enter)

(The part that represents a sleeve will move so that it is in other part's large hole, as shown in Figure 2-3.)

Applying Flush Constraints

The AMFLUSH command, forces two planes to be coplanar, and points their normal vectors in the same direction. The methods for defining planes we described earlier in this

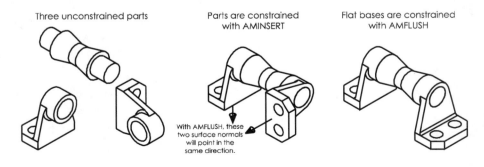

chapter are used in specifying the geometry. As with the other assembly constraints, you can specify an offset distance between the two planes. Only the planes will be aligned—their edges will not be aligned. Three degrees of freedom, two translational and one rotational, will remain.

Applying Angle Constraints

Angle constraints are applied by the AMANGLE command. The constraint controls the angle between two planes, two axes, or one plane and one axis. The techniques for specifying the constraint geometry are as we described earlier in this chapter. After selecting the two geometry sets, you will be prompted to specify the angle between their axes or planes. One rotational degree of freedom is removed when an angle constraint is applied.

The following example illustrates how an angle constraint is applied. Previously, an insert constraint has positioned the 90 degree elbow on a fitting on the base part.

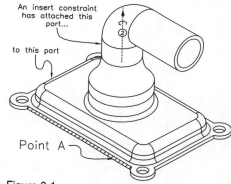

Figure 3-1

```
Command: AMANGLE (Enter)
Select first set of geometry: (Pick point A,
    which is on a planar surface, in Figure 3-1.)
First set = Plane/Vector
Select first set or [Clear/Next/Flip/cYcle]
    <accEpt>: (Enter)
(A direction vector arrow will point away from
    the selected face.)
Select second set of geometry: (Pick point B,
    which is on the surface of a cylinder, in Figure
    3-2.)
Second set = Axis/Vector, (cylinder)
Select second set or [Clear/Flip] <accEpt>:
    (Enter)
(An axis that has a direction arrow pointing to
    the right is in the center of the cylinder.)
Enter angle <0>: 30 (Enter)
(The part with the elbow will rotate so that the
    centerline of the cylinder in the second
    geometry set is 30 degrees from the direction
    vector of the plane in the first geometry set,
    as shown in Figure 3-3.)
```

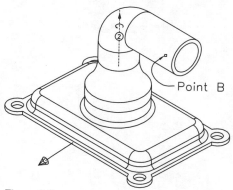

Figure 3-2

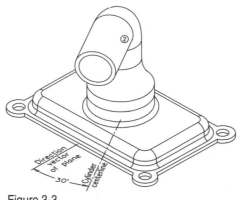

Figure 3-3

Editing Assembly Constraints

When you invoke the AMEDITCONS command, a dialog box titled **Edit 3D Constraints** will be displayed. Initially, this dialog box shows a list of all of parts that have assembly constraints, but most of the buttons are grayed-out. When you pick a part's name, the part will be highlighted in the graphics window and the button labeled Show will be highlighted. You can arrive at this same condition by clicking the Select button, and then picking a point on the part that has the constraints you want to edit.

Once you have specified the part whose constraints you intend to edit, click the Show button to activate all of the options in the dialog box. The number labeled Count refers to the number of constraints attached to the selected part. A count of 2 of 5, for instance, means the part has five assembly constraints and the data shown is for constraint number 2. If the part has more than one constraint, the Show button will be replaced by forward and reverse increment buttons, and you can use them to step through the part's constraints.

Initially the AMEDITCONS dialog box displays only a list of the parts that are constrained.

After specifying a part, click the button labeled Show to activate all of the options in the dialog box.

The type of the current constraint and its Offset or Angle values are displayed below the increment buttons. You can enter new values in the Edit Constraint edit box to change the current offset or angle. The button with the lighting bolt icon updates the assembly. All constraints on the specified part are removed when you select the All button, while just the just the constraint currently shown in the Type area is deleted when you select the Current button.

Each assembly constraint appears twice in the Desktop Browser—once for each of the constraint's pair of parts. When you highlight a constraint's name, the geometry of the constraint (such as planes and their normals, axes, and points) are shown in the graphics window. The shortcut menu displayed when you right-click a constraint's name has a Delete option and an Edit option. When you select Edit, a special version of the `Edit 3D Constraints` dialog box is displayed for you to use in changing the offset or angle values of the constraint.

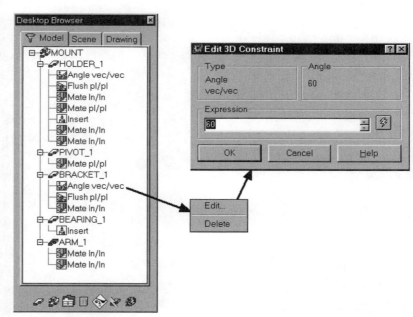

The Browser can become confusingly cluttered when the features of parts are displayed along with assembly constraints. Consequently, you may find it helpful to use the Browser Filter to turn off feature display, as was done in the Browser shown in the near-by figure. To open the dialog box of the filter, right-click in the background area of the Browser, and select Browser Filter from the shortcut menu. Then clear the check boxes of the items, such as features, you do not want displayed.

The AMLISTASSM command gives you information about a part. A command line prompt will ask you to either select an object or enter the name of a part or subassembly. Mechanical Desktop will report the object's part or subassembly name, its definition name, and the number of rotational and translational degrees of freedom that remain.

Exercise

Assembling a Check Valve

In this exercise you will use assembly constraints to put the parts for a flanged check valve together. In an exercise in Chapter 17 you used the AMCATALOG command to import the parts for the check valve into an assembly file. Open your file of the check valve parts, or else locate file md17e204.dwg on the CD-ROM that comes with this book, and open it.

You will begin assembling the valve by constraining the parts in the BODY subassembly. Activate that subassembly. Turn off the visibility of the other subassemblies and parts, leaving just the VA_BODY, VA_SEAT, and four FLATSCR parts. (You can hold down the Ctrl key as you select these objects in the Browser, and then turn their visibility off through the Browser shortcut menu.) Use AMINSERT to constrain any one of the four screw holes inside the valve body to one of the holes in the valve seat. Make certain that the countersunk side of the valve seat holes are away from the valve body. Then use another insert constraint to match another tapped hole in the valve body with the corresponding hole in the valve seat. These two insert constraints will completely constrain the valve seat to the valve body.

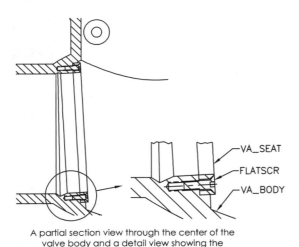

A partial section view through the center of the valve body and a detail view showing the valve seat and flat head screw locations.

Figure 4-1

Next, use AMINSERT to insert the four flat head screws through the valve seat. Select the top rim of each screw head as one geometry object and the top rim of the countersunk hole as the second geometry object. Make certain that the direction vector arrows on the screw head point into the screw (not away from the flat surface of the screw head), and that the vector arrows for the valve seat surface point away from the countersinks. Figure 4-1 is a section view showing the constrained location and orientation of these parts. Constraining the parts in this subassembly is relatively simple, but you may have trouble viewing the parts due to the large size and complexity of the valve body. You will probably have to zoom in very close to be able to see and select objects.

Turn off the visibility of the BODY subassembly. Activate the DISK subassembly, and turn on its visibility. There are just three parts in this subassembly, and they will be easy to constrain to one another. Use the AMINSERT command to constrain the hanger to the valve disk by selecting the edges labeled in Figure 4-2. Then, use AMINSERT again to constrain the one-fourth inch nut to the hanger by selecting the edges shown in Figure 4-2.

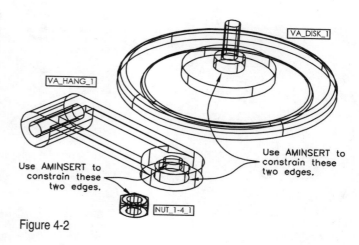

Figure 4-2

The two sides of the nut are not the same, and you must be certain to select the edge on the side that has a ring-like flat face.

Turn off the visibility of the DISK subassembly. Activate the COVER subassembly, which has six separate parts—one VA_COVER, one VA_GASK, and four BOLT3-8's, and make the subassembly visible. Use AMINSERT to position any one of the holes in the gasket to the bottom side of one of the holes in the cover. Then use a second insert constraint to match another hole in the gasket with the corresponding hole in the cover. Invoke AMINSERT four more times to insert the bolts through the holes in the cover and gasket, with the bottom surface of their heads on the top surface of the cover. See Figure 4-3, which is an exploded view of this subassembly.

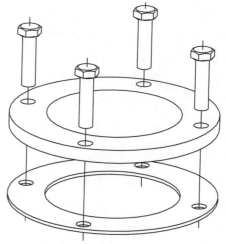

Figure 4-3

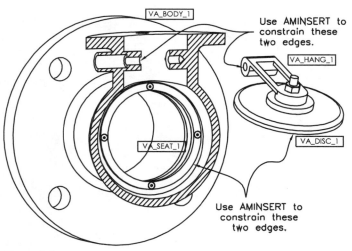

Figure 4-4

Activate the entire assembly so that you can place the subassemblies and the remaining loose parts together, and make all of the subassemblies and parts visible. First, you will place the valve's disk subassembly into the valve's body. Do this with two calls to AMINSERT matching the circular edges shown in Figure 4-4. In Figure 4-4 the valve body has been sliced and the front end removed to clearly show the valve seat that the valve disk is to be against, and the hole that holds the pin the hanger subassembly is to pivot about. These circular edges will be less obvious to you, because of the numerous and confusing edges in the valve body.

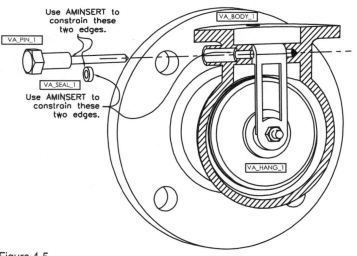

Figure 4-5

In operation, the check valve's disk swings about the pivot pin when water or other fluid pushes against it. We constrained the disk to the valve seat to place it in its initial, closed position, and after applying that constraint, you should delete it.

As shown in Figure 4-5, use AMINSERT to place the valve seal on the valve pin, and use AMINSERT again to place both the valve pin and the valve seal inside the valve body. Although it is not obvious in Figure 4-5, the large diameter of the valve pin and the corresponding cylindrical surface inside the valve body represent threads.

Use the AMINSERT command to constrain the bottom edge of a hole in the gasket that is in the cover subassembly to the top rim of a hole in the top flange of the valve body. Repeat this operation to line up and constrain two other pairs of holes in the valve cover and body. These two insert constraints will also insert the four bolts through the holes in the valve body's flange.

With the cover in place, use AMINSERT to place a washer over the end of each bolt to lie next to the lower side of the valve body flange and place a nut over each bolt to touch the washer. See Figure 4-6. Be certain in constraining the nuts to the washers that the flat raised surface on each nut is next to the washer. You may find it helpful to first constrain the nuts to the washers and then constrain the washers to the valve body.

You are now finished with this exercise, and you should save the file of your constrained assembly model. In Chapter 19 you will create a scene, in which the parts are spread apart, from this model. On the CD-ROM supplied with this book, the model at this stage is in file md18e406.dwg.

Moving and Positioning Parts

Often as you create assemblies, you need to move and reorient parts to obtain a better view of them and to more easily select their edges and faces when applying assembly constraints. You can freely use AutoCAD's MOVE command to move parts, both before and after they have been constrained, and you can use AutoCAD's ROTATE and ROTATE3D to reorient them. Directions in

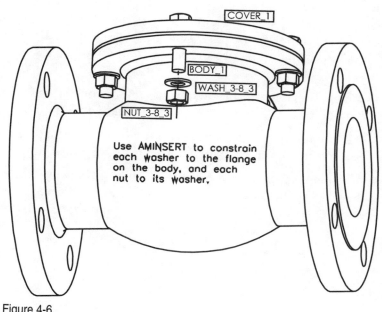

Figure 4-6

these commands are always relative to the User Coordinate System, and your pointing device is restricted the XY plane of the UCS in specifying movements and rotations, unless you use object snaps.

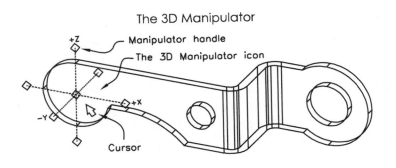

The 3D Manipulator

Manipulator handle

The 3D Manipulator icon

+Z

+X

–Y

Cursor

Mechanical Desktop has a command, AM3DMINIPULATOR, that both moves and rotates parts, and does this independently of the UCS. The command can also create copies, or instances, of a part. When you initiate AM3DMANIPULATOR, a command line prompt will ask you to select one or more parts. The 3D Manipulator icon will appear and be located on an end or center point of one of the selected part's edges, and the screen cursor will assume an arrow-like form.

The manipulator is a local coordinate system having X, Y, and Z axes, and an origin, plus diamond shaped handles located at the origin and at each end of the three axes. Select one of the handles with the cursor and depress the pick button of your pointing device to manipulate the part. Whether the selected part rotates or moves, and whether it moves in a straight line or not, depends on which handle is selected and the direction it is moved.

- When you position the cursor on a handle on the end of an axis, depress the pick button and drag the handle along the axis, the manipulator and the part move linearly.

- When you position the cursor on the handle at the origin and depress the pick button, you can move the part anywhere on the XY plane of the manipulator.

- When you select an end handle and drag it sideways, the part will rotate about the axis that is perpendicular to the movement. For example, when you drag the handle that is at the end of the Z axis in the X axis direction, the part will rotate about the Y axis.

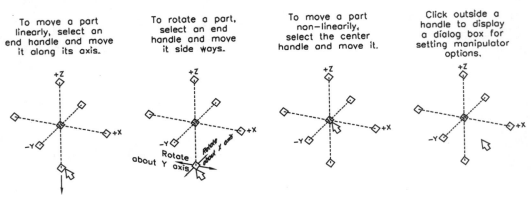

To move a part linearly, select an end handle and move it along its axis.

To rotate a part, select an end handle and move it side ways.

To move a part non-linearly, select the center handle and move it.

Click outside a handle to display a dialog box for setting manipulator options.

AM3DMIPULATOR has a command line option for undoing the last action. Another option is Mode, which is a toggle that is either FOLLOW or FREE. In the FOLLOW mode, which is the default mode, the selected parts move as the 3D Manipulator icon moves. In the FREE mode, though, only the 3D Manipulator icon moves. This is useful when you want to move the icon to another location. You can use AutoCAD object snaps in relocating the origin of the 3D Manipulator. To end AM3DMIPULATOR, choose Exit from the command line options or press the Enter key.

When you press the Enter key as you are moving a handle a dialog box titled either **Move** or **Rotate**, depending on the direction of the cursor's movement, will appear. Options in these dialog boxes allow you to enter a specific distance or a rotation angle, to make copies of the selected parts, and to toggle between the FOLLOW and FREE modes.

When you press the pick button of your pointing device as the manipulator cursor is outside a handle, a dialog box titled **Common Options** is displayed. Options in this dialog box toggle between the

One of these dialog boxes appear when you press the Enter key as you move or rotate the 3D Manipulator icon.

FOLLOW and FREE modes, and set the number of copies to be made from the selected object. The Entity and Face options are useful for positioning the manipulator in the FREE mode. Entity places the manipulator in a default location on a selected part, while Face places it on a selected face. The UCS and WCS options position the manipulator according to the User Coordinate System or the World Coordinate System. The effect these four options have on the manipulator is controlled by the three radio buttons below them. The button labeled Default Position returns the manipulator to its default position and orientation.

When you select the Settings option in the **Common Options** dialog box, a dialog box titled **Configuration** appears. Options in this dialog box allow you to:

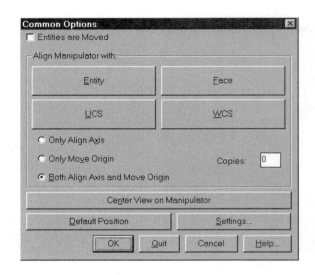

- Have rotations snap to preset angles,

- Control the relative size of the manipulator's axes, handles, and axis labels,

- Control whether the parts will be displayed in wireframe, hidden line, or shaded viewing modes when the manipulator is being used, and

- Set the colors of the manipulator's axes, handles, and axis labels.

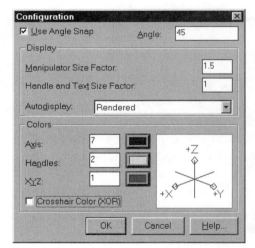

When the Crosshair Color (XOR) check box is selected, the same color used for the AutoCAD crosshairs is used for the manipulator's objects.

CHAPTER 19

Working with Assemblies and Scenes

Obtaining information about an assembly's physical properties, and checking for proper fit between parts is vital in the design of a product. Mechanical Desktop can obtain this information from assemblies, which enables you to make design adjustments before parts are actually manufactured. Mechanical Desktop is also able to spread the parts of an assembly apart, so that individual parts and their relative positions can be seen more clearly.

This chapter covers the following topics.

- Describes how to find the weight, volume, center of gravity, and other mass properties of an assembly, even if the assembly's parts vary in density.

- Explains how to check an assembly to discover interfering parts (i.e., parts that occupy the same space).

- Tells you how to explode an assembly to create what Mechanical Desktop refers to as a scene.

- Shows you how to use explosion factors and tweaks to control the spacing of parts within a scene.

- Explains how to indicate the path of an exploded part with an assembly trail.

Information from Assemblies

Mass Properties of Assemblies

The AMASSMPROP command gives you the same mass (weight), volume, and geometry data for assemblies that the AMPARTPROP command gives for individual parts, except for surface area. Unlike AMASSMPROP, though, AMASSMPROP supplies density (weight per unit volume) data for ten commonly used materials—such as aluminum and steel. Also, you can assign different density values to different parts in an assembly.

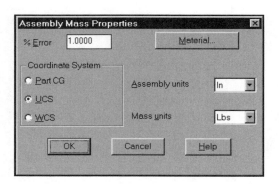

When you invoke AMASSMPROP, you will be prompted from the command line to choose one of two methods for specifying the parts the data is to be based on; you can enter the name of one part or subassembly, or you can select multiple parts via your pointing device.

When you have specified the parts Mechanical Desktop will display the `Assembly Mass Properties` dialog box. The options in this dialog box are as follows.

Percent Error   This option sets the maximum error, expressed as a percentage, in the calculations of the mass properties. Usually, the default 1.0 error percent yields satisfactory results.

Coordinate System   Most mass properties, such as center of gravity and moments of inertia, are based on a point. The three radio buttons in this cluster allow you to specify that the point is to be at the origin of the World Coordinate System (WCS), the origin of the User Coordinate System (UCS), or the selected part's center of gravity (CG). The CG option is not available when multiple parts have been selected.

Assembly Units   Select the system used for linear dimensions in the part from this dropdown list box. You can choose between inches (in), centimeters (cm), and millimeters (mm). The units should match those used in constructing the assembly's parts.

Mass Units   Select the system for measuring mass, or weight, from this dropdown list box. You can choose between pounds (Lbs), grams (g), and kilograms (Kg). The units you select should match the system you have specified for measuring length. Thus, if you selected inches for Assembly units, you should select pounds as Mass units.

Material   This button opens the `Select Material` dialog box.

You will use the `Select Material` dialog box to assign a material to individual parts in the assembly. The dropdown list box contains the names of ten commonly used materials, while the names of the parts you have selected

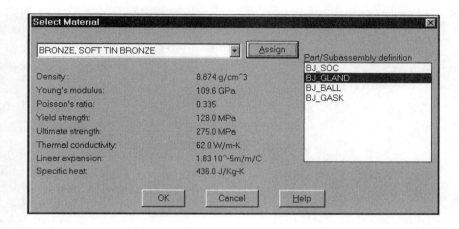

are shown in a list box on the right. To assign a material to a part, highlight the part's name, select a material from the dropdown list box, and press the Assign button. When you select a material, its property data is displayed below the list box. (Except for Density, these properties are not used in computing mass properties.) This data will most likely be in metric units. However, Mechanical Desktop automatically converts the data to the units you have specified in the Assembly Mass Properties dialog box when it computes the part's mass properties. You can assign material properties to just one part or subassembly at a time.

The definitions for the materials listed in the Select Material dialog box are stored in a file named mcad.mat. This file is an ASCII text file that can be read and edited by a text editor, such as Windows' Notepad. Therefore, you can add, modify, and remove materials in this file. A description of the format used for the data is in mcad.mat. Even though density is the only property in this file that is used for computing mass properties, you must include data for the other seven properties. The units for density must be grams per cubic centimeter. If your data is in pounds per cubic inch, you can multiply it by 27.6797 to convert it to grams per cubic centimeter.

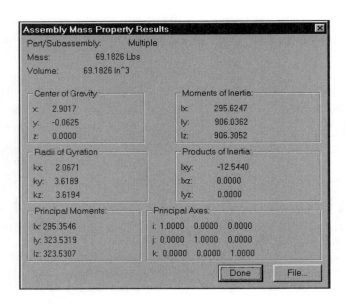

Once you have specified the material of the part, or parts, return to the **Assembly Mass Properties** dialog box. There, press the OK button to bring up the **Assembly Mass Property** Results dialog box. This dialog box displays the mass properties.

Using Attributes to Assign Material Data

Rather than modifying the mcad.mat file, you can assign density values to parts by way of the AMASSIGN command. This is useful when a part is to be made from a material that is not often used. The density value is assigned to just one part, and it only resides in the current assembly file. The steps to assign a density to a part with AMASSIGN are as follows.

1. Invoke AMASSIGN to bring up the **Assign Attributes** dialog box. All of the individual parts and subassemblies will be displayed in a list box.

2. Select the part or subassembly that is to receive the attribute. Then click the Add button to bring up the **Add new Attribute** dialog box.

3. Enter MATERIAL in the Attribute Name edit box, and enter a name for the material in the Attribute Value edit box. Select String as the Column Data type. Click the OK button.

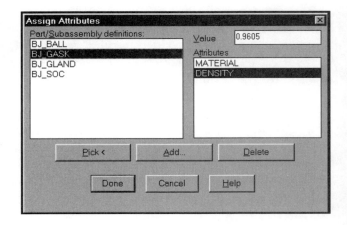

4. With the same part or subassembly highlighted in the **Assign Attributes** dialog box, click the Add button again.

5. Enter DENSITY as the attribute's name, and enter a value for the density in the Attribute Value edit box. Select Real as the Column Data type. Click the OK button.

6. The attributes for the part or subassembly will be displayed in the **Assign Attributes** dialog box. Repeat steps 2 through 5 to assign a material and a density to other parts or subassemblies.

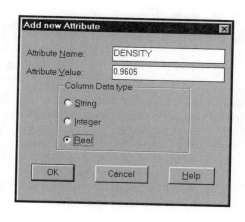

When you invoke the AMLISTASSM command (which is discussed in Chapter 18), the attributes you assigned will be listed.

Finding the Distance between Parts

Use the AMDIST command to find the shortest distance between two objects, or two groups of objects. You will be prompted from the command line to select a set of objects. You can select one or more objects of any type, including AutoCAD objects, but you must select them individually. Then you will be prompted to select a second set of objects. Once you have specified the two sets, you will be given two options for the data output: Display or Line.

The Line option draws an AutoCAD line connecting the two points in the specified groups that are closest to each other. The distance is also given on the command line. The Display option reports the shortest distance between the two groups on the command line and draws a temporary line between the two points. This temporary line disappears when a screen regeneration occurs.

Checking for Interference

The AMINTERFERE command inspects an assembly to determine if two or more parts occupy the same space. When interference is found, Mechanical Desktop will report the names of the parts involved and, if you desire, will create a solid from the overlapping volume. AMINTERFERE uses the command line to issue prompts for user input and to report results. The first prompt is:

```
Nested part or subassembly selection? [Yes/No] <No>: (Enter Y or N, or press Enter.)
```

If you do not select the "Nested part or subassembly selection" option, subassemblies are treated as a single component, and the parts within subassemblies are not checked with each other for interference. On the other hand, if you do select that option, interference between individual parts in an a subassembly can be checked.

Next, you will be asked to select up to two sets of parts or subassemblies. The prompts vary according to your response to AMINTERFERE's first prompt. If you did not choose the "nested part or subassembly" option, the prompts are:

```
Select first set of parts or subassemblies: (Use any object selection method to select one
    or more parts or subassemblies.)
Select second set of parts or subassemblies: (Press Enter, or use any selection method to
    select one or more parts or subassemblies.)
```

If you chose the "Nested part or subassembly selection" option, the prompt to select the first set of objects is:

```
Select first set of parts or subassemblies: (Select parts or subassemblies individually by
    picking a point on them, or press Enter.)
```

When a subassembly is selected, AMINTERFERE will report its name and display prompts to select the entire subassembly or an individual part in the subassembly.

```
Instance = SUB1_1
Enter an option [Down/Next/Accept] <Accept>: (Enter D, N, or A, or press Enter.)
```

With these options you can select all of the components of a subassembly, a subassembly within a subassembly, or a single part within a subassembly. The prompt to select components for the first set of objects is restored when you choose the Accept option. This prompt is repeated until you press Enter. Then prompts to select a second set of objects will appear:

```
Select second set of parts or subassemblies: (Select parts or subassemblies individually by
    picking a point on them, or press Enter.)
```

Selecting a second set of components is optional and can be bypassed by pressing Enter in response to the prompt. When there is just a single set, each component is checked for interference with the other components. When there are two sets, each component in the first set is checked for interference with each component in the second set, but components within the same set are not checked for interference with each other.

As soon as you have specified the components, Mechanical Desktop will report the number of parts and subassemblies that were checked, the number of interference pairs found, and the part and subassembly names involved in each interference pair. You will then be asked if you want 3D solids to be created from the shared volumes, and if you want the interfering components highlighted.

```
Create interference solids? [Yes/No] <N>: (Enter Y or N, or press Enter.)
Highlight pairs of interfering parts/subassemblies? [Yes/No] <N>: (Enter Y or N, or press
    Enter.)
```

If you respond positively to the first prompt, Mechanical Desktop will create an AutoCAD 3D solid from each interfering volume. If you enter a Y in response to the second prompt, Mechanical Desktop will highlight one pair of interfering components, and issue the prompt:

```
Enter an option [eXit/Next pair] <Next pair>: (Enter X or N, or press Enter.)
```

The entire component of each interference pair is highlighted—not just the interference volume. To end the AMINTERFERE command, press the Enter key.

Exercise 1

Checking for Interference

Locate file md19e101.dwg on the CD-ROM that accompanies this book and open it. Figure 1-1 shows the five parts in this file in an exploded view, while Figure 1-2 shows them as they are assembled. Assembly constraints have been applied to the parts.

Make certain that Mechanical Desktop's Model mode is in effect, and use the following command line input to check the assembly for interference.

```
Command: AMINTERFERE (Enter)
Nested part or subassembly selection? [Yes/No] <No>: (Enter)
Select first set of parts/subassemblies: (Use a window or
    crossing selection to select all five parts.)
Select first set of parts/subassemblies: (Enter)
Select second set of parts/subassemblies: (Enter)
Comparing 5 parts/subassemblies against 0 parts/
    subassemblies.
Interference 1:
    SL_4_100_2
    BASE_1
Interference 2:
    SLEEVE_1
    CAP_1
Interference 3:
    SL_4_100_1
    BASE_1
Create interference solids? [Yes/No] <No>: Y (Enter)
Highlight pairs of interfering solids? [Yes/No] <No>:
    (Enter)
```

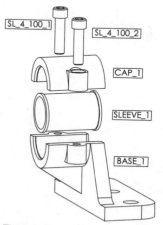

Figure 1-1

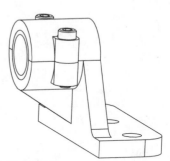

Figure 1-2

In wireframe views, you are able to see three solids within the assembly that designate the space that two parts share. The solids are in the current layer, but their color is red so that you can more easily find them. The two interferences between the body and the cap screws are to be expected since they represent the engagement of the external threads of the screws with the internal threads of the tapped holes in the body.

The interference between the cap and the sleeve, however, indicates a problem. If you move the cap and the interference solid away from the other parts, you will see that only one side of the cap has been counterbored to accommodate the flanges on the sleeve. Therefore, you should activate CAP_1, and add a counterbore to the body with the AMHOLE command.

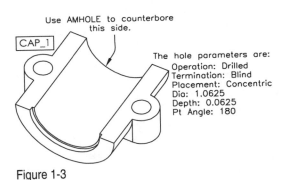

Use AMHOLE to counterbore this side.

CAP_1

The hole parameters are:
Operation: Drilled
Termination: Blind
Placement: Concentric
Dia: 1.0625
Depth: 0.0625
Pt Angle: 180

Figure 1-3

The hole parameters and the edge to select are shown in Figure 1-3. A convenient way to set the hole parameters is to click the Copy Values button in the Hole dialog box, and select the existing counterbore. After adding the counterbore, erase the three interference solids and use the Assembly option of AMUPDATE to reassemble the parts.

Repeat the AMINTERFERE command, selecting just the SLEEVE_1 and CAP_1 parts. Mechanical Desktop will report that the parts do not interfere with each other. That finishes this exercise, and we will not use this assembly model again. On the CD-ROM supplied with this book, the model at this stage is in file md19e103.dwg.

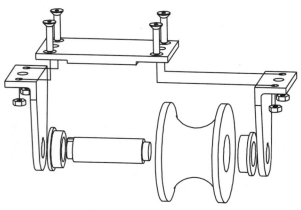

You can create exploded view drawings from assembles, and the relationships between parts can be indicated by trails.

Exploded Assemblies

In manufacturing industries, exploded view drawings are used extensively in service and assembly manuals, because they clearly show the individual parts of an assembly and how they are spatially related. You make exploded view drawings with Mechanical Desktop by first, almost literally, exploding the assembly—the parts are spread apart in space. Then, just as you can with an individual part, you can make drawings from the exploded assembly.

Exploded assemblies are referred to as *scenes* in Mechanical Desktop, and they are created within a special mode: the *Scene mode*. (Note: Mechanical Desktop scenes have no relationship with AutoCAD rendering scenes, which are for defining a particular view and set of rendering lights.) The distance between parts is set by an *explosion factor*. You can also *tweak* the distance between parts, and even move parts sideways and rotate them. Moreover, to more clearly indicate how parts go together, you can connect them with lines that are called *trails*.

Scene Options

To select options for scenes, open the Assembly tab of the **Desktop Options** dialog box launched by invoking AMOPTION. The right half of this tab has three options for scenes.

Lock part positions when a suppressed part is encountered   Suppose a particular feature in a part is used to constrain the part to another part, and then suppose that after a scene has been created the feature is suppressed. (Suppressed features are discussed in Chapter 13.) If this scene option has been selected, the position of the part with the suppressed

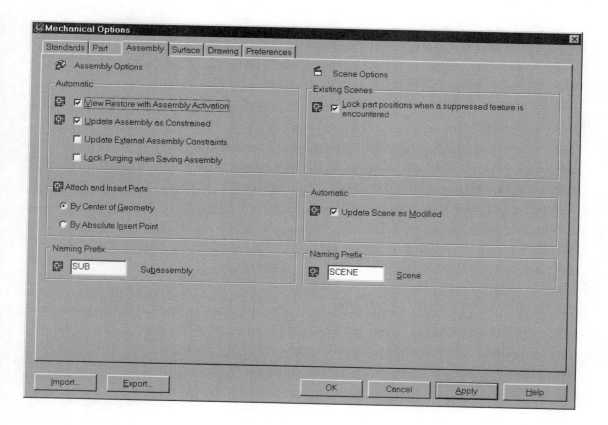

feature will be not changed. However, if this scene option was not selected, the part will lose its explosion factor and move back to its original location.

Update Scene as Modified   When this option is selected, scenes are automatically updated when you change explosion factors and add tweaks. If the check box for this option is cleared, you must use the Scene option of the AMUPDATE command to initiate changes.

Scene Naming Prefix   Enter the default prefix used in naming scenes in this edit box. When you create a scene, you will have an opportunity to override this default prefix.

Creating Scenes

You create a scene by selecting the Scene option of the AMNEW command. Mechanical Desktop will first issue a command line prompt for you to enter a name for the scene. Next it will issue a prompt for you to enter an overall explosion factor for the scene, with 0.0 as the default value. Lastly, you will be asked if you want to activate the scene. If you respond positively, Mechanical Desktop will switch to the Scene mode and activate the scene. If you choose to not immediately activate the scene, you can later invoke the AMACTIVATE command, and select its Scene option. (A shortcut method for activating a scene is to double-click its name in the Desktop Browser.) You can have multiple scenes, and use AMACTIVATE to move from one scene to another.

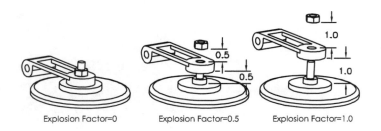

Explosion Factor=0   Explosion Factor=0.5   Explosion Factor=1.0

The look and feel of Scene mode is similar to Model mode. Initially, the Model mode viewpoint will be used, and the parts will be spread apart according to the scene's explosion factor. The explosion factor depends on assembly constraints involving opposing planes. For instance, the planes specified by selecting two round edges for an insert constraint will be moved away from each other by the value of the explosion factor. Movement is always away from the grounded part of the assembly or subassembly. The units for explosion factors are those of the assembly. Thus, when the parts of the assembly are based on millimeters, an explosion factor of 1 represents 1 mm.

In addition to an overall explosion factor for a scene, you can also assign explosion factors on a part-by-part basis with the AMXFACTOR command. This command issues the prompt:

```
Select part or subassembly or [sCene]: (Enter C or select a part)
```

When you choose the sCene option, the explosion factor you set will apply to all of the parts in one specified scene. When you select a part, the following prompt is displayed:

```
Enter new explosion factor for "Selected part's name" or [Reset] <current explosion
    factor>: (Enter R, a positive number, or press Enter)
```

Enter a positive number to set a new explosion factor for the selected part. The Reset option sets the explosion factor of the selected part to equal the overall explosion factor of the scene, and pressing the Enter key accepts the current explosion factor.

When you select a part that is a member of a subassembly in response to AMXFAC-TOR's initial prompt, the following prompt is displayed:

```
Part/Subassembly "Selected part or subassembly's name" [Down/Up] <Continue>: (Enter D or U,
    or press Enter.)
```

Pressing the Enter key will bring up the "Enter new explosion factor" prompt. When you choose the Up option, the entire subassembly is selected, and the explosion factor you enter affects all of the parts in the subassembly. Choosing the Down option selects just the part that was originally specified.

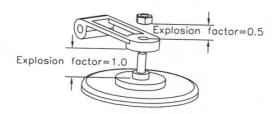

Parts with specific explosion factors

Adding Tweaks

Scenes based entirely on explosion factors seldom have all of the view characteristics you desire. Components, whether they are individual parts or subassemblies, may be either out-of-line or not completely visible, and they may not even respond to explosion factors because their assembly constraints are either not based on planes or they offset one another. You can remedy these problems with the AMTWEAK command. This command enables you to move selected components within a scene in any direction, without regard to their assembly constraints. You can also revolve components. Each tweak is based on the component's current position, and is independent of previous tweaks. Similar to explosion factors, tweaks have no effect on the grounded component of an assembly or subassembly.

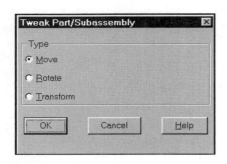

When you invoke AMTWEAK, you will be prompted from the command line to select a part. As with AMXFACTOR, if the part you pick belongs to a subassembly, you can move up to have AMTWEAK affect the entire subassembly, or down to select just the part that was picked. Once you have specified the component that is to be tweaked, Mechanical Desktop displays the `Tweak Part/Subassembly` dialog box.

Use the three radio buttons in this dialog box to select AMTWEAK's options, When you choose one and click the OK button, the dialog box will disappear and prompts for specifying the parameters of the option will appear on the command line.

Move   This option moves the selected component linearly by a specified distance. Its initial prompt is:

```
Select reference geometry: (Select an object that defines a line.)
```

Mechanical Desktop uses the reference geometry to establish the move direction. You can select a straight edge or the round edge of a cylindrical or conical feature on a part. When you select a round edge, the axis of the feature defines the move direction. The object you select does not have to be on the part that is to be tweaked. An arrow pointing in the move direction will appear, and you will be prompted to enter the move distance. If you want to move the component in the direction opposite to that of the arrow, enter a negative number.

Rotate   Use this option to rotate the selected component about an axis. As with the Move option, you will be prompted to select a reference geometry object. The object you select will serve as the axis of rotation. You can select a straight edge or a round edge on any part to define the axis. An arc-shaped arrow will encircle the axis to indicate the rotation direction, and you will be prompted to enter the number of degrees the selected component is to rotate. You must enter a positive number.

Transform   While Transform performs the same move and rotate tweaks of the other two options, it gives you more choices in specifying directions and axes. Also, you can perform any number of moves and rotations until you exit the option. When you select Transform, Mechanical Desktop displays the following command line prompt:

```
Enter an option [eXit/Move/Rotate]<Move>: (Enter a X, M, or R, or press Enter.)
```

When you select the Move option, the following command line prompt appears.

```
Specify start point or [Viewdir/Wire/X/Y/Z]: (Enter an option or specify a point.)
```

If you specify a point, using any AutoCAD method, it will serve as one end of a line and you will be prompted to specify the other end of the line. This line establishes both the direction and distance for moving the component. The X, Y, and Z options move the component the direction of those axes, and the Viewdir option moves the component in the current viewport's line of sight direction. The Wire option uses an existing wireframe object to define the tweak move direction, and you will be prompted to select an object. The object can be an AutoCAD line, polyline, arc, circle, or ellipse. When you select an arc, a circle, or an ellipse, the move direction is perpendicular to the object's plane. When you select a polyline that has multiple segments, the segment the object pick point is in is used to establish the move direction.

If you specified a line for the move direction, by either picking two points or an AutoCAD line or linear polyline segment, the line will also be used to establish the move distance. Otherwise, Mechanical Desktop will issue a command line prompt for the move distance. An arrow indicating the move direction will appear, and you can either accept or flip the arrow's direction.

When you select the Rotate option, AMTWEAK will issue the prompt:

```
Specify center of rotation: (Use any AutoCAD method to specify a point)
```

The axis of rotation will pass through the point you specify. Next, you will be prompted to specify the direction of the axis from that point. Your choices are the UCS X, Y, or Z axes directions, the viewport's view direction, and the direction defined by an AutoCAD wireframe object. An arc-shaped arrow will encircle the axis to indicate the positive rotation direction, and you can accept the indicated direction or reverse it. Lastly, you will be prompted to enter the rotation angle.

After you have performed a move or rotate tweak, the Transform prompt for selecting an option reappears. Select the eXit option to end the AMTWEAK command.

You cannot edit tweaks; you can only delete them. This is done with the AMDELTWEAKS command. From a command line prompt AMDELTWEAKS will ask you to select one component. All of the tweaks of that component will be deleted, and it will return to its pre-tweaked position.

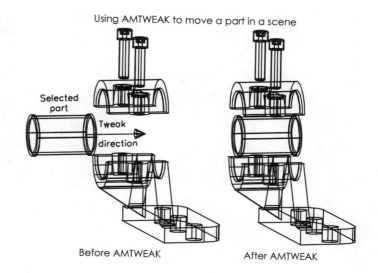

Using AMTWEAK to move a part in a scene

Selected part

Tweak direction

Before AMTWEAK

After AMTWEAK

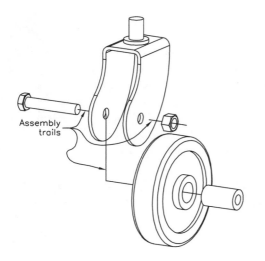

Assembly trails

Creating Assembly Trails

Assembly trails are lines that show the path used in moving a part from its assembled position. Occasionally, MD refers to them as *explosion paths*. Trails are made with the AMTRAIL command on a part-by-part basis. Mechanical Desktop places trails in the AM_TR layer, which has white as its color and CONTINUOUS as its linetype. Trails follow the paths made by explosion factors and tweaks. They are parametric, and therefore, they change as the parts and their positions change.

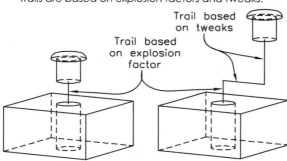

Trails are based on explosion factors and tweaks.

Trail based on tweaks

Trail based on explosion factor

When you initiate AMTRAIL, a command line prompt will ask you to select a reference point on a part or subassembly. You must pick a point on the edge of a face. The trail will extend from the center of circular edges, and from an endpoint on straight and arc-shaped edges. You should not select a point on the assembly's grounded part—although Mechanical Desktop will not issue an error message, neither will it create a trail. Once you have selected a point, Mechanical Desktop will display the **Trail Offsets** dialog box.

The **Trail Offsets** dialog box controls where the trail starts and ends. It is divided into two clusters. The cluster labeled Offset at Current Position is for the reference point end of the trail, while the cluster labeled Offset at Assembled Position is where the reference point would be if the part had not been exploded and tweaked. By default, the trail starts and ends at these two points. When you specify an over shoot distance, the trail will extend beyond the reference point location; and when you specify an under shoot distance, the trail will end before reaching the reference point. You can either enter a distance within the edit boxes or click the Pick buttons to graphically specify a distance.

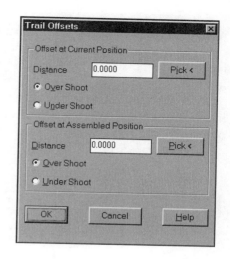

Once you have created a trail for a part, you can modify its over and under shoots by invoking the AMEDIT-TRAIL command. This command displays the same **Trail Offsets** dialog box that is used by the command for creating trails. You can remove trails with the AMDELTRAIL command, which will issue a command line prompt for you to select the trail that is to be deleted.

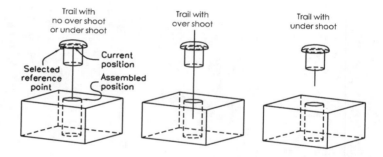

Managing Scenes

Usually scenes automatically update themselves when changes have occurred. You can though force updates by selecting the Scene option of the AMUPDATE command.

When you have the explosion factors and tweaks within a scene as you want them, you can prevent inadvertent changes to them with the AMLOCKSCENE command. This command displays a command line prompt with options to either lock or unlock the active scene. When a scene is locked, you cannot add or modify explosion factors or tweaks. You can, though, create and modify trails.

Occasionally you may want to turn off the visibility of some parts within a scene. For instance, in an assembly that has numerous pairs of bolts and nuts, you may want to turn off the visibility of all but one pair to reduce clutter in the scene. You can control the visibility of parts, subassemblies, and trails by selecting the Scene tab of AMVISIBLE's dialog box.

You can make a copy of a scene with AMCOPYSCENE. Prompts similar to those used in creating a new scene establish a name and an overall explosion factor for the copy. The copy will have all of the original scene's parts, tweaks, and trails. You can remove an unneeded scene by choosing the Scene option of the AMDELETE command.

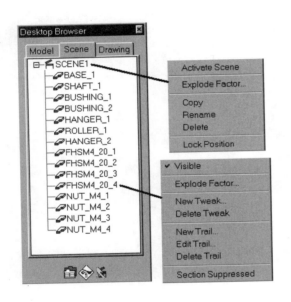

The Scene tab of the Desktop Browser lists the names of all parts within the existing scenes in the file. Those within inactive scenes, though, will be grayed out. You can conveniently access the commands related to scenes that we have discussed in this chapter through right-click shortcut menus. These shortcut menus are especially useful in changing explosion factors and adding tweaks to subassembly parts. When you select a subassembly name, all of the parts in the subassembly will move; and, when you select a part's name, only that part will move.

Exercise 2

Creating a Scene of the Check Valve Assembly

In this exercise you will create a scene from the check valve assembly you added 3D constraints to in an exercise in Chapter 18. Open your file from that exercise, or else retrieve md18e406.dwg from the CD-ROM that comes with this book and open it.

Use AutoCAD's VPOINT command to set a viewpoint that is rotated 320 degrees from the X axis and 50 degrees from the XY plane, and use AutoCAD's UCS command to restore the World Coordinate System. Then, invoke Mechanical Desktop's AMNEW command and select its Scene option. Accept the default name of SCENE1, set the overall explosion factor to 3.0, and activate the scene. When hidden line removal is active, your exploded assembly is likely to look similar to the one in Figure 2-1.

Some of the parts are still hidden within the check valve's body, and some parts have not moved due to the way they are constrained. You will have to vary explosion factors and use tweaks to clean up the scene. Take the following steps to modify the locations of the parts in the COVER_1 subassembly.

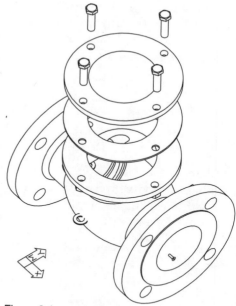

Figure 2-1

- Invoke AMXFACTOR, select any part in the COVER_1 subassembly, choose the Up option to select the entire subassembly, and change its explosion factor from 3 to 1. (In modifying an explosion factor or adding a tweak, you will probably find that selecting the part or subassembly and activating the command from the Browser is easier than selecting it from the graphics area and using the command line.)

- Again invoke AMXFACTOR; and select any one of the BOLT3-8 parts. Decrease its explosion factor from 3 to 2. Repeat this step three more times to decrease the explosion factor of all four bolts.

- Invoke AMTWEAK, select any part in the COVER_1 subassembly, choose the Up option, and move the subassembly, as a single component, 6 inches in the positive Y axis direction. You will probably find that the easiest way do this is with the Transform option of AMTWEAK.

- Set the explosion factor of the washer that is toward the front end of the check valve to 0; then use AMTWEAK to move the washer 1 inch in the negative Z axis direction and 6 inches in the positive Y axis direction. In file md18e406, the name of this washer is WASH_3-8_4.

- Tweak the nut that goes with this washer 2 inches in the negative Z axis direction and 6 inches in the positive Y axis direction. In file md18e406.dwg, the name of this nut is NUT_3-8_3.

- Use AMVISIBLE to turn the visibility of the three other pairs of washers and nuts for the valve cover off.

After making those changes, your scene should look similar to the one in Figure 2-2. Finish modifying the part and subassembly locations with the following operations.

- Increase the explosion factor of VA_SEAT from 3 to 10. The four screws, FLATSCR4, will move with the valve seat because they are constrained to it. Reduce the explosion factor of each screw from 3 to 1.

- Change the explosion factor of the DISK_1 subassembly from 3 to 0. Then tweak the subassembly 6 inches in the minus Y axis direction.

- Reduce the explosion factor of the disk subassembly's NUT_1-4_1 from 3 to 1.

- Use AMTWEAK to move VA_PIN_1 8 inches in the minus Y axis direction.

- Change the explosion factor of VA_SEAL_1 from 3 to 2.

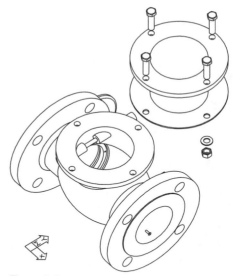

Figure 2-2

Your scene should now look similar to the one shown in Figure 2-3. To complete the scene take the following steps to add some explosion paths.

- Invoke AMTRAIL and select the front bolt hole in the gasket, part VA_GASK_1, as a reference point. Then choose the UP option to select the entire COVER_1 subassembly. Set the trail over and under shoots to zero.

- Add a trail from WASH_3-8_1 that has over and under shoot values of zero.

- Add a trail from the right-hand screw hole in VA_SEAT_1, and another from the head of screw FLATSCR4_2. Use zero over and under shoots.

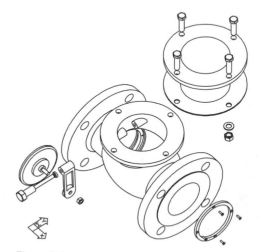

Figure 2-3

- Add a trail from VA_PIN_1. Select the rim of the conical point of the pin as the reference point. Leave all over and under shoot values to zero.

- Add a trail from the hole in VA_HANG_1 that is used in attaching the hanger to the valve disk. Set the over shoot at the current position to 1.5, but leave the other over and undershoot values at zero.

Your finished scene should look similar to the one in Figure 2-4. On the CD-ROM that comes with this book, the scene is in file md19e204.dwg. You will continue to work with this scene in the next chapter as you make a drawing of it.

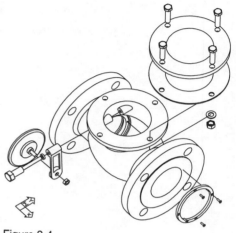

Figure 2-4

CHAPTER 20

Drawings from Assemblies

Drawings of assembled parts are often needed for manufacturing, as well as for service manuals, part manuals, and even catalogs. To accommodate these needs, Mechanical Desktop has a robust set of tools for creating drawings from assemblies. Mechanical Desktop also has tools for storing, retrieving, and displaying information about the individual parts in an assembly.

This chapter covers the following topics.

- Explains how to make both orthographic and exploded view drawings of assemblies.

- Describes how to create and work with a bill of material (BOM) that contains information about each part in an assembly. The fundamental BOM information for a part is its name, item number, and quantity, but you can have it also include information such as the part's material, vendor, cost, and so forth.

- Tells you how to retrieve information from an assembly's BOM and display it as a parts list in the assembly drawing or on a separate sheet of paper.

- Explains how to identify each part in an assembly drawing with a balloon, which consists of a number within a circle and a leader that points to the part.

Creating Drawing Views of Assemblies

Just as in drawings of single parts, you can create both orthographic and axonometric views in drawings of assemblies of parts. Generally, orthographic views are used to show the parts in their assembled position, while axonometric views are used to show the parts in their exploded positions. Views of exploded parts are so common that they have long been referred to as *exploded views*, regardless of their view point. For simple assemblies you may choose to have both orthographic and exploded views on the same drawing sheet. However, since orthographic and exploded views serve different purposes, you will usually have them on different sheets, and therefore, in different paper space layouts. The same commands described in Chapters 14 and 15 for creating and managing views of single parts are used for views in assembly drawings.

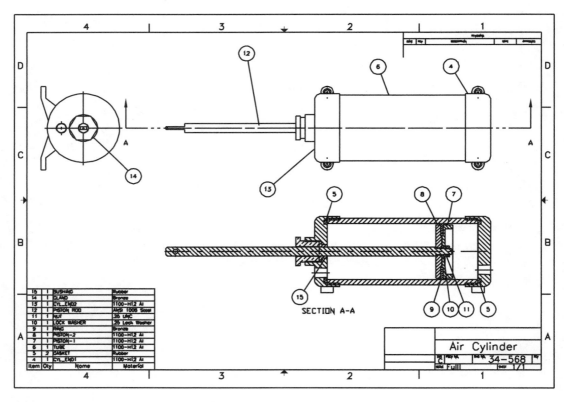

An assembly drawing with orthographic views.

Orthographic Views

The first view you create in a drawing will a Base view, and your data set options are to either select a named scene or to select the specific parts that are to be in the drawing view. Use the Select parts option in creating the base view of a drawing having orthographic views.

Mechanical Desktop does not display dimensions of individual parts in assembly views, regardless of the setting of the system variable **amreusedim**. Any dimensions you want, such as for the assembly's overall length, are added as reference dimensions with the AMREFDIM command.

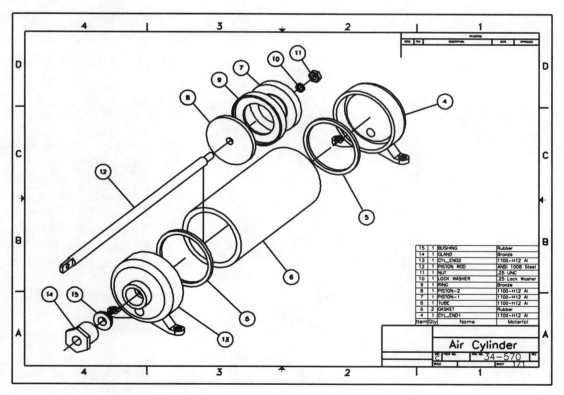

An exploded view assembly drawing.

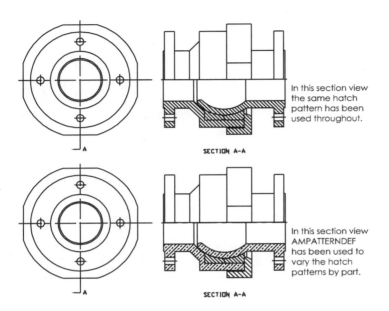

In this section view the same hatch pattern has been used throughout.

SECTION A-A

In this section view AMPATTERNDEF has been used to vary the hatch patterns by part.

SECTION A-A

Section views are commonly used in depicting assemblies. By default, one hatch pattern is used throughout a section view, but to more easily distinguish individual parts, you can assign hatch patterns on a part-by-part basis with the AMPATTERN-DEF command. The command works only in Model mode.

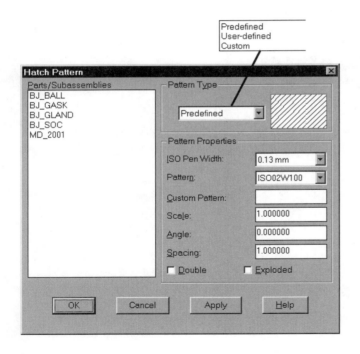

AMPATTERNDEF displays a dialog box titled **Hatch Pattern** for you to use in setting the hatch parameters. The parts and subassemblies of the assembly are listed on the left side of this dialog box, while list and edit boxes for setting a hatch pattern are on the right side. Select a part, set its hatch parameters, and click the Apply button to associate the hatch parameters with the part. Setting hatch pattern parameters with the list and edit boxes on the right side of the Hatch Pattern dialog box works the same as in the dialog box for AutoCAD's BHATCH command. When you have finished setting the hatch patterns for the assembly's parts, click the OK button to exit AMPATTERNDEF. The default hatch pattern will be used for parts that have not had their hatch parameters modified by AMPATTERNDEF. See the discussion of creating section views in Chapter 15 for information about establishing the default hatch pattern.

Exploded Views

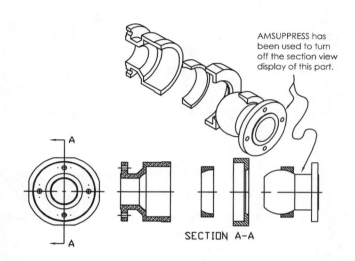

AMSUPPRESS has been used to turn off the section view display of this part.

SECTION A-A

Often exploded views do a better job of showing the components of an assembly than orthographic views. The data set for the base view in exploded view drawings is based on a specified scene. Generally, but not always, exploded views are axonometric, and their viewpoint will be the one that best shows the parts and their relationships, rather than that of a true isometric view. Therefore, you should establish the viewpoint you intend for the exploded view to have in Mechanical Desktop's Scene mode, and select the View option when AMDWGVIEW prompts you for a plane to establish the base view's viewpoint.

To give you additional control over section views based on scenes, whether they are orthographic or axonometric, you can turn off the section view display of specified parts in an assembly. This is done with the AMSUPPRESS command. AMSUPPRESS displays a dialog box titled Instance Suppression. This dialog box lists the name of the active scene, along with all of the parts in the scene and whether or not section views of each part are suppressed. To suppress the section display of a part, select the part's name and click the button labeled Suppress. To clear the suppression of a part's section view display, click the Unsuppress button.

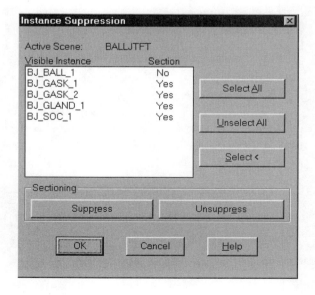

You can also use the Desktop Browser to suppress the section view display of a part, although you must be in the Scene mode to do this. Right-click the name of the part, and select Section Suppressed.

Establishing Drafting Standards

Mechanical Desktop has complete set of tools for managing and using data related to the parts within an assembly. This data, which includes information such as the name, quantity, and material type of each part, can be used to:

* Create a list of the parts within an assembly. This parts list can be displayed on a drawing of the assembly, or printed on a separate sheet of paper.

* Store supplementary information—such as vendor, applicable specifications, and material—for a part.

* Identify parts within a drawing by using leaders and balloons that give the part's item number.

Information about parts is stored in a *Bill of Material* or, as it is more often called, a BOM. Although many people in manufacturing industries often use the terms *BOM* and *parts list* interchangeably, in Mechanical Desktop a BOM is a database that never appears in a drawing, while a parts list is a display of data from the BOM.

Before you begin working with the assembly's BOM, parts list, and balloons, you should establish a drafting standard for them. You will do this through the Standards Tab of the `Mechanical Options` dialog box displayed by the AMOPTIONS command. First, select one of the seven standards from the list box. If the parts in your assembly are based on inch dimensions, you are likely to select the ANSI standard; and if they are based on millimeter dimensions, you will probably select one of the other standards, such as ISO.

After selecting a drafting standard, you will use the shortcut menus displayed by right-clicking items in the tree-like list on the right side of the tab to set the properties of specific drafting symbols. Choose the Properties option from one of these shortcut menus to display a dialog box containing the property parameters that are appropriate for that item and the specified drafting standard. (These dialog boxes for properties are also displayed when you double-click on an item in the list.)

Note: You can also display this list of symbol standards by invoking the AMSYMSTD command. In Mechanical Desktop Release 5, though, this command is no longer documented, and you should instead, use the Standards tab of the Mechanical Options dialog box in establishing symbol properties.

The symbol property standards that affect assembly drawings are as follows.

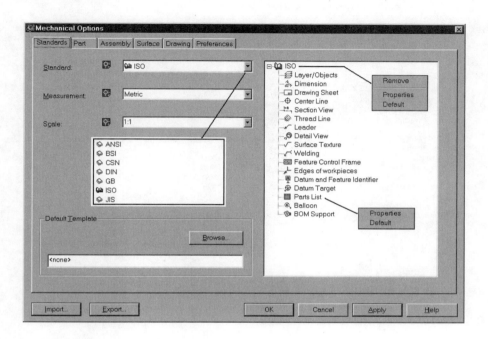

Layer/Objects   Controls the layer and properties of leaders, balloons, parts list components, and so forth.

Leader   Sets the arrowhead size of the leaders of balloons.

Parts List   Establishes the contents and display of a drawing's parts list.

Balloon   Controls the appearance characteristics of balloons.

BOM Support   Controls the contents of the BOM.

The properties of BOMs, parts lists, and balloons are discussed in this chapter's sections on bills of materials, parts lists, and balloons.

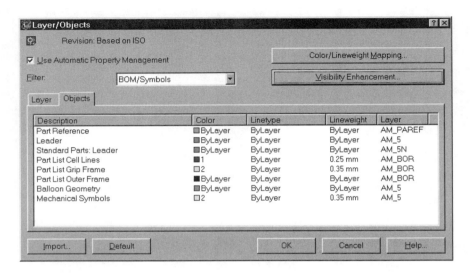

Working with Bills of Materials (BOM)

Mechanical Desktop's BOM is a database of information about the parts within an assembly. This information can be viewed within a dialog box and it can be printed, but it cannot be displayed directly in a drawing of the assembly. Much of the BOM information is, though, used within the parts list of an assembly drawing.

A typical Bill of Materials (BOM)

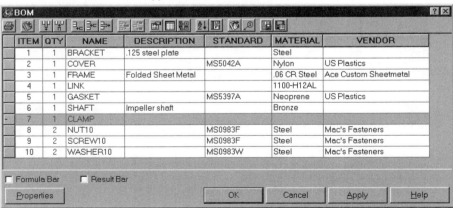

Establishing BOM Properties

Your first step in working with a BOM will be to establish its properties and scope. You will do this through the `BOM Properties` dialog box, which you can open by selecting Properties from the shortcut menu of BOM Support in the symbols list of the Standards tab of the `Mechanical Options` dialog box. You can also open this dialog box through the AMBOM command, which is discussed later in this chapter. Some of the BOM properties, as will be pointed out, also affect the parts list.

The BOM data is arranged in columns, and the `BOM Properties` dialog box uses a table to control the format of those columns. For each BOM column, you can:

- control whether or not the column is displayed in the BOM;
- control whether or not editing the BOM contents of the column is allowed;
- set the text that will be used as the BOM column heading and the parts list heading;
- establish the column's width in the parts list;
- set the alignment (such as right, or centered) of the column's heading, and the parts list heading;
- set the alignment of the data in the column, and in the parts list cells;
- establish that the data is either textual or numeric, and for numeric data you can set its precision.

Some of the columns of the table in the `BOM Properties` dialog box have numbered headings, and those numbers correspond to the numbers in the Format Columns cluster of buttons and edit boxes. For example: Column caption alignment is in the table's column number 3. You can click anywhere in one of the table's rows to activate the options for setting the BOM format for the columns of that row. You can change the contents of the cells in the table's unnumbered columns, such as a caption, by clicking in its cell, and then entering new data. You cannot, however, change the column names.

You can add new rows in this table—and therefore, columns in the BOM—by simply entering data in the cells of the empty bottom row. You can delete a row, except for the rows for the ITEM, QTY, and NAME columns, by highlighting it, and pressing the Delete key of your computer. You can move a row—and therefore, rearrange the columns in the BOM—by picking its horizontal edge on the left side of the table, and dragging it up or down to another location.

When you select the summation option, which is available only for the MASS, PRICE, and DIM columns, the data for all of the parts is added together in the BOM. With this option, you can for example, obtain the total cost of the parts in an assembly.

When you click within a cell in the Formula for Columns column, the formula edit box is opened, and when you click on the equal icon to the left of that edit box, a drop-down list box containing BOM variables for use in the formula is opened. For most assemblies, you will not use formulas in the BOM.

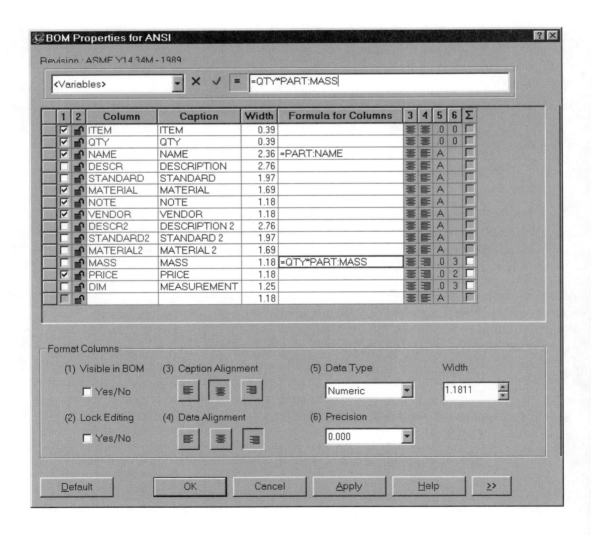

Assigning Material Attributes

Mechanical Desktop automatically assigns data from the assembly catalog to the BOM to set the name, quantity, and item number of each part. (The assembly catalog is discussed in Chapter 17.) One way to assign data to the other BOM part categories, such as the material a particular part is to be made from, is with the AMASSIGN command. This command displays the **Assign Attributes** dialog box.

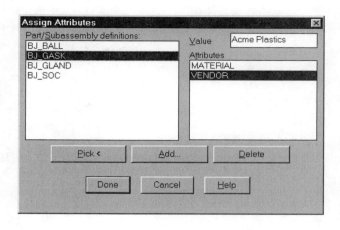

To assign an attribute to a part, select the name of the part in the Part/Subassembly definitions window, and click the ADD button. A dialog box titled **Add new Attribute** will appear. Enter the attribute's name and its value. The attribute's name must be the same as one of the BOM column headings. Also, select the String, Integer, or Real radio button to indicate the attribute value's data type. For example, to assign a value to the MATERIAL attribute of a part, you would enter MATERIAL as the Attribute name, and enter text that describes the material—such as Buna N—as the Attribute Value. Then you would select String as the data type, and click OK to return to the **Assign Attributes** dialog box.

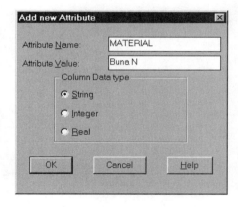

Another, more convenient, way to assign attribute values to parts is through *part references*. A part reference is an associative block that is attached to each part instance in an assembly, and they are used by an assembly's BOM and in inserting balloons. You can add and modify part reference data with the AMPARTREFEDIT command. When you invoke this command, a part reference icon is displayed in the geometric center of each instance, and a command line prompt will ask you to select one of them. To help you identify instances, its part name is displayed when you hold the screen cursor over a part reference icon.

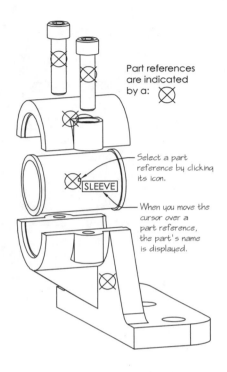

Part references
are indicated
by a: ⊗

Select a part
reference by clicking
its icon.

SLEEVE

When you move the
cursor over a
part reference,
the part's name
is displayed.

As soon as you select a part reference, the **Part Ref Attributes** dialog will appear. In this dialog box, each column name from the BOM Properties dialog box (except for ITEM and QTY) is displayed along with the values attached to them. You can enter values to fields that have none, as well as modify existing values. These values will then appear in the BOM for the assembly.

Mechanical Desktop automatically attaches part references to the part instances within an assembly. You can manually attach a part reference to a non-parametric object, such as a surface. To do this, turn the object into an AutoCAD block (with AutoCAD's BLOCK command), insert the block, and use AMPARTREF to assign attributes to it. The command will prompt you to select a block, and then the **Part Ref Attributes** dialog box will appear for you to use in assigning attribute data to the block.

A third way to add and modify part attribute values is, as explained in the next section, through the BOM itself.

Managing the BOM

The AMBOM command displays the BOM database and inserts an icon for the BOM in the Model mode Browser. The BOM behaves as a spreadsheet type window, although there is no interaction between cells. You can drag the edges of the BOM, as well as those of the individual cells, to change their size. You can move between cells with the tab or up-and-down keys of your keyboard, or by clicking within a cell. Subassemblies are indicated by a plus sign on the left

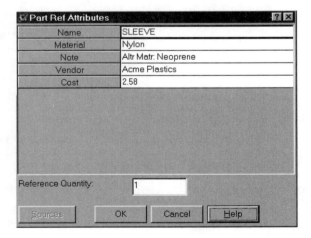

Part Ref Attributes	
Name	SLEEVE
Material	Nylon
Note	Altr Matr: Neoprene
Vendor	Acme Plastics
Cost	2.58

Reference Quantity: 1

Sources | OK | Cancel | Help

end of their row, and you can click that plus sign to display all of the parts in the subassembly.

The attribute data for each part is displayed in columns along the part's row. You can add new attribute values and modify existing values by moving to an attribute's cell and entering or editing its contents. You can also use your computer's Ctrl-C and Ctrl-V key combinations to copy and paste values from one cell to another. Values displayed in red, however, cannot be changed. Part names are from the part definition name as displayed in the All tab of the Assembly Catalog dialog box. (See Chapter 17 for a description of the assembly catalog.) By default, part quantity is calculated by Mechanical Desktop. Through the shortcut menu displayed when you right-click within any cell, though, you can turn off automatic calculation and then edit the Qty column.

Toolbuttons along the top of the window access options for managing the BOM. These options are as follows.

Print   You can obtain a hard copy of the BOM contents with this option. There is no provision for printing the BOM to a file.

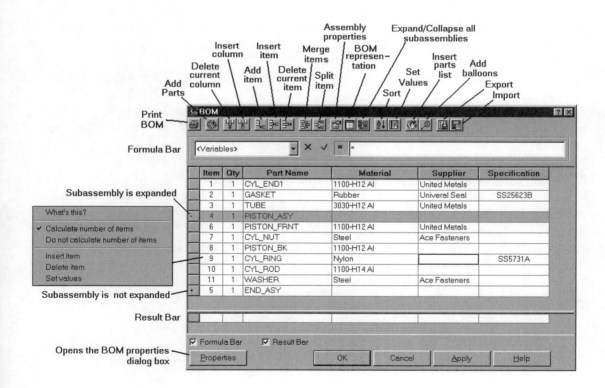

Add Parts   This option adds parts to the BOM. It is available only when AMBOM is invoked from Model mode, and it is functional only when one or more parts have been created since the BOM was last updated.

Delete Column   To remove a column from the BOM, click its heading to highlight the column, and then select this option.

Insert Column   To create a new column, highlight the column that is to precede the new column and select this option. BOM properties dialog box will be displayed for you to set the parameters for the new column. The default name for the new column is NEWCOL.

Add Item   This option adds an empty row at the bottom of the BOM.

Insert Item   This option inserts an empty row above the row of the current cell.

Delete Item   You can remove a part from the BOM database with this option. Select any cell in the row of the part, and select this option. While the part is removed from the BOM database, it is not deleted from the assembly file.

Merge Items   This option combines two or more items in the BOM database. The items must have the same attribute values, including name.

Split Item   Separate an item that has been merged into two items with this option.

Assembly Properties   You can assign or modify attribute values for the entire assembly with this option. You can also change the name of the BOM with this option. By default, the BOM name is the same as that of the drawing file.

BOM Representation   This option offers, in a dialog box, two methods for item numbering in assemblies having subassemblies—Expanded and Structured. Expanded is the default representation. In the structured representation, the item number of each part within a subassembly consist of two numbers separated by a hyphen (or by a character of your choice). The first number is that of the subassembly item number, and the second is the part's number within the subassembly. A comparison of the two representation methods is shown in the following table.

Expanded			Structured	
Item	Name		Item	Name
1	SUB_1		1	SUB_1
3	PART_A		1-1	PART_A
4	PART_B		1-2	PART_B
2	SUB_2		2	SUB_2
5	PART_C		2-1	PART_C
6	PART_D		2-2	PART_D
7	PART_E		2-3	PART_E
8	PART_F		2-4	PART_F

Expand/Collapse All Subassemblies   This button is a toggle that either displays or hides all parts in all subassemblies in the BOM, depending on the current display condition.

Sort   You can rearrange the order of the rows in the BOM with this option. A dialog box is displayed for you to select the column, or columns, the sort is to be based on, and to specify if the sort is to be in an ascending or descending order.

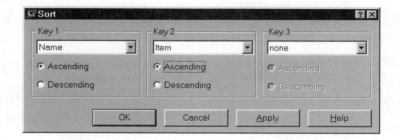

Set Values   You can set an attribute value for several different parts in one step with this option. First, select the cells as you hold down your computer's Ctrl key, or click the heading of a column. The cells must all be within one column. Then select this option, and enter the attribute's value. If the attribute value is a number, either real or integer, you can have the value increment by a specified value in each cell down the column.

Insert Parts List   This option invokes the AMPARTLIST command.

Add Balloons   The AMBALLOON command is invoked by this option.

Export   You can export the BOM database to an external file in one of a variety of formats, including Microsoft Excel, with this option.

Import   This option imports data from a external database into the current BOM.

The Formula Bar checkbox displays the same Formula edit box and Variables list box that are used in the `BOM Properties` dialog box. The Result Bar check box, displays the summation results specified in the `BOM Properties` dialog box. The Properties button displays the `BOM Properties` dialog box.

Working with Parts Lists

Establishing Parts List Properties

The parts list is a table showing the names of the parts used in an assembly, and information about those parts. Usually it placed in a drawing of the assembly, but it is sometimes printed on a separate sheet of paper. The data in the parts list comes from the assembly's BOM, while its format and appearance is controlled by a variety of drafting standard properties dialog boxes.

- The color and layer of the frame around the parts list, and that of the lines separating the data is set by the `Layer/Objects` dialog box.

- The widths of the parts list columns, and the alignment of the text within the cells is controlled by the `BOM properties` dialog box.

- The text within the parts list heading is controlled by the `BOM Properties` dialog box.

- The text style and its font is set by the specified drafting standard. For example, the AutoCAD style name of the parts list text is ACISOTS when the ISO drafting standard is in effect.

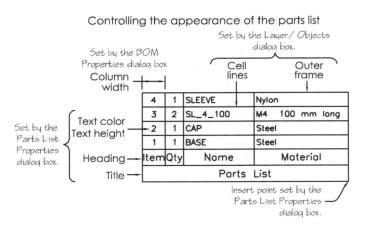

Controlling the appearance of the parts list

The other parameters of the parts list are controlled by the **Parts List Properties** dialog box. One way to open this dialog box is by invoking the AMOPTIONS command, selecting the Standards tab, and double-clicking Parts List in the list of drafting standard objects and symbols.

The **Parts List Properties** dialog box has one tab labeled Standard, and another labeled Custom Blocks. The options in the Standard tab are as follows.

Insert Heading   Select this option to have the column captions—such as Item, Qty, and Name—that are specified in the BOM Properties dialog box displayed

Insert Title   Select this option to display a title, such as "Parts List," for the parts list.

Show Grip Frame   When you select this option, Mechanical Desktop adds a rectangular grip frame that is drawn directly over the parts list outer frame (border).

Heading Gap   This edit box sets the distance between the heading and the parts list.

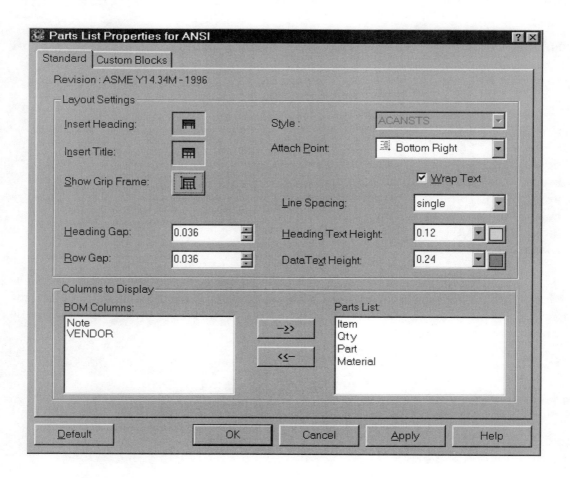

Row Gap   Enter the distance between the cell text and its horizontal edges in this edit box.

Attach Point   Choose between Top Left, Bottom Left, Top Right, and Bottom Right as the parts list's insert point.

Wrap Text   When this check box is selected, parts list data that is too long to fit on a single line in a cell is wrapped to the next line, and the row height is increased to accommodate the new line. When this check box is cleared, parts list data that exceeds the width of a cell extends beyond the borders of the cell.

Line Spacing   Choose between single, double, or triple line spacing in the rows of the parts list. Double and triple spacing increases the height of the rows even if their contents do not require the additional height.

Heading Text Height   Select a height value for the column headings from this list box.

Data Text Height   The value you select in this list box sets the height of the text in the parts list cells.

Columns to Display   The captions of the BOM columns that you do not want displayed are in the list box titled BOM Columns that is located on the left in this cluster. The captions of the BOM columns that you want displayed are in the list box titled Parts List that is on the right. Together, the contents of these two list boxes represent all of the columns in the BOM. To move a column from one list box to the other, highlight it and press the button having the arrows pointing in the direction of the desired movement. The order of the captions in the Parts List box is the order they will appear in the parts list. You can change their order by selectively moving captions between the list boxes.

You can use AutoCAD blocks to create a parts list having a custom appearance. These blocks, which contain attributes, must reside in a separate drawing file. To use these blocks, open the Custom Blocks Tab of the **Parts List Properties** dialog box. The options in this tab are as follows.

Use Custom Blocks for Parts List   Activate this check box to use custom blocks in the parts list rather than the standard one.

Block Name Scheme   Use this list box to specify the file containing the custom parts list blocks.

Attach Point Specify whether the parts list attachment point is to be the Top Right, Top Left, Bottom Right, or Bottom Left corner.

Insert Heading
When this option is selected, the parts list heading uses a custom block.

Filter Empty References References that are not attached to a part are filtered from the parts list when this option is selected.

Evaluate dsk-File
This option reads the specified block scheme for information

Inserting the Parts List

Parts lists are inserted in a drawing by the AMPARTLIST command, which displays the **Parts List** dialog box. Most of the options in this dialog box are duplicates of those in the **BOM** dialog

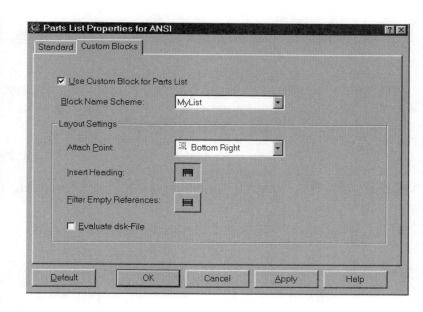

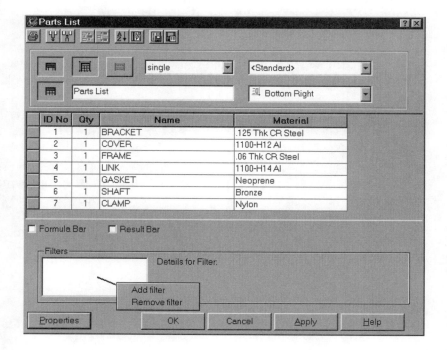

box and the **Parts List Properties** dialog boxes, and we will not describe those options. The edit box containing the words "Parts List" is for entering a title for the parts list.

By default, all of the parts in the BOM are included in the parts list, but you can use filters to exclude certain parts. You select a filter by right-clicking in the Filters pane, and selecting Add Filter from the shortcut menu. A dialog box listing as many as six types of filters is displayed. The filters are as follows.

Ballooned   All parts that are not ballooned are filtered out of the parts list.

Custom   You can create a unique filter by selecting items in the BOM and by using relational operators.

Parts   You specify the parts that are not be in the parts list by manually selecting them.

Sheet   This filter excludes all parts that are not shown in the drawing views of the current layout. This filter is not available in model mode.

Standard Parts   A standard part is one that has been created by Power Pack, which is a Mechanical Desktop add-on program. Often, they are fastener hardware, such as bolts and nuts. You can either filter out all standard parts, or all parts that are not standard parts.

View   Only the parts in a selected drawing view will be displayed in the parts list. You will be prompted to select one drawing view. This filter is not available in model mode.

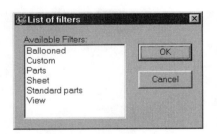

The button labeled Properties displays the **Parts List Properties** dialog box. When you click the OK button, Mechanical Desktop will dismiss the dialog box and prompt you to pick the location of the parts list. An icon for the parts list will be placed in the Desktop Browser, and you can use its shortcut menu to display the **BOM** dialog box, and the **Parts List** dialog box for editing the BOM and the parts list.

Identification of Parts

Individual parts in an assembly draw-ing are generally identified by their item number, and usually the item number is within a circle connected to a leader pointing to the part. Because of their appearance, they are commonly referred to as balloons.

Individual parts are identified by balloons.

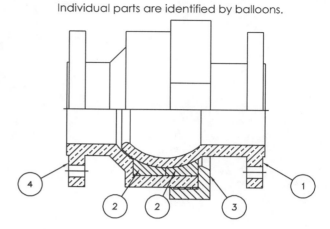

Establishing Balloon Properties

Before you add bal-loons to an assembly drawing, you will use the standard property dialog boxes that are accessed through the Standards Tab of the AMOPTIONS com-mand's **Mechani-cal   Options** dialog box to estab-lish their appearance parameters.   The color and layer of the balloon and its leader is set by the **Layer/ Objects** dialog box, and the leader's arrowhead length is set   within   the **Leader Proper-ties** dialog box. The other appearance parameters of bal-loons are controlled

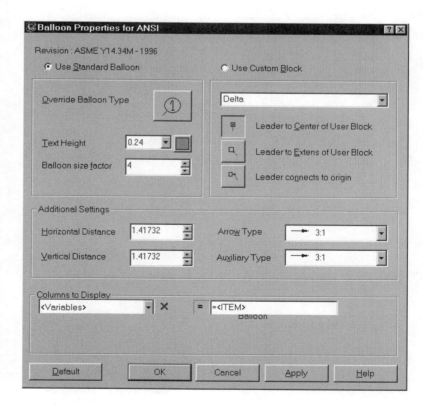

by the **Balloon Properties** dialog box.

The options in the **Balloon Properties** dialog box are as follows.

Use Standard Balloon   Select this option to use a Mechanical Desktop pre-made balloon.

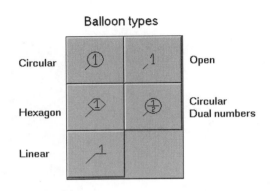

Balloon types

Circular — Open — Hexagon — Circular Dual numbers — Linear

Override Balloon Type   The default balloon is a circle enclosing the data, as shown in this image tile. Click this tile to display four other balloon options. The dual numbered balloon will, by default, display part number and quantity.

Text Height   Select the height of the text within the balloon from this list box. And, specify the color of the text from the accompanying image tile.

Balloon Size Factor   Enter the ratio of the balloon diameter to the text height in this edit box. The ratio cannot be smaller than 2.0.

Use Custom Block   Select this option if you would rather use an AutoCAD block in place of a standard balloon. The names of the blocks currently in the drawing file are displayed in a list box. When you create the block you intend to use as a balloon, you must assign an attribute to it that corresponds to a BOM column heading. Usually, ITEM is the column heading you will use.

Leader to Center of User Block

Leader to Extents of User Block

Leader Connects to Origin   Select one of these three radio buttons to control the end of the leader.

Horizontal Distance

Vertical Distance   When you create balloons, you can have Mechanical Desktop automatically position them. The distance between balloons is controlled by the values in these two edit boxes.

Arrow Type   Select a leader arrow type from this list box.

Use Auxiliary Arrow Type   Occasionally you may attach an additional leader from a balloon's leader. Use this option to specify the arrow type of these auxiliary leaders.

Balloon leader arrowheads

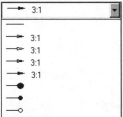

Columns to Display   These two list boxes are similar to the Formula Bar of the **BOM** dialog box. Enter the name of a variable that represents one of the BOM columns in the right-hand edit box. For example, to have the part's name appear in its balloon, enter =<NAME> in the edit box. (You must include the equal sign.) Rather than type-in the name of a variable, you can select one from the list box on the left. By default, the part's item number appears within the balloon.

Inserting Balloons

Use the AMBALLOON command to insert balloons in drawing views. You can insert balloons automatically or manually, and individually or as a group. Balloons are based on part references, so the icons of part references are displayed when you initiate AMBALLOON.

AMBALLOON offers four options on the command line.

Auto   Use this option to create and align multi-ple balloons. You will first be prompted to select the part references. Generally you will use a window or crossing selection method to do this. The balloons and their leaders will be displayed and a command line prompt will be issued for you to align the balloons horizontally, vertically, or by a user specified angle. Select an alignment option and then drag the balloons to their loca-tion. The arrow end of the balloon leaders will be anchored on the part reference locations. You can also create leaderless balloons with this option; they are called *standalone* balloons.

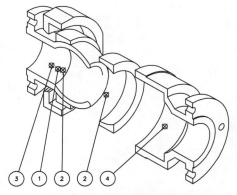

Leaders begin at the part reference icons when the Auto option of AMBALLOON is used.

The Collect option of AMBALLOON

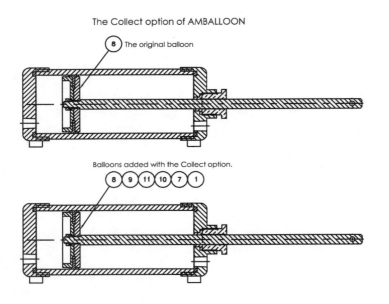

The original balloon

Balloons added with the Collect option.

Collect This option creates multiple leaderless balloons that are placed next to an existing balloon. After selecting the part references to be identified, you will be prompted to select the balloon they are to be attached to.

Manual A part reference in addition to a balloon is created by this option. You will be prompted to pick a point on the screen for the part reference. The `Part Ref Attributes` dialog box will be displayed for you to enter the part reference data, and then you will be prompted to select the start point of the balloon's leader and the location of the balloon.

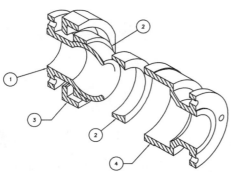

The One option of AMBALLOON allows you to select the start point of each leader as well as the balloon location.

One One balloon at a time is created with this option. All of the part references will be displayed, and you will be prompted to select one. Next, you will be prompted for the starting point of the leader, and then for the next point, and the next, until you press the Enter key to set the center of the balloon. This enables you to have leaders with bends. After creating one balloon, you will be prompted to select another part reference. The AMBALLOON command ends when you have selected all of the part references, or when you press the Enter key in response to the prompt to select a part reference.

Renumber This option changes the numbers within existing balloons and changes the BOM item numbers to match the balloon numbers. You will be prompted to enter the starting item number and the increment between numbers. Then select the balloons one-by-one. The item renumbering will correspond to the balloon selection order.

Reorganize   You can align selected standalone balloons, or realign balloons that are in a line, with this option. You will be prompted to select the balloons that are to be reorganized, and then a command line list of options is offered for you to align them horizontally, vertically, or by angle.

Balloons are placed in the AM_5 layer. Their relative location to the drawing view objects is fixed, so that they move with the view and with the view's objects. You can edit balloons with the AMEDIT command. This command displays a dialog box that enables you to delete the balloon and to change its shape and arrowhead type.

Exercise 1

Creating an Exploded View Drawing of a Check Valve

Open the drawing file of the assembly model you created in Exercise Two of Chapter 19, or else open file md19e204.dwg on the CD-ROM that accompanies this book. Make certain that the viewpoint in the Scene mode is 320 degrees from the X axis and 50 degrees from the XY plane, because we will base the exploded view on that viewpoint. Then activate Layout1 in Mechanical Desktop's Drawing mode and initiate AutoCAD's PAGESETUP command. In the dialog box of this command select the plot device of your choice and set the page size to ANSI C (22 by 17 inches). Leave the other parameters at their default values.

Insert a size C drawing border and title block in the layout. If you do not have one available, you can use the file ansi_c.dwg on the CD-ROM that comes with this book. The size of the drawing border in this file is 21.5 by 15.5 inches.

Once the drawing border and title block are in place, start the AMDWGVIEW command and set the view's parameters as follows.

View Type:	Base
Data Set:	Scene1
Scale:	0.75
Display Hidden Lines:	Off
Display Tangencies:	On

Leave the other view parameters at their default settings. In the command line prompts for establishing the view's direction, select the View option and point the X axis to the right. When you are prompted for the view's location, select a location that leaves room over the title block for the drawing's parts list. Your drawing should look similar to the one shown in Figure 1-1.

Next you will set the standard and the properties of the BOM database. Open the Standards tab of the **Mechanical Options** dialog box. In this tab:

- Select the ANSI standard.

- Open the **BOM Properties** dialog box. Change the width of the ITEM and QTY columns to 0.50, and the width of the NAME column to 3.0. Leave the other settings as they are.

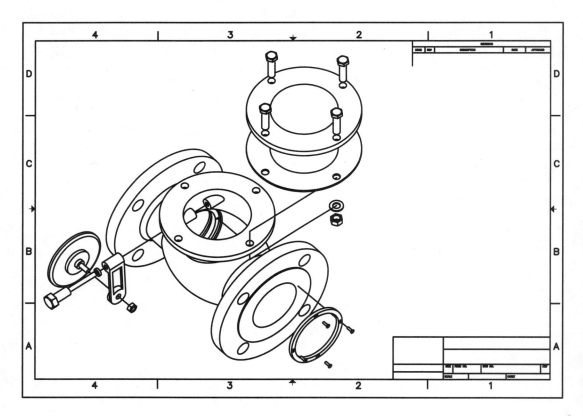

Figure 1-1

- Open the `Parts List Properties` dialog box. Turn on the Insert Heading and Insert Title buttons. (They appear to be depressed when they are on.) Set the Attachment Point to Bottom Right. Set both the Heading and Data Text Heights to 0.12. Leave the Heading and Row Gaps at their default 0.036 values, Line Spacing to Single, and Wrap Text turned on. In the Columns to Display lists, move MATERIAL, NOTE, and VENDOR from the Parts List list to the BOM Column list.

- Open the `Balloon Properties` Dialog Box. Select the Standard Balloon and the default round balloon style. Set Text Height to 0.12, and the Balloon size factor to 3.0. Verify that <ITEM> is the BOM column to be displayed in the balloon, and leave the other settings at their defaults.

- Open the `Leader Properties` dialog box, and set Arrowhead size to 0.16.

Leave the `Mechanical Options` dialog box. Next, you will rename the part definitions to give the parts more meaningful names than the drawing file names they are currently based on. Switch from Drawing mode to Model mode, invoke the AMCATALOG command, and open the All tab of the `Assembly Catalog` dialog box. In the Local Assembly Definitions list box, change the part definition names as shown in the table below. To do this right-click a part's name and select Rename Definition from the shortcut menu. The `Rename Definition` dialog box will be displayed. Enter a new name for the selected part, and choose No Instances from the cluster of Instance Renaming radio buttons.

Part Definition Name Changes

Original Part Name	New Part Name
VA_BODY	VALVE BODY
VA_SEAT	VALVE SEAT
FLATSCR4	#4 UNC FLAT HD SCREW
VA_DISK	VALVE DISK
VA_HANG	DISK HANGER
VA_COVER	VALVE COVER
BOLT3-8	3/8 UNC BOLT
VA_GASK	COVER GASKET
NUT_3-8	3/8 UNC NUT
VA_PIN	DISK PIN
VA_SEAL	PIN SEAL
WASH_3-8	3/8 WASHER

Part Definition Name Changes

Original names   New names

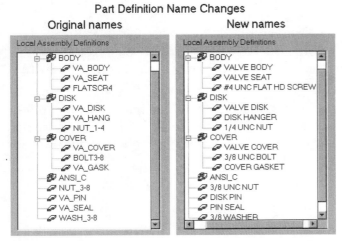

Figure 1-2

These name changes are also shown in Figure 1-2, which shows the before and after appearance of the Local Assembly Definitions list box of the **Assembly Catalog** dialog box.

Return to Drawing mode, and invoke AMBOM to display the **BOM** dialog box. Click the plus marks to the left of BODY, DISK, and COVER to display the parts within those subassemblies. Enter the material and note information shown in Figure 1-3.

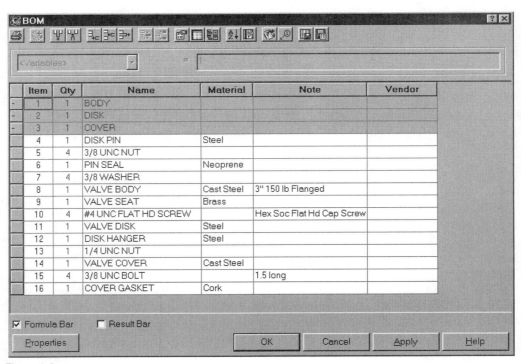

Item	Qty	Name	Material	Note	Vendor
1	1	BODY			
2	1	DISK			
3	1	COVER			
4	1	DISK PIN	Steel		
5	4	3/8 UNC NUT			
6	1	PIN SEAL	Neoprene		
7	4	3/8 WASHER			
8	1	VALVE BODY	Cast Steel	3" 150 lb Flanged	
9	1	VALVE SEAT	Brass		
10	4	#4 UNC FLAT HD SCREW		Hex Soc Flat Hd Cap Screw	
11	1	VALVE DISK	Steel		
12	1	DISK HANGER	Steel		
13	1	1/4 UNC NUT			
14	1	VALVE COVER	Cast Steel		
15	4	3/8 UNC BOLT		1.5 long	
16	1	COVER GASKET	Cork		

Figure 1-3

This information is for documentation purposes, and will not be displayed in the parts list. Sort the parts list using ITEM as the key and Ascending as the sort type. Click the OK button to leave the **BOM** dialog box.

Start the AMPARTLIST command. Accept the default settings of the **Parts List** dialog box, and click its OK button. Insert the parts list above the drawing's title box and next to the right hand border, as shown in Figure 1-4. (You can use an AutoCAD object snap, such as an endpoint snap, to position the parts list.)

Initiate the AMBALLOON command, and choose its One option. Each time you are prompted to pick an object, select a part reference icon; and, when you are prompted to select a start point for the balloon pick a point on the edge of the part corresponding to the part reference. You will notice that some of the part reference icons are not close to the location of their part. To help identify a part reference, hold the screen cursor momentarily over it to display the name of the part it belongs to. You will create 13 balloons to match the 13 parts in the parts list.

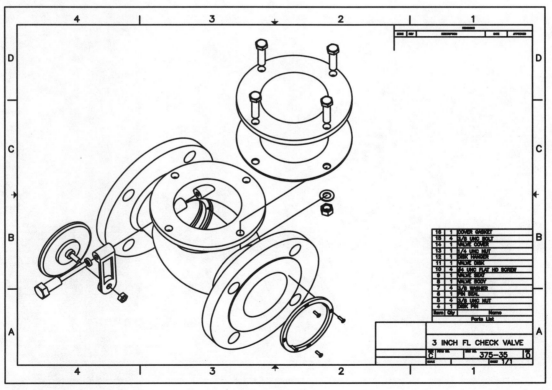

Figure 1-4

Your finished exploded view drawing of the check valve should look similar to the one in Figure 1-5. On the CD-ROM that comes with this book, the finished drawing is in file md20e105.dwg.

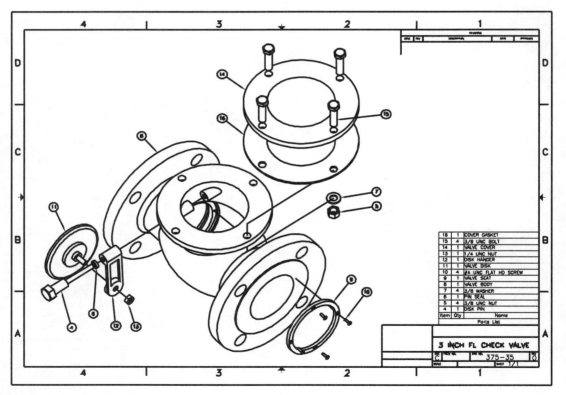

Figure 1-5

APPENDIX A

CD-ROM Files

The files on the CD-ROM are for the book's demonstrations and exercises. Files with .dwg filename extensions are Mechanical Desktop Release 5 drawing files. Files with .xls filename extensions are Microsoft Excel files. You can either copy these files all at one time to your computer or individually as you are working in the chapter they pertain to.

The file copies you make will all have their read-only attribute set, because they are from a CD-ROM. To clear the read-only attribute of a file, highlight the name of the file in Windows' Explorer. Then press the right-hand button of your pointing device to bring up a shortcut menu, and select Properties from that menu. This action will display the Properties dialog box. The attributes of the file will be listed in check boxes near the bottom of the General tab of this dialog box. Click the Read-only attribute check box to clear it.

Also, you can you can use this same method to clear file read-only attributes within Mechanical Desktop's Select File dialog box, and you can clear the read-only attribute of multiple files by using any of Windows' file selection techniques to highlight them.

Table A.1 CD-ROM File List by Chapter

Chapter	File	Chapter	File
Chapter 2	md02e101.dwg	Chapter 13	md_1310.dwg
Chapter 4	md04e105.dwg		md_1310.xls
	md04e206.dwg		md13e107.dwg
	md04e303.dwg		md13e107.xls
Chapter 5	md05e103.dwg	Chapter 15	md15e101.dwg
	md05e204.dwg		md15e103.dwg
	md05e401.dwg	Chapter 16	iso_a3bd.dwg
	md05e503.dwg		md16e101.dwg
Chapter 6	md06e103.dwg		md16e113.dwg
	md06e305 xls	Chapter 17	md17e101.dwg
	md06e305.dwg		md17e104.dwg
Chapter 8	md08e110.dwg		md17e204.dwg
	md08e201.dwg		bolt3-8.dwg
	md08e203.dwg		flatscr4.dwg
	md08e305.dwg		nut_1-4.dwg
	md08e401.dwg		nut_3-8.dwg
	md08e403.dwg		va_body.dwg
	md08e503.dwg		va_cover.dwg
Chapter 10	md10e106 dwg		va_disk.dwg
	md10e204 dwg		va_gask.dwg
Chapter 11	md_1145.dwg		va_hang.dwg
	md11e102.dwg		va_pin.dwg
	md11e207.dwg		va_seal.dwg
	md11e304.dwg		va_seat.dwg
	md11e404.dwg		wash_3-8.dwg
Chapter 12	md12e101.dwg	Chapter 18	md18e406.dwg
	md12e104.dwg	Chapter 19	md19e101.dwg
	md12e205.dwg		md19e103.dwg
	md12e306.dwg		md19e204.dwg
		Chapter 20	md20e105.dwg
			ansi_c.dwg

Mechanical Desktop Power Pack

Power Pack is a Mechanical Desktop add-on application that is included with United States shipments of Mechanical Desktop Release 5, and is available separately outside the United States. You can install Power Pack when you install the United States' version of Mechanical Desktop, or you can add it at a later time. Power Pack uses international standards in creating objects, and when you install it you will be asked to specify the standards that are to be incorporated, with the ANSI, ISO, and DIN standards being the defaults.

Power Pack uses its own commands, rather than modifying Mechanical Desktop commands, and you can conveniently initiate these commands through the Content 3D pull-down menu, and the Content 3D tool bar. Most of the Power Pack commands fall into one of the following categories:

- *Threaded fasteners*

- *Rotating shaft design*

- *Structural steel shapes and standard machine components*

- *Engineering Analysis*

2D versions of the commands in these categories also exist, but this Appendix will focus entirely on the 3D commands.

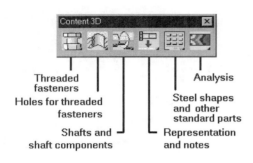

Threaded fasteners

Holes for threaded fasteners

Shafts and shaft components

Analysis

Steel shapes and other standard parts

Representation and notes

Threaded Fasteners

Creating Threaded Fasteners

Power Pack can create threaded fastener components in a wide variety of forms and sizes in accordance with international standards. The Power Pack command AMSCREW3D creates screws and bolts, AMNUT3D creates nuts, and AMWASHER3D creates washers. When you initiate one of these commands, a dialog box will open for you to use in selecting the type of screw, nut, or washer.

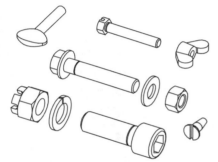

Power Pack can create threaded fastener components in a wide variety of forms and sizes in accordance with international standards.

For example, AMSCREW3D displays the `Select a Screw` dialog box. When you select a type of screw from the list on the left side of this dialog box, specific categories of the screw type are displayed on buttons. And, when you click a button the dialog box will disappear and a command line prompt will ask you to position and orient the screw by selecting two points, by selecting a circular edge, or by selecting a cylindrical surface. When you select two points, the bottom of the screw head is on the first point, and the threaded portion of the screw points toward the second point. Next, a dialog box is displayed for you to specify the size of the screw, and lastly you will be prompted to specify the length of the screw. You can set the length of the screw by dragging the screen cursor, or by selecting a length from a dialog box that lists the standard lengths for the screw type and size you have specified.

The AMNUT3D and AMWASHER3D commands work in a similar manner. Each Power Pack fastener is a base Mechanical Desktop part, and therefore, cannot be edited. By default, threads are not shown on screws and nuts.

You can, though, invoke the AMSTDPREP command, select the threaded fasteners you want changed, and select the Detailed representation option. Even in the detailed representation, though, threads are modeled as parallel circular grooves, rather than as helixes.

Creating Holes for Threaded Fasteners

Power Pack also has a set of commands for creating holes for threaded fasteners.

AMBHOLE3D   Creates blind holes.

AMTHOLE3D   Creates through holes.

AMCOUNTB3D   Creates counterbored holes. Termination options are Through and To Plane.

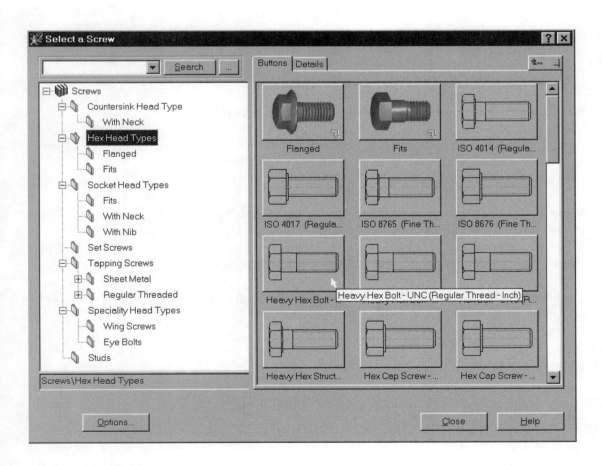

AMCOUNTS3D   Creates countersink holes. Termination options are Through and To Plane.

AMTAPBHOLE3D   Creates blind tapped holes.

AMTAPTHOLE3D   Creates through tapped holes.

Each of these commands use dialog boxes for you to select the type of screw that is be inserted into the hole and for its size, and then displays a dialog box for you to specify the method for placing the hole. The placement method options are:

Concentric   The hole is concentric to an arc or circular shaped edge and starts on the edge's planar face.

Concentric to a Reference Plane   The hole is concentric to an arc or circular shaped edge and starts on a specified plane.

Cylinder Axial   This method starts the hole on a plane having an arc or circular shaped edge, but the hole need not be concentric with the edge. The hole can be offset a specified distance in a specified direction from the plane's center point, or it can be offset a specified distance by a specified angle from a specified direction.

Cylinder Radial   The hole starts on the side of a cylinder. After selecting the cylindrical surface, you specify the distance of the hole from the base of the cylinder, and for its direction into the cylinder.

From Point   This option is similar to the From Hole option of AMHOLE. You will first be prompted to select a plane. Next you specify a point for the X axis direction on that plane and another point for the Y axis direction—they can be the same point. Then you specify the center of the hole by its distance from these points.

On Point   The hole is centered on a selected work point and its axis is perpendicular to the plane of the work point.

Two Edges   You will be prompted to select two different linear edges and then to specify a distance from each edge for locating the hole.

The holes created by Power Pack are the same as those created by AMHOLE, and you can edit them in the same way.

Power Pack also has two commands for making slots—AMSLOT3D makes through slots for metric fasteners and in user specified sizes, and AMBSLOT3D makes blind slots for metric fasteners and in user specified sizes. Creating slots is similar to creating round holes, but your options for locating them are restricted to Two Edges, Concentric, On Point, and From Point. Power Pack slots are extruded Mechanical Desktop features, that have profiles as do other extruded features, and you can use Mechanical Desktop commands to edit them and their profiles.

Creating Threaded Fastener Connections

When you are working with assemblies, you can create all of the threaded fastener components for joining two parts, as well as the screw holes, at one time with the AMSCREWCON3D command. This command displays the **Screw Connection** dialog box, which has buttons for specifying all of the components you are likely to need in the order they will be assembled. When you select a component, the same dialog box displayed when you create a single fastener component appears for you to specify details of

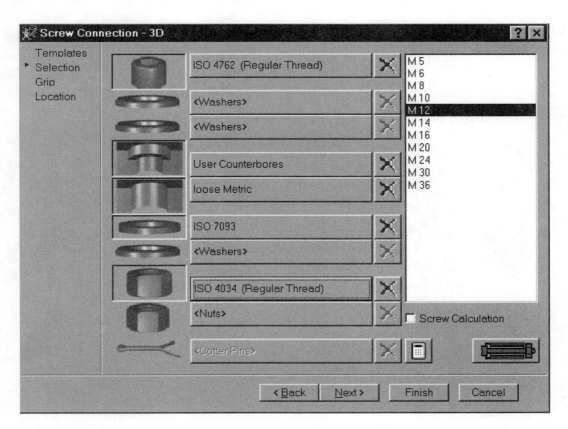

that component. For example, when you select a washer the `Select a Washer` dialog box appears for you to specify the type of washer. For each component you select you will specify its nominal size in the list box of the `Screw Connection` dialog box.

If the two parts do not already have holes for the fastener, you will also specify the parameters for making a hole in each part. When you have selected the components you want, click the Finish button. If you have specified that a hole is to be made in each part, you will be prompted to specify the location of each hole; and if the holes exist, you will be prompted to identify them.

You can create templates for fastener components with the AMSCREWMACRO3D command. Templates are useful when you often use the same components for making connections. The command displays the `Screw Assembly Templates` dialog box for you in creating and managing templates. AMSCREWCON3D and AMSCREWMACRO3D are related commands, and you can move between their dialog boxes by selecting the Back and Next buttons. To create a template, open the `Screw`

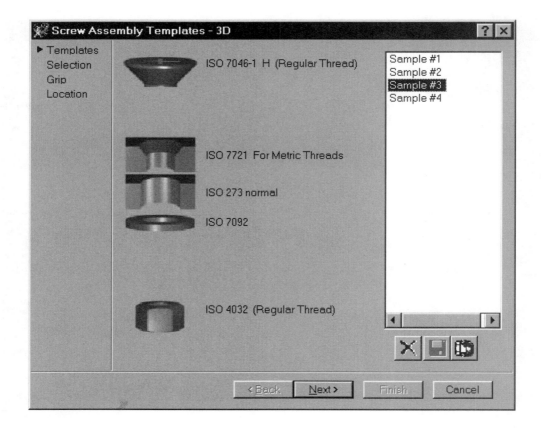

Connection dialog box and select the components you want; then use the Back button to open the **Screw Assembly Template** dialog box and click the Save button. To load a saved template, highlight it and select the Load Template button, or else double-click its name. To remove a template, highlight it and select the Delete Template button.

Rotating Shaft Design

Creating Shafts

Power Pack's AMSHAFT3D command creates solid models of shafts, such as those used in motors and axles. Shafts are built along a centerline and are basically cylindrical, but typically they are not uniform along their axis. Sections along the

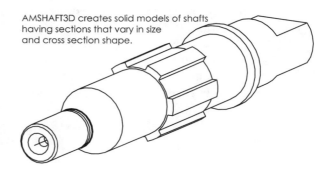

AMSHAFT3D creates solid models of shafts having sections that vary in size and cross section shape.

axis may have different diameters, be tapered, have wrench flats or splines, may be threaded, and so forth. Furthermore, shafts often have grooves for O-rings and other seals, as well as chamfers and fillets.

AMSHAFT3D creates a solid model that can have any of the features a shaft requires, and it can add bearings, gears, and retaining rings to the shaft. It constructs a shaft one feature at a time in the positive X axis direction. The command starts with a command

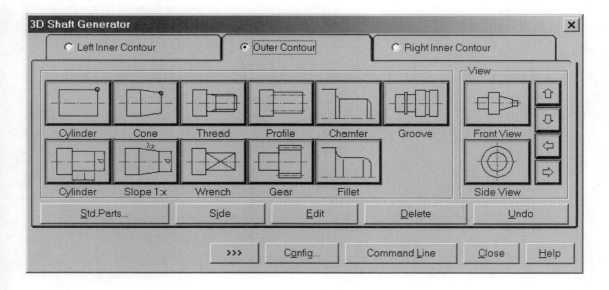

line prompt for you to specify the starting point of the shaft's centerline. Then it prompts for the direction of the centerline (this also establishes the direction of the X axis), and next it prompts for the direction of the Y axis. Then the command displays the `3D Shaft Generator` dialog box. If a shaft exists, you can select it from the initial AMSHAFT3D prompt to redisplay this dialog box to modify and add features to the shaft.

The options in the 3D Shaft Generator dialog box are as follows.

Cylinder   There are two button, one over the other, for creating cylindrical shaped sections in a shaft. When you select the top button, you establish the diameter and length of the section by dragging a point on its surface. When you select the lower button, you establish the diameter and length of the section by entering values on the command line.

Cone   This option creates a tapered section along the shaft. It initial diameter is that of the adjacent section, and you drag the screen cursor establish the other diameter and the length of the section.

Slope   This option is a more general method for creating a tapered section than the Cone option. You will be prompted for the length of the section and for its starting diameter. Then you can enter an end diameter, a taper angle, or a slope value.

Thread   Create a threaded section with this option. The section must be either the first or last section of the shaft. A dialog box is displayed for you to select the diameter and the thread parameters of the section, and to set its length.

Wrench   Use this option to create a section that has a square, hexagon, or flat-on-two-sides cross section shape. A dialog box titled `Wrench Opening` is displayed for you choose the shape of the section, and then a dialog box titled Wrench Size appears for you to specify the section's cross section parameters and its length.

Profile   This option creates a section that has splines or lobes, or is non-circular in cross section. A dialog box titled Profiles appears for you to specify the shape of the cross section. All of the options in this dialog box conform to a internationally recognized standard. After you specify the shape, a dialog box with parameters corresponding to your selection appears for you to specify the size and length of the section.

Gear   You can create spur gears with this option. A dialog box will appear for you to specify the gear's parameters—such as pitch, number of teeth, and pressure angle—and for the gear's length. By default, only one gear tooth is created, but the Config button has an option to have all of the gear's teeth constructed.

Chamfer   This option bevels sharp edges and corners. From the command line you will be prompted to select the edges to be chamfered, and for the chamfer size.

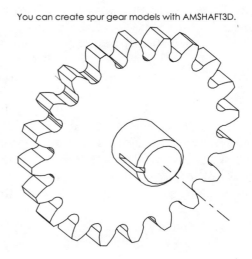

You can create spur gear models with AMSHAFT3D.

Fillet   Use this option to round sharp edges and corners. You will be prompted from the command line to select the edges to be filleted, and for the fillet radius.

Groove   You can create either a groove or a ridge around an existing cylindrical or cone shaped section of the shaft with this option. You will be prompted to select a surface, and then to specify a distance from the start of the section. Lastly, you will be prompted to enter a length and a diameter. If you enter a diameter smaller than that of the existing feature, a groove will be cut around the feature.

Contour   When the tab labeled Outer Contour is selected, all of the diameter dimensions for creating sections refer to the outside surface of the shaft. To hollow-out sections of the shaft, select the tab labeled Left Inner Contour or the one labeled Right Inner Contour. Then the section features you create will be subtracted from the existing features. Left Inner Contour works from left-to-right, and Right Inner Contour works from right-to-left.

View   The buttons in the cluster labeled View enable you to change the model space view direction. The button labeled Front View sets the line of sight to look straight down on the current XY plane, and the button labeled Side View sets the line of sight to look directly toward the YZ plane. The arrow buttons rotate the view direction 15 degrees at a time.

Std Parts   With this option, you can insert O-rings, bearings, keys, and other standard parts on the shaft. You can also insert these parts through the individual commands that are discussed shortly in this appendix.

Side   This option reverses the direction of feature creation. By default, features are created in the positive X axis direction.

Edit   Each section of the shaft is a Mechanical Desktop feature, and you can initiate editing operations for a feature with this option. You will be prompted to select a feature. Then Mechanical Desktop prompts and dialog boxes are displayed for you to change the feature's dimensions. When you have finished, Power Pack automatically updates the model and returns to the **3D Shaft Generator** dialog box.

Delete   You can delete a feature with this option. You will be prompted to select a feature. Features created after the one you select will be deleted as well.

Undo   This option reverses the last operation. You can step back through any number of operations.

>>>   When you click the button that has three arrow heads, the **3D Shaft Generator** dialog box is temporarily dismissed to give you an unobstructed view of the shaft. The dialog box is restored when you press the Enter key.

Config   This option controls whether gears are represented by just one representative tooth, or by all of their teeth.

Command Line   When you click this button, the **3D Shaft Generator** dialog box is permanently dismissed, and a command line prompt will appear listing the shaft generator options.

Close   This option ends the AMSHAFT3D command. You can invoke the command again to resume working on a partially completed shaft.

Standard Parts for Shafts

Power Pack has a set of commands for creating parts that are commonly associated with shafts, and for installing them on a shaft. The geometry and sizes of these parts meet specific international standards. You can invoke the commands individually, or through the Std Parts option of the **3D Shaft Generator** dialog box. The commands are as follows.

AMSHAFTKEY3D   Creates and installs parallel keys, Woodruff keys, and slotted hubs.

AMGROOVE3D   Creates and inserts retaining rings (Circlips) in metric sizes on shafts

AMSEALS3D   Creates shaft seals, O-rings, O-rings in a shaft groove, O-rings in a circular planar groove, and O-rings in a groove within a tube.

AMADJRINGS3D   Creates adjusting rings in metric sizes and installs them on shafts.

AMCENTERHOLE3D   Creates a threaded or non-threaded metric sized hole in the end of a shaft

AMUNDERCUT3D   Creates an external or internal undercut in metric sizes on a shaft

AMROLREAR3D   Creates a ball or cylindrical roller bearing and inserts it on a shaft or in a hole.

AMPLBEAR3D   Creates sleeve bearings in metric sizes

AMSHIMRING3D   Creates sealing rings in metric sizes

Structual Steel Shapes and Standard Machine Components

Creating Steel Shapes

Power Pack's AMSTLSHAP3D command creates steel I's, L's, round bars, rectangular tubes, and so forth in both English and metric sizes. The command displays the `Select a Steel Shape` dialog box for you to choose the basic shape of the part. The shapes are depicted in image buttons, and when you select a shape the buttons change to show specific versions of that shape and their standards. For example, if you choose an L-Shape, the buttons change to show steel L's in sizes that are controlled by standards such as DIN and ANSI that have either equal or unequal length sides.

Once you choose a steel shape, a command line prompt will ask you to specify a point for one end of the part and a second point to establish the direction of the part. Then a dialog box listing all of the available sizes for the shape and standard you selected is displayed for you to specify the part's size. Lastly, you will be prompted to specify the length of the part by dragging the screen cursor or by entering a length value.

Steel shapes are created as an extruded Mechanical Desktop feature, rather than as a base part. Therefore, they are based on a fully constrained profile, they can be edited, and you can add other features to them. Each steel shape you make, though, is a separate part. The dimensions of steel shapes are controlled by active part variables (See Chapter 6 for information about part variables.), with the variable G_L controlling the length of the steel shape.

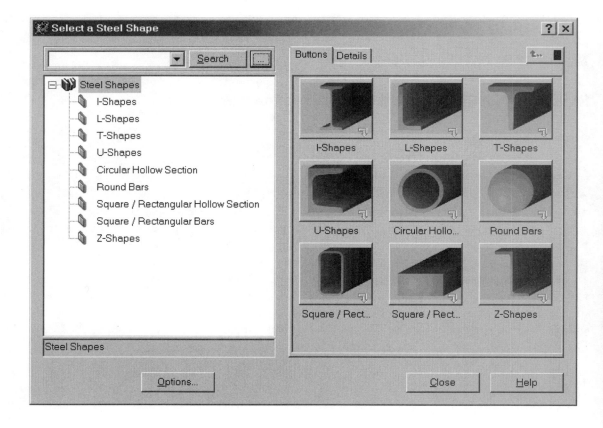

Non-Threaded Fasteners

In addition to the threaded fastener components discussed earlier in this appendix, Power Pack can create an assortment of non-threaded fasteners. The commands that create these parts are:

AMPIN3D   Creates cylindrical pins, taper pins, grooved drive studs, and cotter pins.

AMCYLPIN3D   Creates cylindrical pins, including plain, grooved, and spring pins. (These parts duplicate the cylindrical pins of AMPIN3D.)

AMTAPERPIN3D   Creates taper pins. (These parts duplicate the taper pins of AMPIN3D.)

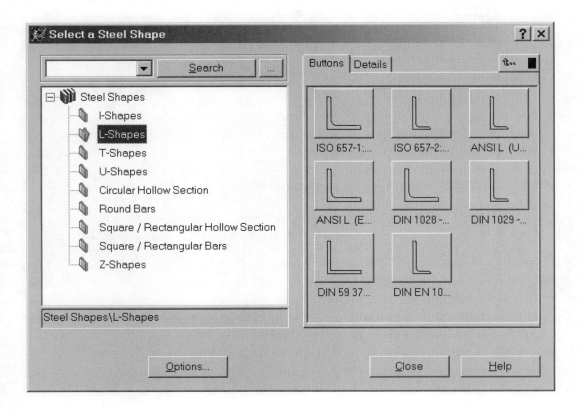

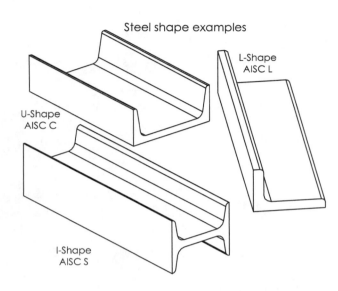

Steel shape examples

U-Shape AISC C

L-Shape AISC L

I-Shape AISC S

AMGROOVESTUD3D   Creates headed grooved drive studs. (These parts duplicate the grooved drive studs of AMPIN3D.)

AMCOTTERPIN3D   Creates cotter pins. (These parts duplicate the cotter pins of AMPIN3D.)

AMPLRIVET3D   Creates plain, button-head rivets.

AMRIVET3D   Creates counter-sunk rivets (These parts duplicate the countersunk rivets of AMCRIVET3D.)

AMCRIVET3D   Creates countersunk rivets.

AMCLEVISPIN3D   Creates headed and headless clevis pins.

Other Standard Machine Component Parts

The following Power Pack commands create standard parts that you may occasionally need.

AMPLUG3D   Creates threaded male plugs in metric sizes

AMLUBRI3D   Creates threaded lubricating (grease) plugs in metric sizes

AMSEALRING3D   Creates seal rings in metric sizes. This command operates differently than the other commands for creating standard parts. From the command line, it asks you to position the seal ring, and then it displays a dialog box for you to specify its size.

AMDRBUSH3D   Creates drill bushings.

AMDRBUSHHOLE3D   Creates a hole for a drill bushing and a drill bushing to match the hole, and inserts the bushing in the hole.

Standard Part Library

You can create all of Power Pack's standard parts, including threaded fasteners and their holes, through the AMSTDPLIB command. The advantages of this command over those that more directly create parts are that you can filter-out parts that are not within a certain standard, you can create 2D versions of the parts, and you can search for a particular part.

AMSTDPLIB displays the **Standard Parts Database** dialog box. Initially the names of the available standards are listed in image buttons and in an outline-type list. (The available standards are those you specified when you installed Power Pack.) When you select a button, or click a standard in the list, the components available for that standard are shown graphically in buttons, as well as in the list. You can keep expanding the list until you come to the part you want. For example, if you wanted to create an unhardened ground dowel pin having inch dimensions, you would select the ANSI standard, then fasteners, then pins, then cylindrical, and finally select the pin you want. Some of the parts in the library, such as springs, are only available as 2D objects.

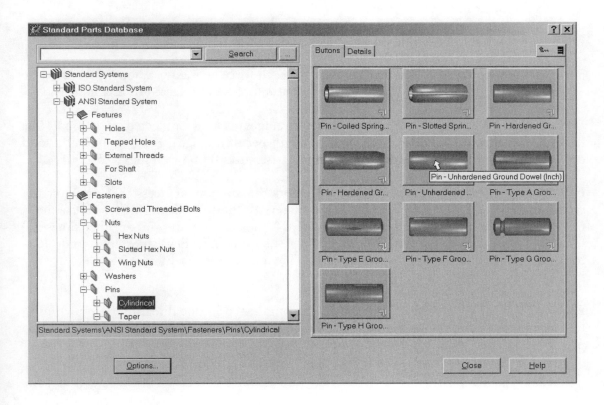

Engineering Analysis

Finite Element Analysis

Finite Element Analysis, which is usually shortened to the acronym FEA, is a mathematical method for finding the stresses and deformations in an object that are caused by external forces. The Power Pack command AMFEA3D performs FEA computations on Mechanical Desktop 3D solid model parts. Although it is easy to find stresses and deformations with AMFEA3D, stress analysis is a complex subject that requires specialized knowledge and experience to produce accurate and reliable results. Consult an engineering text book or handbook for information about material properties, stresses, and FEA.

Some terms you will encounter as you work with the AMFEA3D command are:

Force A fundamental directed (or vector) action that changes the motion of an object. The unit of force is a pound in English systems and a Newton in metric systems.

Stress The quantity of force that acts on a unit of area within a body. In English systems, the units of stress are commonly pounds per square inch, and are Newtons per square millimeter in metric systems.

Load A external force acting on an object.

Support Newton's third law requires that for each force acting on a body there must be an equal and opposite force. In FEA these reaction forces are referred to as supports.

Deformation The distance that an object stretches as it is subjected to a load. The related term strain is an object's change in length per unit length. For example, if a load causes a 100 mm long rod to deform 0.5 mm, its strain is 0.005 mm/mm (0.5/100).

E-Modulus A material property that represents the amount of stress that permanently stretches an object. (The stress exceeds the material's limit of elasticity.) It's full name is modulus of elasticity, and it is sometimes called Young's modulus, and at other times the material's elastic limit. Its units are pounds per square inch in English Systems and Newtons per square millimeter in metric systems. The higher the modulus value, the stronger the material.

Poisson's Ratio As an object is stretched or compressed in one direction (lateral strain), it is also deformed in the perpendicular direction (axial strain). Poisson's ratio is the ratio of lateral strain to axial strain. It is a dimensionless material property.

Specific Gravity   In the FEA Calculation dialog box Specific Gravity is another term for the density of a material. It is a material property that represents the material's weight per unit volume. The units of density are typically pounds per cubic inch in English systems, and kilograms per cubic decimeter in metric systems.

When you invoke the AMFEA3D command, you will be prompted from the command line to select a 3D part. Once you do, the `FEA Calculation 3D` dialog box is displayed for you to set the analysis parameters, perform the calculations, and view the results. Your steps in performing a Finite Element Analysis are as follows.

1. Assign loads and supports to the part. Loads and supports are divided into three different types.

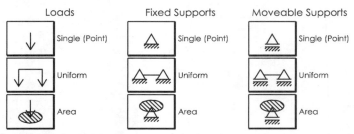

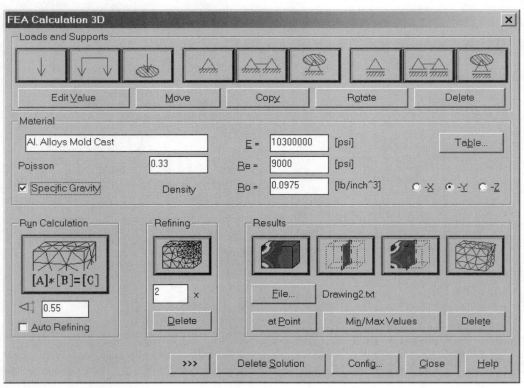

Single (or Point)   The force or support is concentrated on a point on the part.

Uniform   The force or support is spread along an edge on the part.

Area   The force or support is spread over an area on the part.

Power Pack sometimes refers to these as the analysis boundary conditions. A moveable support is one that is not fixed to the part. A rectangular plate resting on two sawhorses is an example of a part with two movable uniform supports.

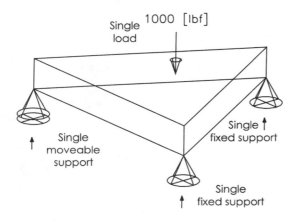

When you assign a point load or support, you will be prompted from the command line to select a surface, and then to select a point on that surface. As an option you can use a dialog box to help position the point. Once the point is established, command line options permit you to specify the angle of the load or support. The default angle is perpendicular to the specified surface. When you are assigning a point load, you will also be prompted to enter the value of the load. Power Pack displays loads as arrow icons and supports as cone-shaped icons.

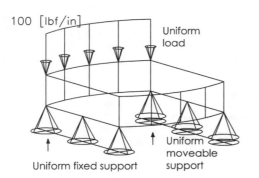

You will also be prompted to select a surface when you are assigning a uniform load or support. Then, a prompt will ask you to pick two points on the surface. Use object endpoint or midpoint snaps to select points on the surface's edge. The uniform load or support will be along the surface edge between the two points. As an option, you can have the load or support encompass the entire edge of the specified surface. Next, you will specify whether the directions of the distributed forces are parallel to one another or are normal (perpendicular) to the surface. If you specify that they are to be parallel to one another, you will specify the angle of the load or support through command line prompts. If you are assigning a uniform load, you will also be prompted for a force per length value. Loads are shown on the part as a series of connected arrows, and supports as a series of connected cones.

When you assign an area load or support, you will also be prompted to select a surface. Then, a dialog box with options for defining the border of the load or support's area will be displayed. One of the options in this dialog box is for the load or support to extend over the entire selected surface. Power Pack indicates an area load or support with one large, or main, arrow (or cone for supports) positioned somewhere in the area, and numer-

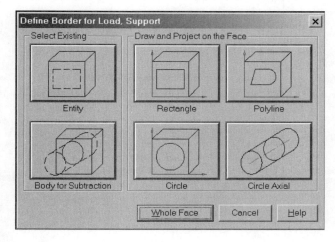

ous small arrows throughout the area. And you will be prompted to specify the location of the main arrow after you have specified the load or support area. Next, you will specify whether the direction of the lines of force are parallel with each other or are normal to the specified surface, and if they are parallel with each other for their direction. Lastly, when you are assigning an area load, you will be prompted to enter a force per unit area value.

Buttons in the Loads and Supports section of the **FEA Calculation 3D** dialog box allow you to edit load values, move loads and supports, copy loads and supports, rotate lines of force, and delete loads and supports.

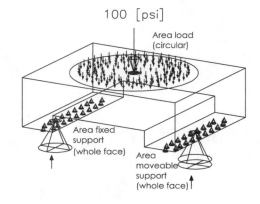

2. Assign material properties to the 3D part. Although you can enter material data in the provided edit boxes, the most convenient way to assign material properties is to click the Table button and select a material from a

list of commonly used metals. The material property units must match the units of the dimensions of your model. If you want the weight of the object to be used in the analysis, select the Specific Gravity check box.

3. Initiate the FEA calculations by clicking the Run Calculation button. After extensive computer calculations, a mesh network is created within the part, and the force values of the supports are displayed. The mesh is an object type named AMG3FEMMESH that is in the AM_FEA-AM_8 layer, and at the conclusion of its creation Power Pack offers a command line option for you to move it away from the part.

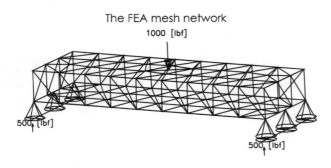

The FEA mesh network
1000 [lbf]
500 [lbf]
500 [lbf]

You can change the default size of the elements within the mesh by entering a value in the edit box below the Run Calculation button. Larger values create a coarser mesh.

The Refining button allows you to make the mesh smaller (increase its density) in the neighborhood of a selected point. The degree of refinement is controlled by the edit box below the button. Its default refining factor of 2, for instance, means that there will be twice as many mesh elements near the point. You must re-run the FEA calculation for the refinement to take effect. You can delete refinement points by selecting the Delete button.

4. Display the FEA results. A variety of options are available to you for displaying the results of the FEA calculations. The options for displaying stress indicate the various levels of stress as colored isolines or isoareas and display a table showing the stress values represented by the colors next to the model. You can also print the FEA results to a file.

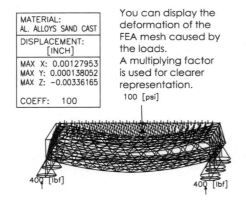

MATERIAL:		
AL. ALLOYS SAND CAST		
DISPLACEMENT:		
[INCH]		
MAX X: 0.00127953		
MAX Y: 0.000138052		
MAX Z: −0.00336165		
COEFF: 100		

You can display the deformation of the FEA mesh caused by the loads. A multiplying factor is used for clearer representation.
100 [psi]
400 [lbf]
400 [lbf]

One option for displaying the stress results of the FEA calculations is to show the stress in the part's surface. Another way is to slice through the part and view the stress on a plane within the interior of the part. Command line options are displayed for you to define the cutting plane, and to make multiple cuts if you want. You can also combine the surface stress display with a cutting plane. And, with all of these options you can move the stress display away from the part.

You can also view the deformation, of the FEA mesh that the loads cause. Since deformations (or as they are often called, displacements) are usually very slight, a multiplication factor is used to give a clearer representation of the distortion. A table showing the maximum displacement in the X, Y, and Z directions, along with the multiplication factor is displayed next to the deformed mesh.

Other Calculations

In addition to Finite Element Analysis, Power Pack has commands for performing other engineering calculations and analyses. These commands are:

AMBEARCALC For roller bearings. Calculates limiting values, dynamic and static load ratings, and fatigue life in revolutions and in hours. You can also initiate this command as an option when you are creating a bearing.

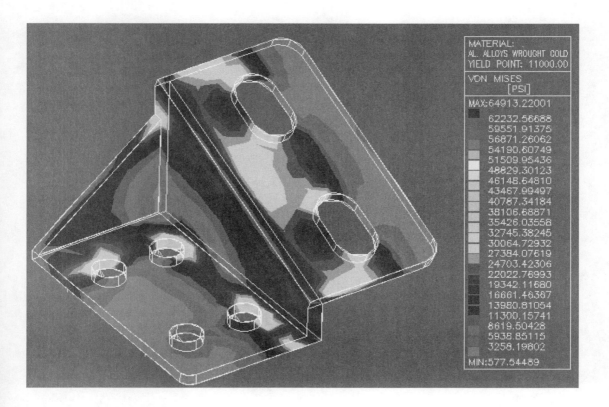

AMSHAFTCALC   Calculates deflection lines, bending and torsional moments, and factors of safety for symmetrical shafts.

AMSCREWCALC   Calculates factors of safety for threaded fastener connections. You can also access these calculations as an option when you are creating a threaded fastener connection.

INDEX

Numerics

T

Design
with Authority

THREE TOOLS FOR YOUR SUCCESS

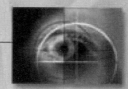

Cadenceweb.com

Design professionals use Cadenceweb.com as their online resource for placing the most important information about the design industry on their desktops. Visit us on the web to get your free subscription to CADENCE magazine and the industry's most respected MCAD Newsletter.

CADENCE Magazine

Covering the most important trends in design technology, CADENCE magazine is recognized as the industry's most trusted, unbiased resource for the design professional.

CADENCE MCAD Newsletter

Every two weeks Robert Green, noted industry expert, management consultant and CAD trainer, explores the financial and technical aspects of managing a CAD group. His newsletter complements his Manager's VPOINT column published in CADENCE magazine every other month.

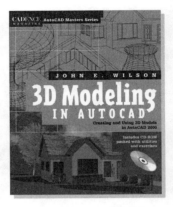
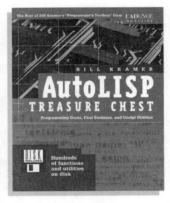